THE ULTIMATE WWII QUIZ BOOK

THE
ULTIMATE
WWII
QUIZ BOOK

Originally published in two volumes: *The World War II Quiz & Fact Book*
and *The World War II Quiz & Fact Book: Volume 2*

TIMOTHY B. BENFORD

BARNES
&NOBLE
BOOKS
NEW YORK

Contents

THE ULTIMATE WWII QUIZ BOOK

VOLUME ONE

For my wife, Marilyn

Contents

Foreword

Well before it ended, the Second World War was recognized as the single event that affected more lives than any other in human history. More than four decades after it began, there is hardly a person alive whose life has not in some way been directed or altered by its consequences. Books and films covering every aspect of the conflict have continued to be enormously popular. Millions of words, in a multitude of languages, retrace the various campaigns, examine closely the political and military leaders, and attempt to enlighten an audience now accustomed to watching history being made while sitting comfortably in its living room.

But, even if the convenience of television had been available for remote coverage of the conflict, it is very likely that all those books and all those words would have still been written about it. Beyond its scope and size, World War II was different, perhaps a psychological turning point in the evolution of mankind, bringing about an awakening of human interests and feelings unlike any war preceding it. It is even possible that the classification of events as being pre- or post–World War II will eclipse the time standards of B.C. and A.D. in measuring mankind's often flawed progress on this planet. It may not happen in this century, or even this millennium, but it will happen. Provided we don't first destroy earth in a final holocaust.

Between 1939 and 1945, events took place that changed our lives. Sometimes they happened in the chambers of power in Washington, Berlin, London, Tokyo, or Rome. More often than not they happened on a beachhead, in a forest, on a previously unknown island, or in the ruins of a devastated city. Enormous numbers of people died, twice as many civilians as military personnel. Many of those who survived came out of the war with determination to change the course of future history, and have been trying with various degrees of success ever since.

This book ventures to present both the great events and the trivial, if anything about world war can be considered trivial, as a collection of facts, vignettes, and occurrences. Not only is it informative and entertaining, it also makes vividly real once again the details of a great convulsion that shook the world, with all the human tragedy—and the occasional saving humor—that accompanied it.

Introduction

There was never a problem of what to include. The problem was what not to put in. As one can imagine, there is an abundance of anecdotes, vignettes, items of interest, facts and just plain trivia that came out of the war years. However, space does not permit use of it all.

I began this project by collecting information of an unusual or extreme nature. There are over 1,000 pieces of information in question-and-answer form plus 50 photographs and the Appendix. Some of the material shatters popular myths, but the majority of it underscores the folly of war. Nothing here is original, save the information I gathered from individuals who participated in the war, and I suspect that even much of that has previously been recorded elsewhere. My co-authors of this work are the people listed in the bibliography. My task was to edit their labors for this presentation. And herein may exist my future frustrations: contradictions.

Despite the millions of words written about the war, despite the talents of some of the leading historians of this century, contradictions abound. I've spent an extraordinary amount of time checking and confirming various details that appear differently in major works. Sometimes this happened when information was published too soon after the war and in later years was corrected by other authors. Every effort has been made here to publish the most accurate and confirmed information available. If the reader finds an error, it is mine and mine alone.

FACT: Approximately 700 journalists followed U.S. forces in all theaters of the war. Over 450 participated in the Normandy invasion on D-Day alone. This photo, taken on Iwo Jima, shows a series of foxholes scooped in the volcanic ash that served as a press and photo headquarters for newsmen covering that conflict. Empty ration boxes served as desks for the Coast Guard combat photographers. Small sign says "Iwo Jima Press Club."

Multiple Choice

Q. Identify the type of aircraft that was produced in larger amounts than any other during the war.

> a. Japanese Zero
> b. Messerschmitt BF-109E
> c. B-24 Liberator
> d. DC-3 (including C-53 and C-47 versions)

A. The Messerschmitt BF-109E, with nearly 36,000 produced.

Q. Which American entertainer traveled the most to entertain troops during the war?

> a. Gary Cooper
> b. Bob Hope
> c. Joe E. Brown

A. Joe E. Brown traveled over 150,000 miles. He was named Father to All Men Overseas by the National Father's Day Committee in 1944.

Q. Which unit was nicknamed the Red Devils?

> a. Russian Sixth Army
> b. U.S. 1st Infantry
> c. British 6th Airborne

A. The British 6th Airborne.

Q. Identify the only U.S. Navy ship sunk by enemy gunfire on D-Day.

    a. U.S.S. *Corry*
    b. U.S.S. *Augusta*
    c. U.S.S. *Butler*

A. The *Corry*, by gunfire from German gun batteries on Utah Beach. Thirteen members of her 294-man crew died.

Q. Identify the first U.S. Army Air Force aircraft type to see action in Europe.

    a. Grumman Wildcat
    b. Lockheed P-38
    c. Douglas Havoc

A. The Douglas A-20G Havoc, a ground attack bomber, on July 4, 1942.

Q. How did U.S. Admiral Thomas C. Hart, commander-in-chief of the Asiatic fleet, depart from the Philippines on December 26, 1941?

    a. Russian fishing boat
    b. U.S. submarine *Shark*
    c. P-40 Flying Tiger, which he flew

A. Via the *Shark,* headed for Java, where the Asiatic fleet was reorganizing.

Q. Identify Hitler's chauffeur.

    a. Victor Lutze
    b. Erich Kempka
    c. Hugo Blaschke

A. Kempka. Lutze was Hitler's SA chief of staff and Blaschke was the Fuehrer's dentist.

FACT The flag that flew aboard the U.S.S. *Missouri* during the surrender ceremonies in Tokyo Bay on September 2, 1945, was the same flag that had flown over the U.S. Capitol in Washington, D.C., on December 7, 1941.

Q. Identify the first U.S. Navy ship named in honor of a black.

    a. *Emmons*
    b. *Harmon*
    c. *Baldwin*

A. A mess attendant killed saving his shipmate's life during the Guadalcanal campaign, Leonard Roy Harmon was posthumously awarded the Navy Cross and was the first black to have a ship named in his honor. His mother christened the destroyer escort *Harmon* on July 25, 1943.

Q. Who commanded the Big Red One during the Sicily campaign?

    a. George Patton
    b. Walter Bedell Smith
    c. Terry Allen

A. Terry Allen commanded the U.S. 1st Infantry Division, the Big Red One.

Q. What was the U.S. VI Corps code name for the plan to break out from Anzio by way of Cisterna and Valmonte, Italy?

    a. Buffalo
    b. Crawdad
    c. Grasshopper

A. Buffalo. Crawdad was the plan to go along the coast to the northwest. Grasshopper was the plan for an eastward breakout. The plan to go via Campoleone was Turtle.

FACT   The 130-ton white plaster cast model of the U.S. Marine Corps War Memorial remained in sculptor Felix de Weldon's Warwick, Rhode Island, studio from 1954 until October 1981. The bronz sculpture was unveiled at Arlington National Cemetery in 1954, but no home for the plaster original was found until de Weldon donated it to the Marine Military Academy. Valued at $3.5 million, the 108-piece model takes four months to assemble. It was delivered to the MMA in Harlingen, Texas, by nine eighteen-wheel flatbed trucks. Dedication was on February 19, 1982, the thirty-seventh anniversary of the assault on Iwo Jima.

Q. Which Russian newspaper did Soviet troops prefer for rolling cigarettes?

    a. *Pravda*
    b. *Izvestia*
    c. *Red Star*

A. Red Star had a reputation for burning better and as a result was more popular.

Q. Who said, "He who holds Paris holds France"?

    a. Charles de Gaulle
    b. The Duke of Windsor
    c. Adolf Hitler

A. Hitler.

Q. Who was the last commander of the Afrika Korps?

    a. Jurgen von Arnim
    b. Sepp Dietrich
    c. Gustav Fehn

A. Von Arnim was commander of Axis troops in North Africa, Dietrich was an SS panzer commander in the Normandy and Ardennes campaigns. The last commander of the Afrika Korps was General Gustav Fehn.

Q. What was the unofficial name for the allied ships' assembly area as they got under way for the French coast in June 1944?

    a. Piccadilly Circus
    b. Swine Lake
    c. Hero Harbor

A. Piccadilly Circus.

FACT   For a time during the Battle of Britain RAF pilots were ordered to destroy German air-sea rescue seaplanes marked with the Red Cross, to prevent the rescued German pilots from fighting another day. The order met stiff resistance among RAF pilots.

Q. Which tank was produced in greater numbers than any other?

    a. German Panther
    b. British Churchill
    c. American Sherman

A. There were only 384 Panthers built and 5,640 Churchills. Of the twenty-six different tank models used by both Allies and Axis powers, the Sherman, with 49,000 units made, was by far the leader. Russia produced 40,000 T34/76 tanks for number two position. Despite its high production numbers, the Sherman got low grades as a weapon. Some 3rd Armored Division commanders called them "deathtraps."

Q. Where did the largest tank battle in history take place?

    a. Tunisia
    b. Ardennes Forest
    c. Kursk

A. Around the Kursk salient in July 1943, where the Russians and Germans employed approximately 3,000 tanks. Germany lost more than 400 tanks in the conflict.

Q. What was the name of the bridge at Sant'Angelo, Italy, over the Rapido?

    a. Brooklyn Bridge
    b. London Bridge
    c. Mussolini Bridge

A. London Bridge.

Q. Which was the only major surrender after D-Day that was *not* accepted in the name of the Allied powers?

    a. Rome
    b. Paris
    c. Berlin

A. Paris. It was accepted in the name of the Provisional Government of the French Republic, according to instructions de Gaulle had given General Leclerc.

Q. The first Allied troops to cross the Strait of Messina and set foot on the Italian peninsula were under the command of:

    a. Mark Clark
    b. Bernard Law Montgomery
    c. George Patton

A. The Eighth Army, under Montgomery, did it on September 3, 1943.

Q. How many .50-caliber machine guns were on board B-17 Flying Fortresses?

    a. Eight
    b. Thirteen
    c. Between fifteen and twenty

A. Thirteen.

Q. How many Japanese troops were killed trying to prevent the U.S. from retaking the Philippines in 1945?

    a. 100,000
    b. 250,000
    c. 450,000

A. The Japanese lost 450,000 troops.

Q. When did the U.S. *officially* declare that war with Germany had ended?

    a. May 7, 1945
    b. January 1, 1946
    c. October 19, 1951

A. October 19, 1951. Britain, France, Australia and New Zealand declared war with Germany as officially ended on July 9, 1951.

FACT   The first British air raid of the war, on September 6, 1939, resulted from a disastrous false alarm. British Spitfires mistakenly shot down two British Hurricanes. There were no German aircraft over England.

Q. When did Japan sign the peace treaty with the U.S. and forty-eight other nations (except the U.S.S.R.), officially ending its role as a belligerent?

    a. August 15, 1945
    b. September 2, 1945
    c. September 8, 1951

A. September 8, 1951, at San Francisco, California.

Q. How many of the 2,000-plus German Navy crew members survived the sinking of the battleship *Bismarck?*

    a. Less than 50
    b. 110
    c. Almost half

A. The British rescued 110 German sailors and officers.

Q. How many aircraft did Japan produce during the war?

    a. 35,000
    b. 65,000
    c. over 80,000

A. Approximately 65,000, of which 9,000 were left at the end of the war.

Q. When did Josef Stalin become Premier of the Soviet Union?

    a. 1927
    b. 1931
    c. 1941

A. On May 7, 1941. Though he controlled the U.S.S.R. well before that, he had not held the title of Premier.

FACT British commandos who crossed the English Channel and attacked Germans in France (killing two) the day the German-French armistice was signed were almost prevented from landing back in England because they carried no identification. One boatload was delayed at Folkestone harbor for several hours.

U.S. Army Photo

Q. Identify the island on which war correspondent Ernie Pyle was killed.

      a. Okinawa
      b. Iwo Jima
      c. Ie-shima

A. Seen here with a tank crew of the 191st Tank Battalion, Fifth Army, in the Anzio beachhead area in Italy in 1944, Pyle was killed on the Pacific island of Ie-shima, off Okinawa. Pyle is seated center, with goggles, in photo.

Q. How many Russian aircraft were destroyed by the Germans during the first seventy-two hours of Operation Barbarossa?

    a. None
    b. Under 1,000
    c. Nearly 2,000

A. The Germans succeeded in destroying approximately 2,000 Russian planes in what had only three days earlier been touted as the largest air force in the world.

Q. Which Nazi is credited with issuing the first order for the extermination of Jews?

    a. Himmler
    b. Goering
    c. Ribbentrop

A. Goering, in a letter to Reinhard Heydrich on July 31, 1941, in which he asked for a "final solution of the Jewish question." (This is the earliest known *written* order.)

Q. What were British casualties in the sinking of the aircraft carrier *Ark Royal?*

    a. One
    b. Half the crew
    c. All

A. One casualty. She sank on November 14, 1941, two days after being torpedoed by U-81 off Gibraltar.

FACT After the war it was learned that the U.S. shot down Japanese Admiral Yamamoto's plane with the help of Ultra intelligence. The British charged that the U.S. compromised the security of the code-breaking, but the U.S. denied the charges and defended its position. Previously secret wartime messages released to the U.S. National Archives in 1981 substantiate the British position. American fighter pilots talked over the air so much about the Yamamoto incident that the Japanese suspected their codes were being read and immediately changed them. It took four months for the U.S. to crack the new code.

Q. How many aircraft carriers did Japan lose during the war?

    a. Ten
    b. Twenty
    c. Thirty

A. Twenty, including five escort carriers, between May 7, 1942 (*Shoho* in the Battle of the Coral Sea), and July 24, 1945 (*Kaiyo* in Beppu Bay, Japan).

Q. Which Italian city was subjected to the worst bombing raid (in Italy) of the war?

    a. Rome
    b. Naples
    c. Turin

A. Turin, on November 20, 1942, by the RAF.

Q. When did the U.S. Eighth Air Force bomb Berlin for the first time?

    a. 1942
    b. 1943
    c. 1944

A. On March 4, 1944, three months before the Allied invasion of France.

Q. Who was Supreme Allied Commander, Mediterranean Theater?

    a. General Sir Harold Alexander
    b. General Carl A. Spaatz
    c. General Sir Henry Maitland Wilson

A. Wilson. Alexander was commander of Allied armies in Italy, and Spaatz was commander of U.S. Strategic Air Forces in Europe.

FACT   The U.S. 2nd Armored Division employed a tank equipped with a loudspeaker rather than guns to get German villages and towns to surrender. Lieutenant Arthur T. Hadley, a psychological warfare specialist, commanded the tank.

Q. Name the first American general to command four field armies.

       a. Dwight Eisenhower
       b. Louis A. Craig
       c. Omar N. Bradley

A. During the drive into Germany the First, Third, Ninth, and Fifteenth armies were under the command of Omar N. Bradley. Their combined strength was nearly a million men. In this November 1944 photo, Eisenhower, Craig and Bradley (from left to right) appear delighted with the war's progress as they meet in Butgenbach, Belgium.

Q. Name the German general who while chief of the Luftwaffe general staff committed suicide because of abuse and scorn he received from Hitler.

    a. Hans Jeschonnek
    b. Robert Ritter von Greim
    c. Ernst von Falkenhausen

A. Greim committed suicide on May 24, 1945. He had replaced Goering as head of the Luftwaffe; but it was Jeschonnek who as chief of staff was unable to tolerate the abuse from Hitler and ended his own life on August 18, 1943. Falkenhausen, who served as governor-general in occupied Belgium and northern France, was a conspirator in the July 20, 1944, plot to kill Hitler.

Q. Which Axis power suffered most from the Allied use of incendiary bombs?

    a. Germany
    b. Japan
    c. Italy

A. Japan by far. Building construction in Japan was over 80 percent wood and wood product, while in Germany stone and brick were the primary building materials. However, the U.S. and Great Britain dropped almost a million and a half incendiaries on Hamburg, Germany, in July and August 1943, causing the infamous "firestorms."

Q. What was responsible for the loss of the one and only U.S. lighter-than-air craft during the war?

    a. A German U-boat
    b. Bad weather
    c. Friendly fire

A. U-boat 134 gained the distinction of shooting down the only airship lost by the U.S. during the war when it successfully defended itself from attack by Airship K-74 off the Florida Keys on July 18, 1943.

Q. Which Allied general was code-named Duckpin?

    a. Devers
    b. Eisenhower
    c. Truscott

A. Supreme Commander, Allied Expeditionary Force in Europe, General Dwight D. Eisenhower was Duckpin.

Q. Identify the first type of naval vessel captured by a U.S. Navy boarding detail in the war.

    a. Japanese destroyer
    b. Italian destroyer
    c. German U-boat

A. On June 4, 1944, U.S. Navy Captain Daniel V. Galley of the U.S.S. *Guadalcanal* sent a detail to board German U-boat 505 off the African coast. It was the first enemy ship so captured since 1814. Abandoned by its crew, U-505 was towed to the U.S.

Q. Who said, "At the moment the situation in Italy is such that not a single Luftwaffe aircraft dares show itself"?

    a. U.S. General Carl Spaatz
    b. Luftwaffe chief Hermann Goering
    c. British Air Chief Marshal Sir Arthur Tedder

A. World War I air ace and Luftwaffe commander-in-chief, Reichsmarschall Hermann Goering on May 28, 1944. He made the pronouncement to Hitler.

Q. The U.S. 93rd Infantry Division was:

    a. All American Indian
    b. All black Americans
    c. German-speaking Americans

A. It was an all-black American division.

FACT U.S. submarines sank more enemy tonnage than all other naval and air combatants combined.

Q. Where did the Germans launch their last panzer offensive in North Africa?

    a. Djebel Bou-Aoukaz
    b. Maknassy
    c. Medenine

A. The successful assault by German armored units resulted in the capture of Djebel Bou-Aoukaz, Tunisia, on April 30, 1943. The attack had begun on the 28th.

Q. When was General Eisenhower named Supreme Commander, Allied Expeditionary Force?

    a. 1942
    b. 1943
    c. 1944

A. On Christmas Eve, December 24, 1943.

Q. Which country suffered the greatest merchant marine losses in the war?

    a. Britain
    b. Japan
    c. Germany
    d. U.S.

A. Britain, with 4,786, was followed by the others: Japan 2,346; Germany 1,595; U.S. 578. A total of 11,700 merchant ships of all nations were sunk between 1939 and 1945.

Q. How long after Britain declared war on Germany was it before RAF planes flew over Germany?

    a. The same day
    b. Not for three months
    c. Almost one year later

A. The same day, September 3, 1939. The RAF dropped six million propaganda leaflets on northern German cities but no bombs.

Q. When did the first Allied air raid on Germany take place?

    a. The day after war was declared
    b. One month after the start of war
    c. Not until the end of "the phony war"

A. The day after war was declared, when RAF bombers flew toward Germany's North Sea navy bases. However, of the twenty-nine planes in the mission, seven were shot down, ten couldn't locate their targets, one bombed neutral Denmark by mistake and three bombed British ships in the North Sea. Eight planes succeeded in reaching their targets but did little damage.

Q. The Anglo-American organization responsible for gathering intelligence in the Middle East was known as:

    a. The Ankara Committee
    b. The Cairo Committee
    c. The Suez Section

A. The Ankara Committee. The other two are fictitious.

Q. The name of the Allied operation to capture Sardinia was known as:

    a. Brakestone
    b. Brimstone
    c. Stonewall

A. Brimstone.

Q. When did Italy formally declare war on Germany?

    a. It didn't
    b. In September 1943, when the Allies invaded
    c. In October 1943

A. King Victor Emmanuel read the declaration on October 13, 1943, and Italy was then recognized "officially" as a co-belligerent by the Allies.

FACT Once Italy joined the Allies against the Germans, only seven of its sixty-one divisions were actually involved in combat.

Q. The first Italians to fight as Allied co-belligerents were in the:

    a. Army
    b. Navy
    c. Air force

A. The 1st Italian Motorized Group became part of the U.S. Fifth Army on October 31, 1943.

Q. What was the code name for the Canadian attack on the so-called Hitler Line in Italy?

    a. Camel
    b. Chesterfield
    c. Lucky Strike

A. Chesterfield.

Q. Who was the commander of the Hermann Goering Division in the Sicily campaign?

    a. Major General Paul Conrath
    b. Lieutenant General Adolph Steiner
    c. Brigadier General Carl Muller

A. Major General Paul Conrath. The other two are fictitious.

Q. Who was Carl Johann Wilberg?

    a. An Allied spy in Berlin
    b. Admiral Canaris's code name
    c. A BBC broadcaster who spoke German

A. An Allied spy who remained in Berlin up to the end informing on troop movements and conditions. He was a member of the Office of Strategic Services (OSS).

Q. Which Allied nation can claim that its ships were the vanguard of the Normandy invasion?

    a. France (free forces)
    b. United States
    c. Britain

A. Britain. Twelve minesweepers cleared the waters close to the French shore on June 5 at night.

Q. Who said, "Paris is worth 200,000 dead"?

    a. A German General
    b. A British politician
    c. A French Resistance leader

A. "Colonel Rol," of the French Resistance.

Q. General Chaing Kai-shek was code-named:

    a. Moss Bank
    b. Kingpin
    c. Peanut

A. The Allied code name for French General Henri Giraud was Kingpin. French Premier Pierre Laval was Moss Bank. Peanut was the official code name for Chiang Kai-shek. It was also the nickname U.S. General Joseph Stilwell used to display his contempt for the Chinese leader.

Q. What was the production rate that the American aircraft industry reached in 1944?

    a. One plane a day
    b. One plane every hour
    c. One plane every six minutes

A. One plane every six minutes!

Q. Which U.S. division is credited with securing the first U.S. beachhead in France?

    a. 1st Infantry
    b. 4th Infantry
    c. 29th Infantry

A. The 4th Infantry Division on D-Day.

FACT Hitler had two horoscopes,—one from November 9, 1918, and the second from the day he took power, January 30, 1933—that predicted the outbreak of war in 1939, victories until 1941, difficulty in April 1945 and peace in August. Both horoscopes also noted that Germany would begin to rise again in 1948.

Q. Identify the Frenchman who is credited with bringing information to the Allies that led them to change plans and liberate Paris.

   a. Roger Gallois
   b. Charles de Gaulle
   c. Georges Eugène Haussmann

A. Gallois succeeded where even de Gaulle failed. Haussmann, appointed by Napoleon III, had designed the "modern" Paris with its broad and beautiful boulevards.

Q. Who accepted the surrender of the German commander of Paris when the city was liberated?

   a. A French lieutenant
   b. An American GI
   c. A British medic

A. Lieutenant Henri Karcher "of the Army of General de Gaulle" accepted the surrender of General Dietrich von Choltitz.

Q. What was the name of the directional device used to correct RAF bomber accuracy by sending a beam from England?

   a. Elbow
   b. Oboe
   c. Hobo

A. Oboe.

Q. What was the nickname given to the machine the British built to decode messages they received on the Enigma code machine?

   a. The Bomb
   b. The Thing
   c. Our Friend

A. The Bomb.

FACT Hitler's bunker in Berlin was surrendered to the Russians by Luftwaffe doctor Captain Walter Hagedorn.

Q. How many Allied ships did German U-boats sink between 1939 and 1945?

    a. 1,400
    b. 2,800
    c. 3,900

A. More than 2,800, at a cost to Germany of 630 U-boats and 27,491 submariners.

Q. When did the Polish Navy surrender to the Germans?

    a. October 1, 1939, a month after war began
    b. The crews scuttled their ships instead
    c. It didn't have a chance to surrender

A. October 1, 1939. However, some ships made their way to Britain and sailed with the Royal Navy.

Q. Where did the idea for partitioning Germany after the war originate?

    a. Britain
    b. France
    c. U.S.A.
    d. Soviet Union

A. On January 15, 1944, a cabinet committee that was chaired by future Prime Minister Clement Attlee in Great Britain made the recommendation.

Q. On May 13, 1944, an American destroyer escort sank a Japanese submarine that was:

    a. Carrying a peace offer to the U.S.
    b. Returning to Tokyo with plans for an atom bomb that it received from Germany
    c. Operating in the Western Hemisphere

A. Japanese submarine Ro-501, one of the few of its class to operate in the Western Hemisphere, was sunk. There were no peace offers or atom bomb plans aboard.

U.S. Army Photo

Q. Name the U.S. general who said, "When the going is tough, in a brawl or battle, there is no better fighting partner than the man from Down Under."

     a. Matthew Bunker Ridgway
     b. Robert Lawrence Eichelberger
     c. Joseph Stilwell

A. General Robert L. Eichelberger, commenting on the spirit and ability of the Australian troops in the Buna campaign. He is seen here inspecting a Japanese saber at Mokmer Airstrip, Biak Island, Dutch New Guinea, on June 30, 1944.

Q. What was the Allied code name for the U.S. Army?

 a. Destiny
 b. Challenge
 c. Force

A. Destiny.

Q. Identify the European city that was proclaimed an open city on August 14, 1943.

 a. Prague
 b. Lourdes
 c. Rome

A. Rome. However, the Vatican was bombed by Allied aircraft on November 5.

Q. What was the Allied code name for the Russians?

 a. Laundress
 b. Ecuador
 c. Ali Baba

A. Laundress was the name of the Vichy French. The Greeks were known as Ecuador in Allied codes. Ali Baba was the code name of the Russians.

Q. How did Polish General Wladislaw Sikorski die?

 a. In an airplane crash near Gibraltar
 b. As a suicide in England
 c. Facing a Russian firing squad

A. Sikorski and several other Polish exile leaders were killed in a plane crash near Gibraltar on July 4, 1943.

FACT A Jewish battalion from Palestine fighting in North Africa was almost totally wiped out during the German offensive against Bir Hacheim in June 1942. Less than fifty of the just over 1,000 troops survived. The Palestinians, along with Free French troops, kept the Germans from reaching Tobruk.

Q. Which country sent in the first troops to assist the Partisans in Yugoslavia?

    a. U.S.
    b. Great Britain
    c. Soviet Union

A. The first assistance for Tito's communist Partisans came from Great Britain in May 1943.

Q. What German site was the target of the first major daylight air raid on the Ruhr?

    a. Gestapo headquarters
    b. A synthetic rubber plant
    c. Port facilities

A. The synthetic rubber plant at Huels.

Q. Where was the site of the only wartime meeting between Generals Douglas MacArthur and George Marshall?

    a. Washington
    b. Goodenough Island
    c. Tokyo

A. On Goodenough Island off New Guinea.

Q. Luftwaffe efforts to supply Axis troops in Africa resulted in fifty-one transports and sixteen escort fighters being shot down in a period of less than fifteen minutes, an event that was known as

    a. Bloody Sunday
    b. Palm Sunday Massacre
    c. The Europe-to-Heaven Run

A. More than seventy U.S. and RAF fighters, supplied with Ultra intelligence, easily mauled the Germans on Palm Sunday, April 18, 1943, in what became known as the Palm Sunday Massacre.

FACT   Messerschmitt designed two long-range bombers *named* after the city that was their intended target: New York.

Q. When did the U.S. officially declare its neutrality after war began in Europe?

    a. It didn't
    b. September 5, 1939
    c. December 7, 1939

A. September 5, 1939.

Q. What was the code name for the German air and sea invasion of Crete?

    a. Mercury
    b. Silver
    c. Gold

A. Mercury.

Q. Prime Minister Winston Churchill's plan for an invasion of northern Norway was known as:

    a. Mars
    b. Jupiter
    c. Saturn

A. Jupiter.

Q. The B-29 that dropped the first atom bomb on Japan was part of:

    a. Special Services, Pacific
    b. 509th Composite Group
    c. Allied Pacific Air Wing (APAW)

A. The 509th Composite Group, Twentieth Air Force. (The plane was named *Enola Gay*. See Appendix for what became of her.)

Q. German casualties from the Allied raids on Dresden on February 13–14, 1945, were:

    a. 35,000
    b. 100,000
    c. 135,000

A. One hundred thirty-five thousand people were killed.

Q. Who captured the German High Command headquarters at Zossen?

    a. Patton's Third Army
    b. Montgomery's Desert Rats, the 7th Armored
    c. Rybalko's Soviet 3rd Guards

A. Colonel General Pavel Rybalko's 3rd Guards captured the head-quarters intact. However, the German senior military personnel had moved to Rheinsberg, about fifty miles northeast of Berlin.

Q. Identify the last German strongpoint in Paris to surrender on liberation day, August 25, 1944.

    a. The Louvre
    b. Notre Dame
    c. Luxembourg Palace

A. Luxembourg Palace, home of the French Senate, at 7:35 P.M.

Q. How many aircraft did the Russians employ when they began their attack across the Oder that began the Battle of Berlin on April 16, 1945?

    a. Under 2,500
    b. About 6,500
    c. Over 9,000

A. About 6,500, which came in to finish the job started by the thirty-five-minute artillery bombardment.

Q. Who was head of the American OSS in France in August 1944?

    a. Colonel David Bruce
    b. Joseph Grew
    c. Major James F. Hollingsworth

A. David Bruce. Grew was U.S. ambassador to Japan in 1941; Hollingsworth, of the 67th Armored Regiment, was wounded in a heroic tank charge crossing the Elbe on the road to Berlin.

Q. Identify the head of the political arm of the Gaullist Resistance in Paris in 1944.

    a. Claude Guy
    b. André Tollet
    c. Alexandre Parodi

A. Alexandre Parodi. Guy was de Gaulle's aide, and Tollet was head of the Comité Parisien de la Libération.

Q. Who commanded the 6th Parachute Regiment (German) in Normandy on D-Day?

    a. Baron von der Heydte
    b. Count Klaus Schenk von Stauffenberg
    c. A noncom, senior officer present

A. Baron von der Heydte.

Q. What was the size of the Soviet cavalry?

    a. Under 10,000
    b. just over 100,000
    c. 600,000

A. 600,000.

Q. Identify the first ground recaptured from the Germans in the war.

    a. Calais, France
    b. Siddi Barrani, Egypt
    c. Smolensk, U.S.S.R.

A. Smolensk, U.S.S.R., in August 1941.

Q. When did the U.S. seize Axis ships that were in American ports?

    a. March 1941, while the U.S. was neutral
    b. December 8, 1941, when war with Japan was declared
    c. After Germany declared war on the U.S.

A. While still officially neutral, the U.S. seized Axis ships in U.S. ports in March 1941.

FACT The first ship sunk as a result of German mines in the Thames estuary was a Japanese passenger ship, the *Terukuni Maru*, on November 21, 1939.

Q. How many Russian guns opened fire on April 16, 1945, as they began the attack on Berlin?

    a. 5,000
    b. 10,000
    c. 20,000

A. There were 20,000 guns in a bombardment never previously equaled on the Eastern Front. (The firepower and unleashed energy were so great they created a hot wind that howled through the forest, bent saplings and lifted small objects into the air.)

Q. Hitler's order to destroy industries, communications and transportation that he feared were in jeopardy of falling into Allied or Russian hands was known as the:

    a. Denial Decree
    b. Nero Decree
    c. Phoenix Decree

A. Issued on March 19, 1945, as the U.S. 70th Division crossed the Saar River, the order was known as the Nero Decree because it resembled the order for the destruction of Rome by the infamous emperor.

Q. Identify the last U.S. airfield to be captured by the Japanese.

    a. Laohokow, China, March 1945
    b. Ormoc Bay, Philippines, 1942
    c. Kunming, China, 1943

A. Laohokow, China, near the end of March 1945. The U.S. Fourteenth Air Force destroyed anything of value prior to withdrawing, to deny Japanese use of the base.

Q. Which airborne operation was the largest of the war?

    a. German drop on Crete
    b. Allied drops in Operation Market Garden (Holland)
    c. Allied drops on Wesel

A. The British 6th and the U.S. 17th paratrooper drops on Wesel, March 24, 1945, which required approximately 40,000 paratroopers and just over 5,050 planes.

Q. When did the first V-2 bombs fall on London?

    a. October 10, 1943
    b. September 8, 1944
    c. January 1, 1945

A. September 8, 1944, in West London.

Q. When did Germany launch the last V-2 bomb against Great Britain?

    a. January 1945
    b. March 1945
    c. May 1, 1945

A. March 27, 1945. More than 2,850 people died from the bombs during their nearly seven months of terror, and another 6,000 sustained serious injuries.

Q. What was the percentage of U.S. Marine casualties during the initial assaults on Mount Suribachi, Iwo Jima?

    a. 10 to 20 percent
    b. 20 to 30 percent
    c. 40 to 50 percent

A. With progress measured in yards, as on Peleliu, and with half of their armored vehicles knocked out of action, the Marines sustained 20 to 30 percent casualties on February 19–20, 1945.

Q. When did the first U.S. Navy vessels return to action in Manila Bay after being driven out by the Japanese in 1942?

    a. 1943
    b. 1944
    c. 1945

A. Not until February 14, 1945, when PT boats began night reconnaissance missions.

FACT The Molotov cocktail, a popular and easily made explosive, got its name from the Finns, who used them extensively against the Russians in the winter of 1939–40.

Q. Who said, "The destruction of Dresden remains a serious query against the conduct of Allied bombing"?

    a. Franco of Spain
    b. Goering of Germany
    c. Churchill of Great Britain

A. The British Prime Minister, Winston Churchill, in commenting on what is considered the most devastating incendiary raid (February 13–14, 1945) of the war. More than 100,000 people were killed by the U.S. and British bombers.

Q. When did Hitler make his last radio broadcast of the war?

    a. One week after D-Day, June 1944
    b. January 30, 1945
    c. Two weeks before he died

A. On the twelfth anniversary of his taking control of Germany, January 30, 1945. He made his last appearance in public on March 20, when he presented medals to Hitler Youth who had performed with merit in combat.

Q. What was the relationship of casualties between the U.S. 77th Division and the Japanese troops involved in the battle on Leyte between December 20 and 31, 1944?

    a. 10,006 Japanese vs. 520 U.S.
    b. 3,107 Japanese vs. 302 U.S.
    c. 5,779 Japanese vs. 17 U.S.

A. It was 5,779 Japanese vs. 17 U.S.

Q. Name the island that was captured to open the way to Antwerp, and identify the Allied nation's troops that did it.

The island was: The troops were:
a. Water Island   a. Canadian
b. Walter Island   b. Polish
c. Walcheren Island   c. French

A. The Canadian First Army, on November 8, 1944, captured Walcheren Island.

Q. Identify the site of the last Allied air raid of the war in Europe.

    a. Kiel
    b. Berlin
    c. Nuremberg

A. Royal Air Force Mosquitoes bombed Kiel on May 2, 1945, the last attack in Europe by bombers.

Q. When did Nazi Propaganda Minister Joseph Goebbels become Reich Minister of War?

    a. 1942
    b. 1943
    c. 1944

A. On July 25, 1944.

Q. Which army was first to cause Germany to fight on soil Germany had held prior to the war?

    a. Russia
    b. United States
    c. Great Britain

A. The Soviets engaged the Germans on the East Prussian border at the Sesupe River on August 17, 1944.

Q. What Continental European city was the target for the only long-range Luftwaffe air attack in the war?

    a. Brussels
    b. Amsterdam
    c. Eindhoven

A. Eindhoven, on September 19, 1944, when approximately 100 bombers raided.

FACT When Adolf Hitler was told that France and Britain had declared war on Germany as a result of the invasion of Poland, the Fuehrer slumped in his chair and was silent for a few moments. Then, looking up at the generals around him, he asked, "Well . . . what do we do now?"

Q. Identify the general who led U.S. troops back to the Philippines on October 20, 1944.

    a. MacArthur
    b. Krueger
    c. Eichelberger

A. Lieutenant General Walter Krueger and the U.S. Sixth Army landed on the east coast of Leyte, establishing two beachheads. Four hours after the landing General MacArthur came ashore. He had indeed returned.

Q. Which naval battle is considered the greatest in history?

    a. Midway
    b. Leyte Gulf
    c. Coral Sea

A. The Battle of Leyte Gulf. The Japanese lost thirty-four ships, including four aircraft carriers and three battleships. The U.S. lost six ships, including one light aircraft carrier (*Princeton*) and two escort carriers (*Gambier Bay* and *St. Lo*).

Q. During the attack on Pearl Harbor, what was the first target hit by a Japanese bomb?

    a. Ford Island
    b. Hickham Field
    c. Battleship Row

A. Ford Island.

Q. Where was Japanese Admiral Yamamoto during the attack on Pearl Harbor?

    a. Tokyo
    b. With the attack force off Hawaii
    c. Aboard his flagship, *Nagato,* in Japanese waters.

A. He was aboard the *Nagato.*

Q. Identify the first Japanese aircraft carrier sunk by the U.S. in the war.

    a. *Shoho*
    b. *Shokaku*
    c. *Zuikaku*

A. The *Shoho,* during the Battle of the Coral Sea.

Q. Which type of ship was the largest lost by the U.S. in the battle for Okinawa?

    a. Destroyer
    b. Light cruiser
    c. Heavy cruiser
    d. Escort carrier
    e. Fleet carrier

A. Of the thirty-six ships lost, none was larger than a destroyer. The Japanese lost just under 200 ships of various sizes, up to the world's largest battleship, the *Yamato.*

Q. Where and when was Heinrich Himmler captured?

    a. Berlin, May 1945
    b. Bavaria, June 1945
    c. Bremervorde, May 1945

A. In Bremervorde by the British on May 21, 1945, while using false identity papers. He escaped justice by committing suicide while in captivity two days later at Lüneburg.

Q. Which one of the following countries stated it would be a non-belligerent on September 2, the day after war began in 1939?

    a. Italy
    b. Soviet Union
    c. Japan

A. Benito Mussolini made the declaration for Italy.

FACT The first planned bombing of Berlin by the Russians, on August 8, 1941, resulted in failure. Five planes on the mission could do nothing more than bomb a section of railroad on the outskirts of the city. Two planes were downed by German antiaircraft fire.

Q. With whom did France sign an armistice on the day that the Pé-tain government set up its headquarters in Vichy, June 24, 1940?

    a. Russia
    b. Germany
    c. Italy

A. The Italians. The document was signed in Rome.

Q. Identify the Norwegian King who fled to England on May 5, 1940.

    a. King Oscar III
    b. King Haakon VII
    c. King Erich V

A. King Haakon VII. The German invasion of his country had begun less than a month earlier, but despite strong Norwegian resistance, the monarch was advised to leave. Belgian King Leopold III, who remained in his country, became a German prisoner on May 28.

Q. Who conceived the idea for Radio Werewolf, the propaganda broadcasts intended to encourage last-ditch resistance in Germany?

    a. Hitler
    b. Himmler
    c. Goebbels

A. Joseph Goebbels. The program made its broadcasting debut on April 1, 1945, and was responsible for the slogan that lived through the cold war years into the 1950s: *Besser tot als rot,* which translates to "Better dead than Red."

Q. Who said, "I made a mistake and I shall pay for it, if my life can still serve as payment"?

    a. Benito Mussolini
    b. Erwin Rommel
    c. Isoroku Yamamoto

A. Mussolini, not very long before he died.

Q. The Japanese code name for the attack on Pearl Harbor was:

    a. Operation A
    b. Operation P
    c. Operation Z

A. In a discussion with his chief of staff in December 1940, Admiral Isoroku Yamamoto used the code name Operation Z for the possible attack on Pearl Harbor.

U.S. Army Photo

Q. Who said: "That is the biggest fool thing we have ever done. The bomb will never go off" in remarks concerning the atom bomb:

    a. Admiral King, USN
    b. General Arnold, USAF
    c. Admiral Leahy, USN

A. President Trumen's Chief of Staff, Admiral William Leahy, during a conversation with the President in 1945. In photo above, King, Arnold and Leahy check a wall map during a Joint Chiefs of Staff meeting.

Code Names

Q. Which American plane was known as the Flying Prostitute and why?

A. The Martin Marauder, a medium weight bomber, was known as the Flying Prostitute because it had no visible means of support. It was also called the Widow Maker for a time after it began service in 1942 because it was said to be unsafe.

Q. What was the code name for the breakout at St. Lo, Normandy?

A. Cobra.

Q. Which American unit was called the Rag-Tag Circus?

A. Because of the varied collection of enemy, civilian and other vehicles they used, the U.S. 83rd Infantry Division became known as the Rag-Tag Circus. Major General Robert C. Macon was the commander.

Q. What was the American equivalent of British Ultra called?

A. Magic.

Q. Who was Cicero?

A. A German agent who worked as a valet at the British Embassy in Turkey. Among other information he passed on was the meaning of the code name Operation Overload—the invasion of Europe. His name was Elyesa Bazna.

Q. What did the British call the DC-3?

A. The British and the Allied air forces in general termed the DC-3 and its modified versions—the C-47 and C-53—the Dakota.

Q. What was Operation Bolero?

A. The transfer of U.S. troops from America to England.

Q. Who was Iva D'Aquino?

A. Tokyo Rose. An American born to Japanese parents, she broadcast propaganda to American forces on behalf of Japan.

Q. Who was irreverently known as the Berlin Bitch by Allied troops in Europe?

A. Germany's answer to Tokyo Rose, Axis Sally.

Q. What was the code name for the Allied amphibious assault on the French Riviera?

A. Operation Anvil-Dragoon. Originally called Anvil, it was changed to Dragoon by the time of the actual invasion.

Q. Who was Lord Haw-Haw?

A. William Joyce, who was executed by the British for his radio broadcasts from Germany during the war.

Q. Who was known throughout Germany as the Voice of the High Command?

A. Lieutenant General Kurt Dittmar, a Wehrmacht officer who broadcast the latest news from the fronts during the war. He surrendered to the U.S. 30th Infantry at Magdeburg by making his way across the Elbe on April 23, 1945. (Dittmar told U.S. intelligence two things: the National Redoubt was a myth and Hitler was still in Berlin.)

Q. Who was Colonel Britain?

A. Douglas Ritchie, who was introduced at the end of BBC news as the voice of Supreme Headquarters, Allied Expeditionary Force. Remember those famous lines: "Our messages for our friends in occupied France tonight are . . ."?

Q. What was Winston Churchill's code name?

A. Colonel Warden.

Q. Who was Colonel Valerio?

A. Italian partisan commander Walter Audisio, the man who read the death sentence to Mussolini and ordered him and his mistress shot.

Q. Who was Colonel Rol?

A. Henry Tanguy, the communist leader in the Resistance in Paris.

Q. Who was named the Spy of the Century?

A. General Reinhard Gehlen, the man in charge of the German Army's intelligence and espionage network in the East. He later worked for the U.S. Army, the CIA and West Germany's espionage organization, the BND.

Q. What was the White Death?

A. The Finnish ski troops who in their white uniforms inflicted heavy casualties on the invading Soviets and nearly drove them out after the Russian attack on November 30, 1939.

Q. Who was Grofaz? (The term is an abbreviation for *grosster Feldherr aller Zeiten,* which means the greatest general of all time.)

A. Never as fond of their Fuehrer as people in other parts of Germany, the name Grofaz was sarcastically used by Berliners when speaking of Hitler.

Q. What was the Hooligan Navy?

A. The U.S. Coastal Picket Patrol. Organized in May 1942, it consisted of auxiliary yachts and motorboats under 100 feet in length. The civilian owners were often skippers who could not pass Navy qualifying exams. They were armed with small guns and depth charges to hunt U-boats. By February 1943 there were 550 of them, but they failed to make any "kills."

Q. What was General Patton's Navy?

A. The ships under Admiral H. Kent Hewitt that aided Patton with his "leapfrog" techniques along the coast of Sicily. Used to land his troops at points along the coast and to transport supplies, they helped Patton beat Monty to Messina.

Q. What was the U.S. Mystery ship project?

A. Heavily armed vessels disguised as peaceful merchantmen. Also known as the Q ship project, it accomplished nothing of significance and cost the lives of approximately one quarter of the sailors who volunteered. The ships were copied from those used for this purpose in World War I.

Q. What was the Schwarze Kapelle (Black Orchestra)?

A. The group of Germans, including Abwehr chief Admiral Wilhelm Canaris, that worked to overthrow Hitler and the Nazis.

Q. What was the Red Orchestra?

A. The Soviet spy ring active in Berlin during the war. The Luftwaffe squads that hunted for secret radio transmissions used the term "orchestra" to mean transmitter.

Q. What were the WASPS?

A. Nearly 2,000 American women who piloted every kind of plane the U.S. could produce, from Mustangs to B-29s, generally on delivery or ferry missions, between 1942 and 1944. Almost all of these women were experienced civilian pilots with more prewar flying hours to their credit than their male counterparts.

Q. What did the initials WAVES stand for?

A. Women Appointed for Voluntary Emergency Service, a branch of the U.S. Navy.

Q. What were the U.S. Women's Coast Guard Reserve members known as? Why?

A. They were the SPARS, from the motto of the U.S. Coast Guard— *Semper Par*atus—always ready.

Q. Which U.S. aircraft carrier was known as the Fighting Lady?

A. The U.S.S. *Yorktown,* also known as the Lucky Y because despite all the action she saw she received only one hit from the enemy.

Q. What ship was known as the Evil I?

A. Because of her ability to be in the way of Japanese torpedoes and bombs all too frequently, the U.S. aircraft carrier *Intrepid* had the nickname.

Q. What was the nickname of the battleship U.S.S. *Missouri?*

A. Mighty Mo.

Q. Which U.S. destroyer in the Pacific was nicknamed G. Q. Johnny?

A. The U.S.S. *Johnston,* because of the numerous general quarters alerts in combat.

Q. What was the bill in the U.S. Congress with the official designation of HR-1776 commonly known as?

A. Despite the patriotic designation, bill HR-1776 was better known as Lend-Lease.

Q. What was the Red Ball Highway?

A. The route, non-stop, heading northeast, that the seemingly endless convoy of U.S. Army supply trucks rolled along on to the Rhine and the Western Front. The trucks themselves were called the Red Ball Express.

Q. What was the Tokyo Express?

A. The name U.S Marines applied to the Japanese ships coming through the Slot in the Solomon Islands.

Q. What was the Caesar Line?

A. The German defense line protecting Rome.

Q. What were Rommel's asparagus?

A. Poles about six to twelve inches in diameter and eight to twelve feet long, approximately seventy-five feet apart. They were intended to deny the Allied airborne troops good landing zones during D-Day.

Q. Who was Smasher Karl?

A. Wehrmacht Lieutenant General Karl Weidling, who Hitler once ordered shot and then appointed commandant of Berlin in April 1945. On May 2, 1945, Weidling surrendered Berlin to the Russians.

Q. What was kickapoo joy juice?

A. The name GI's gave to the unusual alcoholic drink they managed to make during the campaign in Italy. (In the Pacific just about anything U.S. servicemen managed to brew was dubbed jungle juice.)

Q. Which branch of the U.S. military was known as the Silent Service?

A. The Navy's submarine fleet.

Q. What and when was Big Week?

A. February 19 to 25, 1944, when the Allies had over 6,000 bombers pounding at Germany. The Luftwaffe lost over 450 planes trying to stop the raids.

Q. During the campaign in North Africa what was known as Black Saturday?

A. June 13, 1942, Rommel's ambush of 300 British tanks under the command of General Sir Neil Ritchie. The Desert Fox destroyed 230 of them.

Q. What was the name of the RAF plan to employ all available aircraft against the Luftwaffe as it approached Coventry?

A. Operation Cold Douche, which had little success.

Q. What was the German Kondor Mission?

A. Their intelligence operation in Cairo, Egypt.

Q. What was P. C. Bruno?

A. The code name for the French cryptographic service prior to occupation by the Germans. It functioned from the Chàteau Vignolle approximately twenty-five miles from Paris.

Q. By what name did Hitler and the German High Command identify the counteroffensive in the Ardennes Forest that the Allies called the Battle of the Bulge?

A. Watch on the Rhine.

Q. What was Eagle Day?

A. The 1,000-bomber, 700-fighter-plane raid on London on August 15, 1940, by the Luftwaffe.

FACT Italian dictator Benito Mussolini is credited with creating the term Axis as it applied to that group of nations in the war. On November 1, 1936, after reaching a secret agreement with Hitler, Mussolini gave a speech in Milan in which he said, "The vertical line between Rome and Berlin is not a partition but rather an axis round which all European states animated by the will to collaboration and peace can also collaborate."

Q. What was the Battalion of Heaven?

A. Chasseurs Parachutistes, the 4th SAS Regiment, the French unit that employed airborne drops behind German lines in Europe after the Normandy invasion. They practiced guerrilla and commando-style tactics.

Q. What was the Cactus Air Force?

A. The name adopted by the Navy and Marine pilots operating out of Henderson Field during the Guadalcanal campaign.

Q. Who were the Martians?

A. The Allied personnel from SHAEF in London who were responsible for the evaluation of intelligence.

Q. Which plane did Allied bomber crews nickname Little Friend?

A. The longest-range fighter escort in action during the war, the Mustang.

Q. What was the name of the Lockheed Lodestar that carried De Gaulle back to France?

A. The *France,* piloted by Colonel Lionel de Marmier.

Q. What was General Hideki Tojo's nickname?

A. Razor Brain.

Q. Who was nicknamed the Fuehrer's Brown Eminence?

A. Martin Bormann, who owned and wore only brown boots rather than the black boots that others in Hitler's circle were fond of.

Q. Which American general did the Chinese affectionately call Old Leather Face?

A. General Claire Chennault.

Q. Identify the British General nicknamed Jumbo.

A. General Sir Henry Wilson.

Q. Which American general was known as Vinegar Joe?

A. General Joseph Stilwell.

Q. What was FDR's code name?

A. Victor. The American President was also known as Admiral Q in certain messages. President Truman was code-named Kilting.

Q. Who was Popski?

A. Lieutenant Colonel Vladimir Peniakoff, the British commando who became a legend from Africa to Italy leading Popski's Private Army.

Q. Which Allied general was known as the Impatient Lion?

A. Jacques Leclerc of the Free French.

Q. Identify the Italian general nicknamed Electric Whiskers by his own troops.

A. Bergonzoli, who was captured by the British in the African campaign. The name referred to his red beard.

Q. Who was known as the Father of the Royal Air Force?

A. Air Marshal Lord Hugh Trenchard, who developed the RAF between 1919 and 1929. He came out of retirement in 1939 at age sixty-six.

Q. Who is known as the Father of the Atomic Bomb?

A. Dr. Robert Oppenheimer. He was denied security clearance nine years after he headed the team that developed the bomb.

Q. What name and rank did the British give to the body deposited off the Spanish coast in the hopes the Axis would think it was a dead secret courier?

A. Major Martin. The body had an attaché case replete with "secret" communications indicating the British would land in Greece or Sardinia instead of Sicily. The Germans believed the ploy, but the Italians were not convinced.

FACT   In an effort to thwart Allied bombing raids on Germany, reproductions of Berlin, Hamburg and other areas were built near enough to the actual sites to confuse aircraft. However, they were far enough away to provide safety for the inhabitants. There were no less than five copies of Berlin alone sprinkled across the German landscape in giant scale.

Q. What were Flash and Thunder?

A. The passwords that were used by the 82nd Airborne in addition to tin toy snappers to identify friendly troops after the drop on Normandy.

Q. What was the real name of the Dutch Intelligence Service officer known as Captain Harry who jumped with the 82nd Airborne in Nijmegen, Holland?

A. Arie D. Bestebreurtje. Actually he participated in several missions with U.S. forces, and was involved in the planning for the airborne drop on Tempelhof Airport in Berlin.

Q. Who were known as the Golden Pheasants?

A. The select group of Nazi officials who were permitted to wear the gilded swastika.

Q. To whom did FDR refer as Uncle Joe?

A. Joseph Stalin. However, the Allied code name for Stalin was Glyptic.

Q. What was the name of Hitler's private train?

A. Amerika.

Q. What was the name of the private train Reichsfuehrer Heinrich Himmler used?

A. Steiermark.

Q. What period of the war did German submariners call the Happy Time?

A. The summer and fall of 1940, when they were sinking an average of eight ships per U-boat per month.

Q. What did Rommel call Devil's Gardens?

A. The extensive German minefields at El Alamein.

FACT   The U.S. Selective Service Act, which had been law for one year in 1940, was continued in 1941 by a margin of one vote in the House of Representatives, less than four months before the attack on Pearl Harbor.

U.S. Army Photo

Q. What was the real name of French General Jacques Leclerc?

A. Philippe François Marie Leclerc de Hautecloque. After joining the Free French he changed it to protect his family still in France. In photo above Leclerc (right), as commander of the French 2nd Armored Division, is congratulated by U.S. General Walton H. Walker on the beach at Normandy on July 31, 1944.

Q. What were the Stalin Organs?

A. Rockets fired from launchers with an ear-splitting screech. Their Russian name was Katushkas. Fired at night, they produced a long white trail.

Q. What was the Sitzkrieg?

A. The period from September 1939, when war was declared on Germany, and the start of actual fighting by Britain and France early in 1940. In the English-speaking world it was called the phony war.

Q. What does blitzkrieg mean?

A. Lightning war, which was popularized after the rapid German advance on Poland in 1939.

Q. What significance did Wagner's "Twilight of the Gods" have for members of the Berlin Philharmonic Orchestra?

A. They knew that the night they were requested to play it would be the night Armament and War Production Minister Albert Speer had made arrangements for them to flee Berlin to the West rather than be captured by the Russians.

Q. What was a Fuehrer Paket?

A. The packages of food Hitler gave as gifts to important military personnel he summoned to his headquarters at Rastenburg.

Q. What was Hitler's dog named?

A. Blondie.

Q. What was Big B?

A. For the Eighth Air Force fliers who flew the missions, Berlin was Big B.

FACT During the Battle of Britain Churchill sent the last seventy tanks on the island to British forces fighting in North Africa. He felt that if the situation in Great Britain got to a point where the tanks would be a crucial ingredient, the battle would already be lost. In justifying their movement to Egypt he said: "I have not become the King's First Minister to preside over the liquidation of the British Empire."

Q. What was the German code name for the operation that involved penetrating U.S. lines with English-speaking troops in U.S. uniforms?

A. Greif. It was under the command of SS commando Otto Skorzeny and intended for widespread use during the Battle of the Bulge.

Q. What was the German code name for the bombing of Coventry, England, on November 14–15, 1940?

A. Moonlight Sonata.

Q. The Allied scheme that involved the Man Who Never Was had two code names. What were they?

A. Mincemeat and Trojan Horse. Carried out in 1943, it was conceived to mislead the Germans about Allied invasion intentions in Italy.

Q. How did Churchill sign his correspondence with FDR?

A. Former Naval Person, which he seemed to delight in. Churchill had been in charge of the Admiralty at times during both World Wars.

Q. Which German general was nicknamed Unser Giftzwerg (our poison dwarf)?

A. Colonel General Gotthard Heinrici, the short, tough general ordered to hold the Russians on the Oder River as commander of Army Group Vistula. The name was used by those who liked him as a compliment and by those who disliked him, including Hitler, as derogatory.

Q. What was the Night of the Long Knives? When was it?

A. The changing of the guard for Hitler. On June 30, 1934, his SS murdered eighty-three members of the SA, his former personal army.

Q. What were the eight code names used for the subdivided sections of Omaha Beach on D-Day?

A. They were Easy Red, Fox Red, Fox Green, Charlie, Easy Green, Dog Green, Dog White and Dog Red.

Q. Which island did the Marines call the Killing Ground?

A. Tarawa.

Q. What battle was known as the Great Marianas Turkey Shoot?

A. The Battle of the Philippine Sea, June 19–21, 1944. So named by an aviator because U.S. forces destroyed 346 Japanese planes and two carriers. The U.S. lost thirty planes and no ships. It marked virtually the end of significant Japanese carrier opposition.

Q. What were the circumstances under which the following bulletin was transmitted by accident on June 4, two days before the D-Day invasion: "Urgent Press Associated NYK Flash Eisenhower's HQ announced Allied landings in France"?

A. An Associated Press teletype operator had been trying to build up transmitting speed and the perforated tape was somehow mixed in with "live" tape.

Q. What did the coded message Ham and Jam mean?

A. Sent by British 6th Airborne paratroopers, it was the message indicating that the unit had captured two vital bridges over the Caen Canal and Orne River.

Q. Which U.S. Army division was known as the Victory Division?

A. The 5th Armored Division.

Q. Name the U.S. division whose unusual tactics earned it the name Hell on Wheels.

A. The 2nd Armored, which confused the Germans from North Africa onward.

Q. Which division was known as the Screaming Eagles?

A. The 101st Airborne Division.

FACT   Boise City, Oklahoma, holds the distinction of being the only mainland U.S. town bombed during the war. However, the incident was not the result of Axis ability to penetrate U.S. defenses. A U.S. Air Force bomber on a training mission from Dalhart, Texas, knocked out the local Baptist church and another building—which were over forty miles from the target range. No casualties resulted in Boise City, but the future flight status of the pilot and crew were seriously questioned.

Q. What and when was Kristalnacht?

A. On November 10, 1938, a "spontaneous" anti-Jewish demonstration was staged because German diplomat Ernst von Rath had been assassinated by a Jew. Stores and shops were ruined, synagogues burned, Jews beaten and arrested.

Q. By what name did the Allied troops know the peaceful-looking seacoast area of Vierville?

A. Omaha Beach, Normandy.

Q. What were Ascension Day Rations?

A. The extra portions of food the German government issued to Berliners on April 20, 1945, Hitler's birthday. They were properly called crisis rations, and many Germans believed they had gotten the extra food because the government expected them to "ascend into heaven" before the Russians captured the city.

Q. Identify the code names of the three Paris transmitters used by the Resistance to communicate with the Allies.

A. Apollo Black, Montparnasse Black and Pleyel Violet.

Q. What was the Eagle's Nest?

A. Hitler's mountain retreat at Berchtesgaden.

Q. What was the name of Hitler's headquarters at Rastenburg?

A. Wolf's Lair.

Q. What was the Little Red School House?

A. SHAEF (Supreme Headquarters Allied Expeditionary Force) in Reims, France.

Q. Who were the Devils in Skirts?

A. The British 51st Highland Division.

Q. Identify the U.S. division known as the Railsplitters?

A. The 84th Infantry Division.

Q. What was the U.S. 4th Infantry Division called?

A. The Ivy Division.

Q. Which U.S. division was called the Blue and Gray?

A. The 29th Division.

Q. What were the German Goliaths?

A. Miniature robot tanks with over a half ton of explosives. Guided by remote control, they were intended to be sent among Allied troops and vehicles and set off.

Q. What was the name of the ersatz coffee Parisians turned to during the occupation?

A. Café National.

Q. What was Paname?

A. A French slang word for Paris. It first came into general use after Edith Piaf sang it in a song prior to the war.

Q. What was the official name of General de Gaulle's Free French provisional government?

A. Comité Français de Libération Nationale (CFLN).

Q. What was the Red Plan the French underground was to execute upon hearing the BBC message "The dice are on the table"?

A. The cutting of all phone and communication lines in advance of D-Day.

Q. What was General von Choltitz's headquarters in Paris code-named at the time of the city's liberation?

A. Located in the Hotel Meurice on the Rue de Rivoli across from Tuileries Gardens, the headquarters code name was Hypnose.

Q. What are the three code names used for the forty-, thirty-, and nine-ton bridges the Allies constructed near Monte Cassino, Italy?

A. The forty-ton bridge was Amazon, the thirty-ton was Blackwater and the nine-ton was Congo. They crossed the Rapido River.

Q. What were the German Werewolves?

A. Commando troops the Allies feared would operate from the National Redoubt after the end of hostilities. The name Werewolves was used by propaganda Minister Joseph Goebbels.

Q. What were the Chindits?

A. British Major General Orde Wingate's forces in the China-Burma-India theater. Chindit was a bastardization of the Burmese word for lion, *chinthe*. Wingate's Chindits successfully foiled the Japanese in their efforts to capture India.

Q. What was the popular name of the special American combat infantry team known as the Galahad Force that was commanded by Brigadier General Frank D. Merrill?

A. Merrill's Marauders.

Q. When did the U.S. succeed in breaking the Japanese Purple code?

A. In September 1940. It enabled the U.S. to read the most confidential messages Tokyo sent to its diplomatic corps for more than fourteen months before the attack on Pearl Harbor.

Q. What was the Carpetbagger Squadron?

A. The Army Air Force unit that dropped arms and supplies to the Resistance fighters in the Fortress Europe. They flew over 300 missions from January 1943 to the end of the war in Europe.

Q. Which German aircraft was known as the Flaming Coffin?

A. The Heinkel He-177, Germany's only heavy bomber. About 1,000 were produced.

Q. Which British plane did the Germans nickname Stachelschwein (porcupine)?

A. The well-armed Short Sunderland Flying Boat, which had great success in anti-U-boat warfare.

FACT One of the most unusual devices for identification used by any nation was the employing of fireworks by the U.S. Regimental Combat Team during the North African invasion. In an effort to convince the Vichy French at Oran that the invasion force was U.S., not British, the Americans shot firework bombs that exploded into 100-foot-wide U.S. flags overhead. (The French were hostile to the British, who had recently attacked their fleet in the harbor.) The U.S. troops also used loudspeakers which identified the Americans as not being British troops.

Q. What was Plan Green?

A. The code name the French underground gave to the operation to smash German railroad traffic.

Q. What was the German code name for the invasion of Russia?

A. Barbarossa.

Q. What was Operation Eclipse?

A. The Allied plan for the occupation of Berlin, including the sectors that were to be occupied by the major powers. Prior to November 1944, it was also known as Operation Rankin, Case C and Operation Talisman.

Q. What was Operation Punishment?

A. When the Yugoslavs overthrew their government and repudiated the treaty of "alliance" with Germany in the spring of 1941, Hitler ordered the savage bombing of Belgrade, killing 17,000, which he termed Operation Punishment.

Q. What was the German and Italian code name for the attack on Malta?

A. Operation Herkules. It was called off when the Germans succeeded in taking Tobruk. The Malta-bound troops were given to Rommel.

Q. What was the German code name for the planned invasion of England?

A. Operation Sea Lion.

Q. What was Operation Roundup?

A. The code name for the 1943 Allied plan to invade Europe.

Q. What was Plan Jael?

A. The operation to convince the Germans that the Normandy D-Day landings would take place elsewhere. Jael was an Old Testament woman accused of treachery. It was renamed Plan Bodyguard after a quote that appears elsewhere in this book.

Q. What was Operation Fortitude?

A. The code name for the cover plan for the D-Day invasion to convince the Germans it would take place at Pas de Calais. This was different from Plan Jael in that it indicated a specific area.

Q. What was Operation Gambit?

A. The British submarine mission that went in close to the French coastline in advance of the Normandy landings in June 1944. They functioned as navigational markers for British and Canadian troops. Two subs, X-20 and X-23, were involved.

Q. What was the code name for the Allied invasion of North Africa?

A. Operation Torch.

Q. What was Operation Jubilant?

A. The plan for Allied airborne drops on prisoner of war camps as the Allies pushed deeper into Germany.

Q. What was the code name for the proposed Allied airborne attack on the German naval base at Kiel?

A. Operation Eruption.

Q. What was the German code name for the plan to take Moscow?

A. Typhoon.

Q. What was the code name for the plan that would have dropped U.S. airborne troops on the trio of airfields around Rome?

A. Giant II, which was never employed.

Q. What was Operation Yellow?

A. German's actions against Belgium, Holland and Luxembourg.

Q. What was Operation Puakenschlag?

A. Operation Paukenschlag (roll of the drums) was the name for U-boat assaults on U.S. coastal and Caribbean shipping from January to July 1942.

Q. What was the naval portion of the D-Day invasion code-named?

A. Operation Neptune.

FACT The most destructive single bombing mission of the war took place March 9–10, 1945, when 334 B-29s raided Tokyo and left 1.25 million people homeless. This raid caused more damage than the atom bombs on Hiroshima and Nagasaki.

U.S. Army Photo

Q. Which German commander was called Smiling Albert by the Allies?

A. Field Marshal Albert Kesselring, shown here while being held as a witness by the Allies during the Nuremberg war crimes trials in November 1945.

Q. What was A-Day?

A. The Allied code name for the beginning of the assault on Berlin, April 16, 1945.

Q. What was the code name for the evacuation at Dunkirk?

A. Operation Dynamo.

Q. What was the German code word that indicated the Russian attack on Berlin?

A. Clausewitz.

Q. What was Operation Beggar?

A. The plan to drop guns and supplies to the Resistance fighters in Paris in August 1944. Instead, the planes brought food and coal to the French city on August 26 after it was liberated.

Q. What was Operation Diadem?

A. The liberation of Rome.

Q. What was the Allied code name for Great Britain?

A. Wildflower.

Q. Which Allied air operation was known as Soapsuds?

A. The bombing of Ploesti, Rumania, on August 1, 1943.

Q. Operation Venerable, the Allied plan to open the French port of Bordeaux, was known earlier by what name?

A. Operation Independence.

Q. What was the England-to-Russia air shuttle bombing known as?

A. Operation Frantic.

Q. What was Fanfare?

A. The Allied code name for all operations in the Mediterranean.

Q. What was the code name for the U.S. invasion and liberation of the Philippines?

A. Excelsior.

Q. What was the Allied operation to paralyze the German transportation system called?

A. Operation Clarion.

Q. What was Operation Baytown?

A. The invasion of Italy by the British Eighth Army via Messina.

Q. What was Fat Boy?

A. The code name for the plutonium atom bomb dropped on Nagasaki.

Q. What was Little Boy?

A. The code name for the uranium atom bomb dropped on Hiroshima.

Q. What was Operation Crossbow?

A. The code name for Allied air raids against Germany's V-1 launch sites.

Q. What was the code name for the deceptive operation to make the Germans believe the Allies had an invasion fleet off the coast of Boulogne on D-Day?

A. Operation Glimmer.

Q. What was the code name for the Allied raid on Dieppe, France, in 1942?

A. Operation Jubilee. However, it was originally called Operation Rutter.

Q. What were Zeal, Thumb and Pearl often used as code names for?

A. Information from the Enigma code machines. Rather than risk using the code name Ultra for such information passed on to field commanders below the rank of commanding generals, the British used a series of code names.

Q. What was the English-French operation against Dakar in 1940 code named?

A. Menace.

Q. What was the Garibaldi Partisan Division?

A. Two Italian divisions that fought along with Tito's troops against the Germans in Yugoslavia after Italy declared war on Germany.

Q. What was Piccolo Peak?

A. A hill in the battle for Salerno that General Mark Clark had assigned a regimental band to defend. The name came *after* the troops were assigned.

Q. What was the code name for the unsuccessful 1943 attempt to kill Hitler by placing a bomb in his plane?

A. Flash. Many of the same German officers who would later take part in the July 20, 1944, attempt were involved in this.

Q. What was the German generals' code name for the plot to kill Hitler in 1944?

A. Operation Valkyrie, which failed on July 20, 1944.

Q. What was the code word the German generals in the plot to kill Hitler awaited as news that the mission had succeeded?

Q. Ubung. Because it was sent out prematurely, several conspirators quickly ordered SS, Gestapo and other Nazis in their area arrested. Their fast action earned them death sentences.

Q. What was the code name for the plan to capture or kill Field Marshal Rommel in France in 1944?

A. Operation Gaff.

Q. What was called a great crusade?

A. The Allied efforts to wrest Europe from the grasp of the Nazis. Dwight Eisenhower popularized it.

Q. What was Special Operations Executive?

A. The British organization, established in 1940, that organized subversion and sabotage in German-occupied countries.

Q. What was known as the Gibraltar of the South Pacific?

A. Rabaul on New Britain island.

FACT   The United States was asked to join the Tripartite Pact alliance with Japan, Germany and Italy "in the spirit of the new order. . . in which . . . the natural geographic divisions of the earth established in complementary fashion" would be the goal. Japan extended the invitation on October 13, 1940.

Q. What did Gustav mean in the German code with regard to Tempel-hof Airport?

A. It was the warning that Allied planes were heading for the airport.

Q. What was Duroc?

A. Named for one of Napoleon's generals, Duroc was the underground control center for the French Resistance in August 1944. It covered approximately 300 miles of tunnels and sewers of the metro system and sanitation department.

Q. What was Exchange 500?

A. The largest telephone and communications center in Germany, linking Hitler, OKW and other bases with field commanders in Germany and conquered territories.

Q. What was PLUTO?

A. Pipe Line Under the Ocean, the trans-Channel fuel transport line from England to France that fed the Allied supply lines after the Normandy invasion.

Q. What were the artificial harbors constructed for Operation Over-lord called?

A. Mulberry.

Q. What was the Manhattan Engineer District?

A. Established in August 1942, it was the name of the U.S. project that worked to build the atom bomb. It was also known as the Manhattan Project.

Q. What were Millennium and Millennium II?

A. Code names for the thousand-bomber raids on Cologne and Bremen.

Q. What were Maybach I and Maybach II?

A. Mayback I was the headquarters of OKH, the German Army High Command. Maybach II was the German OKW, Armed Forces High Command, and Hitler's headquarters, located in Zossen.

Q. What were Bangalore torpedoes?

A. Devices used to destroy barbwire obstacles, usually lengths of pipe filled with explosives.

Q. What is a MOMP?

A. Navy lingo for Mid Ocean Meeting Point.

Q. What is Condition Zed?

A. Complete watertight integrity on a ship.

Q. In U.S. jargon what does SOPA stand for?

A. Senior Officer Present Afloat.

Q. What was AMGOT?

A. Allied Military Government of Occupied Territories.

Q. What was Eisenhower's Circus Wagon?

A. The trailer he used in England during the planning for D-Day.

Q. Who was Jade Amicol?

A. Colonel Claude Ollivier, chief of the British Intelligence Service in occupied France.

Q. What did membership in the Caterpillar Club say about a pilot?

A. That the American pilot had successfully bailed out of an aircraft. Possession of a parachute ripcord handle was considered proof.

Q. What weapon was known as the Earthquake bomb?

A. The ten-ton bombs in the Allied arsenal. The first one was dropped on Germany in March 1945.

Q. Who was General Bor?

A. General Tadeusz Komorovski, leader of the Polish underground in Warsaw, which began an aggressive campaign against the Germans on August 1, 1944, because they believed the Russians were about to arrive.

FACT The *Queen Mary,* with 10,000 U.S. troops aboard and en route to Great Britain, sliced the British cruiser *Curaçao* in half in October 1942. The *Curaçao* was escorting the *Queen,* which made a course correction but did not alert the warship. Casualties aboard the two halves of the cruiser were 338 killed. The *Queen,* fearing U-boats, did not stop to participate in rescue operations.

Q. What was the Night and Fog Decree?

A. An order, authorized by Hitler, to eliminate all persons considered a threat to German security throughout Fortress Europe. The eliminations, however, were to be conducted in a discreet manner whereby victims would simply disappear into the "night and fog," leaving no trace.

Q. What did the designation CV indicate with regard to U.S. aircraft carriers?

A. The *C* designated the ship as a carrier, while the *V* represented heavier than air, the aircraft on carriers. Thus the CV classification was for ships that were carriers of heavier-than-air planes.

Q. Identify the London hotel that became known as the Blitz Hotel.

A. Because it was the home away from home for numerous British and foreign dignitaries, monarchs, heads of state in exile and the leading newsmen from the U.S., the Savoy earned the name.

Q. Which U.S. air base was known as Cochran's Convent and why?

A. Avenger Field, near Sweetwater, Texas. It was the home of the Women's Air Force Service Pilots (WASP's) and the only all-female U.S. air base in history. The nickname was a lighthearted tribute to one of the two women responsible for female pilots having an opportunity to contribute their skills to the war, Jacqueline Cochrane. The other aviatrix who worked at putting women in the sky for the war effort was Nancy Harkness Love.

Q. What was the cipher used by U.S. military attachés during the war until it was compromised?

A. The Black Code, which had been copied by an Italian spy working in the U.S. Embassy in Rome in August 1944. Passed on to the Germans, it was "read" by the enemy for a full year before being changed.

FACT   The U.S. submarine *Tullibee*, March 26, 1944, off Palau in the Carolines, fired two torpedoes at a Japanese transport. One of the torpedoes began a full circle and hit the submarine, sinking it. Only one crewman survived.

Messages
and Quotations

Q. Kilroy was here. Who said it? What did it mean?

A. James J. Kilroy, a rivet inspection checker at the Fore River Ship-yard in Quincy, Massachusetts, wrote the legend next to work he checked rather than make small chalk marks that piece workers could erase and thereby hope to have counted twice. As a result, ships departed the yard with the words that would become an al-most cult-slogan throughout the war. U.S. servicemen, amused at the legend, scratched, painted, wrote and carved "Kilroy was here" on thousands of buildings, monuments, vehicles and toilet walls.

Q. Who sent the historic message "Air Raid, Pearl Harbor—This is no drill"?

A. An unidentified caller contacted CINCPAC Headquarters by phone prior to 7:58 A.M. on December 7, 1941, with the message "Enemy air raid, not drill." Rear Admiral Patrick Bellinger sent out at 7:58 from Ford Island: "Air Raid, Pearl Harbor—This is no drill." At 8 A.M. Commander Vincent Murphy at CINCPAC Head-quarters sent out "Air raid on Pearl Harbor. This is no drill." Bel-linger is credited with the message picked up by a West Coast radio station and carried across the country to Washington.

Q. Who gave the signal "All ships in harbor sortie"? Where? When?

A. Rear Admiral William R. Furlong aboard the minelayer *Ogala* al-most at the same moment someone telephoned CINCPAC head-quarters "Enemy air raid, not drill." Both of these alerts went out from Pearl Harbor minutes before Admiral Bellinger's historic message.

Q. Who said, "Believe me, Lang, the first twenty-four hours of the invasion will be decisive . . . for the Allies as well as Germany it will be the longest day"?

A. Field Marshal Erwin Rommel to an aide in April 1944.

Q. "Uncommon valor was a common virtue." Who said it, where and when?

A. Admiral Chester Nimitz, after the capture of Iwo Jima.

Q. Who said, "Show this gentleman out through the back door"?

A. Soviet Commissar for Foreign Affairs Vyacheslav Molotov to his secretary after receiving the German declaration of war from Count Werner von der Schulenburg. Hostilities had already begun.

Q. Who said, "Pearl Harbor will never be attacked from the air"?

A. United States Admiral Charles H. McMorris, on December 3, 1941, four days before it happened.

Q. Who said, "But, sir, I think we might be going a bridge too far"?

A. Lieutenant General Frederick Browning, deputy commander, First Allied Airborne Army, at the final conference at Montgomery's headquarters before Operation Market Garden, the drop on Holland.

Q. At whom did Hitler scream *"Brennt Paris?"* ("Is Paris burning?")?

A. His chief of staff, Generaloberst Alfred Jodl, on August 25, 1944. He continued: "Jodl, I want to know . . . is Paris burning? Is Paris burning right now, Jodl?"

Q. Who responded to the German surrender ultimatum with one word, "Nuts"? Where and when?

A. U.S. General Anthony Clement McAuliffe while acting commander of the 101st Airborne at Bastogne during the Battle of the Bulge in 1944.

Q. What was the American retort to the British quip "You Yanks are overpaid, oversexed and over here"?

A. "You're underpaid, undersexed and under Eisenhower."

Ullstein Photo

Q. Who called Hitler's Atlantic Wall a "figment of Hitler's cloud cuckoo land"?

A. The man who was once his favorite general, Field Marshal Erwin Rommel. He made the comment after inspecting it and seeing its numerous deficiencies. Rommel and other senior staff officers are seen above on May 29, 1944, eight days before the Normandy invasion began, on an inspection trip to the Atlantic Wall.

Q. Who said, "I'll put an end to the idea that a woman's body belongs to her . . . the practice of abortion shall be exterminated with a strong hand"?

A. Adolf Hitler, in *Mein Kampf*. And he followed through by sentencing women who had abortions to hard labor. A second offense brought death. This only applied to Aryan women, however.

Q. Who claimed he had secured Peace in Our Time?

A. British Prime Minister Neville Chamberlain after visiting Hitler at the Munich Conference. Germany invaded Czechoslovakia less than six months later.

Q. To whom was the Cromwell quote "You have sat too long here for any good you have been doing. Depart, I say, and let us have done with you. In the name of God, go" repeated in 1940?

A. To British Prime Minister Neville Chamberlain in Parliament by Conservative member Leopold Amery. It signified the displeasure with the government's handling of the war up to that time. Two days later Chamberlain was out, Churchill in.

Q. East Wind, Rain—what did it mean?

A. This was the coded weather broadcast signal Japan may or may not have sent to its intelligence forces abroad to indicate that Japanese-U.S. relations were in danger. Along with similar codes it was intended for use between mid-November and December 7, 1941.

Q. What did "Climb Mount Niitaka" mean?

A. It was the coded message to the Japanese fleet on December 2, 1941, that irrevocably ordered the attack on Pearl Harbor.

FACT The German Navy developed magnetic mines which remained on the sea floor and were activated by the magnetic field generated by a ship passing overhead. This was a great improvement over moored contact mines, which could be located by minesweepers, their cables cut and then destroyed by small arms fire. Britain overcame the magnetic mines through the use of an electric cable around ships' hulls, thereby countering the magnetic field.

Q. Who prepared the following message: "Our landings in the Cherbourg-Havre area have failed to gain a satisfactory foothold and I have withdrawn the troops. . . . If there is any blame or fault attached to the attempt, it is mine alone"?

A. General Dwight D. Eisenhower, Supreme Allied Commander. It was Ike's *"other"* message "that was never sent" in the event the Normandy invasion failed.

Q. Who said; "If I was commander of the Allied forces right now, I could finish off the war in fourteen days"?

A. Field Marshal Erwin Rommel on D-Day, June 6, 1944, as he raced back to his Army Group B from his home in Germany.

Q. What were the two messages that came over the transport ships' loudspeakers that most D-Day veterans still remember?

A. The command "Away all boats," and the Lord's Prayer.

Q. Who said; "Two kinds of people are staying on this beach, the dead and those who are going to die. Now let's get the hell out of here"?

A. Colonel George A. Taylor, the 16th Infantry Regiment's commanding officer, to men on Omaha Beach on D-Day.

Q. Who said; "I hope Vichy drives them back into the sea" when he was informed that the Allies had invaded North Africa?

A. General Charles de Gaulle, who had not been told of the planned invasion. (The United States did not recognize de Gaulle's position as head of the French provisional government but did recognize the Vichy government and had negotiated with Admiral Jean Darlan to eliminate resistance to the landings.)

Q. Who said, "There are only two rules of war. Never invade Russia. Never invade China"?

A. Field Marshal Sir Bernard Law Montgomery.

Q. Who said, "The last man who sees Hitler wins the game"?

A. Rommel to an aide when discussing the Fuehrer's ability to change his mind or make a decision.

Q. Who said; "There'll be no Dunkirk here"? Where?

A. British General L. J. Morshead, commander at Tobruk.

U.S. Army Photo

Q. Who said, "Compared to war, all other forms of human endeavor shrink to insignificance. God, how I love it"?

A. U.S. Army General George Patton, who also said, "Peace is going to be hell on me," in a letter to his wife. In the August 26, 1944, photo above, Patton confers with officers of the 5th Division, under his command, on the progress in crossing the Seine River in France.

Q. Who said, "Firing [General Sir Claude] Auchinleck was like killing a magnificent stag"?

A. Winston Churchill, after he fired Auchinleck as commander in North Africa.

Q. Who said, "Suppose my neighbor's home catches fire, and I have a length of garden hose . . ." about what?

A. FDR at a press conference prior to asking Congress to pass Lend-Lease.

Q. Who said, "All the same, a formidable people, a very great people . . . to have pushed this far"? About whom?

A. Charles de Gaulle, when visiting Moscow. The rest of the quote is "I don't speak of the Russians, I speak of the Germans."

Q. Who said the following about whom? "His ardor and daring inflicted grievous disasters upon us . . . a great general."

A. Winston Churchill about Erwin Rommel.

Q. Who said, "My Fuehrer, I congratulate you! Roosevelt is dead. It is written in the stars. The last half of April will be the turning point for us"?

A. Propaganda Minister Joseph Goebbels, on April 13, the day after Roosevelt died. Hitler would take his own life seventeen days later, and Goebbels and his wife and six children would be dead a day later.

Q. Who said, "The hand that held the dagger has struck it into the back of its neighbor"? About what?

A. FDR, commenting on Italy's entry into the war against the Allies on June 10, 1940, made the statement in a speech at the University of Virginia.

Q. Who said, "I only wish Herr Reichsmarschall, that we were issued similar razor blades!"—about what, to whom?

A. Rommel to Goering when the latter brushed off reports that the British were destroying Rommel's panzers with American shells. Goering said, "All the Americans can make are razor blades and refrigerators."

Q. Who said, "Praise the Lord and pass the ammunition," and when?

A. Chaplain Howell Forgy, aboard the *New Orleans* during the attack on Pearl Harbor, popularized the remark which, according to U.S.M.C. Major Louis E. Fagan was uttered in 1689 by the Reverend Dr. Walker during the defense of Londonderry from the forces of King James II.

Q. Who said, "I'm too old a bunny to get too excited about this"? About what?

A. General Hans von Salmuth, Commanding Officer of the German Fifteenth Army, when told that the second part of the coded message announcing the invasion of Europe had been intercepted. He continued to play bridge with other officers.

Q. Who said, "Hitler has missed the bus"?

A. British Prime Minister Chamberlain, commenting on the "phony war." The full quote was "After seven months of war I feel ten times as confident of victory as I did at the beginning. Hitler has missed the bus."

Q. Who said, "Berlin is no longer a military objective"?

A. Supreme Allied Commander Dwight D. Eisenhower, on April 14, 1945, when he announced that the Anglo-American drive toward Germany's capital would be halted. Some troops were only forty-five miles away.

Q. Who created the motto "The Fuehrer commands, we follow"?

A. Dr. Joseph Paul Goebbels, Germany's Propaganda Minister.

Q. "That Bohemian corporal, Hitler, usually decides against himself." Who said it?

A. Field Marshal Gerd von Rundstedt upon learning that Rommel, who was his junior, would be redesigning the anti-invasion defenses of the European coast—under orders from Hitler.

FACT   The worst air raid on Paris came the day after liberation on August 26, 1944. Nearly 150 planes of the Luftwaffe bombed the city for thirty minutes, destroying 597 buildings, killing 213 and injuring almost 1,000 people.

Q. Who frequently included the following quote when he apologized to his guests for serving vegetarian meals: "The elephant is the strongest animal. He also cannot stand meat"?

A. Adolf Hitler.

Q. "Where have you come from?" Who asked it?

A. Major General Josef Reichert, Commanding Officer of the German 711th Division to two British paratroopers who landed on the lawn of his headquarters and were promptly captured. One of them, however, responded, "Awfully sorry, old man, but we simply landed here by accident."

Q. Who said, "It is assumed that there are no enemy [aircraft] carriers in waters adjacent to Midway"?

A. Japanese Admiral Chuichi Nagumo, on June 4, 1942, prior to the start of the Battle of Midway.

Q. Who wrote the following in Latin in the customs station in Belgium as he left: "Ungrateful Belgium, you will not possess my bones"?

A. General Ernst von Falkenhausen, German governor-general of Belgium, who had done his utmost to prevent the SS and Gestapo from their campaign of horror in that country. Falkenhausen was sentenced to twelve years in prison by the Belgians after the war but was released within a month as an act of clemency. One of the conspirators in the plot to kill Hitler, he had been imprisoned in Dachau also but escaped death when the U.S. liberated the death camp.

Q. Who popularized the phrase "unconditional surrender"?

A. FDR, at the Casablanca Conference, January 24, 1943. He is said to have believed that the term was an expansion of General Grant's initials (U.S.) after Grant's demand for unconditional surrender of Fort Donelson in February 1862.

Q. What did the following message mean: "The Italian Navigator has just landed in the New World. The natives are friendly"?

A. Sent by Nobel prize-winner physicist Arthur Compton, it informed Washington that the U.S. had successfully produced a controlled chain reaction with the atom.

Q. Who sent the following message: "Our casualties heavy. Enemy casualties unknown. Situation: we are winning"? About what?

A. U.S. Marine Corps Colonel David Shoup to the Navy ships off Betio during the initial engagements of the Tarawa campaign.

Q. What did the following mean: "The long sobs of the violins of autumn"?

A. It was the first half of the message on the BBC announcing the D-Day invasion to the French underground and, because they knew what it would be, to German counterintelligence.

Q. What was the second half of the D-Day message broadcast to the French underground troops re the Normandy landings?

A. "Wounds my heart with a monotonous languor." Both the first and second parts of the message are from a nineteenth-century poem by French poet Paul Verlaine, "Song of Autumn."

Q. Whose wartime diary contains the following, dated November 25, 1941: "The President predicted that we were likely to be attacked perhaps next Monday . . . the question was how we should maneuver them into the position of firing the first shot"?

A. U.S. Secretary of War Henry L. Stimson's. It covered events discussed in a cabinet meeting over the possibility of hostilities with Japan.

Q. What was the legend above the portico on the Reichstag?

A. Dem Deutschen Volke (To the German people).

Q. What did the BBC code message "It is hot in Suez" indicate?

A. Sabotage by the French of railroad equipment and tracks. It was broadcast at 6:30 P.M. the night before D-Day.

Q. Which American unit posted the following sign and where was it: "Truman Bridge, Gateway to Berlin"?

A. At Barby, Germany, on the east bank of the Elbe. The rest of the sign read, "Courtesy of the 83rd Infantry Division." It went up less than twenty-four hours after Harry S. Truman took the reins of government in April 1945.

Q. Who asked, "Does anybody here know the road to Paris?"

A. Captain Raymond Drone of the 2nd French Armored Division on August 24, 1944, as he set out to become the first French officer to return to Paris with a small column of men and vehicles.

Q. Who sent the following message to Hitler on April 22, 1945: "My Fuehrer, in view of your decision to remain in the fortress of Berlin do you agree that I take over at once the total leadership of the Reich?"

A. Hermann Goering, who was promptly arrested by the SS for his grab at power.

Q. Who said, "A million men cannot take Tarawa in a hundred years"?

A. Japanese Admiral Keji Shibasaki. To his boast 5,600 Marines responded by taking Tarawa in seventy-two hours.

Q. Of whom did Churchill say, "A man of genius who might well have become also a man of destiny"?

A. British Major General Orde Wingate, who was killed in a plane crash on March 24, 1944. The other "man of destiny" the PM referred to was Charles de Gaulle.

Q. Who said, "Gee, I didn't know our bombers had done *that* much damage in Rome"?

A. An unidentified American GI who, upon entering the Eternal City, had his first glimpse of the ruins of the Colosseum.

Q. What did Hitler say after seeing tanks being tested at Kumersdorf?

A. "That's what I need. That's what I want to have." The date was February 1935.

Q. Who said, "If the Germans ever get here they will never go home"?

A. Mussolini, in 1940, discussing the "advantage" of having German troops on Italian soil.

FACT Six Japanese cities were destroyed by a single 855-plane B-29 raid on August 2, 1945, that dropped several tons of jellied gasoline and magnesium bombs. This was four days before the first atom bomb was dropped.

U.S. Army Photo

Q. When did U.S. President Franklin D. Roosevelt first publicly announce the Four Freedoms?

A. During his State of the Union address to Congress in January 1941. He had been elected to an unprecedented third term the previous November and would go on to yet a fourth term. The Four Freedoms are freedom of speech, freedom of worship, freedom from fear, and freedom from want.

Q. Who said, "Never have so few been commanded by so many"?

A. Major General Maxwell Taylor, who with his staff of the 101st Airborne landed amid a small group of enlisted paratroopers during the Normandy airborne drop.

Q. Who said, "If bombs drop on Germany, my name is Meyer"?

A. Head of the German Luftwaffe, Hermann Goering, in 1939. The Reichsmarschall regretted the remark on August 24, 1940, when the RAF succeeded in bombing Berlin for the first time.

Q. What battle did this Churchill quote describe: "I had hoped that we were hurling a wildcat onto the shore, but all we got was a stranded whale"?

A. The Allied landings at Anzio and Nettuno, Italy.

Q. Who said, "Hoist the colors and let no enemy ever haul them down"?

A. MacArthur upon returning to Corregidor.

Q. "Two eyes for an eye." Whose battle cry was this?

A. The Red Army's as it pushed toward Berlin.

Q. Who said, "I do not understand the words, but by God I like your spirit"?

A. Stalin to Churchill during a meeting in Moscow between the two heads of state. The Soviet leader had insulted the ability of the British to fight. Churchill burst into a torrent of oratory that was so forceful and fast the interpreters were unable to keep up.

Q. Who radioed the memorable message of the sinking of the Japanese aircraft carrier *Shoho*—"Scratch one flattop"?

A. Navy pilot Lieutenant Commander Robert Dixon during the Battle of the Coral Sea, May 4–8, 1942. The *Shoho* marked the first time the U.S. had sunk a Japanese ship larger than a destroyer.

Q. Who said, "Saw steamer, strafed same, sank same, some sight, signed Smith"?

A. Captain Fred M. Smith, U.S. Army Air Force, flying a P-38 during the campaign in the Aleutians. Smith sent the witty message after an encounter with a Japanese destroyer.

Q. Who said, "If Hitler were to invade hell, I should find occasion to make a favorable reference to the devil"?

A. Winston Churchill, after being questioned about his kindly remarks about Russia (he was widely known as an anti-communist) and Britain's support of her after the German invasion.

Q. Who said, "It is more likely that the United States ... will be attacked by the not-well-known but very warlike inhabitants of the planet Mars"?

A. Mussolini, in an address to the Italian people on February 23, 1941, in which he denied that the Axis powers had any plans to attack the U.S.

Q. Who said, The "British, the Jewish, and the Roosevelt administration [are] the three most important groups ... pressing this country toward war"?

A. American aviation hero Charles Lindbergh during an address in Des Moines, Iowa, on September 12, 1941. This is the worst side of Lindbergh; he performed valuable and unheralded service later as a flier in combat situations.

Q. Who said, "This is not the end. It is not even the beginning of the end. But it is, perhaps, the end of the beginning"?

A. Prime Minister Winston Churchill in remarks about the British victory in Egypt on November 10, 1942.

Q. Where does the following inscription appear?

> We Polish soldiers
> For our freedom and yours
> Have given our souls to God
> Our bodies to the soil of Italy
> And our hearts to Poland.

A. At the Polish cemetery established after the battle for Monte Cassino, where 1,200 Poles died.

Q. Who said, "I give the gift of myself to France. ... The fighting must stop"?

A. Marshal Henri Pétain, upon becoming Premier on May 17, 1940, as German troops were overwhelming the French.

Q. What was the last message Hitler sent via teletype out of the bunker in Berlin before he committed suicide?

A. "Where is Wenck? Where is Steiner?" He was referring to the two generals on whom the final defense of the city had fallen. The message was transmitted by Gerda Niedieck, a teletype operator.

Q. Where did the message "Good luck to you all" come from before the Berlin telegraph office closed down on April 22, 1945?

A. Tokyo. It was the last message received.

Q. Who said, "I am insulted by the persistent assertion that I want war. Am I a fool? War! It would settle nothing"?

A. Adolf Hitler during an interview on November 10, 1933.

Q. Which well-known American broadcast newsman made the following quip after Italy joined the war: "Italy looks like a boot and behaves like a heel"?

A. Walter Winchell.

Q. Who made the following predictions about World War II: "Japan will attack the Hawaiian Islands and damage the American fleet... they will employ a pincers movement against the Philippines"?

A. Similar in content to predictions by Billy Mitchell, which would come years later, the above comments were published in *The Valor of Ignorance* by American author Homer Lea in 1909.

FACT The United States resettlement of Americans of Japanese ancestry which began after the December 7, 1941, attack on Pearl Harbor was still being investigated by the U.S. government forty years later. Hearings in Washington, D.C., by the Commission on Wartime Relocation and Internment of Civilians heard charges that the ten resettlement camps "behind barbed wire fences" were incarceration centers. The defense of the action included testimony by former Assistant Secretary of War John McCloy who said: "There has been, in my judgment, at times a spate of quite irresponsible comment to the effect that this wartime move was callous, shameful and induced by racial or punitive motives. It was nothing of the sort." One CWRIC member, William Marutani, an American of Japanese ancestry who became a judge in Pennsylvania, challenged McCloy's comments with the question: "What other Americans fought for this country while their parents, brothers and sisters were incarcerated?"

Quotes on War in General

"In time of war the first casualty is truth."
—Boake Carter

"In wartime, truth is so precious that she should always be attended by a bodyguard of lies."
—Winston Churchill

"Never think that war, no matter how necessary, nor how justified, is not a crime."
—Ernest Hemingway

"Better pointed bullets than pointed speeches."
—Otto von Bismarck

"War can only be abolished through war."
—Mao Tse-tung

"There are no warlike peoples, just warlike leaders."
—Ralph Bunche

"The way to win an atomic war is to make certain it never starts."
—Omar Bradley

"Diplomacy has rarely been able to gain at the conference table what cannot be gained or held on the battlefield."
—Walter Bedell Smith

"War is too important to be left to the generals."

—*Georges Clemenceau*

"In war, when a commander becomes so bereft of reason and perspective that he fails to understand the dependence of arms on divine guidance, he no longer deserves victory."

—*Douglas MacArthur*

"War hath no fury like a non-combatant."

—*C. E. Montague*

"You furnish the pictures, I'll furnish the war."

—*William Randolph Hearst*

"War would end if the dead could return."

—*Stanley Baldwin*

"Do not needlessly endanger your lives until I give you the signal."

—*Dwight D. Eisenhower*

"When women have a voice in national and international affairs, war will cease forever."

—*Augusta Stowe-Gullen*

"The day when nobody comes back from a war it will be because the war has at last been properly organized."

—*Boris Vian*

FACT   The legendary Allied convoy lines to Murmansk and Archangel, Russia, were actually safer than similar convoy runs to Britain. The percentage of ships lost in the Arctic was 7.2 vs. 22.6 bound for Britain. However, one of the ships lost in the Arctic, the HMS *Edinburgh*, went down with 372 Russian gold bars which was payment for war materiel. In late summer 1981 a salvage team had recovered one hundred of the bars, valued at more than $20 million, and expected to bring up the rest. The U.S. government had no claim for the treasure as it had settled its claim and been compensated years earlier.

The War on Land

Q. Name the three American beaches at Normandy on D-Day?

A. There were only *two:* Utah and Omaha. The British had three: Gold, Juno and Sword.

Q. Who was the American baseball player who performed espionage for the U.S. while on a visit to Japan as a member of a U.S. baseball team in 1934?

A. Morris (Mo) Berg, who was joined on the trip by Babe Ruth and Lou Gehrig. Berg took photographs of restricted areas that were later used by U.S. pilots on bombing missions. He was the only player on the trip with a letter of introduction to the U.S. diplomatic and consular officers from Secretary of State Cordell Hull.

Q. Where was the first battle contact by Allied airborne troops in France on D-Day?

A. At the Caen Canal and Orne River bridges, by the British 6th Airborne. It lasted about fifteen minutes and ended in favor of the Allies.

Q. Name the famous British actor who died when the Germans shot down a commercial airliner they thought Winston Churchill was aboard.

A. Leslie Howard, who was nominated twice for Academy Awards. He also played Ashley Wilkes in *Gone With the Wind*.

U.S. Army Photo

FACT: The Ludendorff railroad bridge at Remagen, Germany, the only Rhine crossing that had not been destroyed, collapsed ten days after the first Allied troops began to cross it in March 1945. Four hours after this photo was taken, on March 17, the bridge crumbled. Some 400 troops of the U.S. First Army were on it at the time.

U.S. Coast Guard Photo

Q. How many Allied troops participated in the Normandy invasion?

A. There were nearly 3 million combat and support personnel from the Allied powers involved in the operation. About 1.7 million were from the U.S.

Q. Identify the SS officer who commanded the German incident on the radio station at Gleiwitz which Germany used as an excuse for invading Poland.

A. Alfred Naujocks, who personally received the orders from Reinhard Heydrich less than a month before the incident on September 1, 1939.

Q. What was the first battle in the Pacific where the Japanese defended territory the Empire held prior to its conquests in the war?

A. Kwajalein, the largest atoll in the world, measuring eighteen miles wide by 78 miles long.

Q. Who was the head of the branch of the Signal Corps responsible for producing U.S. propaganda films?

A. Colonel Frank Capra, who was aided by Lieutenant Colonel Darryl F. Zanuck, Major John Huston, and Lieutenant Colonel Anatole Litvak, among others. In all, 132 members of the Screen Directors Guild were among the 40,000 Hollywood people in uniform.

Q. Who was the French general who escaped from a German prison camp in France and was smuggled to Gibraltar by the Allies?

A. General Henri Honoré Giraud, who became the military chief of North Africa and was a serious threat to de Gaulle as the Frenchman who would lead all Free French forces. Captured in May 1940, he escaped from occupied France in April 1942.

Q. Name the Russian general who "captured" Berlin?

A. Colonel General Vasili I. Chuikov, commander of the Eighth Guards Army, who once advised Chiang Kai-shek.

Q. Who succeeded Mussolini as Italian Premier?

A. General Pietro Badoglio, an anti-Facist, in July 1943. He surrendered to the Allies in September and declared war on Germany in October.

FACT The U.S. Navy fleet which was to come under attack at Pearl Harbor left the U.S. West Coast for maneuvers around Hawaii on April 2, 1940. On May 7, President Roosevelt ordered it to remain indefinitely in Hawaii.

Q. Who offered to recognize the Soviet claims in the Dardanelles and permit the U.S.S.R. freedom in the Balkans in return for a "common policy of self-protection" against Germany?

A. Winston Churchill, through Britain's ambassador to Moscow. This was in 1940, when Germany and the Soviet Union were still on "good terms." The proposal was never renewed.

Q. Name the German commando who rescued Mussolini on September 12, 1943.

A. Otto Skorzeny, who had been asked by Hitler himself to bring the Italian dictator back to Berlin. Shorzeny's ninety men landed by glider in the Abruzzi Mountains and overwhelmed the garrison of 250 men guarding Mussolini.

Q. What was the pact that Germany, Italy and Japan signed on September 27, 1940?

A. The Tripartite Pact. It obliged the signatories to come to each other's aid in the event the U.S. joined the war.

Q. Who was the American Vice President when the U.S. entered the war in December, 1941?

A. Henry A. Wallace, who was elected with FDR in the 1940 election.

Q. Which of the three British beaches at Normandy was the costliest?

A. Juno, which was the task of the Canadian troops.

Q. Identify the medical equipment that was taken everywhere Hitler went.

A. A complete set of dental tools and supplies. He had taken poor care of his teeth in his younger days.

Q. Name the first German city captured by U.S. troops.

A. Aachen, which is famous in history as the fortress of Charlemagne.

FACT American aviation hero Charles Lindbergh resigned his commission as a U.S. Army Air Corps reserve colonel on April 28, 1941, after President Roosevelt criticized a speech Lindbergh had made. FDR called the Lone Eagle an appeaser and a defeatist. After Pearl Harbor, however, he served with distinction.

Q. Identify the only amphibious invasion thrown back with a loss.

A. The Japanese attempt to take Wake Island on December 11, 1942. A few days later they tried again and succeeded.

Q. Which battle was America's worst defeat in the war?

A. The Ardennes Forest, just before Christmas 1944, when approximately 12,000 out of 16,000 troops of the 106th U.S. Infantry Divisions were killed, wounded or captured by the Germans.

Q. Identify the Frenchman who ran the Resistance for de Gaulle until he was captured and killed in June 1943.

A. Jean Moulin, known as Max. Captured initially in 1940 by the Nazis, he slit his own throat and thereafter wore a scarf to conceal the ugly scar. His second capture in 1943 was by the Gestapo.

Q. Identify the highest-ranking traitor in the war.

A. General Andrei Andreyevitch Vlasov, a hero during the attack on Moscow, was captured by the Germans and cast his lot with them. He built up an army of Soviet prisoners who fought for Germany until May 1945. Captured by Patton and turned over to the Russians, he was hanged.

Q. Identify the Norwegian whose name became a synonym for traitor.

A. Vidkun Quisling, who, after the Germans captured Norway in April 1940, proclaimed himself Prime Minister in their behalf. The Nazis rejected him within the week but did return him to that post in 1942. He was executed as a traitor by the Norwegians after the war.

Q. Identify the Italian commander who invaded Egypt from Libya in September 1940.

A. Marshal Rodolfo Graziani, who was pushed 500 miles back into Libya by Wavell's Army of the Nile.

FACT Despite the fame the German panzer divisions earned with blitz tactics, only four divisions were totally mechanized. The other eighty-six German divisions at the outbreak of war depended largely on horses for mobility. By war's end slightly more than 2.7 million horses had been used by the German war machine on all fronts.

Ullstein Photo

FACT: Through the efforts of Germany's armaments minister, Albert Speer, left, the German Army was better equipped as late as 1944 than it had been when the Nazis invaded Russia in 1941. With Speer in this May 1945 photo after the German surrender are Admiral Karl Doenitz, Hitler's successor, and General Alfred Jodl, chief of operations at OKW and Hitler's personal chief of staff. Speer and Doenitz were sentenced to prison terms at the Nuremberg trials. Jodl was hanged.

Q. Identify the German general, second in command to Rommel, who was captured in November 1942 when Montgomery drove the Germans out of Egypt.

A. General Ritter von Thoma was captured along with 30,000 Axis troops.

Q. Which countries produced the heaviest, which the lightest tanks?

A. Germany's 74.8-ton Tiger II tanks, which measured 33'9", were the largest. Italy's L-3 at 3.4 tons and 10'5" in length was the smallest. The largest/heaviest tank in the U.S. arsenal was the 41.1-ton, 28'10"-long Pershing. Germany had another 74.8-ton tank, the Elephant, but it was a tiny 22'3" in length compared to the Tiger II.

Q. Who was the first British general to land in Normandy?

A. Major General Richard Gale, commander of the 6th Airborne.

Q. Who designed the SS uniforms and insignia?

A. Carl Diebitsch, who was later the artistic director of the first profit-making business run by the SS, the porcelain factory at Dachau.

Q. Of the 4,500 Japanese troops on Betio Island in the Tarawa Atoll how many lived to be taken prisoner?

A. Seventeen. The rest followed orders to fight to the last man.

Q. To what concentration camp did General Patton order the residents of a nearby village be brought to view the conditions they claimed to know nothing about?

A. Ohrdruf, on April 13, 1945. The next day the mayor and his wife hanged themselves.

Q. Identify the French general who conquered Monte Cassino in Italy.

A. Alphonse Juin.

Q. Who was the commissar of Kharkov, the city known as the Soviet Pittsburgh?

A. Nikita Khrushchev, who called the Kremlin and demanded that the Soviet Army be withdrawn in the face of German strength.

Q. Identify the Axis general responsible for defending Sicily.

A. General Alfredo Guzzoni, commanding general of the Italian Sixth Army.

U.S. Army Signal Corps Photo

Q. Identify the two highest-ranking Axis officers captured in North Africa.

A. German General Jurgen von Arnim, seen here the day after his capture on Cape Bon Peninsula following the surrender of Tunis and Bizerte, and Italian Field Marshal Alessandro Messe. Behind Von Armin in photo is German General Kramer.

Q. What was the name of the site near Kiev where the SS murdered almost 34,000 Jews by gunfire?

A. Babi Yar ravine. The Jews were told to assemble for resettlement. The Germans, who expected no more than 6,000 to appear, were surprised that so many actually turned up.

Q. What were the four things that Eisenhower said won the war for the Allies?

A. The bazooka, the jeep, the A-bomb and the DC-3.

Q. Why was the city of Lidice leveled?

A. On May 29, 1942, two Czech freedom fighters tossed a bomb into the car of Reinhard Heydrich, chief of the security police, and the SD "Hangman" Heydrich died on June 4. In revenge the Nazis killed 1,331 Czechs and selected the village of Lidice to be burned down, the ruins dynamited and leveled off.

Q. Which British ground commander held the distinction of never having lost a battle?

A. The man whom Eisenhower considered an inadequate strategist, Bernard Law Montgomery.

Q. Who was Colonel Count Klaus Schenk von Stauffenberg?

A. The German officer who placed the bomb in Hitler's headquarters at Rastenburg. The original plan was to kill Hitler, Goering and Himmler at Berchtesgaden, but it was postponed twice because Hitler was alone both times. Finally, on July 20, 1944, the plan was carried out, but failed. While four Germans were killed in the explosion, Hitler survived, the plot was aborted and the plotters were eventually caught and executed.

Q. Who was Stauffenberg's chief co-conspirator in the plot to kill Hitler on July 20, 1944?

A. General Friedrich Olbricht, deputy commander of the Home Army in Germany.

Q. Who was the Japanese commander on Iwo Jima?

A. Lieutenant General Tadamichi Kuribayashi, who commanded over 20,000 troops to defend the eight-square-mile island when the U.S. Marines invaded in 1945.

U.S. Army Photo

Q. Which Allied general at one time advocated celibacy for those serious about pursuing a military career?

A. When Bernard Law Montgomery was a young officer he held that belief. Here Montgomery chats with his boss, Dwight D. Eisenhower, in Holland on November 29, 1944.

Q. Of the approximately 75,000 men on the Bataan Death March, how many were Americans?

A. Twelve thousand. Most of the rest were Filipinos.

Q. How many Allied prisoners of war actually marched, or walked, on the Death March?

A. About half of those involved rode in trucks and suffered little. However, the atrocities to many who did walk were enough to justify the name Death March. Seven to ten thousand died.

Q. Which branch of the German armed forces was known as the Nazi Service because of the high number of party members in it?

A. The Luftwaffe, which was under the command of Reichsmarschall Hermann Goering.

Q. Identify the village in France where the 101st Airborne first exchanged fire with the enemy?

A. According to division records it was at Foucarville, behind Utah Beach, where eleven troopers attacked machine gun, anti-tank gun and dugout positions.

Q. What was the name of General Eisenhower's British chauffeur?

A. Kay Summersby.

Q. What song did the British troops in the Africa campaign "steal" from the Afrika Korps and take as their own?

A. "Lili Marlene."

Q. What was the name of the site where German scientists worked on rocket research?

A. Peenemunde, in Poland.

FACT For the low-level bombing that Lieutenant Colonel Jimmy Doolittle's B-25s had to perform in their attack on Japan in 1942 it was discovered that the regular bombsights were ineffective. Captain C. R. Greening, a pilot in the 17th Bombardment Group, which flew the mission, created a device for a cost of approximately fifteen cents per bombsight which worked perfectly.

U.S. Army Photo

Q. What kind of children's toy did American paratroopers use to exchange identification signals after the D-Day drops into Fortress Europe?

A. Tin snapper cricket toys. A single snap required two in answer. The 82nd Airborne, however, added a password just to be sure. This group happily displays a Nazi flag captured near St. Marcouf, France.

Q. Name the two French ports that remained in German hands until they surrendered at the end of the war.

A. Lorient and St. Nazaire. In contrast, Carentan was the first French town liberated by the Allies on June 12, 1944. This photo shows U.S. troops moving through Carentan streets and away from St. Lô and Paris (note sign on wall above GI at far right).

Q. Who led the Japanese suicide charge on Attu Island against U.S. 7th Division troops?

A. Colonel Yasuyo Yamasaki, on May 29, 1943, screaming "Japanese drink blood like wine."

Q. Identify the first U.S. forces from the Normandy beaches to link up with U.S. airborne forces dropped before the beach invasions began.

A. Troopers from the 101st Airborne and soldiers from the 4th Division, behind Utah Beach.

Q. On what grounds did the Germans justify the right to use Soviet POW's to work in essential war production?

A. By noting that the Soviets were not signers of the Geneva Convention, and therefore should not come under its protection.

Q. What was the name of Mussolini's mistress?

A. Clara Petacci. She, along with the Duce, was shot by Italian partisans near Lake Como on April 28, 1945.

Q. Who signed Clark Gable's discharge papers in June 1944?

A. Fellow actor, and future President of the United States, Captain Ronald Reagan.

Q. Where did Hitler do his famous "jig," which was actually the work of clever Allied film editing?

A. Though it was reported to have been done at Compiègne, site of the French surrender, Hitler was recorded on film at his headquarters at Bruly-de-Pesche, Belgium, after having received word that Marshal Pétain was asking for an armistice.

FACT On September 11, 1944, U.S. submarines sank two Japanese transport ships that had over 2,218 U.S., British and Australian prisoners of war. These troops were survivors of the building of the bridge on the River Kwai. Nearly 1,300 of the POWs were killed when the *Rakuyo Maru* and the *Kachidoki Maru* sank within minutes. The U.S. submarines rescued 159, and Japanese ships picked up another 792 and reimprisoned them. Only 606 of the original 2,218 survived the war.

National Archives Photo

FACT: Japan's ambassador in Washington, Admiral Kichisaburo Nomura, advised Tokyo that the U.S. was reading the Japanese diplomatic code on May 20, 1941, more than six months before the hostilities between the two countries began. Tokyo responded by telling its Washington embassy to have all sensitive messages handled by only one person. As a result, on December 7, 1941, Nomura (right) checks the time as he and special envoy Saburo Kurusu wait in the U.S. State Department to see Secretary Cordell Hull. Only a relatively short time before they arrived did the two Japanese diplomats themselves receive the slowly decoded message that war was to begin this day.

Q. Who was the only general to land with the first wave of troops on Normandy?

A. Brigadier General Theodore Roosevelt, 4th Division, on Utah Beach.

Q. Which German units got closest to Moscow, and how close did they get?

A. The 3rd and 4th Panzer Groups got to within twenty-five miles of the Russian capital in December 1941.

Q. Identify the Norwegian king who, with his ministers, set up a government in exile in Britain.

A. King Haakon VII.

Q. Identify the European monarch who died under questionable circumstances after a visit with Adolf Hitler.

A. King Boris III of Bulgaria, who had never been one of the Axis powers' great supporters, died on August 28, 1943. Though his death was listed as by natural causes, it is believed he was assassinated.

Q. Who stopped Rommel in North Africa?

A. British General Sir Claude Auchinleck at El Alamein. Churchill replaced him with Generals Alexander and Montgomery, who followed with several successes.

Q. Identify the SS division responsible for protecting Hitler at his Rastenburg headquarters.

A. The Gross Deutschland Division.

Q. What did the initials SHAEF stand for?

A. Supreme Headquarters Allied Expeditionary Force. General Dwight D. Eisenhower, U.S. Army, commanded.

FACT Heinrich Himmler ordered the creation of an extermination camp at Auschwitz, Poland, on April 27, 1940. Of the 3.3-million Jews in Poland less than 10 percent would be alive by the time the exterminations at Auschwitz ended on October 30, 1944. In addition, the camp was responsible for the deaths of Jews transported there from other occupied areas.

Q. Where was the heaviest concentration of German troops on D-Day?

A. At La Roche-Guyon, the headquarters of Field Marshal Erwin Rommel's Army Group B, the most powerful German military presence in France. There were more than three German soldiers per villager.

Q. Who were the first victims of poison gas extermination at Auschwitz?

A. Russian prisoners of war on September 3, 1941.

Q. Where was the only place in Paris where the Tricolor was visible during the German Occupation?

A. At Les Invalides, the Army Museum.

Q. Where and when did the French Tricolor fly for the first time after the German occupation of Paris in 1940?

A. At the Prefecture of Police on the Ile de la Cité across from Notre Dame, August 19, 1944. It had not been flown from a public building in over four years and two months. Paris would be liberated six days later.

Q. Where did Soviet troops raise their country's flag in Berlin?

A. Atop the Reichstag building, on April 13, 1945, while the battle of Berlin was still going on.

Q. When did German troops occupy Athens?

A. April 27, 1941. The Nazi flag was hung from the Parthenon before 9 A.M.

Q. Who was the first member of the U.S. Congress to enlist after Pearl Harbor?

A. Representative Lyndon Baines Johnson of Texas, later senator, senate majority leader and President of the United States.

Q. Who was the only member of the U.S. Congress to vote no after FDR said that "a state of war existed" between the U.S. and Japan?

A. Representative Jeanette Rankin (R., Mont.). She had also voted no against the resolution for war with Germany in 1917.

U.S. Army Photo

Q. Name the German town where the Western Allies and the Russians linked
up in April 1945.

A. At 4:40 P.M. on April 25 in Torgau on the Elbe, Lieutenant William D.
Robertson of Los Angeles, U.S. 69th Division, First Army, met soldiers of
Marshal Koniev's First Ukrainian Army on the twisted and sloping girders
of a blown-out bridge spanning the Elbe. In photo, Robertson and Soviet
Lieutenant Sylvashko re-enact their first embrace. However, Lieutenant
Albert Kotzebue, also of the U.S. 69th, and a patrol of troops crossed the
Elbe at 1:30 P.M. and reported meeting Russian soldiers in Strehla. This
would have been three hours before Robertson's Torgau meeting, which is
considered the official meeting.

USIS Photo

FACT: Charles de Gaulle was nearly shot by a German Navy officer, Lieutenant Commander Harry Leithold, as Leithold watched the French general's return to Paris from the Kriegsmarine headquarters on the Place de la Concorde. However, after capturing de Gaulle in the sights of his submachine gun, Leithold realized that the crowd around the man outside would easily seize and kill him. Leithold decided that the tall Frenchman in the vehicle wasn't worth it, no matter who he was. Later in a POW camp Leithold saw a newspaper photo of de Gaulle and realized who it was he had almost shot. Other snipers, even after the German surrender, continued to break up crowds at the world-famous square. Parisians in photo above scatter as shots rang out on August 26, 1944.

Q. Name the first geographic area to be awarded a medal during the war.

A. The island of Malta, which received the George Cross from Britain for its heroic stand against the Axis.

Q. What was the worst military disaster ever suffered by a European nation in the Orient?

A. The fall of Singapore on February 15, 1942, along with the surrender of more than 70,000 troops and civilians.

Q. Identify the Polish general who led troops that had been liberated from POW camps in Russia and fought in the Middle East.

A. General Wladyslaw Anders, whose troops also had the distinction of capturing the abbey at Monte Cassino.

Q. Identify the only two civilian activities in Berlin that did not cease during the attack, surrender and occupation of the city.

A. The seventeen breweries and the weather bureau operated without interruption.

Q. Identify the Japanese general who did what was thought impossible and crossed the Owen Stanley Mountains in New Guinea.

A. General Horii, who drowned in a river crossing when the Australians and Americans counterattacked in September–October 1942. The Japanese had come to within thirty miles of Port Moresby.

Q. Identify the first American unit to cross the Rhine.

A. A unit of the 9th Armored Division, First Army, crossed the Ludendorff bridge at Remagen on March 7, 1945.

FACT   At the outbreak of war in Europe, Dwight D. Eisenhower was a lieutenant colonel on the staff of General Douglas MacArthur in the Philippines. By the time the Japanese attacked Pearl Harbor, Eisenhower had accepted command of a tank regiment in a division headed by General George S. Patton. Prior to his first assignment to London during the war, Ike had only been to Europe once previously, to write a guidebook on American war monuments. He rose from lieutenant colonel to general in less than eighteen months.

Q. Identify the Egyptian military officer who located a mansion on the Rue des Pyramides that was to be used by Erwin Rommel once the field marshal arrived in Cairo.

A. Anwar el-Sadat, who, along with Gamal Abdel Nasser, was part of the anti-British Free Officers Movement in the army.

Q. Identify the two generals, one from the allies, the other from the Axis, who had a fondness for parakeets.

A. Montgomery of the British and Blumentritt of the Wehrmacht. Both men kept several of the birds with them whenever possible.

Q. Name the site where the British first defeated the Japanese in a land battle.

A. At Sinzweya, Burma, on February 23, 1944.

Q. Who was the youngest general in the German Army?

A. General Walther Wenck, forty-five, former chief of staff to Guderian and the man all Berliners depended on to save the city from the Russians.

Q. What was the first U.S. offensive in the Pacific against Japanese ground troops that resulted in a U.S. victory?

A. Guadalcanal, which was also Japan's first land defeat.

Q. Who was the Allied general the Germans respected above all others?

A. General George Smith Patton. They simply couldn't believe the allies would not use him to lead the D-Day invasion, and they waited for "Army Group Patton" to storm the Pas de Calais instead of Normandy.

FACT The largest aircraft carrier of any navy became part of the Japanese fleet on November 11, 1944, when the *Shinano* (with a thirty-centimeter-thick deck over concrete) went on-line. However, this ship recorded the briefest period of sea duty of any major ship in the war. The U.S. submarine *Archerfish* torpedoed her and she sank on November 29 in the Kumano Sea. The sinking of the 59,000-ton leviathan was the largest submarine kill of the war.

U.S. Army Photo

FACT: Hitler created an award for German mothers, the Mother's Cross, that was awarded in bronze, silver and gold, depending on the number of children they bore for the Reich. The *Mutterkreuz* was an amalgam of the Iron Cross, the Nazi Party Badge and the Pour le Mérite. To earn the gold version the German mother had to have eight or more children. Initiated in 1938, it was intended to honor women much in the same way soldiers earned citations for exceptional service. The *Mutterkreuz* awards were given out each year on the anniversary of Hitler's own mother's birth, August 12.

U.S. Army Photo

FACT: Not all French citizens hated the Germans or gave wholehearted support to the underground Resistance movement. In photo above two
women are paraded through the Paris streets with their heads
shaved, barefooted and with swastikas painted on their heads. This
was the price they paid for collaborating with the enemy. This scene
was recorded on August 27, 1944.

U.S. Army Photo

FACT: U.S. General Courtney Hicks Hodges was forced to leave the U.S. Military Academy at West Point in 1906 because he failed geometry. He immediately enlisted as a private in the Army and was commissioned as a second lieutenant in 1909, only one year behind his former classmates. During World War II the U.S. First Army, while under his command, liberated Paris, defeated the Germans in the Ardennes, made the first Rhine crossing at Remagen and met the Russians on the Elbe.

Q. Which Allied army had the greatest representation of foreign units in it?

A. The British Second Army, under Sir Miles Dempsey, included Irish, Scottish, Polish, Czech, Belgian, Dutch, U.S. and British units.

Q. What area did Churchill frequently refer to as "the soft underbelly" of Europe?

A. The Balkans.

Q. Identify the first German officer to sight the Normandy invasion fleet.

A. Major Werner Pluskat, who commanded four batteries of the German 352nd Division with its twenty guns over Omaha Beach. When he called division headquarters and was asked where the ships were heading he replied, "Right for me."

Q. Who were the three army group commanders directly under Eisenhower in Europe?

A. Generals Bradley, Montgomery and Devers.

Q. Identify the U.S. General who was smuggled into Italy to negotiate the surrender of the Italians.

A. General Maxwell D. Taylor, artillery chief of the 82nd Airborne, who went via a British PT boat, Italian corvette and land vehicles into occupied Rome to meet with General Carboni. This was prior to the invasion of Italy.

Q. Which Allied commander boasted that his army had liberated more square miles of Europe, traveled farther than any other and caused more German casualties?

A. Patton.

FACT The Russians turned on more than 140 large antiaircraft lights at 4 A.M. on Monday, April 16, 1945, as they began their bombardment across the Oder which started the battle for Berlin. The lights were intended to confuse defending German troops but actually provided German artillery with a better view of the advancing Russians.

U.S. Army Photo

Q. Identify the U.S. Army unit that broke the deadlock after the Normandy invasion and crossed the St. Lô-Périers road.

A. The VII Corps of the First Army under General J. Lawton "Lightning Joe" Collins. Within two days after their success on July 25, 1944, they were well on their way down the Cotentin Peninsula. Collins, like his boss, Omar Bradley, was known as a GI's general.

Q. What became of Karol Wojtyla, the Polish student who remained on Gestapo execution lists for years because of helping Jews escape?

A. Ordained a priest in 1946, he became Pope John Paul II in 1978.

Q. Identify the only U.S. Army division to employ a captured German plane and use it for scouting.

A. The 83rd Infantry Division. The plane was a Messerschmitt 109, which they painted olive green.

Q. Where did the first Axis assault on a U.S. mainland military base take place?

A. At Fort Stevens, Oregon, on June 22, 1942, when a Japanese submarine fired at the coastal outpost. The last time a U.S. mainland military outpost had been fired on was during the War of 1812. There were no casualties in the Fort Stevens incident.

Q. Identify the first U.S. mainland civilian location to come under enemy fire in the war.

A. The oil fields west of Santa Barbara, California, which were fired on by Japanese submarine I-17 on February 23, 1942.

Q. What was the common name for the British explosive called Explosive C?

A. Plastic.

Q. What company, famous for expensive fast cars, designed the Tiger tanks for Germany?

A. Porsche.

FACT The debate about the U.S. decision to drop the atom bomb on Hiroshima and Nagasaki frequently calls attention to the fact that more destruction was caused by a B-29 raid on Tokyo, March 9–10, 1945, than the later atomic raids. More than 83,000 people died in the Tokyo raid, which employed incendiary bombs, as against 70,000 deaths in Hiroshima and 20,000 in Nagasaki. However, the Tokyo raid employed more than 275 B-29s, while only one bomb-dropping plane was used in each of the atom bomb raids.

U.S. Army Photo

Q. Where and when did units of Patton's Third Army first cross the Rhine?

A. At Oppenheim, near Mainz, on Thursday, March 22, 1945. Shown here are the members of the first tank crew of the 41st Tank Battalion, 11th Armored Division, Third U.S. Army, on the day of the crossing. The five men are: Corporal William Hasse, Palisades Park, N.J.; Private Marvin Aldridge, Burlington, N.C.; T/4 John Latimi, Bronx, N.Y.; Corporal Vincent Morreale, Trenton, N.J.; and Corporal Sidney Meyer, Bronx, N.Y. Name of the tank? *Flat Foot Floosie.*

Q. Because of the relatively large number of Japanese troops who surrendered, which battle is considered a turning point in the psychological aspect of the war in the Pacific?

A. Saipan. Although most of the Japanese 27,000-man force on that island fought to the death, several hundred were captured, a previously unheard of situation.

Q. Identify the husband and wife team credited with breaking the Japanese Purple Code.

A. Lieutenant Colonel William Friedman, chief of the U.S. Army Cryptanalysis Bureau in World War II, and his wife, Elizabeth, who was a cryptanalyst with the U.S. Navy. She also broke the Japanese Doll Woman Case code, which dealt with the locations of Allied warships.

Q. Who was the Vichy French Prime Minister when Germany occupied France totally in 1942?

A. Pierre Laval, who supported the move.

Q. Where was Rommel on June 6, 1944, during D-Day?

A. He had returned home to be with his wife on her birthday.

Q. Name the most decorated soldier in World War II.

A. By the time he was twenty years old Audie Murphy had become the most decorated U.S. soldier *ever*. He received the Congressional Medal of Honor and twenty seven other decorations.

Q. Who were: "Soldiers in sailor uniforms, with Marine training, doing civilian work at WPA wages"?

A. The thousands of plumbers, carpenters, electricians, power equipment operators and other civilian craftsmen who became Navy 'engineers' in the Construction Batallions. They were called Seabees (CBs) and were involved in every operation in the Pacific during the war.

Q. Identify the Japanese general who defended Saipan against the U.S. Marines.

A. General Yoshitsugu Saito commanded 32,000 troops there when the assault began on June 15, 1944.

Q. What was the German National Redoubt?

A. During the final weeks of the war in Europe, rumors that the Germans were gathering for a last-stand battle or holdout in the mountainous southern part of Germany persisted. They proved to be groundless but had greatly influenced Allied thinking.

Q. When did the Allies invade the French Riviera?

A. On August 15, 1944, French and American troops under General Alexander Patch landed on the southern coast of France at St. Tropez.

Q. What was the delightful surprise the U.S. Marines found on Guam when it was reoccupied?

A. Guam had been the Japanese main liquor distribution center for the Central Pacific. Scotch, beer, bourbon, rye and sake were left for the leathernecks in great amounts.

Q. Name the Russian general who committed suicide rather than surrender to the Germans near Vyazma in April 1942.

A. General Mikhail G. Yefremov of the Thirty-Third Army.

Q. What was the name of the Spanish legion that Franco sent to help the Germans against the Russians at Leningrad?

A. The Blue Legion, made up of about 14,000 Spanish troops. They arrived at the front in September 1941.

Q. From which country did the Allied troops involved in the raid on Dieppe come?

A. Canada. There were 3,369 casualties out of just over 5,000 troops.

Q. Which member of Hitler's inner circle was born in Alexandria, Egypt?

A. Rudolf Hess.

Q. What was the name of the Italian secret service?

A. Servizio Informazione Segreto, known commonly as SIM.

Q. What was the name of the Japanese secret police in Tokyo, often compared to the German Gestapo?

A. Kempeitai.

Q. Identify the only American labor union to violate the AFL and CIO pledge of not striking during the war.

A. The United Mine Workers, who, under John L. Lewis, walked off their jobs four times.

Q. What were the American casualties as a result of the Japanese attack on Pearl Harbor and other areas of Oahu?

A. A total of 2,403, including sixty-eight civilians.

Q. Who helped the Germans violate the Treaty of Versailles and build an army in excess of 100,000 men?

A. In a secret agreement, the Soviet Union allowed Germans to train in Russia while the Germans trained Soviet officers and built arms plants for the U.S.S.R.

Q. Who was responsible for German espionage before and during the war?

A. Admiral Wilhelm Canaris, chief of the Military Intelligence Service (Abwehr).

Q. Which campaign is considered the greatest with regard to scope and number of personnel involved?

A. Operation Barbarossa, the German thrust to conquer Russia. Germany alone committed 300 divisions to it.

Q. Who commanded the Japanese Fourteenth Army that defended the Philippines from the U.S.?

A. General Tomoyuki Yamashita, Japan's most revered soldier.

Q. What was Karinhall?

A. Goering's palatial estate.

Q. How was Karinhall destroyed?

A. Before leaving for Hitler's birthday celebration on April 20, 1945, and only after a convoy of no fewer than twenty-four trucks had departed with his antiques, furniture, paintings, etc., the Reichsmarschall himself pushed the plunger destroying the estate. "Well, that's what you have to do sometimes when you're a crown prince," he told those around him. The Russians were expected to capture the area at any time.

Q. Which Allied airborne troops were considered expendable and actually had firecrackers attached to them set to explode upon landing during the D-Day invasion?

A. The hundreds of life-size rubber "paratrooper" dolls dropped to confuse the Germans.

Q. Who is credited with development of tanks as strategic war weapons?

A. General Heinz Guderian, who also created the blitzkrieg.

Q. How long did it take Germany to conquer France?

A. Twenty-seven days.

Q. How many rooms were in Hitler's bunker beneath the Chancellery in Berlin?

A. Including bathrooms, lounges in hallways, and storage areas, there were thirty-two rooms.

Q. Identify the first Allied troops to invade Fortress Europe by sea on D-Day.

A. At 4:30 A.M., 132 troops from the 4th and 24th U.S. Cavalry landed on the two rocky islands called Iles St. Marcouf, about three miles off Utah Beach, to destroy heavy gun emplacements that did not exist. Nor were there any enemy troops. However, nineteen men died in minefields.

Q. Identify any two of the Luftwaffe's five pilots who scored more than 250 "kills."

A. Erich Hartmann, 352
Gerhard Barkhorn, 301
Gunther Rall, 275
Otto Kittel, 267
Walter Nowotny, 255

FACT The allied air forces managed to overpower the German Luftwaffe not because heavy bombing had reduced the Reich's output of aircraft but because of a shortage of qualified German pilots. Overall armament production in Germany remained high until February 1944.

Q. How many days did the Germans occupy Paris?

A. From June 15, 1940, to August 25, 1944—1,524 days. During a 1940 visit to the city Hitler, center, took time to be photographed with his architect and armaments minister, Albert Speer (left), and sculptor Arno Breker. Breker, wearing an SS death's-head overseas cap, would later execute a larger-than-life marble bust of Hitler that Goering requested as a gift for his own birthday on January 12, 1944.

Q. Who replaced Montgomery as commander of the British Eighth Army when the hero of El Alamein was called to England in preparation for the D-Day invasion?

A. General Sir Oliver Leese.

Q. What was Dr. Joseph Goebbels' actual title?

A. Reichsminister for Public Enlightenment and Propaganda. In addition, he was the Gauleiter of Berlin.

Q. Name the American general who formally surrendered Bataan to the Japanese.

A. General Edward P. King, Jr., at 12:30 P.M. on April 9, 1942.

Q. What was the German *Fahneneid?*

A. The allegiance oath that the armed forces swore to the Fuehrer. Many officers who opposed Hitler felt they could not violate their oath.

Q. What was the name of the law that made the families of German generals responsible for the generals' actions?

A. Sippenschaft (apprehension and arrest of kin). After the plot to kill Hitler, SS Reichsleiter Robert Ley wrote the law. It was also designed to discourage surrender or failure to accomplish objectives. It was passed in August 1944.

Q. What was the Nazi Family Hostage Law?

A. An act by which all male relatives of an identified Resistance fighter would be executed. Female members of the family were sent to concentration camps, and children were placed in youth prisons. It was first issued in France on July 19, 1942. However, if the identified Resistance fighter surrendered, his family could escape the penalty.

FACT   During what is known as the Battle of the Atlantic over 2,600 ships were sunk for a total of 15 million tons. Great Britain lost nearly 60,000 sailors and seamen. Germany lost 28,000 U-boat sailors and 785 submarines. U.S. losses were only a fraction of these.

Q. What was Hitler's infamous Commissar Order?

A. That all Soviet commissars captured were to be shot. The date was March 21, 1941, three months before Operation Barbarossa actually began.

Q. Which American unit made the greatest advances on D-Day?

A. The 4th Division, which moved inland from Utah Beach quicker than the most optimistic estimates.

Q. What did the initials CBI stand for with reference to a theater of operation?

A. The China-Burma-India Theater.

Q. What did Britain plan as the prelude to Operation Crusader, its counteroffensive against the Germans in North Africa?

A. The assassination of Erwin Rommel. Six officers and fifty-three commandos came ashore from the submarines *Torbay* and *Talisman.* Rommel's murder was one of four missions they were to execute. All were failures.

Q. What was *Der Weg zur Ewigkeit* (the Road to Eternity)?

A. The road between Berlin and Zossen, headquarters of the German High Command. Its official designation was Reichsstrasse 96.

Q. Identify the only father and son in the U.S. forces to have landed at Utah and Omaha beaches on June 6, 1944.

A. General Theodore Roosevelt, Jr., on Utah, and his son, Captain Quentin Roosevelt, on Omaha.

Q. Name the German allies who supplied fifty-two divisions for the 1942 summer offensive against Russia.

A. To reinforce its own troops Germany asked for, and got, Spanish, Hungarian, Slovakian, Italian and Rumanian divisions. Germany had lost 1.3 million troops in the first year of war with Russia.

Q. Which German army was responsible for the zone that included the five Normandy beaches where the Allies landed?

A. The Seventh Army, commanded by Colonel General Friedrich Dollmann. Because of bad weather he canceled a practice alert the night of June 5, 1944. For reasons never properly explained, this was the only German army not notified that intelligence knew the invasion was expected "within 48 hours."

Q. What was the largest U.S. land campaign of the war in the Pacific?

A. Lingayen Gulf and Luzon, where more U.S. troops than had participated in Italy or North Africa were involved.

Q. Identify the one-armed leader of the Hitler Youth.

A. Thirty-two-year-old Arthur Axmann, who ordered several hundred youngsters to resist the Russians to the death in the battle for Berlin. Nearly all obeyed.

Q. Which defeat resulted in the greatest U.S. surrender in history?

A. The Philippines in 1942.

Q. Identify the other three countries that participated in Operation Barbarossa with Germany against Russia.

A. Hungary, Rumania and Finland.

Q. Identify the Swedish Red Cross official that Heinrich Himmler secretly met with to discuss negotiating peace in April 1945.

A. Count Folke Bernadotte. The meetings were not successful.

Q. Who made the initial recommendation that Germany be divided into three sectors for occupation at the end of hostilities?

A. British Foreign Secretary, later Prime Minister, Anthony Eden in 1943.

Q. Identify the U.S. army charged with the assault on Salerno.

A. The U.S. Fifth Army, General Mark Clark commanding.

Q. Who was the head of the French underground army in 1944 prior to the liberation of Paris?

A. General Alfred Mallaret-Joinville, a communist.

Q. Identify the three countries occupied by U.S. Marines in the Atlantic.

A. On July 7, 1941, five months before its neutrality was to abruptly end, the U.S. Government occupied Trinidad, Iceland and British Guiana in order to free British troops for service elsewhere.

Agence France-Presse Photo

Q. Identify the Swedish consul general who arranged for the release of 532 political prisoners in Paris's Fresnes Prison in exchange for five times as many German POW's from the Allies as the Germans prepared to evacuate Paris.

A. Raoul Nordling, who was assisted by German Abwehr agent Emil Bender, an avid anti-Nazi. Nordling convinced Major Josef Huhm, chief of staff of the German occupation authority in France, that he could guarantee the deal. In fact Nordling had no authority, and he had no intention of seeing the swap accomplished by *both* sides.

Q. Who was commander-in-chief of the Polish Army when Germany invaded in 1939?

A. Marshal Edward Smigly-Rydz, who led an army capable of mustering 1,800,000 men. However, approximately 800,000 actually got to their divisions before the war in that country was over.

Q. Who was the British commander of the Army of the Nile when war in Europe broke out?

A. One-eyed General Sir Archibald Wavell.

Q. When did Field Marshal Erwin Rommel leave Africa for the last time?

A. On March 9, 1943. He was replaced by General Jurgen von Arnim. Rommel's last battle in Africa was on March 6, an offensive action against the British at Medenine that failed.

Q. At precisely what time on June 6, 1944, did the Allied invasion of Normandy begin?

A. At 12:15 A.M., when American and British Pathfinders dropped out of the sky to illuminate the way for the airborne divisions.

Q. Identify the American general criticized for taking too long to move off the beaches at Anzio before the Germans had a chance to mount a staunch defense?

A. Major General John P. Lucas of the U.S. VI Corps. He was replaced by Lieutenant General Lucian Truscott of the 3rd Division.

Q. Identify the Big Three heads of state who met in Cairo in November 1943.

A. Generalissimo Chiang Kai-shek of China joined President Roosevelt of the U.S. and Prime Minister Churchill of Great Britain.

FACT The greatest U.S. naval loss at sea was the July 30, 1945, sinking of the cruiser *Indianapolis* with a loss of nearly 900 men, mostly to sharks. The Japanese submarine I-58 scored with two torpedoes. It was the last major U.S. ship lost in the war. The *Indianapolis* was returning from delivering the uranium to Tinian Island that would be used in the first atom bombing of a Japanese city seven days later.

Q. Identify the hotel in Cairo where Churchill, Roosevelt and Chiang Kai-shek held their historic conference.

A. The Mena House, which is the closest hotel to the Pyramids of Giza. So close, in fact, that the distance can be walked in a short time.

Q. Identify the heads of state who participated in the Casablanca Conference.

A. President Roosevelt of the U.S. and Prime Minister Churchill of Great Britain. General Charles de Gaulle, who would eventually become Premier of France, was there also but not included in the major discussions.

Q. Who were the three world leaders in attendance at the Teheran Conference?

A. Once again President Roosevelt of the U.S. and Prime Minister Churchill of Great Britain were there, but this time Soviet Premier Joseph Stalin was also present.

Q. What was the task of the 813th Pionierkompanie of the Wehrmacht in Paris in August 1944?

A. Placing explosives at various bridges and monuments including the Eiffel Tower and Les Invalides. Hitler wanted the Allies to liberate ruins, not a city.

Q. Who was largely responsible for developing amphibious landing techniques in the Pacific?

A. Marine General Holland McTyeire Smith ("Howling Mad" Smith). He commanded the operations in the Gilbert and Marshall Islands, the Marianas and the Volcano Islands, from Tarawa to Iwo Jima.

FACT U.S. General George S. Patton became commander of the U.S. II Army Corps on the same day, March 6, 1943, that German Field Marshal Erwin Rommel began his last battle in North Africa. However, Patton turned command of the II Corps over to General Omar Bradley less than six weeks later. Patton was assigned to plan the Sicily invasion. Rommel had returned to Germany to defend against the expected Allied invasion of France.

French Tourist Office Photo

FACT: The world was horrified to learn that Hitler had ordered the beautiful bridges crossing the Seine destroyed as German troops withdrew from Paris. However, over seventy years earlier the French themselves passed laws installing special metal pans under *every* bridge in France for demolition purposes. The pans were designed to hold explosives so the French could destroy the bridges in a war emergency. The Germans in 1944 found the pans intact and prepared to use them. Above is a recent photo of Pont Alexander III, considered to be the most beautiful of the Seine bridges in Paris.

Q. What country did the members of Detachment 101 come from in the Burma campaign?

A. General Frank Merrill arranged for a tribe of Burmese natives, called Kachins, to participate in the struggle against the Japanese. The unit's war record reports killing 5,447 enemy and sustaining seventy Kachin and fifteen American losses.

Q. How many Allied personnel were evacuated during the nine days of Dunkirk?

A. There were 338,226 evacuated in more than a thousand boats of all shapes and sizes; 68,111 left behind were taken prisoner, wounded or killed.

Q. Who was the American commander during the battle for Cassino?

A. General Mark Clark, who was criticized for ordering the monastery bombed.

Q. When did the U.S. 36th Infantry Division make its combat debut?

A. The 36th Division, formerly the Texas National Guard, saw combat in World War II for the first time at Salerno, Italy.

Q. Where was the first British offensive in Southeast Asia?

A. On the Arakan coast of Burma on September 21, 1942.

Q. Identify the camp where the survivors of the Bataan Death March were imprisoned for the first three months.

A. Camp O'Donnell, some sixty miles from the Bataan Peninsula.

Q. Name the three Resistance political groups in Paris.

A. The three were the Paris Liberation Committee, the National Resistance Committee and the Military Action Committee.

Q. What was the overriding reason for the campaign to capture Guadalcanal?

A. The Japanese were building an air base that would threaten Australia with land-based bombers.

FACT   The British 1st Airborne Division lost 75 percent of its personnel in the attack on Arnhem during Operation Market Garden.

Q. Which campaign is considered "the most spectacular series of victories ever gained over a British army"?

A. The German campaign to capture Tobruk in 1942, according to the history of the campaign as it is recorded in the official South African version.

Q. Identify the German general given the command of Army Group Vistula and ordered to hold the Russians on the Oder River as they attacked Berlin.

A. Colonel General Gotthard Heinrici, considered a brilliant defensive officer but disliked by Hitler for holding religious beliefs.

Q. Into what mountain was the tunnel fortress on Corregidor built?

A. Malinta Hill.

Q. Identify the SS general who met Allen Dulles of the OSS to try and negotiate peace in March 1945.

A. General Karl Wolff, smuggled into Zurich, Switzerland. He also met with General Lyman Lemnitzer on the same trip.

Q. What were U.S. Marine Corps casualties at Tarawa?

A. Eleven hundred. The Japanese lost over 4,600 troops, while only seventeen Japanese surrendered. In addition to the 1,100 U.S. troops killed, another 2,292 were wounded.

Q. Who did General Heinrici replace as commander of Army Group Vistula?

A. Reichsfuehrer Heinrich Himmler, who proved to be inept as a military commander and permitted himself to relinquish the post because of his other many jobs and his poor health. (Himmler was also Minister of the Interior, chief of the Gestapo, head of the SS and commander of the Training Army.)

Q. Identify the general who was commander-in-chief of the French Army when Germany invaded Poland.

A. General Maurice Gamelin. He was replaced by General Maxime Weygand on May 19, 1940, as a result of his inability to stop the German blitzkrieg.

Ullstein Photo

FACT: On the eve of the liberation of Paris Heinrich Himmler, seen here shaking hands with Hitler, ordered a squad of SS to remove a particular tapestry from the Louvre. It depicted the invasion of England, created nine centuries earlier for William the Conqueror. The Nazi plan to invade England never came to pass, but Himmler thought the tapestry would be appreciated by Hitler. The SS were unable to get it, however, because of heavy fire from the French Resistance. Others in photo, from left: Marshal Keitel, Admiral Doenitz, and Marshal Milch.

Q. What was the name of the German intelligence organization that succeeded the Abwehr?

A. The Amt Mil.

Q. How long did it take for the Allies to recover from the German thrust in the Ardennes and push the Germans back behind their borders?

A. The recovery was rather swift, but it still took five weeks to recapture the lost ground.

Q. What is the historic significance of the British offensive against the Germans at El Agheila, Libya, on January 6, 1942?

A. It marked the first British victory over the Germans in the war. The British Eighth Army caused nearly 40,000 German casualties.

Q. Who was SS Gruppenfuehrer Heinrich Muller?

A. The head of the Gestapo, under Himmler.

Q. What was the German paramilitary construction organization called that included both engineers and workers.

A. The Todt Organization.

Q. When did the last Polish troops surrender after the German invasion?

A. On September 17, 1939, about 52,000 Polish troops surrendered at Warsaw. The last organized Polish resistance was southeast of Warsaw, at Kock, which surrendered on October 6. Approximately 17,000 Poles were involved.

Q. Which U.S. unit spearheaded the Sicily invasion?

A. The 505th Parachute Regimental Combat Team, on July 9, 1943. It was part of the 82nd Airborne Division.

FACT   General Joseph Stilwell served as chief of staff to Supreme Commander Chiang Kai-shek in China, commander of U.S. forces in the China-Burma-India theater, and subordinate to the British commander in India, all at the same time. This made him responsible to Washington, China and London simultaneously.

U.S. Army Photo

Q. Identify the first three U.S. generals to land during the Normandy invasion in 1944.

A. The first three were Matthew B. Ridgway, 82nd Airborne; Maxwell D. Taylor, 101st Airborne; and James M. Gavin, 82nd Airborne, pictured here.

Q. Name the location in the Middle East where Free French and Vichy French troops fought each other, and when did it happen?

A. In June 1941 in Vichy French Syria. The British felt if they employed Free French units the Vichy troops would be reluctant to kill other Frenchmen. Units of the Free French that General de Gaulle consigned to the Middle East Command were used. The British were wrong, and several Frenchmen on both sides died before the Vichy French surrendered.

Q. Identify any three of the multinational armies General Alexander commanded in the battle for Cassino.

A. They included a brigade of Palestinian Jews, Poles, Moroccans, Greeks, Senegalese, Italians, Algerians, Brazilians, Indians, South Africans, Canadians, French, New Zealanders, British and Americans.

Q. Who was Hitler's personal bodyguard in the last days of the war?

A. SS Colonel Otto Gunsche.

Q. How many hours after General MacArthur had been notified of the Pearl Harbor attack was Manila attacked?

A. Between eight and nine hours. Yet, as at air bases at Pearl Harbor, his planes remained on the ground and were easy targets.

Q. Who was the head of German Military Intelligence (Abwehr) in France in 1944?

A. Colonel Friedrich Garthe.

Q. What do the initials COSSAC stand for?

A. Chief of Staff, Supreme Allied Commander.

Q. Why did Canada wait seven days, until September 10, 1939, to follow Britain, Australia, New Zealand and India in declaring war on Germany?

A. Because Canada was expecting large shipments of war materiel from the U.S. The U.S., which was neutral, could not send such materiel to a belligerent. The delay permitted the delivery.

Q. Who became German Fuehrer upon the death of Hitler?

A. Admiral Karl Doenitz.

Q. Identify the town in Sicily that Patton raced and beat Montgomery to.

A. After conquering most of the island, including Palermo, Patton captured Messina, which had been Montgomery's objective, and he delighted in welcoming the field marshal upon his late arrival.

Q. What was the area of beachhead involved in the Normandy landings?

A. Approximately sixty miles along the Cotentin Peninsula.

Q. What German general was responsible for creating a limited scorched-earth plan to be used as the Germans withdrew from Paris?

A. Generalleutnant Gunther Blumentritt, chief of staff to Generalfeldmarschall Gunther von Kluge, commander of OB West (Oberbefehlshaber West).

Q. How long did it take Germany to conquer Belgium?

A. Seventeen days.

Q. How long did the Dutch hold out against the German invasion?

A. Five days.

Q. What was the ABDA Command?

A. The short-lived effort that combined American, British, Dutch and Australian forces in the Pacific. Each nation had its own idea of what the ABDA should do; as a result it was terminated after less than two months in the early part of 1942.

Q. What was the function of the London Controlling Section (LCS)?

A. Created by Winston Churchill, its purpose was to deceive the Germans about Allied plans and operations through the use of stratagems, lies and misleading acts.

FACT Italy signed two documents marking its end of participation in the war as a member of the Axis. The first, on September 3, 1943, was not publicly announced, in order to avoid a German move at seizing control of the country. The second, public announcement came five days later.

Q. Which high-ranking Nazi claimed he told Hitler to end the war three times and even considered murdering Hitler?

A. Albert Speer said he brought the subject up in October 1944 and again in January and March of 1945. He told General Gotthard Heinrici, commander of Army Group Vistula, that he had considered introducing poison gas into the ventilating system of the Fuehrerbunker. During the meeting with Heinrici, Speer produced a pistol, saying it was "the only way to stop Hitler." But Speer never attempted an assassination.

Q. Identify the U.S. Marine commander of the Guadalcanal invasion.

A. Major General Alexander A. Vandergrift of the 1st Marine Division.

Q. Identify the Norwegian location where the Germans produced heavy water for atomic research.

A. Rjukan. From there it was sent to the Kaiser Wilhelm Institute for research in Germany.

Q. Besides Hitler, his new wife Eva Braun, and Joseph and Magda Goebbels, identify some of the other people who committed suicide in the bunker.

A. OKH chief of staff, General Hans Krebs; Hitler's adjutant, General Wilhelm Burgdorf; and Captain Franz Schedle of the SS bunker guards.

Q. Where was Bloody Nose Ridge?

A. On Peleliu, in the Pacific. It took Marine and Army personnel one month to capture the island from the Japanese. More than 11,000 Japanese were killed by the attacking force of 45,000 Americans.

Q. Which British unit went into battle on D-Day accompanied by wailing bagpipes?

A. The 1st Special Service Brigade commandos under Lord Lovat. The piper was William Millin, who played "Blue Bonnets over the Border" more than once that day.

Q. How many concentration camps did the Nazis operate in Germany and occupied countries?

A. More than thirty, of which Auschwitz, Buchenwald, Belsen, Dachau and Ravensbruck were the most infamous.

Q. Identify the U.S. Marine Corps general who commanded the V Marines in the invasion of Iwo Jima.

A. Major General Harry Schmidt.

Q. Who had the distinction of announcing officially to the world that the Allies had invaded France on D-Day?

A. Colonel Ernest Dupuy, press aide to the Supreme Allied Commander. It was announced at 9:30 A.M. June 6, 1944.

Q. Name the "impregnable" fort in Belgium that the Germans captured in thirty hours?

A. Fort Eben Emael. German paratroopers had trained in advance of the attack at a replica. One sergeant and eighty men assaulted and captured it.

Q. Which two U.S. generals threatened to quit if Eisenhower appointed Montgomery Land Forces Commander?

A. Omar Bradley and George Patton. Monty had sought the role more than once, but Ike refused to relinquish command. Monty believed so strongly in the post, however, he once offered to serve subordinate to Bradley.

Q. Identify the German gun introduced in the North African campaign that sliced through British armor almost effortlessly?

A. The 88 millimeter.

Q. How many anti-personnel and anti-marine mines and obstacles had the Germans laced the European shoreline with in hopes of foiling the D-Day landings?

A. There were reportedly over a half million lethal devices awaiting Allied troops.

Q. What was the obvious difference between U.S. Army A rations and C and K rations?

A. A rations indicated the meal was prepared in an area where it could be refrigerated and was, as a result, better than the K or C rations. C rations included Spam and nine other meat compounds, dehydrated eggs and potatoes and an assortment of other "almost foods."

Q. How did the German S mines react when stepped on?

A. They snapped into the air and detonated at the victim's midriff.

Q. Name the German commanding general of Paris who failed to follow Hitler's orders and destroy the city.

A. General Dietrich von Choltitz, commandant of Festung Paris (Fortress Paris), delayed giving the order that would have set off explosions in a number of architectural treasures, including the Eiffel Tower, because he didn't want to be remembered in history with that stigma. Because the city was liberated without the destruction Hitler wished, Choltitz was tried in absentia for treason by a Nazi court in April 1945. The order to destroy Paris had been given on August 23, 1944.

Q. Name the Japanese commander who defeated MacArthur's army in the Philippines.

A. Lieutenant General Masahara Homma, who was executed after the war for his role in the Death March at Bataan.

Q. Identify the German city that was the target of the first thousand-bomber raid in the war.

A. Cologne, on May 30–31, 1942. The RAF air armada took off from fifty-two airfields in Britain.

Q. What was the significance of the London *Daily Telegraph*'s crossword puzzles in May and June 1944?

A. Several of the answers turned out to be code names for the Normandy invasion. From May 2 through early June compiler Leonard Sideny Dawe coincidentally used Overlord, Utah, Omaha, Mulberry, Neptune and others.

Q. Who created the comic character Sad Sack, and where did it first appear?

A. U.S. Army Sergeant George Baker created him, and millions of servicemen followed Sad Sack adventures in *Yank* magazine.

FACT   The Allies used more than 10,000 code names for various persons, places and operations during the war.

U.S. Army Photo

Q. Who created "Willie and Joe," and where did the cartoon appear?

A. Bill Mauldin's two hapless GI's were found in the pages of the U.S. military newspaper *Stars and Stripes*. The best antics of Willie and Joe appeared in Mauldin's postwar book *Up Front*. Photo above shows some of the 15,000 copies of the extra edition of the paper that came off the presses of *The Times* of London on May 7, 1945. *Stars and Stripes* was the first newspaper to hit the London streets with the full story of the German surrender.

Q. What was the name of the official Nazi Party newspaper in Berlin?

A. *Voelkischer Beobachter.*

Q. Identify the trio of newspapers in Paris that collaborated with the Germans.

A. The three were a weekly, *Je Suis Partout,* and two dailies, *Le Petit Parisien* and *Paris-Soir.*

Q. What was the name of the Nazi newspaper that Propaganda Minister Goebbels had published during the last six days before Berlin surrendered?

A. *Der Panzerbar (The Armored Bear),* which was intended to raise morale among the citizens defending the city against the Russians. The more famous Nazi newspaper *Voelkischer Beobachter* had been the last of Berlin's regular newspapers to cease publishing.

Q. What was the name of the German-language newspaper printed in Paris during the German occupation?

A. *Pariser Zeitung,* which ceased to go to bed in August 1944 after 221 editions.

Q. What was the headline in the *Atlanta Constitution* on President Roosevelt's desk when he died on April 12, 1945, at Warm Springs, Georgia?

A. "9th 57 Miles from Berlin," which reported the progress of the U.S. Ninth Army.

Q. Name the three Resistance newspapers in Paris that began publishing in August 1944.

A. The three were *Libération, Le Parisien Libéré* and *Défense de la France.*

Q. Which newsman broke the story about General Patton slapping a shell-shocked soldier?

A. Drew Pearson. Although other correspondents agreed not to file the stories about two separate incidents, Pearson did not feel so obligated.

Q. Identify the future U.S. senator who was sued by Adolf Hitler for copyright infringement over *Mein Kampf.*

A. Alan Cranston (D., Calif.), who after reading both the original in German and the U.S. version decided too much had been edited out and promptly published *Adolf Hitler's Own Book*. Cranston was a news correspondent at the time in the 1930s, and the book sold a half million copies before a U.S. injunction forced him to discontinue offering it.

Q. Who was Adolf Hitler's German publisher?

A. Max Amann, an early Nazi and friend.

Q. Who actually made Winston Churchill's famous "We shall fight on the beaches" speech on the BBC in June 1940?

A. Churchill made the speech in Parliament but permitted actor Norman Shelley to re-create it on the air, as the PM was busy with the evacuation of Dunkirk. Shelley's imitation was good enough to fool Churchill's closest friends. It is the only time the PM permitted such an act.

Q. Identify the U.S. newsman who made the last broadcast from Paris before the German occupation in 1940.

A. Larry Lesueur of CBS, on June 10, which was his thirtieth birthday. Lesueur also has the distinction of making the first broadcast out of liberated Paris on August 25, 1944.

Q. How did the premature message of the liberation of Paris come to be broadcast?

A. CBS newsman Charles Collingwood had recorded the story in advance and forwarded it to London for use at the appropriate time. However a mixup resulted in it being broadcast on August 23, two full days before the actual liberation. It was carried throughout the world.

Q. In what languages did the BBC broadcast coded messages after the regular news?

A. French, Norwegian, Dutch and Danish.

Q. What radio station did Allied troops tune in when they wanted to hear the latest hits after the D-Day landing?

A. Radio Paris and the sexy-voiced Axis Sally.

FACT: The two most recognizable voices Americans heard on their radios broadcasting from London belonged to Winston Churchill and Edward R. Murrow, above. The dapper Murrow was not above lying in the gutter so that his microphone could pick up the sounds of bombs and sirens. By the time this 1941 photo was made, he was already a legend in broadcasting. By the end of the war Murrow had flown as an observer on twenty-five combat missions. His CBS broadcasts from England opened with "This . . . is London."

Q. What were the British islands that came under the control of an Axis power?

A. The Channel Islands, which had fallen to the Germans at the end of June 1940 and were not liberated until May 9, 1945. They are approximately eighty miles off the southern English coast and some forty miles from Cherbourg, France.

Q. Identify the last European capital to be liberated in May 1945.

A. Prague, Czechoslovakia, by the Russians.

Q. Identify the Yugoslav monarch deposed by Tito when the Partisan resistance leader declared the People's Republic of Yugoslavia?

A. King Peter II on November 23, 1943.

Q. Identify the Associated Press newsman who was ordered to leave the European theater of war for scooping the world with the news that the Germans had surrendered.

A. Edward Kennedy earned that distinction for his violation of the official release time when he broke the story on May 7, 1945.

Q. Name the only two countries whose declarations of war against the U.S. were not "accepted."

A. During the month of December 1941, diplomatic exchanges of declarations of war between Allied and Axis powers and various sympathizers were relatively rapid and, obviously, accepted. However, the U.S. refused to accept the Slovakia declaration on December 12, and then on the 14th refused to accept the Croat declaration against the U.S.

Q. Name the only bridge in Florence, Italy, that was not destroyed by the retreating Germans in August 1944.

A. The historic fourteenth-century Ponte Vecchio.

Q. Identify the three former French premiers who were liberated by U.S. troops from confinement in Austria in May 1945.

A. The three were Edouard Daladier, Paul Reynaud and Léon Blum. In addition, former Austrian Chancellor Kurt von Schuschnigg and French generals Weygand and Gamelin were also liberated.

Q. Who was the commanding Japanese general of the Okinawa defense against the Americans in 1945?

A. Lieutenant General Mitsuru Ushijima, who committed suicide on June 22, 1945, and became one of the approximately 110,000 Japanese who died during the eighty-one-day conflict. U.S. Marine and Army losses were 12,520 killed and over 36,000 wounded.

Q. When was Athens free of German troops?

A. The Germans began to withdraw on October 2, 1944, and were completely out by October 14, the same day British troops landed on the island of Corfu.

Q. Identify the U.S. Marine Corps division that established the first beachhead on Peleliu Island on September 15, 1944.

A. The 1st Marine Division, in a campaign where progress was gauged in yards, sometimes feet. The U.S. Army sent troops from the 81st Division to assist the Marines on September 23. The island was not secured until October 14.

Q. What was the last major amphibious operation of the war?

A. The invasion of Okinawa. About 60,000 U.S. troops (two Marine and two Army divisions) were involved.

Q. Identify the U.S. troops that invaded the island of Ie-shima during the Okinawa campaign.

A. The U.S. 77th Division assaulted the island on April 16, 1945.

Q. Identify the German city near a salt mine where U.S. troops uncovered a tremendous amount of buried Nazi treasure.

A. When the U.S. 90th Division captured Merkers, they discovered art, gold and other valuables (much of which was Nazi plunder from occupied countries) buried in the nearby salt mine. The discovery was in April 1945.

FACT Rommel and his army were surrounded by German troops on September 15, 1939, and ordered to surrender. He declined the offer. However, Major General Juliusz Rommel was the military commander of Warsaw, not the German general and future field marshal of North Africa fame.

U.S. Coast Guard Photo

FACT: U.S. war correspondent Ernie Pyle covered the war in both the Atlantic and Pacific theaters. After he was killed, one of his manuscripts was auctioned for over $10 million during a War Bond drive in Indianapolis, Indiana. Sharing a cup of coffee somewhere in the Pacific, en route to the Ryukus, are Pyle and U.S. Coast Guard commander, former heavyweight boxing champion of the world, Jack Dempsey.

Q. Identify the Japanese Army major that led the abortive attempt to stage a coup in Tokyo during April 1945 when he learned that the Emperor had prepared a surrender speech.

A. Though Japan would not surrender for over four months, Major Kenji Hatanaka and other officers could not even consider the possibility. When the April 14–15 plot failed, Hatanaka committed suicide.

Q. Identify the three countries Germany invaded on May 10, 1940.

A. The three were Belgium, Holland and Luxembourg.

Q. Identify the first country to join the original Axis powers of Germany, Japan and Italy.

A. Bulgaria, on March 1, 1941.

Q. Identify the neutral country that had an official two-day mourning period after the death of Adolf Hitler.

A. Portugal, where flags were flown at half staff on April 30 and May 1, 1945. Another country that followed diplomatic protocol was Ireland. Prime Minister Eamon de Valera actually expressed his condolences to German representatives in Dublin on May 2, 1945.

Q. Identify the location that has the distinction of being the only North American territory occupied by an Axis power during the war.

A. The Aleutian Islands, where a Japanese invasion force of approximately 1,800 troops landed unopposed on June 7, 1942, on Attu and Kiska.

Q. Name the German general who because of his ability to always agree with Hitler and seek approval was called "Lackey" by other army officers.

A. Field Marshal Wilhelm Keitel, Chief of the Supreme Command of the German Armed Forces. A little wordplay with his name changed it to *Lakeitel,* which in German means "lackey."

FACT The total number of aircraft used by both sides during the war was approximately 675,000 planes, of which 475,000 were employed by the Allies.

Q. When was the American flag raised on Iwo Jima?

A. February 23, 1945. The invasion began February 19, the battle lasted twenty-six days.

Q. Who provided the flag that was raised on Mount Suribachi, Iwo Jima?

A. The first flag, a small one that a U.S. Marine had brought with him and lashed to an iron pipe, was replaced by the battle ensign from LST-779 down on the beach. This is the flag in the famous Associated Press photo by Joe Rosenthal.

Q. Name the servicemen who raised the flag on Iwo Jima.

A. The *first* flag-raising on Mount Suribachi was by Marines H. O. Hansen, E. I. Thomas, H. B. Shrier, J. R. Michaels and C. W. Lindberg. It is recorded in U.S. Navy Photo 304841.

Q. Where was the closest American flag to the Japanese homeland raised during combat?

A. On the northern end of Okinawa in mid-April 1945 by the U.S. 6th Marine Division. They also raised the same flag on the southern end of the island on June 21.

Q. Identify the military unit that was the first to occupy Japan.

A. The U.S. 4th Marines.

Q. What two teams were playing a football game at the Polo Grounds in New York when the broadcast was interrupted with the news of the Pearl Harbor attack?

A. The Dodgers and the Giants. Ward Cuff of the Giants had caught a Dodger kickoff and brought it to the Giants' twenty-seven-yard line. It was 2:26 P.M., and radio station WOR broadcast the news that the Japanese had attacked the U.S. Naval Base at Pearl Harbor in Hawaii.

FACT Claus von Bulow, the Rhode Island financier who on March 16, 1982, was convicted of twice trying to kill his heiress wife with insulin injections so he could collect a $14 million inheritance and marry his mistress, had been a page at the wedding of Reichsmarschall Hermann Goering in the 1930s.

Q. Name the Australian Prime Minister who died in July 1945 after leading his country since 1941.

A. John Curtin. His passing marked the fourth death of a head of state of a major World War II combatant in three months. Roosevelt, Mussolini and Hitler had preceded him.

Q. What was the only industry that provided its products free of charge to the U.S. Government throughout the war?

A. The film industry. Prints of all features were provided at no cost for entertainment of servicemen. Over 43,000 prints were furnished.

Q. Where did the U.S. Army get its first taste of combat against the Germans?

A. At Kasserine Pass, Tunisia, against Rommel's Afrika Korps, which had created a bulge in Allied lines. About 2,400 inexperienced U.S. troops surrendered.

FACT The most decorated World War II veteran ever elected to Congress was Sen. Daniel Ken Inouye (D-Hawaii) who was awarded the Distinguished Service Medal, Bronze Star, Purple Heart with clusters, and five Battle Stars. Inouye is a third-generation American whose ancestry is Japanese.

The Air War

Q. Who was the ace of aces among all the combatant nations in the war?

A. Luftwaffe Major Erich Hartmann, with 352 "kills." Several German pilots recorded over 100 "kills," and five had more than 250. This was due in part to the fact that they did not rotate tours of duty with rest periods as the Allies did, and they counted aircraft shot on the ground.

Q. Who won fame in the Battle of Britain as the "legless air ace"?

A. Squadron Leader Douglas Bader, who lost both legs in a crash in 1931. In 1939, wearing artificial legs, he rejoined the service. He is credited with twenty-three "kills."

Q. What was the name of the airfield the U.S. Marines built on Guadalcanal?

A. Henderson Field, after Major Loften R. Henderson of the Midway-based Marine Aircraft Group, who was killed during the Battle of Midway. They used abandoned Japanese equipment to convert a level piece of ground that the Japanese had cleared for use as an airstrip.

Q. Identify the bombsight that is credited with much of the success the U.S. had in precision bombing.

A. The Norden.

U.S. Navy Photo

Q. Identify the major Midwestern U.S. city that named an airport in honor of the first U.S. Navy ace of the war.

A. Chicago, the Windy City, named O'Hare Airport for Lieutenant Edward "Butch" O'Hare, who downed five Japanese planes on February 20, 1942. O'Hare was stationed on the aircraft carrier *Lexington*. While flying from the *Enterprise* during activity in the Central Pacific in 1944 he lost his life. His 1942 combat action won him the Congressional Medal of Honor.

Q. How did the Japanese get aerial photos of Hickam Field and Pearl Harbor?

A. By having agents take private sightseeing plane rides from John Rogers Airport. Their task was duplicated hundreds of times by ordinary tourists.

Q. Identify the aircraft considered by many to have been the best torpedo bomber of the war.

A. The Italian Savoia-Marchetti Sparviero, which was called the Damned Hunchback. It was also used as a transport and reconnaissance plane. More than half of the Italian Air Force's bombers were Damned Hunchbacks.

Q. Who was Britain's top ace, including pilots from throughout the Commonwealth?

A. Major Saint John Pattle from South Africa with forty-one "kills."

Q. Identify the pilot who flew more combat missions than anyone else in the war.

A. Luftwaffe ace Hans-Ulrich Rudel. According to German records, he flew 2,530 combat missions. He is the only German ever awarded a Knight's Cross to the Iron Cross with Golden Oak Leaves and Swords and Diamonds, the second highest degree of Iron Cross. (The highest degree is Great Cross of the Iron Cross, which was also only awarded once, to Hermann Goering.)

Q. Name the other three Japanese cities bombed at the time of Doolittle's raid on Tokyo in April 1942.

A. Kobe, Nagoya and Yokohama were the three.

Q. How many women served as pilots in the Soviet Air Force?

A. More than 5,000, of whom Lieutenant Lilya Litvak with seven "kills" and Lieutenant Katya Budanova with six "kills" were the top two fighter aces.

FACT The wearing of Star of David cloth identification badges for Polish Jews began on November 23, 1939, less than three months after the war began. The order was extended to Jews in all Baltic States on July 8, 1941.

Q. Who founded the Free French Air Force?

A. General Charles de Gaulle.

Q. Identify the two aircraft involved in the last dogfight in the European theater.

A. A Piper Cub unarmed spotting plane named *Miss Me* of the U.S. 5th Armored and a German Fieseler Storch, also a spotting plane, met in the sky over Germany in April 1945. Lieutenant Duane Francies, pilot, and his observer, Lieutenant William Martin, dove on the Storch and fired their .45 Colts, bringing the German plane down. They landed and captured the pilot and German observer. It was the only German plane shot down with a handgun.

Q. Who was the American Army Air Force officer that Reichsmarschall Hermann Goering offered a $5,000 reward for?

A. Tail gunner Clark Gable, who may or may not have quipped after hearing it, "Frankly, Herr Reichsmarschall, I don't give a damn!"

Q. Where did the Japanese introduce the kamikaze plane?

A. The Battle for Leyte Gulf. In Japanese, *kamikaze* means "divine wind" and refers to the typhoon that struck the invading Mongol fleet prepared to invade Japan in the Middle Ages.

Q. What was the name of the B-29 that dropped the second atomic bomb on a Japanese city? Name the city and when it was done.

A. On August 9, 1945, Major Charles W. Sweeney diverted his plane, named *Bock's Car,* from its primary target, Kokura, and bombed the secondary target, Nagasaki. The plane, along with the *Enola Gay,* was part of the 509th Composite Group, 313th Wing, of the Twentieth U.S. Air Force.

Q. Which English ace earned the best record?

A. Captain James E. Johnson, with thirty-eight "kills."

Q. What was the name of Adolf Hitler's pilot?

A. Hans Baur.

Q. Identify the only Rumanian-built fighter plane to see action during the war.

A. The I.A.R. 80. Production began in 1941.

Q. After the famous raid on Tokyo by Lieutenant Colonel James Doolittle, when was the next time U.S. bombers attacked Japan?

A. Not until more than two years later, on June 15, 1944. This time B-29s from a base in China dropped 221 tons of bombs on the Yawata ironworks on the island of Kyushu.

Q. Identify the all-female fighter group in the Soviet Air Force.

A. The 586th Fighter Aviation Regiment, 122nd Air Division, which flew more than 4,400 combat missions.

Q. Identify the aircraft considered the best French fighter of the war.

A. The Dewoitine D-520. France had only produced thirty-six of them that were in service before the armistice with Germany. Under occupation, approximately 870 were produced for use by the Luftwaffe and the Italians, Bulgarians and Rumanians.

Q. What is considered the most significant result of the Battle of the Bismarck Sea with regard to air power?

A. The fact that the Japanese troop convoy heading for New Guinea with reinforcements was wiped out, and more than 6,000 troops and 102 planes were destroyed. The U.S. Fifth Air Force was under the command of Major General George C. Kenny.

Q. Identify the two types of RAF planes credited with winning the Battle of Britain.

A. The Spitfire and the Hurricane.

Q. Identify the first type of monoplane fighter to operate from a U.S. aircraft carrier.

A. The Brewster Buffalo.

Q. Which aircraft was the first monoplane deck fighter in the Japanese navy?

A. The Mitsubishi A5M4, produced in 1937 and taken out of service in 1942. The Allied code name was Claude.

Q. Which aircraft holds the distinction of being the first monoplane used by the RAF?

A. The Avro Anson. It was also the first aircraft in RAF service to boast retractable landing gear.

U.S. Navy Photo

Q. Who was the U.S. Army Air Force commander in Hawaii on December 7, 1941:

    a. William Farthing
    b. Frederick L. Martin
    c. William W. Outerbridge

A. General Frederick L. Martin. Colonel William Farthing was commander of Hickam Field and Lieutenant William W. Outerbridge was the skipper of the U.S. destroyer *Ward,* the ship that sank the first ship at Pearl Harbor, a Japanese midget submarine. A destroyed U.S. B-17 sits on the runway at Hickam in this photo.

Q. Name the Australian-built fighter plane that was designed and (a prototype) built in four weeks.

A. The CA-12 Boomerang. Because of the difficulty in obtaining U.S. or British aircraft to fend off the Japanese, the Australians instantly created one of their own. A total of 250 Boomerang fighters were produced.

Q. Who was the leading Irish ace fighting for Britain?

A. Colonel Brendan E. Finucane, who is credited with thirty-two "kills."

Q. Identify the well-known German aviatrix who landed a Fieseler Storch in the heart of Berlin during the height of the battle for the city.

A. Hanna Reitsch, who had taken over the controls from General Ritter von Greim, wounded in the approach. They had been called to Berlin by Hitler.

Q. When did U.S. personnel participate as full crews for the first time in a bombing mission over occupied Europe?

A. On July 4, 1942, U.S.-crewed planes joined an RAF raid on Luftwaffe airfields in Holland. The U.S. lost two of the six planes that participated.

Q. Other than British, which nations had the greatest and which had the least number of squadrons in the RAF by the time the Allies invaded France?

A. There were forty-two Canadian squadrons, the most, and one Yugoslav squadron among the 487 in the RAF. A total of 157 squadrons in the RAF were international by D-Day.

Q. Name the aircraft that was the backbone of the Polish Air Force when the Germans invaded.

A. Poland had 125 P.Z.L. P-11c aircraft, first produced in 1933, as her total fighter plane power in September 1939. For seventeen days these outdated planes engaged in more modern aircraft of the Luftwaffe before the surrender. Only seven were left at the end, but they had shot down 126 German aircraft.

Q. Identify the type of U.S. aircraft that the Japanese nicknamed Whistling Death.

A. The Chance-Vought F4U-1 Corsair, which went into service in 1943. It is credited with more than 2,000 successful missions.

Q. Identify the Japanese jet-engine air bomb piloted by a kamikaze pilot and carried by a larger plane to its target.

A. The Yokosuka MXY7, code-named Baka by the Allies. Japan produced five versions and a total of 852 of these suicide bombs.

Q. Identify the Italian plane that participated in the Battle of Britain with the Germans and was also used by the Japanese against the Chinese.

A. The Fiat Cicogna light bomber. Italian pilots flew them over Britain, but in China the pilots were Japanese. Tokyo purchased seventy-five Cicognas from Italy in 1938.

Q. Identify the top Canadian ace of the war.

A. Major George F. Beurling, with thirty-one "kills."

Q. Who was the immediate object of Rudolf Hess's flight to Britain?

A. The Duke of Hamilton, whom he had met at the 1936 Olympics and hoped would deliver him to Britain's leaders to discuss peace.

Q. How many U.S. military aircraft from all services were based on Oahu on December 7, 1941? How many got aloft?

A. Of the approximately 390 aircraft at various bases, thirty-eight got into the sky, and ten of these were shot down.

Q. Which country developed the first single-engine low-wing fighter plane that had retractable landing gear?

A. The Soviet Union developed the Polikarpov, which was known as the Rata during the Spanish Civil War.

Q. Who was France's top ace?

A. Pierre Closterman, with thirty-three "kills." He rose from the rank of sergeant to major in the Free French Air Force, which was based in England.

Q. Identify the only Allied jet aircraft to enter service during the war.

A. The Gloster Meteor III, which made its inaugural flight on March 5, 1943, but didn't face enemy aircraft until July 1944. They actually faced V-1 bombs but not piloted planes.

Q. What type Allied aircraft is credited with scoring the first "kill" against a German plane?

A. A Lockheed A-29 Hudson, American made, but in service for the British Coastal Command. A Hudson was also the first American plane to sink a German U-boat.

Q. What was the proper name of the most famous Japanese aircraft produced during the war?

A. The Mitsubishi A6M3 Zero, which was known to the Allies as Zeke. Japan manufactured 10,449 of them, including 465 modified versions as kamikazes.

Q. Who was Italy's top air ace of the war?

A. Major Adriano Visconti, with twenty-six "kills." Despite Italy's inferior air power due to lack of aircraft, its pilots were considered among the finest in the war.

Q. Identify the first German city to suffer a bombing raid in the war.

A. On September 4, 1939, the RAF bombed Brunsbüttelkoog.

Q. Identify the type of fighter plane General Claire Chennault's Flying Tigers used.

A. The Curtis P-40 Warhawk. In England it was called the Tomahawk and the Kittyhawk.

Q. Who was the Soviet air ace of aces?

A. Colonel Ivan N. Kozhedub, with sixty-two "kills."

Q. What was the name of the Free French fighter group that fought in Russia with the 1st Soviet Air Division?

A. Normandie, which functioned from early 1943 on. Four members of this group were honored as Heroes of the Soviet Union. Each had over ten "kills" to his credit.

Q. Where and when did the RAF and the Luftwaffe first meet in air combat?

A. Over Aachen on September 20, 1939, when the Germans shot down two enemy planes and the British scored one enemy plane. Aircraft involved were Messerschmitts and Battles.

Q. Where did the four dive-bombers that were accidentally shot down trying to land at Pearl Harbor come from on the night of December 7, 1941?

A. The carrier *Enterprise*. They had landed earlier in the day but had been sent out to search for the Japanese fleet. Returning in the dark, they were mistaken for enemy planes.

Q. Who was Japan's ace of aces in the war?

A. Hiroyishi Nishizawa with 87 "kills."

Q. What plane was the first all-metal fighter produced by Italy?

A. The Fiat G-50 Freccia, designed in 1937. Used in the Spanish Civil War on a limited basis, the Freccia saw action in Greece, Belgium, Libya, the Balkans and the Aegean Sea. Approximately 675 were manufactured.

Q. Identify the type of RAF plane that dropped the first 8,000-pound bomb on Germany.

A. A Halifax, the night of April 10–11, 1942.

Q. When did U.S. aircraft participate in the first totally American air raid on Germany?

A. On January 27, 1943, bombing the German port of Wilhelmshaven.

Q. How much were the American volunteers in Chennault's Flying Tigers paid for their participation in China?

A. They earned $600 per month plus $500 for each "kill."

Q. Did the French Air Force ever actually bomb a German city during its brief combat service in the war?

A. Yes, Berlin, on June 7, 1940.

Q. What were the names of the three old Gladiator biplanes that defended Malta from the Germans?

A. *Faith, Hope* and *Charity*.

FACT   In the early offensives of the North African campaign most of Rommel's troops were Italian.

Q. Who was America's ace of aces?

A. Major Richard I. Bong, forty "kills."

Q. What was the largest flying boat produced during the war?

A. The German Blohn & Voss Bv222C Wiking. Designed in 1940 by Lufthansa for use in passenger service across the Atlantic, these huge six-engine aircraft were put to military use in September 1941 as troop and materiel transports. Fourteen were manufactured.

Q. What was the first Japanese heavy bomber to have a tail-gun turret?

A. The Nakajimi Ki-49-II, code-named Helen by the Allies. Just over 800 were manufactured. It first saw combat on February 19, 1942, in the bombing of Port Darwin, Australia.

Q. Identify the Italian city that was the object of the first RAF daylight raid from British bases.

A. Milan, on October 24, 1942. The trip was just over 2,800 air miles.

Q. What city was the target of the most destructive RAF air raid of the war?

A. Hamburg, Germany, on July 27–28, 1943, when nearly 750 RAF bombers dropped over 2,400 tons of bombs, many of which were incendiaries that created fire storms with winds of over 150 miles per hour. Official records put the death toll at 20,000 and the injured at more than 60,000.

Q. Who was Australia's top ace?

A. Captain Clive R. Caldwell, twenty-eight "kills."

Q. How many aircraft did the Luftwaffe use in the Battle of Britain?

A. They used 3,550, including 2,000 bombers.

FACT Anti-Hitler German officers tried and failed twice to kill Hitler during one week in March 1943. In the second attempt Colonel Rudolph von Gertsdorff had to flush the fuse of a bomb down a toilet when Hitler left a meeting before the bomb could be detonated. The incident took place at the Zeughaus exhibition hall in Berlin.

Q. What was the Central Aircraft Manufacturing Company (CAMCO)?

A. The cover name for the American volunteer organization General Claire L. Chennault recruited to fight the Japanese for China. The fighting units were called the American Volunteer Group (AVG) when they began training in September 1941. After Pearl Harbor they became a legend as the Flying Tigers.

Q. What was the strength of the French Armée de l'Air (Air Force) when war began?

A. Counting those attached to French colonies, there were 3,600 aircraft. Only 1,400, however, were in the mother country.

Q. What were the strengths of the RAF and the Luftwaffe at the start of the Battle of Britain?

A. The RAF had 704 serviceable aircraft vs. 2,682 for the Luftwaffe.

Q. What was the fastest propeller fighter plane ever built?

A. The U.S.-made Mustang.

Q. Name the type of Japanese torpédo bomber credited with sinking the U.S. aircraft carriers *Lexington, Yorktown* and *Hornet*.

A. The Nakajima B5N2, 144 of which participated in the Pearl Harbor attack. It was code-named Kate by the Allies.

Q. Name the site in Italy that was the target of the first U.S. air attack?

A. Naples harbor on December 4, 1942, bombed by U.S. B-24s.

Q. Who was New Zealand's top air ace?

A. Lieutenant Colonel Colin F. Gray, twenty-seven "kills."

Q. Where were the Luftwaffe headquarters in Paris located?

A. In the Luxembourg Palace on the Left Bank on Rue de Vaugirard.

Q. Who first used rockets in air combat in the Pacific?

A. The Flying Tigers, which became the U.S. Fourteenth Air Force.

Q. When did the U.S. Eighth Air Force make its combat debut?

A. In August 1942, from bases in England against targets in Germany.

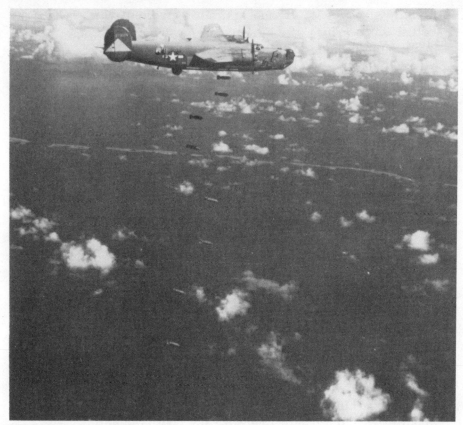

FACT: The American B-24 Liberator was used more extensively in the Mediterranean than in Germany because it had less armament and tend-
ed to catch fire when hit. In this photo, the famous Seventh Air Force
in action over Truk atoll in the Pacific drops 500-pound bombs on
Japanese positions. The name of the particular plane in this photo is
the *Kansas Cyclone.*

Q. Identify the type of Japanese aircraft credited with sinking the British ships *Prince of Wales* and *Repulse* on December 10, 1941, in the Gulf of Siam.

A. The Mitsubishi G3Mi, code-named "Nell." A long-range medium bomber, it ended the war serving as a transport. Over 1,000 were built.

Q. What was the seagoing version of the RAF Spitfire known as?

A. The Seafire.

Q. How many tons of bombs did Britain drop on Germany?

A. Just over 645,920 tons.

Q. Where and when did the first B-29 Superfortress debut in a combat theater?

A. The first of the sixty-ton B-29s was sent to India in April 1944 and participated in its first raid on June 5, 1944 (the day Rome was liberated and one day before the Normandy invasion), on the railroad yards of Bangkok.

Q. Identify the first fighter designed for carrier use by the British?

A. The Fairey Fulmar. It was introduced to aircraft carrier service aboard the *Illustrious* in 1940 with the 806th Squadron.

Q. When did Boeing produce the last B-17 Flying Fortress for the U.S.?

A. April 9, 1945, at its Seattle, Washington, plant.

Q. Which Japanese aircraft, code-named Betty by the Allies but nicknamed Flying Lighter by U.S. pilots, brought the Japanese delegation to Ie-shima to negotiate the surrender?

A. The Mitsubishi G4M1 Navy medium bomber. It was the most widely produced of the Japanese medium bombers (2,446 were made).

Q. Identify the other British cities that the Luftwaffe raided during the same moonlight period of 1940 when they bombed Coventry.

A. Birmingham and Wolverhampton, along with Coventry, were Luftwaffe targets in November 1940.

Q. What position did Generalfeldmarschall Hugo Sperrle hold in August 1944?

A. Commander in Chief of the Luftwaffe, Western Front.

Q. When did the first U.S. heavy bombers begin operations against Germany from England?

A. August 1942.

Q. Identify the British fighter-bomber that was fast enough to intercept Germany's V-1 bombs.

A. The Hawker Tempest. It is credited with intercepting and destroying over 600 V-1 bombs.

Q. What was the name of the plane that President Roosevelt boarded in Miami on January 11, 1943, for the start of his trip to the Casablanca Conference?

A. The *Dixie Clipper*. When FDR boarded the plane, he became the first U.S. President to fly while in office. The pilot for the historic flight was Howard M. Cone, a Pan Am employee and Naval Reserve lieutenant.

Q. Which aircraft did Japan depend on to defend Tokyo during the last months of the war?

A. The Kawasaki Ki escort fighter–night fighter. The 10th Division depended on Nick, as the Allies called her, to repel the U.S. B-29s. Over 1,700 were produced.

Q. What was the last aircraft to leave Dunkirk?

A. A Westland Lysander with the name of *Lizzie*.

Q. Was the V-1 or V-2 known as the buzz bomb?

A. The V-1. Both were developed at Peenemunde.

Q. What was the maximum bomb load for a B-17, and what was the typical load for a mission over Germany?

A. Capable of carrying 17,600 pounds of bombs for short distances, the B-17 more frequently carried between 4,000 and 5,000 pounds on long-range raids.

Q. Which aircraft was the most used to train British pilots?

A. The De Havilland Tiger Moth.

Q. How did the Americans and British divide the bombing of Germany?

A. The British bombed at night and the Americans bombed during the day.

Q. Where did the U.S. launch the first air attack against the Japanese in the war?

A. In the Marshall and Gilbert islands on February 1, 1942, when a U.S. task force of two aircraft carriers and fifteen other ships initiated the largest U.S. offensive to date.

Q. Which aircraft was Japan's first low-wing monoplane fighter?

A. The Nakajima Ki-27, code-named Nate by the Allies. Introduced against the Russians in the Manchurian incident, it ceased to be manufactured in August 1940. However, the 3,400 planes in Japanese army flight groups saw considerable action through 1942.

Q. Whom did Churchill appoint as Minister of Aircraft Production?

A. Canadian entrepreneur Lord Beaverbrook.

Q. What other name was the German Junkers 87 more commonly known by?

A. The Stuka dive-bomber.

Q. What were the U.S. squadrons of the RAF called before they were reorganized under U.S. command on September 29, 1942?

A. The three U.S. units were the Eagle Squadrons.

Q. Identify the type of seaplane Japan produced in greater numbers than all others.

A. The Aichi E13A1, code-named Jake by the Allies. It was first used offensively on December 7, 1941, against the U.S. at Pearl Harbor. Catapulted from ships, its primary function was reconnaissance. Over 1,400 were produced.

FACT The U.S. Navy ordered all ships to engage Axis ships discovered within twenty-five miles of the Western Hemisphere from April 18, 1941, on. The reasoning was that any ship so located could be considered hostile.

Q. How many bombing missions did Britain fly on all fronts during the war?

A. The RAF flew 687,462, dropping more than 1,103,900 tons of bombs.

Q. When did Germany launch the first V-1 bombs against London?

A. In June 1944, one week after the Allied landings at Normandy, France. They killed approximately 6,000 persons. (Hitler, bent on revenge against the English people, failed to use the V-1 against the critical military objectives of Southampton or Portsmouth, where the supply lines to France were being fed.)

Q. What was the name of the first U.S. jet plane flown during the war, and where did it fly?

A. The Bell XP-59 introduced U.S. aviation to the jet age on October 1, 1942, at Muroc in the Mojave Desert in California. The first U.S. jet fighter, the Lockheed P-80 Shooting Star, flew for the first time on January 8, 1944, but not in combat until June 1950 in Korea.

Q. Identify the type of Japanese aircraft responsible for downing ten U.S. B-29 Superfortresses on February 19, 1945.

A. The Nakajima Ki4411, produced in 1942. These high-altitude army interceptor-fighters were code-named Tojo by the Allies. Some 1,225 were produced.

Q. What were the aircraft losses of the British and Germans in the Battle of Britain?

A. The British lost 915 planes vs. 1,733 for the Germans.

Q. On what date did a German plane first drop a bomb on London?

A. August 25, 1940, in the financial center of London, the City. Previously the Luftwaffe bombed the docks and areas where war production was being carried out. There is evidence that the bomb was a stray hit, not intentional. The British retaliated by bombing Berlin.

Q. What type aircraft was the most produced by the U.S. in the war?

A. The Consolidated B-24 Liberator, which was used by the Army, Navy, RAF and other Allies. There were 18,188 of them produced.

Q. Who was the Deputy Supreme Commander at Supreme Headquarters Allied Expeditionary Force?

A. British Air Chief Marshal Sir Arthur Tedder, who is shown in photo above with the Supreme Commander, U.S. General Dwight D. Eisenhower, as the future U.S. President makes his VE-Day speech from Reims, France, in May 1945.

Q. Identify the RAF pilot who racked up the highest score during the Battle of Britain.

A. Sergeant Pilot Josef Frantisek, a Czech. He was one of many foreigners in the RAF, including Poles, Americans and others from the dominion. About 20 percent of the RAF was non-English.

Q. Where did the first Luftwaffe action in North Africa take place?

A. At Benghazi, on February 12, 1941.

Q. Which city suffered more damage from bombing, London or Berlin?

A. An area equal to ten times that destroyed in London was destroyed in Berlin by Allied bombings. Approximately 52,000 people, five times more than in London, were killed.

Q. Who originated the idea of a bombing raid on Tokyo that James Doolittle carried out?

A. Captain Francis S. Low, a submarine staff officer, submitted a plan for using Army bombers from aircraft carriers.

Q. Which country had the war's first jet engine bomber?

A. Germany, with the Arado Blitz, which went into service late in 1944.

Q. What enemy target marked the debut of the F6F Hellcat fighter on September 1, 1943?

A. Marcus Island, approximately 1,200 miles southeast of Tokyo.

Q. Who produced the only jet fighter aircraft flown in combat during the war?

A. Germany. The Messerschmitt Sturmvogel made its combat appearance by attacking a De Havilland Mosquito in July 1944. Approximately 360 Me-262 jets saw combat. (The world's first jet aircraft was a Campini N-1, which, piloted by Mario de Bernardi, connected Milan and Rome on August 28, 1940.)

FACT The B-29 Superfortress never flew on a mission against Germany. However, virtually all types of U.S. planes active in Europe saw action in the Pacific against Japan.

FACT: The Japanese had presented "Good Friendship" medals to various American citizens prior to the war. Lieutenant Colonel Jimmy Doolittle, in a ceremony just before his B-25s departed on their famous raid, attached several of the medals to bombs the planes would carry and drop on Japan. In photo above Doolittle attaches medal to the fin of a 500-pound bomb aboard the deck of the aircraft carrier *Hornet*.

Q. Which country produced the only rocket-propulsion fighter plane in the war?

A. Germany. The Messerschmitt Komet made its debut on July 28, 1944. About 350 of them were in service, and more were destroyed on landing than were shot down by the Allies. This is not to be confused with a jet aircraft.

Q. Identify the French rail center that was the first independent air-raid target of the U.S. Eighth Air Force.

A. Rouen on August 17, 1942. Until that time U.S. and RAF bombers had bombed jointly. The British did, however, provide Spitfire protection for the U.S. planes during the Rouen raid.

Q. What were Japanese aircraft losses in the 1941 attack on the Philippines?

A. Seven fighter planes. The U.S. losses were fifty-six fighters, eighteen B-17s and twenty-five other aircraft.

Q. What were Japanese vs. American air losses during the Okinawa campaign?

A. The Japanese lost over 7,800 aircraft, including a large number of kamikazes, as opposed to approximately 800 for the U.S.

Q. What was the last major Luftwaffe air raid during the war?

A. The January 1, 1945, raid on Allied air and naval bases in the Low Countries and France. Of 800 planes involved in the action, 364 were shot down, while the Allies lost 125 planes.

Q. What was the first target of a joint air raid by combined RAF and Russian aircraft?

A. A train on the outskirts of Dresden, Germany, on April 16, 1945.

Q. In which theater of war was the first helicopter rescue ever accomplished?

A. The China-Burma-India theater in April 1945, when U.S. Army Air Force Captain James L. Green was plucked out of the mountains. Green, who himself had been on a search-rescue mission for pilots, crashed in the mountainous jungle in Burma. Seriously injured, he was lifted to safety a week later by Lieutenant R. F. Murdock in a Sikorsky YR-4.

Q. Name the three Japanese sites that were targets for the last air raids of the war.

A. On August 14, 1945, five days after the second atomic bomb had been dropped, U.S. B-29s raided Akita, Isesaki and Kumagaya. The next day, August 15, all hostile actions ceased as VJ-Day was announced by the Allies.

Q. What was the main difference between the Japanese and German suicide plane pilots?

A. The Japanese kamikazes did not expect to return from a mission, while the German Sonderkommando Elbe pilots had the option to parachute to safety if appropriate. In all, Germany mustered approximately 300 volunteers (mostly from the Luftwaffe) for its suicide force. Their first action was against Allied bombers, which they crashed into in mid-air, on April 7, 1945.

Q. When Malta was bombed for the first time on June 11, 1940, was it German or Italian aircraft that were involved?

A. Italian. The British had only three old Gladiator biplanes with which to defend the island.

Q. When did the first German air raid on England take place?

A. On September 6, 1939, five days after Germany invaded Poland and two days after Great Britain declared war on Germany. The first air raid on London was January 12, 1940.

Q. When was Helsinki, Finland, bombed in the war for the first time?

A. November 30, 1939, by Russia.

Q. Who succeeded Goering as commander-in-chief of the Luftwaffe?

A. General Robert Ritter von Greim, after Goering's bold bid for power during the last days of the Third Reich. Greim committed suicide on May 24, 1945.

FACT   The Japanese kamikaze pilots were responsible for sinking or damaging more than 300 U.S. Navy ships and causing approximately 15,000 casualties.

U.S. Army Photo

FACT: U.S. General Douglas MacArthur was an eighth cousin of British Prime Minister Winston Churchill and a sixth cousin of U.S. President Franklin D. Roosevelt. All three wartime leaders had a common ancestor, Sarah Barney Belcher of Taunton, Massachusetts. MacArthur is seen here (right) with General George C. Kenny, commanding general of the Far Eastern Air Forces, aboard a transport bound for Labuan Island, British North Borneo. As remarkable as the MacArthur-Churchill-Roosevelt relationship was, consider this: At the outbreak of World War I, three of the most powerful European thrones were occupied by first cousins: George V of England, Wilhelm II of Germany and Nicholas II of Russia.

Q. When and how was the U.S. mainland bombed by a piloted aircraft during the war?

A. Catapulted from submarine I-25, a Lieutenant Fujita, flying a Yokosuka E14Y1, dropped four 167.5-pound phosphorus bombs along the timber coast of the State of Oregon in 1942. The Allied code name for the E14Y was Glen.

Q. Which nation is credited with employing the first major airborne operation, independent of other armed forces, in the war?

A. Germany, on May 20, 1941, when they attacked Crete.

Q. Which German city had the unfortunate distinction of being the "most bombed"?

A. Berlin.

Q. How long is Nagasaki, Japan, expected to have recordable amounts of radiation from the atomic bomb dropped there in 1945?

A. According to Dr. Shunzo Okashima of the Nagasaki Medical School, traces will remain for 24,360 years. However, at 540.7 pico curies per kilogram, he says it is not dangerous.

FACT: Germany launched more than 8,000 V-1 flying bombs against London starting on June 13, 1944. However, many were shot down by the R.A.F. over the English Channel. One that went amok after launching actually turned around and hit the Fuehrerbunker. About 2,425 managed to make it to targets in London. Starting on September 8, the first of 1,100 German V-2 rockets began to fall on England.

Naval Operations
and Sea Battles

Q. What is considered the last classic battle between capital ships in the Atlantic ?

A. The battle between the German battle cruiser *Scharnhorst* and the British battleship *Duke of York* on December 26, 1943. The *Scharnhorst* was sunk after engaging British and Norwegian destroyers protecting a convoy en route to Murmansk. The *Duke of York,* three cruisers and six destroyers then finished the great ship off. Only thirty-six survived out of a crew of 1,900.

Q. Identify the U.S battleship that President Roosevelt, Admirals Leahy and King and Generals Marshall and Arnold were aboard when a U.S. destroyer fired a torpedo that exploded in its wake.

A. The *Iowa,* en route to the Teheran Conference, missed being hit when the *William D. Porter* discharged the torpedo by accident while performing a drill.

Q. Identify the British ship Winston Churchill was aboard when it was hit by two German torpedoes on October 30, 1939.

A. H.M.S. *Nelson.* He was in conference with several Royal Navy senior officers. However, both torpedoes failed to explode.

Q. From what aircraft carrier did James Doolittle launch his historic raid on Tokyo?

A. The *Hornet.*

Q. What was the significance of the flag raised on the Japanese carrier *Akagi* on Dec. 6, 1941?

A. It was the same flag that had flown on Admiral Heihachiro Togo's ship in the 1905 Japanese victory over the Russians.

Q. Who was the personal assistant to Admiral John Godfrey, director of naval intelligence in the British Admiralty?

A. Lieutenant Commander Ian Fleming, who years later would create James Bond.

Q. Identify the first German ship sunk in the war.

A. A submarine, U-39, sunk in the Atlantic by Royal Navy destroyers, on September 14, 1939.

Q. Identify the two famous British ships sunk in the Gulf of Siam on December 10, 1941.

A. The battleship *Prince of Wales* and battle cruiser *Repulse*. They had arrived at Singapore only eight days earlier as part of Britain's plan to exhibit its Far East strength. The Japanese lost three aircraft in the attack.

Q. Name the first Japanese ship sunk by the U.S. in the war.

A. The merchant ship *Atsutasan Maru,* on December 15, 1941, sunk by the U.S. submarine *Swordfish.*

Q. Identify the flagship of the Italian fleet in 1941.

A. The *Vittorio Veneto.*

Q. Identify the only Russian battleship sunk in the war.

A. The *Marat,* in September 1941.

Q. Where did the first Axis hostile action against Canadian territory take place?

A. At Vancouver Island in June 1942, when a Japanese submarine fired on a radio station there.

FACT A pair of German U-boats loaded with mines intended for placement in New York harbor were sunk by the Allies before they could complete their mission. However, the Germans did manage to mine ship lanes along the East Coast. The first ship lost from such mines was a merchant vessel, the *Robert C. Tuttle,* on June 15, 1942.

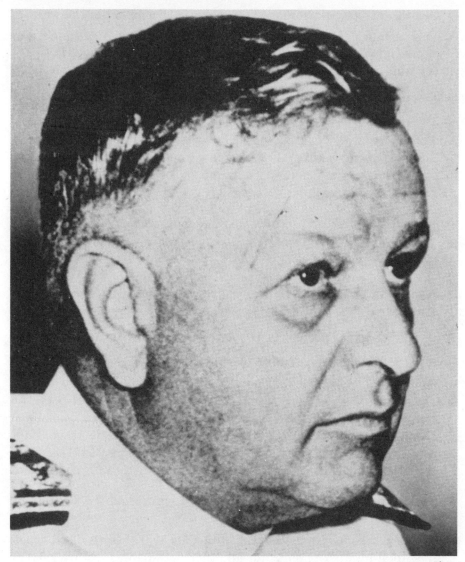

U.S. Navy Photo

Q. Who was the U.S. Navy's Commander-in-Chief, Pacific, on December 7, 1941?

A. Admiral Husband E. Kimmel. He had replaced Admiral James O. Richardson less than nine months earlier, on February 1. Though never formally charged with dereliction of duty or errors of judgment, he was humiliated and in some areas made the scapegoat for the disastrous attack on Pearl Harbor. Kimmel's book, *Admiral Kimmel's Story,* published thirteen years after the attack, details his fall from grace and subsequent battles to set the record straight.

Q. Identify the highest-ranking U.S. Navy officer killed in the war.

A. Rear Admiral Isaac C. Kidd, who died manning a machine gun aboard his flagship, the U.S.S. *Arizona,* on December 7, 1941. Every rank in the U.S. Navy is represented by the more than 1,100 men entombed in that ship.

Q. Who was Guenther Prien?

A. The German U-boat captain who attacked the British fleet at Scapa Flow in October 1939, sinking the *Royal Oak.* His skillful efforts made him a hero in Germany, while in Britain the episode greatly reduced morale.

Q. Identify the first British warship sunk in the war.

A. The fleet carrier H.M.S. *Courageous,* on September 17, 1939, off Ireland by a U-boat.

Q. Name the Japanese admiral who commanded the Pearl Harbor strike force?

A. Admiral Chuichi Nagumo.

Q. Identify the German officer who led the only naval action taken against the Allies on D-Day.

A. Lieutenant Commander Heinrich Hoffman, in the lead E-boat of a trio from the 5th Flotilla broke through a haze off the beaches at Normandy and confronted the invasion convoy. The three ships attacked with eighteen torpedoes and quickly retreated. One ship, the Norwegian destroyer *Svenner,* was sunk with thirty casualties.

Q. Which country had the largest navy and which had the smallest in the war?

A. The U.S. was by far the largest, with over 19,000 ships of all types. The total number of ships for all other nations was just over 5,500. New Zealand, with four ships, was the smallest.

FACT The 2nd Battalion, 12th Regiment, of the U.S. Army's 4th Division used a tourist guide map of Paris that one of its officers traded two packs of cigarettes for in order to locate the unit's objective, the Prefecture of Police, during the liberation of Paris.

FACT: The idea of adding wooden stabilizers to the torpedo fins carried by Japanese aircraft so that the weapons would not hit the forty-five-foot bottom of Pearl Harbor was conceived by Commander Minoru Genda. It was the general opinion in U.S. Navy circles that the harbor was not deep enough for a torpedo-plane attack, as an approximately seventy-foot depth was considered minimal for success.

Q. Who was the first black to be commissioned in the U.S. Navy?

A. Ensign Bernard Robinson, in June 1942.

Q. Identify the first city to come under naval bombardment in the war.

A. Danzig. The German battleship *Schleswig-Holstein* attacked it approximately an hour after the dawn attack on Poland, September 1, 1939.

Q. Who was Commander C. H. Lightoller, R.N.R.?

A. One of the most distinguished participants in the Dunkirk rescue. He was the senior surviving officer of the *Titantic* and had been the major witness in the investigation of that disaster.

Q. Name the six Japanese aircraft carriers that launched planes against Pearl Harbor.

A. *Akagi, Kaga, Shokaku, Zuikaku, Horyu,* and *Soryu,* carrying a total of 423 combat planes.

Q. Name the Japanese naval officer who scouted the U.S. military operations at Pearl Harbor in October 1941.

A. Lieutenant Commander Suguru Suzuki, who was sent on the mission as a passenger aboard the *Taiyo Maru* out of Japan.

Q. Name the only Italian ship actually sunk twice during the war.

A. The cruiser *Gorizia,* which was scuttled and sunk off La Spezia on September 8, 1943, then salvaged, restored and sunk in June 1944 by the Allies. A similar fate awaited the German cruiser *Koenigsberg,* sunk in April 1940 and then again in September 1944.

Q. Identify the first major warship of any country sunk by aircraft bombing in the war.

A. The German cruiser *Koenigsberg* (8,350 tons) while docked in Bergen, Norway, was hit by two bombs from British Blackburn Skuas on April 10, 1940.

Q. Identify the U.S. ship sunk in the Atlantic on December 6, 1941, the day before hostilities began in the Pacific.

A. The merchant ship *Sagadahoc,* which was torpedoed by the Germans.

Q. Of the ninety-six warships in Pearl Harbor on December 7, 1941, how many were sunk or heavily damaged?

A. Eighteen. In addition to the warships the U.S. Navy had forty-nine other ships present, for a total of 145. An odd example is the U.S.S. *Chengho* (IX-52) which was a Chinese junk motor yacht that the Navy acquired on July 23, 1941, for use by the 14th Naval District (see Appendix for complete list of the 145 ships present). In photo above, the battleship *Oklahoma,* with its fourteen-inch guns and very little deck above water, is seen after the attack.

Q. Identify the city that was the target of the only action in which the German battleship *Tirpitz* had an opportunity to fire her mammoth guns.

A. Sister ship to the *Bismarck,* the *Tirpitz*'s only hostile firing of her eight fifteen-inch guns was against Spitzbergen, Norway, in September 1943.

Q. Who was responsible for creating the operational plans for the attack on Pearl Harbor?

A. Rear Admiral Ryunosuke Kusaka.

Q. Identify the first U.S. flagship captured in the Atlantic after war began in Europe.

A. The *City of Flint,* a cargo ship en route to Britain, was challenged and captured by the German pocket battleship *Deutschland.* The Germans contended that its cargo was war materiel.

Q. Identify the other ships involved in the famous battle between the *Hood* and the *Bismarck* on May 24, 1941.

A. The Royal Navy was represented in the engagement by *Hood* and the *Prince of Wales.* The Kriegsmarine's *Bismarck* was joined by the *Prinz Eugen.* These four giant ships fired at each other from 26,000 yards for about twenty minutes. *Hood* was sunk, and the *Bismarck,* which was hit and leaking oil, left a trail which led to her sinking within days.

Q. Identify the first U.S. ship attacked by enemy fire in 1941.

A. A German U-boat torpedoed the *Robin Moor,* a freighter, on May 21, 1941.

FACT   By 1945 the pure Aryan composition of the Waffen SS was only a myth. Approximately 500,000 non-Germans filled the ranks of no less than twenty-seven of the forty Waffen SS divisions. This meant that over half of the service's strength was from other areas of Europe. In addition, there were Americans and Asians who served, but the largest numbers of non-Germans in the Waffen SS were Russian (nearly 100,000). Some of the countries represented included France (20,000); Holland (50,000); Norway (6,000); Denmark (6,000); Finland (20,000).

Q. Give the location and conditions of the sinking of the *Graf Spee*. When did it happen?

A. After fending off the three British cruisers *Exeter, Achilles* and *Ajax,* the *Graf Spee* made port in the neutral harbor of Montevideo, Uruguay. Rather than be captured upon leaving, the ship was scuttled by explosives in the River Plate. The date was December 17, 1939.

Q. Who was the captain of the *Graf Spee?*

A. Captain Hans Langsdorff, a veteran of the Battle of Jutland in World War I. Brokenhearted over the loss of his ship, he covered himself with a German Imperial Navy flag and shot himself on December 20, 1939, in Argentina.

Q. Identify the secret rendezvous base for the Japanese fleet preparing for the Pearl Harbor attack.

A. Tankan Bay in the Kuriles.

Q. Which area of Italy was the target of the amphibious invasion called Avalanche?

A. Salerno.

Q. Which U.S. Navy ship is credited with firing the first shot ever against a German ship?

A. The destroyer U.S.S. *Niblack,* on April 10, 1941, nearly eight months before the U.S. was officially in the war. The destroyer had just completed rescue operations involving the crew of a torpedoed Dutch ship. It dropped depth charges when it was believed the U-boat it had located was preparing to attack.

Q. What is considered the worst naval defeat experienced by the Allies during the war?

A. The Battle of the Java Sea, from February 27 through March 1, 1942, when the Japanese sank a total of ten U.S., British and Dutch ships.

Q. Name the first non-military U.S. ship sunk after the conflict began in 1939.

A. A U.S. merchant ship, the *City of Rayville,* made contact with a mine in the Bass Strait off Cape Otway, Australia, on November 8, 1940.

Q. Which naval battle is considered the greatest sea engagement of all time?

A. The Battle for Leyte Gulf. Japanese Vice Admiral Jisaburo Ozawa's fleet was sacrificed in an effort to lure away U.S. Admiral William Halsey.

Q. Identify the last ship to leave France in 1940 before the capitulation.

A. The Polish passenger liner *Batory,* which sailed for Britain on June 22 with the survivors of the Polish army who had fought in France. It departed from the port of St. Jean de Luz.

Q. Identify the first U.S. Navy ship hit by Japanese gunfire in 1941.

A. The gunboat *Tutuila,* which was on river duty near the Chinese capital of Chungking on July 30, 1941, more than four months before Pearl Harbor. The Japanese claimed the hit was unintentional but that the boat was too close to Chinese targets they were attacking. Japan apologized two days later.

Q. Name the first U.S. Navy ship sunk in 1941.

A. The U.S.S. *Reuben James,* escorting a convoy from Halifax, was sunk by the German submarine U-562 on October 31, 1941, thirty-eight days before Pearl Harbor. One hundred and fifteen lives were lost.

Q. Who sighted and reported the position of the *Bismarck?*

A. Early in 1941 the U.S. sent England some Catalina flying boats along with seventeen Navy pilots to train the British. Ensign Leonard B. "Tuck" Smith, the American co-pilot of Catalina Z-209, sighted the *Bismarck* on May 26 at 10:30 A.M. and radioed its location to the British fleet. The U.S. was officially neutral at the time.

Q. Why was the pocket battleship *Deutschland* renamed the *Lutzow?*

A. Because of Hitler's fear of the psychological effect if a ship named *Deutschland* was sunk by the enemy.

FACT　Civilian deaths in the war were more than double those of military personnel. In total, over 50 million people (civilian and military) died.

Q. Identify the Polish destroyer that participated in the Allied invasion of Normandy.

A. The *Poiron,* which was part of the convoy defense that escorted British and Canadian troops to their three beaches.

Q. Which battle holds the distinction of being the greatest aircraft carrier engagement of the war?

A. The Battle of the Philippine Sea. The Allied fleet had fifteen carriers against the Japanese fleet strength of nine. Overall fleet sizes were Allies 112 ships, Japan 55.

Q. Identify the first naval battle in which opposing ships never saw each other.

A. The Battle of the Coral Sea, May 3–8, 1942.

Q. Name the only U.S. battleship to get under way during the Japanese attack on Pearl Harbor.

A. The *Nevada,* which had already received a torpedo hit in her forward section. The oldest battleship in the Navy at the time, the *Nevada* later saw action at Normandy and Iwo Jima and was used as a target ship in the 1946 atom bomb tests off Bikini Island. She was sunk by the U.S. Navy during weapon tests in 1948.

Q. Who was PT boat commander Lieutenant John D. Buckley?

A. The U.S. Navy officer who on March 11, 1942, transported General Douglas MacArthur and Admiral F. W. Rockwell to Mindanao, where they took a B-17 to Australia.

Q. How was Admiral Yamamoto killed?

A. Acting on information received from Ultra code breakers, U.S. Navy P-38 planes shot him down after he took off from Rabaul on an inspection tour in April 1943.

FACT Carpet bombing was employed for the first time during the breakout at St. Lo after the Normandy landings. However, more than 100 troops of the 30th Division and Lieutenant General Lesley J. McNair, an observer, were killed when a portion of the 5,000 tons of explosives fell on U.S. troops by mistake.

Q. Identify the French admiral who became head of the Vichy government in February 1941.

A. Jean Louis Darlan. He was assassinated by a French monarchist in Algiers on December 24, 1942.

Q. Which naval battle is considered the U.S. Navy's worst defeat ever in a fair fight?

A. Savo Island, August 9, 1942. Despite fair odds, the U.S. Navy lost four heavy cruisers and one destroyer, 1,270 men killed and 709 others wounded. The Japanese lost thirty-five men and had another fifty-seven wounded. There was negligible damage to their ships in this battle that lasted thirty-two minutes.

Q. Identify the German military officer who first suggested to Hitler a cross-channel invasion of England.

A. Grand Admiral Erich Raeder, commander-in-chief of the German Navy, on May 21, 1940. Nearly two months later Hitler authorized the actual planning.

Q. Identify the high-ranking Philippine government official who escaped from the islands aboard the U.S. submarine *Swordfish* on February 21, 1942?

A. President Manuel Quezon.

Q. Which amphibious operation was the largest undertaken in the war?

A. The invasion of Sicily, with 1,375 ships directly involved, plus thirty-six more covering. Even the Normandy invasion exceeds it only if follow-up echelons are counted.

Q. In total, how many Allied convoys, including how many ships, were involved in the D-Day invasion at Normandy?

A. Fifty-nine convoys. U.S. Navy records say 5,000 ships; British records say 4,500.

Q. Identify the two largest battleships in the Japanese fleet at the outbreak of war.

A. The *Yamoto* and the *Musashi*. At 72,809 tons, they were the largest in the world.

Q. Name the French battleship the British sunk at Mers el-Kébir, near Oran, on July 3, 1940.

A. The *Bretagne*. In addition, the French lost two destroyers and the new battle cruiser *Dunkerque*. Over 1,300 French sailors died.

Q. Which branch of the U.S. military had the highest casualty rate?

A. The submarine command, with a rate of nearly 22 percent.

Q. What were the German one-man U-boats called?

A. *Biber,* or, in English, Beaver. They are credited with sinking at least a dozen merchant ships and nine naval vessels. The Allies sank seven of the twenty-nine-foot subs on one day, July 7, 1944.

Q. Identify Rear Admiral Kirk's flagship, which led the American task force on D-Day.

A. The heavy cruiser U.S.S. *Augusta,* which four months before Pearl Harbor transported President Roosevelt to Newfoundland to meet with Winston Churchill.

Q. Who commanded the Japanese carrier force in the Battle of the Coral Sea?

A. Vice Admiral Shigeyoshi Inouye.

Q. How many ships did the French scuttle at the Toulon navy base rather than let them fall into German hands?

A. Seventy ships.

Q. Identify the first U.S. submarine sunk in the war.

A. The *Sealion,* on December 10, 1941, at Cavite Naval Station in the Philippines while being overhauled. Badly damaged by the Japanese air raid, she was sunk by three U.S. Navy depth charges after being stripped of still useful equipment. The first U.S. submarine sunk while underway was the S-26 on January 24, 1942, off Panama.

FACT Major James Stewart, later colonel, flew twenty missions over Germany. In the postwar years he was promoted to general, attaining the highest rank of any member of the entertainment field who served in the war.

Q. Identify the British liner sunk by the Germans on the first day of the war in Europe.

A. The *Athenia*, with a loss of 112 lives, including twenty-eight Americans.

Q. Identify the task force that brought the first waves of troops to hit Omaha Beach.

A. Task Force O, Rear Admiral John L. Hall commanding.

Q. For which battle did Japan assemble its most powerful fleet in its history?

A. The Battle of Midway. It included eleven battleships and eight aircraft carriers. The total fleet consisted of more than a hundred ships.

Q. Which U.S. admiral was in command at the Battle of Midway?

A. Rear Admiral Frank Fletcher, who had to shift his flag to the cruiser *Astoria* after his flagship, the carrier *Yorktown*, had been badly damaged.

Q. Identify the U.S. river whose approaches were mined by the Germans.

A. The Mississippi, in July 1942. The mining was performed by a U-boat.

Q. How many submarines did the U.S. lose in the Pacific?

A. Forty-nine. The first was *Sealion*, three days after Pearl Harbor, the last was *Bullhead*, on August 6, 1945, the day the atom bomb was dropped on Hiroshima.

Q. Who replaced Admiral Erich Raeder as commander-in-chief of the German navy?

A. Admiral Karl Doenitz, on January 31, 1943.

FACT The Japanese super battleship *Musashi*, 72,809 tons, 862 feet long (it was the same size as the *Yamato* but didn't have the feared eighteen-inch guns), was sunk in the battle of Leyte Gulf. The giant ship took twenty torpedo hits and seventeen bombs before going down along with half of her 2,200-man crew.

Q. Name the British destroyer responsible for capturing U-110 on May 10, 1941, the first submarine captured during the war.

A. H.M.S. *Bulldog,* under the command of Commander John Baker-Cresswell. This was not officially acknowledged until 1966 for security reasons. The British were able to get a German code machine (Enigma), cipher books, and other important information off the boat. However, the boat itself sank while being towed back to Scapa Flow.

Q. In total, how many naval battles were fought during the eight-month Guadalcanal campaign?

A. Six.

Q. Who were the two top Japanese officers in the Battle of Midway?

A. Admiral Isoroku Yamamoto was the overall commander, with Vice Admiral Chuichi Nagumo in charge of the carrier force.

Q. How many submarines did the U.S. lose in the Atlantic?

A. Three: S-26 on January 24, 1942; R-12 on June 12, 1943; and *Dorado* on October 12, 1943.

Q. What was the German Navy's U-boat strength when the war began?

A. There were forty-five battle-ready U-boats out of a total fleet of fifty-seven. Nine others were being built.

Q. What was the German U-boat strength during the Battle of the Atlantic?

A. Germany had 409 U-boats in operation in February 1943 and reached its peak in May that year, when there were 425 U-boats at large.

Q. Where and when did the British fleet score its first victory against the Axis in the war?

A. In mid-March 1941 in the Battle of Cape Matapan against the Italians in the Mediterranean.

Q. On the night of August 1–2, 1943, the Japanese destroyer *Amagiri* nearly changed the course of world history. How?

A. It knifed in two and sank PT-109 commanded by then Lieutenant John F. Kennedy.

U.S. Navy Photo

Q. Identify the U.S. admiral who ordered all ships to turn their lights on during the Great Marianas Turkey Shoot so returning pilots at night could locate aircraft carriers.

A. Vice Admiral Marc Mitscher, from his flagship *Lexington*. Eighty aircraft that had used up their fuel crashed in the water, but nearly all the pilots were rescued. A pensive Mitscher and the cap he made famous are seen aboard the *Lexington*.

Q. Identify the future Nixon cabinet member who was Lieutenant John F. Kennedy's commanding officer in the Solomon Islands.

A. Future Attorney General John Mitchell.

Q. What future U.S. Supreme Court Justice co-authored the official report on the loss of PT-109, commanded by then Lieutenant and future U.S. President John F. Kennedy?

A. While an intelligence officer for the flotilla that PT-109 was assigned to, Lieutenant Byron R. White co-authored the report. In 1962 Kennedy appointed him to the highest judicial bench in the land.

Q. What was the name of the U.S. ship on which the five Sullivan brothers perished?

A. U.S.S. *Juneau,* during the naval battle for Guadalcanal, November 12–15, 1942. It had been launched from the Federal Shipyard at Kearny, New Jersey.

Q. What ship did Prime Minister Winston Churchill arrive aboard for his meeting with President Roosevelt in August 1941 for the signing of the Atlantic Charter?

A. H.M.S. *Prince of Wales.*

Q. What was the historical significance of Japan's defeat at Midway?

A. It was her first ever naval defeat.

Q. Name the three U.S. submarines that sank the most enemy tonnage in the Pacific.

A. *Flasher* sank 100,231 tons, twenty-one ships; *Rasher,* 99,901 tons, eighteen ships; *Barb,* 96,628 tons, seventeen ships.

Q. Name the three most successful U.S. submarines in the Pacific based on the number of ships sunk.

A. *Tautog,* twenty-six ships for 72,606 tons; *Tang,* twenty-four ships for 93,824 tons; *Silversides,* twenty-three ships for 90,080 tons.

FACT Three times as many bombs were dropped on Germany during the last eleven months of the war (after D-Day) than in all the years before.

Q. Who was Germany's most successful U-boat captain?

A. Lieutenant Commander Otto Kretschmer, credited with sinking forty-four Allied ships for a total of 266,629 tons. In addition, he sank one Allied destroyer. (Lieutenant Commander Guenther Prien, the most famous U-boat captain, sank twenty-eight ships for 160,939 tons, plus the British battleship *Royal Oak* at Scapa Flow.)

Q. What did the British change the name of the German submarine U-570 to after they captured it?

A. It went into the Royal Navy as the *Graph* after it was captured on its first combat patrol on August 27, 1941. It surfaced within range of RAF patrol planes, who depth-charged it, knocking out its lights and causing internal leaks. The crew panicked and forced the captain to surrender.

Q. Why are submarines called boats?

A. In the early development of the submarine as a combat weapon they were known as submersible torpedo boats.

Q. How much larger was the U.S. Navy at the end of the war than it had been on December 7, 1941?

A. It had twenty-one additional aircraft carriers, six more battleships, nearly 130 more submarines, seventy escort carriers and additional ships in every category.

Q. Name the only aircraft carrier in the German Navy at the outbreak of war.

A. The 23,200-ton *Graf Zeppelin,* which had been launched in 1938 but still wasn't commissioned. It could accommodate forty-two planes.

FACT   In the Battle of Leyte Gulf six of the seven ships in Japanese Admiral Nishimura's Southern Force C were sunk by Admiral Jesse B. Oldendorf's Seventh Fleet ships, which included five U.S. battleships that survived Pearl Harbor: *West Virginia, Tennessee, California, Maryland* and *Pennsylvania.* In a classic naval maneuver, Oldendorf's dreadnoughts formed a battle line at the entrance of Surigao Strait.

Q. Identify the British aircraft carrier whose Swordfish torpedo planes attacked the British cruiser *Sheffield* while tracking the German battleship *Bismarck.*

A. The fourteen Swordfish planes from the British aircraft carrier *Ark Royal* did it. However, all torpedoes missed.

Q. Name the five U.S. aircraft carriers and the six escort carriers lost in the war.

A. The five, alphabetically, were *Hornet, Lexington, Princeton, Wasp, Yorktown.* The six escort carriers were *Bismarck Sea, Block Island, Gambier Bay, Liscome Bay, Ommaney Bay,* and *St. Lo.*

Q. Identify the only U.S. aircraft carrier sunk in the Atlantic during the war.

A. The escort carrier *Block Island* was sunk by a U-boat on May 29, 1944, off the Azores.

Q. With regard to battleships and aircraft carriers, what were the strengths of the U.S. and Japan in December 1941?

A. The U.S. had nine battleships and three carriers in the Pacific fleet. Japan had ten battleships and ten carriers. Japan had more sea power in the Pacific than the combined Pacific fleets of the Americans, British and Dutch.

Q. Identify the only two battleships in the German Navy when the war began in 1939.

A. The *Gneisenau* and *Scharnhorst.* Three "pocket" battleships were also in the fleet: the *Deutschland, Graf Spee* and *Admiral Scheer.* (Though the *Bismarck* and *Tirpitz* had been launched in the spring of 1939, they were commissioned later. There were also two old battleships, the *Schlesien* and *Schleswig-Holstein* in reserve.)

Q. In what battle were the Royal Navy cruisers *Fiji* and *Gloucester* sunk?

A. The Battle of Crete. Two British battleships, the *Valiant* and *Warspite,* were hit also but survived.

Q. Identify the first U.S. ship struck by a Japanese kamikaze.

A. The escort carrier *Santee* during the Battle of Leyte Gulf. The first ship sunk as a result of a kamikaze was the escort carrier *St. Lo* in the same battle. (Some escort carriers such as the *Santee* were converted into aircraft carriers from tankers.)

Q. Where did the U.S. and Japanese meet for the first time in a major naval action?

A. At the Battle of Makassar Strait on January 24, 1942. Four U.S. destroyers attacked and sank four Japanese transport ships, causing heavy casualties.

Q. How successful was the U.S. submarine force in relation to its size?

A. Despite the fact that less than 2 percent of U.S. Navy personnel were crew, back-up and staff attached to the submarine fleet, the force is credited with 55 percent of Japan's maritime losses.

Q. Identify the German admiral who was killed at Christmas in 1943 when the battleship *Scharnhorst* was sunk.

A. Rear Admiral Erich Bey, along with nearly the entire ship's crew.

Q. What was the name of the Royal Navy submarine that is credited with sinking the Italian troop transports *Oceania* and *Neptunia* in September 1941?

A. The H.M.S. *Upholder.*

Q. Which amphibious assault was the largest in the Pacific war?

A. Okinawa. It was also the last amphibious assault.

Q. Under what circumstances was the U.S. aircraft carrier *Lexington* sunk?

A. Badly damaged in the Battle of the Coral Sea, the *Lexington,* a converted battle cruiser, was sunk by U.S. Navy fire rather than be left to the marksmanship of the Japanese.

FACT The greatest damage to the U.S. Navy in the Pacific war was not caused by the Japanese. A typhoon approximately 500 miles off the east coast of the Philippines on December 17–18, 1944, took a toll that included: 769 lives; damage to eight aircraft carriers; the capsizing of three destroyers; the loss of 150 planes (off the carriers) and a number of other ships.

Q. Identify the four German fleet commanders during the war.

A. The four were Admiral Gunther Lutjens, who was lost when the *Bismarck* was sunk; Admiral Hermann Boehm and Admiral Wilhelm Marschall, both of whom were removed from command because of differences with Berlin; and Admiral Otto Schniewind.

Q. Where were the three aircraft carriers of the Pacific fleet during the attack on Pearl Harbor?

A. The *Saratoga* was en route to the U.S. for repairs; the *Lexington* was involved in delivering twenty-five scout bombers to Midway; the *Enterprise,* returning to Pearl after having delivered planes to Wake, sent eighteen planes ahead, which arrived during the Japanese attack.

Q. How did hostilities between Japan and the U.S. begin in the Philippines?

A. Twenty-two planes from the carrier *Ryujo* engaged the American seaplane tender *William B. Preston* in Davao Gulf, Mindanao, on December 7 (December 8, Manila time).

Q. Identify the flagship of the U.S. Pacific fleet on December 7, 1941.

A. The battleship *Pennsylvania,* which was in dry dock at the Navy Yard across from Ford Island and Battleship Row.

Q. How did the German battleship *Gneisenau* meet its end?

A. In February 1942 the *Gneisenau,* the *Prinz Eugen* and the *Scharnhorst* managed to slip away from the Norwegian coast. The *Gneisenau* was bombed by the RAF after it had made port in Germany and was rendered useless.

Q. Identify the first ship sunk at Pearl Harbor on December 7, 1941.

A. A Japanese midget submarine, sighted by a Catalina flying boat, was sunk by depth charges from the U.S. destroyer *Ward* at 6:45 A.M., more than an hour before the air attack. A second midget sub was sunk at 7:00 by another PBY.

Q. Besides her historic action at Pearl Harbor, why else is the date December 7 significant with regard to the U.S. destroyer *Ward?*

A. She was sunk at Ormac Bay in the Philippines on December 7, 1944, exactly three years after the "Day of Infamy."

Q. Name the U.S. battleships moored at Battleship Row on December 7, 1941.

A. *Nevada, Arizona, Tennessee, West Virginia, Maryland, Oklahoma,* and *California.* The *Pennsylvania* was in Drydock One across the harbor. Only the *Arizona,* now a memorial, and the *Oklahoma* were totally lost. The others were repaired and saw action in the war. The photo above, taken by the Japanese, was made as the attack on Pearl Harbor began. Note the ripples in water from a bomb that missed its target.

Q. Identify the four Japanese aircraft carriers sunk or damaged at Midway.

A. Sunk: *Akagi, Kaga, Soryu.* Damaged: *Hiryu.*

Q. Who sighted the first submarine of the Japanese strike force near Pearl Harbor? Where? When?

A. At daybreak on December 6, Lieutenant James O. Cobb sighted and radioed ashore the presence of a submarine off Diamond Head. It submerged before an attack could be undertaken.

Q. Identify the German supply ship the British boarded in Norwegian waters to free nearly 300 British merchant navy personnel in February 1940.

A. The *Altmark,* which had been a tender to the pocket battleship *Graf Spee.* Though Norway protested this violation of her neutrality it wasn't a strong protest. The Norwegians had themselves conducted a search of sorts and had not discovered the British mariners, who were hidden below decks.

Q. When did the first official contact occur between the Japanese and Americans at Pearl Harbor?

A. At 3:42 A.M. on December 7 the mine sweeper *Condor*'s watch officer, Ensign R. C. McCloy, advised Quartermaster B. C. Uttrick that he had sighted a white wave about 100 yards to port of the ship. They identified it as the wake of a submarine periscope and contacted the destroyer *Ward.* However the sub escaped further detection.

Q. Who is credited with originating the concept of the kamikaze?

A. Vice Admiral Takijiro Ohnishi, who, during a senior staff meeting on October 19, 1944, first proffered the idea of planes with 550-pound bombs crashing onto American aircraft carriers.

FACT When the Germans invaded the U.S.S.R. their attack strength was three times as great as Napoleon's and included approximately 620,000 horse-drawn pieces of equipment and cavalry. The Germans also had 3,350 tanks. However, the Russians are believed to have had nearly 10,000 tanks. In all, Russia used more than 21,000 tanks in the war.

Navy Department Photo

Q. Identify the Japanese carrier-borne dive bombers that the Allies called "Val" and which made up the first wave against the U.S. fleet at Pearl Harbor.

A. Aichi D3A1. One hundred and twenty-six of them participated in the first wave. The "Val" sank more enemy ships than any other dive bomber in World War II. The one in the photo above was destroyed after it was unsuccessful in pulling out of a dive.

Q. Identify the German passenger ship that was stalked by a U.S. Navy warship until the German captain elected to scuttle rather than be sunk or seized in 1939.

A. On December 19, 1939, while neutral, the U.S. cruiser *Tuscaloosa* followed and broadcast the position of the German liner *Columbus* in an effort to attract British warships. The U.S. ship had followed the *Columbus* since it left Mexico. The Germans scuttled off Cape May, New Jersey. No German protest was filed.

Q. What was the Japanese strength on Okinawa in April 1945?

A. Lieutenant General Mitsuru Ushijima had over 100,000 troops and 3,000 planes, many of which were the dreaded kamikazes.

Q. What was the name the German blockade-running ship *Odenwald* used while disguised as an American vessel?

A. *Willmoto.* The German ship was intercepted and captured by the U.S. destroyer *Somers* and cruiser *Omaha* in the Atlantic in early November 1941.

Q. Name the hospital ship in Pearl Harbor that the Japanese fliers recognized and did not attack.

A. The U.S.S. *Solace,* with its white hull and large red crosses was moored in East Lock.

Q. How and where was Japan's largest battleship, the 72,809-ton *Yamato* sunk?

A. On April 7, 1945, during the battle for Okinawa, the *Yamato* and an eight-ship screen boldly charged the U.S. fleet. She and five of the escort ships were sunk in less than two hours.

Q. Prior to December 7, 1941, when had so many U.S. battleships been together in port?

A. Not since the July 4 weekend that same year, also at Pearl Harbor.

FACT There were 4,500 newspapers in Germany when the Nazis rose to power in 1933. By 1939, on the eve of war, the number was approximately 1,000, and they were controlled by or in sympathy with the Nazis.

Q. Who was commander-in-chief of the German Navy in 1939?

A. Admiral Erich Raeder, who hoped war would not begin before 1942, by which time he expected to have the navy at full combat strength.

Q. Identify the first Japanese ship captured by the U.S. in 1941.

A. A sampan sighted in the restricted waters at the mouth of Pearl Harbor at 6:48 A.M. on December 7, an hour before hostilities. The skipper of the sampan cut his engines and displayed a white flag when challenged by the destroyer *Ward*.

Q. Identify the Japanese admiral who led a squadron of kamikaze planes against U.S. ships at Okinawa.

A. Admiral Ugaki, with an eleven-plane group on August 15, 1945. He flew a Yokosuka D4Y2, code-named Judy by the Allies. Just over 2,000 of them were manufactured.

Q. What does CINCLANT stand for?

A. Commander-in-Chief Atlantic Fleet.

Q. What prompted Germany to issue the *Laconia* Order, which forbade U-boats from picking up survivors of ships?

A. The September 12, 1942, incident when an American aircraft attacked U-boats that had picked up over 1,100 survivors from the British transport *Laconia*. The ship had nearly 2,000 Italian POW's aboard when it was torpedoed and sunk. The Germans sent out a message for rescue assistance to ships of all flags, with assurances that they would not attack Allied ships that responded. Despite the flying of a giant Red Cross flag on one of the U-boats, the American attack was carried out. The Germans managed to pass the 1,100 survivors to the Allies, but the *Laconia* Order officially prevented any future operations of this scale between hostile nations on the high seas.

FACT   Even though hostilities between Britain and Germany had been a fact since early September 1939, Britain didn't restrict or confiscate German-bound shipments from England until November 21.

Q. Identify the first U.S. battleship launched after war began in Europe.

A. The U.S.S. *Washington,* on June 1, 1940. It was the first battleship added to the navy since the early 1920s.

Q. What was the Japanese hospital ship *Awa Maru* allegedly carrying when she was sunk by the U.S. submarine *Queenfish* on April 1, 1945?

A. According to an Associated Press story on May 3, 1979, the *Awa Maru* was sailing under a mercy-mission agreement with the Allies. However, over the years it has been suggested that the ship was actually transporting more than $5 billion in booty that the Japanese had collected during the war. Only one person of more than 2,000 aboard survived. (The *Awa Maru* had been many miles off the course the Allies agreed to for safe passage. Further, the *Queenfish* was not aware of the mission, the *Awa Maru* was hidden by fog and traveling at a speed equal to a warship's when the submarine fired four torpedoes. China began salvage operations in 1979 at the sinking site 190 feet below the surface in the Taiwan Strait. No mention was made of the treasure.)

Q. What was the name of the first U.S. Liberty Ship ever built?

A. The S.S. *Patrick Henry,* launched in September 1941. By the end of the war the U.S. produced and launched over 2,740, many in record time.

Q. Identify the two Japanese ships sunk in the December 11, 1941, invasion of Wake Island.

A. The destroyer *Hayate,* hit by shore batteries, and the destroyer *Kisaragi,* which was sunk by fire from U.S. Marine aircraft.

FACT The only U.S. aerial photographs taken of the Japanese attack on Pearl Harbor were made by Staff Sergeant Lee Embree aboard one of the twelve B-17 bombers that were arriving from California. Thinking the large aerial camera he swung out of a hatch was a gun, Japanese planes avoided the B-17.

U.S. Army Photo

Q. When was VE-Day?

A. May 8, 1945. The actual surrender was at 2:41 A.M. on May 7 in a school-house at Reims. However, the ceremony was repeated in Berlin, above, with Russian participation on May 8, which is the historical day the war in Europe ended. Seated center is Field Marshal Wilhelm Keitel with General Hans-Juergen Stumpff of the Luftwaffe to his right (left in pho-to) and Admiral Hans von Friedeburg of the Kriegsmarine. Picture was taken at Russian Headquarters in Berlin.

U.S. Army Photo

Q. When was VJ-Day?

A. August 15, 1945, is the day the war with Japan ended. However, the actual surrender was signed aboard the U.S. battleship *Missouri* in Tokyo Bay on September 2, 1945, and is celebrated as VJ-Day.

Q. How successful were the German Wolf Pack U-boat tactics off the U.S. Atlantic coast in early 1942?

A. Very. Eighty-seven ships were sunk during the first four months. After Allied ships only moved in convoy, the U-boats began activity in the Gulf of Mexico and sank forty-one ships in May alone.

Q. Name the Italian battleship sunk by German aircraft while en route from La Spezia to Malta on September 9, 1943.

A. The *Roma.* Italy had signed the armistice with the Allies the day before and was considered an enemy of the Reich.

Q. Which U.S. battleships sustained the least and which the greatest loss of life in the attack on Pearl Harbor?

A. Four crew members were killed aboard the *Maryland.* More than 1,100 were killed on the *Arizona.*

Q. Identify the two British battleships sunk at Alexandria by the Italians on December 19, 1942.

A. The *Queen Elizabeth* and the *Valiant.*

Q. Name the last major U.S. ship damaged in action in the war.

A. The battleship *Pennsylvania,* on August 12, 1945, two days before the war ended, was hit by a torpedo off Okinawa. The *Pennsylvania* was the only battleship present at Pearl Harbor on December 7, 1941, that was not seriously damaged.

Q. Name the ship the Japanese surrender was signed on.

A. The battleship *Missouri,* then Admiral Halsey's flagship.

Q. How was Admiral Sir Bertram Ramsay, Allied Expeditionary Force Naval Commander, killed?

A. In a plane crash in Paris on New Year's Day 1945.

FACT   The highest rate of casualties ever sustained by a United States Marine Corps regiment in one battle was 2,821 out of 3,512 in eighty-two days of the Okinawa campaign in 1945 by the 29th Marine Corps Regiment.

Q. What was the last naval surface engagement of World War II?

A. The action between the Japanese cruiser *Haguro* and a quintet of British destroyers in Malacca Strait. The *Haguro* was sunk there on May 17, 1945.

Q. Name the first U.S. aircraft carrier lost in the war.

A. Commissioned on March 30, 1922, and designated CV-1 (meaning she was the first U.S. aircraft carrier), the *Langley* was sunk near Java on February 27, 1942. She was at that time functioning as a seaplane tender. Hit by bombs from Japanese planes and badly damaged, she was ordered sunk by friendly fire.

Q. Identify the British aircraft carrier sunk by German U-boat U-81 near Gibraltar on November 15, 1941.

A. The *Ark Royal*.

Q. What was the aircraft carrier strength of Japan vs. the U.S. when hostilities began in 1941?

A. The Japanese had ten carriers, the U.S. had seven, of which only three were in the Pacific.

Q. Which aircraft carrier was the newest in the U.S. fleet when war was declared in December 1941?

A. The *Hornet*. Though completed prior to the outbreak of war, she had not yet made her maiden voyage.

Q. Identify the first U.S. Navy chaplain awarded the Congressional Medal of Honor.

A. Lieutenant Commander Joseph T. O'Callahan for his performance aboard the aircraft carrier *Franklin* after she was involved in a Japanese kamikaze attack off Japan in March 1945.

Q. Which nation suffered the greatest loss of life in a single ship sinking during the war?

FACT The RAF marked the anniversary of Adolf Hitler's tenth year in power by conducting its first daylight raid on Berlin. The attack took place while the official ceremonies were under way.

A. Germany, when approximately 6,500 troops drowned during the evacuation of Danzig, April 16, 1945. A 5,320-ton merchant ship, the *Goya,* was hit by Allied torpedoes and because it was very much overweight sank almost instantly. This is the greatest single maritime loss in history, not only the war.

Q. Which country accomplished the largest mining of a seaway during the war?

A. The U.S. on January 25, 1945, when the coastal waters of Saigon, Penang and Singapore, among others, were filled with more than 360 mines dropped by B-29s.

Q. When did the first civilian merchant ship make a channel crossing between England and France since the last one in 1940?

A. In January 1945. After May 1940, only military ships, such as those involved in the raid on Dieppe and the Normandy invasion, had made the trip.

Q. Who was the British vice admiral who commanded a task force that became part of the U.S. Third Fleet in the Pacific, marking the first U.S.-British joint naval operations in that theater?

A. H. B. Rawlings, whose carrier task force linked up with U.S. naval forces on July 17, 1945.

Q. Name the last U.S. ship to be sunk by a Japanese kamikaze plane.

A. The destroyer *Callaghan,* off Okinawa on July 28, 1945.

Q. What became of the *Prinz Eugen,* Germany's only major fighting ship to survive the war?

A. Built in 1938, the *Prinz Eugen* served the Kriegsmarine with distinction. It survived bombing, torpedoing, striking a mine and the battle in which the *Bismarck* was sunk. She was turned over to the Allies at Copenhagen on May 9, 1945. She came to an inglorious end as a target ship during the United States atomic tests off Bikini Island in the Pacific in 1946. Another ship with a proud war record to participate in the Bikini tests was the U.S. battleship *Nevada,* present at Battleship Row in Pearl Harbor on December 7, 1941.

Historic Dates

Q. When, where and how did the United States sink the first German U-boat after entering the war?

A. Ensign William Tepuni, USNR, piloting a Lockheed-Hudson of Squadron VP-82, sank U-656 on March 1, 1942, off Cape Race, Newfoundland.

Q. When did the Japanese high command begin to plan the attack on Pearl Harbor?

A. In January 1941, more than ten months before it took place.

Q. When did U.S. and German warships first exchange gunfire in 1941?

A. September 4, 1941. The U.S.S. *Greer,* responding to a signal from a patrol plane, tracked U-652 for several hours. The patrol plane, British, dropped depth charges. The U-boat commander, Lieutenant Georg W. Fraatz, thought it was from the destroyer and fired two torpedoes. The *Greer*'s commander, Lieutenant Commander Frost, then attacked with depth charges. Neither side scored a hit. This was three months before the U.S. was officially at war.

Q. When did the Battle of Britain end?

A. October 31, 1940. It had begun on August 12.

Q. When did the Jews in the Warsaw ghetto offer the first armed resistance against the Germans?

A. January 18, 1943.

U.S. Air Force Photo

Q. When did Adolf Hitler commit suicide?

A. On April 30, 1945, in his bunker beneath the Chancellery in Berlin. In photo above a tired-looking Lieutenant Harmon Smith, a U.S. navigator who was shot down on a bombing mission over Germany on January 7, 1944, reads about Hitler's death in *Stars and Stripes* after having been freed from a POW camp.

Q. Where and when did the U.S. sustain its first casualties in 1941?

A. In the torpedoing of the destroyer *Kearney* on October 17, 1941, by a U-boat off the coast of Iceland. Eleven U.S. Navy personnel were killed. Pearl Harbor was still several weeks away.

Q. When was Rome liberated?

A. June 5, 1944, one day before the Normandy invasion.

Q. When was the armistice between France and Germany?

A. June 20, 1940.

Q. When did the armistice between France and Germany actually take effect?

A. On June 25, 1940.

Q. When did the German naval war begin with Russia?

A. On June 15, 1941, German ships were ordered to conduct the "annihilation of Russian submarines without any trace, including their crews." This was seven days before Hitler's invasion of Russia and at a time when the two countries were still allied.

Q. What was the date of Rudolph Hess's flight from Germany?

A. May 10, 1941.

Q. Identify the first U.S. Navy vessel to sink a German U-boat, and when?

A. The destroyer *Roper* sank U-85 off Wimble Shoal near Hatteras in April 1942.

Q. When did Winston Churchill become First Lord of the Admiralty?

A. On September 3, 1939, the same day Britain declared war on Germany. Churchill had served as First Lord of the Admiralty for a time in World War I also, and news of his reappointment was signaled from ship to ship: "Winston is back."

FACT When Japan surrendered to the Allies in 1945 it still had over 2 million combat-ready troops and 9,000 aircraft. However, its navy had been all but eliminated.

Q. When did Winston Churchill become Prime Minister of Britain?

A. On May 10, 1940, upon the resignation of Neville Chamberlain. Churchill headed a coalition government made up of Conservative, Labour and Liberal ministers.

Q. When was James Doolittle's raid on Tokyo?

A. The morning of April 18, 1942, while an air-raid drill was in progress.

Q. When was Berlin bombed for the first time?

A. August 25, 1940, by the Royal Air Force. (The attack so shocked the Nazis that they cancelled a victory parade scheduled in Paris, fearing it would be too great a target for the RAF.)

Q. When did the heaviest and most severe Luftwaffe raid on London take place?

A. The night of May 10–11, 1941, when over 1,400 were killed and another 1,800 injured. Westminster Abbey and the House of Commons were among sites hit by bombs.

Q. When did the last air raid by the Western Allies on Berlin take place?

A. On Saturday, April 21, 1945, at 9:25 A.M. by the U.S. Eighth Air Force.

Q. When was the German battleship *Tirpitz* sunk?

A. November 12, 1944. The sister ship to the *Bismarck,* the *Tirpitz* was a constant target for the Royal Navy and RAF. The death blow came from five-ton bombs dropped by the RAF at Tromso Fjord. Over 900 sailors died when she capsized.

FACT During the Battle of Midway a Japanese admiral and two aircraft carrier captains bound themselves to parts of their ships and went down with them rather than abandon the carriers. Captain Taijiro Aoki of the *Akagi* and Captain Tomeo Kaku of the *Hiryu,* along with Admiral Yamaguchi, who was aboard the *Hiryu,* made the ultimate sacrifice. Both of these carriers had participated in the Pearl Harbor attack.

Q. When did the U.S. Navy provide escort cover for a British convoy for the first time?

A. On September 17, 1941. The U.S. was to officially remain neutral for more than two months.

Q. What was the first major amphibious assault of the war in the Pacific? When?

A. Guadalcanal on August 7, 1942. Exactly eight months after the attack on Pearl Harbor, the 1st Marine Division invaded not only Guadalcanal but its sister islands of Tulagi, Gavutu and Florida.

Q. Why is September 15, 1940, known as Battle of Britain Day?

A. Because it marked the turning point in the proportion of Luftwaffe and RAF losses. The RAF lost twenty-six aircraft while downing sixty planes of the Luftwaffe.

Q. When and how was the U.S. aircraft carrier *Hornet* sunk?

A. On October 26, 1942, during the Battle of the Santa Cruz Islands north of Guadalcanal. Damaged by dive bombers, the *Hornet* was sunk by Japanese destroyers.

Q. When did the Allies invade Sicily?

A. July 10, 1943, in Operation Husky. It was captured on August 17.

Q. When did the 82nd Airborne Division make its combat debut?

A. In Operation Husky, the invasion of Sicily, July 1943.

Q. When did the 101st Airborne Division make its first combat jump?

A. D-Day, June 6, 1944.

FACT In November 1981 an American veterans group, the 6th Marine Division Association, announced plans to have Sugar Loaf on Okinawa dedicated as a memorial to the American and Japanese servicemen who fought in that historic World War II battle. Edward L. Fox, president of the Marine group, said it was seeking support from Japanese veterans. "Only in the event the Japanese are unable to participate will we undertake this as a strictly American project." (From a conversation with the author in December 1981.)

National Archives Photo

Q. When was the U.S.S. *Arizona* commissioned?

A. In 1916. The 608-foot dreadnought was the third U.S. Navy vessel to carry that name. In honor of the personnel who perished aboard her on December 7, 1941, no other U.S. Navy ships will ever carry that name. The earth-shattering explosion when the *Arizona* blew up occurred at 8 A.M., about fifteen minutes after the attack began. It is remembered by survivors as the most stunning single moment that day.

Q. When was the monastery at Monte Cassino bombed?

A. On February 15, 1944, 254 Allied planes bombed the historic site where St. Benedict is entombed.

Q. When did the Allies capture Cassino, Italy?

A. May 18, 1944.

Q. When did the B-29 Superfortress, made by Boeing, first bomb Japan?

A. On June 15, 1944. The first B-29 bombs fell on Toyko on November 24. The planes were used only in the Pacific.

Q. When was Saipan declared captured?

A. July 9, 1944. However, Japanese holdouts caused havoc for months after.

Q. What was the "darkest day" for U.S. submariners in the war?

A. October 24, 1944, when three subs, *Tang, Shark II,* and *Darter,* were all lost. *Tang* was hit by one of her own torpedoes that went amok off the coast of China; *Shark II* was sunk in Formosa Strait; *Darter* ran aground on a reef in Palawan Passage, bordering the South China Sea. This was the only day that the U.S. had lost more than one submarine.

Q. When did the Germans learn exactly how the Americans, British and Soviets would divide up Germany and occupy her?

A. In January 1945, five months before the end came. A copy of the secret plan had been captured from the British.

Q. When did Corregidor fall?

A. May 6, 1942.

FACT The United States Navy gathered what is considered by many to be the greatest exhibition of naval strength ever for the Japanese surrender ceremonies in Tokyo Bay in September 1945. The armada that made its way to the waters of the Japanese capital include twenty-three aircraft carriers, twelve battleships, twenty-six cruisers, and 313 destroyers and other ships, for a grand total of 374 vessels.

Q. When was Corregidor retaken by U.S. forces?

A. February 26, 1945. Nonetheless, there were over 50,000 Japanese who did not surrender until the end of the war.

Q. When was Vienna captured by the Red Army?

A. April 13, 1945.

Q. When did the German "blitz" on London begin?

A. The first bombs fell on the city on August 24, 1940.

Q. When did the Battle for Berlin begin?

A. At 4 A.M. on Monday, April 16, 1945, when the Russian artillery barrage began.

Q. When did the U.S. and RAF discontinue strategic bombing of Germany?

A. April 16, 1945, because few targets essential to the German war machine still existed.

Q. When did German troops in Italy surrender?

A. April 29, 1945.

Q. When and where was the first atom bomb tested?

A. At 5:30 A.M. on July 16, 1945, at Alamogordo Air Base, New Mexico.

Q. When did the Soviet Union declare war on Japan?

A. August 9, 1945, the day the U.S. dropped the second atomic bomb.

Q. When did the first Soviet troops actually penetrate the defenses around Berlin and reach the city?

A. Units of Marshal Koniev's armies entered the southern area of Berlin on April 22, 1945.

FACT In a remarkable test of vessels of the same class going against each other, the U.S. submarine *Batfish* scored kills against three Japanese submarines in a four-day period off the Philippines in February 1945.

Q. Where and when did the Flying Tigers make their combat debut?

A. Over Kunming, China, on December 20, 1941.

Q. When did the Italians overthrow Mussolini?

A. On July 25, 1943, the Fascist Grand Council voted nineteen to seven to put command of Italy's armed forces under King Victor Emmanuel III.

Q. When did Italy sign the armistice with the Allies?

A. September 8, 1943. From that time on Italian troops vigorously fought against Germany.

Q. When did Italy officially announce that it was out of the war as a member of the Axis?

A. At 8 P.M. in the evening of September 8, 1943.

Q. When was the Nazi flag raised on Mount Elbrus, the highest peak in the Caucasus Mountains.

A. August 21, 1942.

Q. When was the U.S. Eighth Air Force created?

A. January 28, 1942, under the command of General Carl Spaatz.

Q. When did the U.S. declare war on Germany and Italy?

A. The Germans, followed quickly by the Italians, declared war on the U.S. on December 11, 1941. The U.S. Congress responded with its own war vote that same afternoon.

Q. When were the Germans halted and reversed in their campaign against Russia?

A. On December 5, 1941, when certain panzer units were within twenty-five miles of Moscow. The Russians mounted a counteroffensive on December 6 and began their push that would not end until forty-one months later, in Berlin.

FACT The U.S. Navy trained naval personnel from fourteen different countries at its Submarine Chaser Training Center in Miami, Florida, during 1942–43.

Q. When did the Luftwaffe bomb Moscow?

A. July 21, 1941, one day short of a full month after war between the two former allies was declared.

Q. When did the Soviet Air Force first bomb Berlin?

A. August 8, 1941, using Ilyushin IL-4 medium bombers.

Q. When was Crete invaded by the Germans?

A. On May 20, 1941. It marked the first time that paratroopers and gliders constituted the main body of an attack force. Over 22,700 German airborne troops participated.

Q. What was the date of the Soviet-German non-aggression pact?

A. August 23, 1939.

Q. On what date did the invading German troops reach the sea at Abbeville, France?

A. On May 21, 1940, eleven days after they had crossed the Belgian and Dutch frontiers, thus ending the "phony war" that had existed since September 1939.

Q. When did General Charles de Gaulle announce the formation of the Free French government?

A. On October 27, 1940. The power of the government was to be in the care of the general and his defense council.

Q. When did the RAF execute its first air raid on Italy?

A. The night of June 11–12, 1940. Ten planes bombed the Fiat plant at Turin and the surrounding area; two bombed Genoa.

Q. When did the invasions of Denmark and Norway begin?

A. April 9, 1940. Denmark surrendered the same day.

FACT All during the war U.S. forces in other services envied the legendary meals enjoyed by the Navy. However, many simply would not believe that the U.S. Navy actually had a ship whose sole purpose was to make ice cream for sailors in the South Pacific, yet it was true. The ship was capable of producing over 5,000 gallons of ice cream per hour.

Q. When did RAF planes first enter air space over Berlin?

A. During the night of October 1–2, 1939, on a propaganda leaflet–dropping mission.

Q. When did Warsaw surrender to Germany?

A. September 27, 1939, less than four weeks after the war began.

Q. When did the Russians begin to occupy Poland?

A. September 17, 1939.

Q. On what date did France enter the war?

A. September 3, 1939.

Q. When did Ireland announce its neutrality?

A. On September 2, 1939, the day after the German attack on Poland and the day before Britain, France, Australia, New Zealand and India declared war on Germany.

Q. When did Lithuania, Latvia and Estonia fall to the Soviets?

A. In June 1940.

Q. When was Paris declared an open city?

A. On June 13, 1940.

Q. When did Singapore surrender?

A. February 15, 1942.

Q. Where and when did the first saturation bombing raid take place?

A. May 30, 1942, by 1,000 RAF planes on the German city of Cologne.

Q. When were the first Grumman F6F Hellcats used in combat?

A. On August 31, 1943, from the carrier *Yorktown* for the battle of Marcus Island in the Pacific.

FACT In a remarkable display of precision bombing on October 31, 1944, RAF planes bombed the Gestapo headquarters at Aarhus, Denmark, without damaging two hospitals that were hardly 100 yards away.

U.S. Army Photo

Q. Name the twelve Allied and Japanese signers of the instrument of surrender aboard the *Missouri*.

A. The ten Allied signers were General Douglas MacArthur, for the Allied powers; Admiral Chester Nimitz for the U.S.; General Hsu Yung-chang, for China; Admiral Sir Bruce Fraser, for the U.K.; General K. Derevyanko, for the Soviet Union; General Sir Thomas Blamey, for Australia; Colonel Moore Gosgrove, for Canada; General Jacques Leclerc, for France; Admiral C. Helfrich, for the Netherlands; and Air Vice Marshal Sir L. M. Isitt, for New Zealand. The two Japanese signers were Foreign Minister Mamoru Shigemitsu, on behalf of the Emperor of Japan, and General Yoshijiro Umezu, for the Imperial General Headquarters. This formal signing officially ended 1,364 days, five hours and fourteen minutes of World War II in the Pacific. The exact time of signing was 9:04 A.M.

Q. When did the invasion of Salerno, Italy, begin?

A. At 3:30 A.M. on September 9, 1943, by the U.S. Fifth Army under General Mark Clark.

Q. When did the Allies invade Anzio and Nettuno, Italy?

A. January 22, 1944.

Q. When did CINCPAC issue the order to "Cease all offensive operations against Japan"?

A. August 15, 1945. However all ships maintained full defensive alert until the formal surrender was signed on September 2.

Q. When did General Douglas MacArthur fulfill his pledge and return to the Philippines?

A. October 20, 1944, at Palo, Leyte. He returned 948 days after having been ordered to leave by President Franklin Roosevelt.

Q. What was the date the atomic bomb was dropped on Hiroshima?

A. August 6, 1945, by a B-29 named *Enola Gay*. The pilot was Colonel Paul W. Tibbets, the co-pilot was Captain Robert Lewis, the plane's actual commander.

U.S. Marine Corps Photo

Q. When did the U.S. amphibious landings on Okinawa begin?

A. At 8:30 A.M., April 1, 1945, Easter Sunday. The battle lasted eighty-two days. In the photo above, Marine Corporal Fenwick H. Dunn gives the candy from his K rations to an aged woman on Okinawa.

FACT: More than 7.5 million Europeans were pressed into forced labor for the Third Reich when calls for volunteers fell short of manpower needs. In addition, approximately 2 million prisoners of war were also forced to work in the Nazi war machine. The poster shown here was used in early years to recruit French workers by suggesting that helping the Nazis would save Europe from the Russians.

Appendix

The Fastest Fighter Planes of the War

There were sixty-four different versions of fighter planes, land-based and carrier-borne, produced by Allied and Axis powers during the war. In addition, there were fighter-bombers. Below are the nineteen fastest fighters that had maximum speeds over 400 miles per hour.

Plane/Country	Maximum Speed	Maximum Range
Messerschmitt Me-263, Germany	596 mph (rocket)	N.A.
Messerschmitt Me-262, Germany	560 mph (jet)	650 miles
Heinkel He-162A, Germany	553 mph	606 miles
P-51-H, United States	487 mph	850 miles
Lavochkin La-11, Russia	460 mph	466 miles
Spitfire XIV, Great Britain	448 mph	460 miles
Yakovlev Yak-3, Russia	447 mph	506 miles
P-51-D Mustang, United States	440 mph	2,300 miles
Tempest VI, Great Britain	438 mph	740 miles
Focke-Wulf FW-190D, Germany	435 mph	560 miles
Lavochkin 9, Russia	429 mph	1,078 miles
P-47-D Thunderbolt, United States	428 mph	1,000 miles
Lavochkin La-7, Russia	423 mph	392 miles
F4U Corsair, United States	417 mph	1,015 miles
Yakovlev Yak-9P, Russia	416 mph	889 miles
P-38-L Lightning, United States	414 mph	460 miles
Typhoon, Great Britain	412 mph	510 miles
Lavochkin La-5FN, Russia	401 mph	528 miles
Messerschmitt Me-109G, Germany	400 mph	460 miles

U.S. Ships Present at Pearl Harbor, December 7, 1941

Although most references agree that there were ninety-six *warships* in Pearl Harbor during the Japanese attack and that eighteen of them were sunk, it is rarely mentioned that the U.S. Navy and Coast Guard had forty-nine *other* ships there at the time. The complete list of 145 ships includes:

Allen (DD-66)	*Hulbert* (AVD-6)	PT-42
Antares (AKS-3)	*Hull* (DD-350)	*Pyro* (AE-1)
Argonne (AG-31)	*Jarvis* (DD-393)	*Rail* (AM-26)
Arizona (BB-39)	*Keosangua* (AT-38)	*Raleigh* (CL-7)
Ash (YN-2)	*MacDonough* (DD-351)	*Ralph Talbot* (DD-390)
Avocet (AVP-4)	*Manuwai* (YFB-17)	*Ramapo* (AO-12)
Aylwin (DD-355)	*Marin* (YN-53)	*Ramsay* (DM-16)
Bagley (DD-386)	*Maryland* (BB-46)	*Reedbird* (AMc-30)
Blue (DD-387)	*Medusa* (AR-1)	*Reid* (DD-369)
Bobolink (AM-20)	*Monaghan* (DD-354)	*Reliance* (USCG)
Breese (DM-18)	*Montgomery* (DM-17)	*Rigel* (AR-11)
Cachalot (SS-170)	*Mugford* (DD-389)	*Sacramento* (PG-19)
California (BB-44)	*Narwhal* (SS-167)	*St. Louis* (CL-49)
Case (DD-370)	*Navajo* (AT-64)	*San Francisco* (CA-38)
Cassin (DD-372)	*Neosho* (AO-23)	*Schley* (DD-103)
Castor (AKS-1)	*Nevada* (BB-36)	*Selfridge* (DD-357)
CG-8 (USCG)	*New Orleans* (CA-32)	*Shaw* (DD-373)
Chengho (IX-52)	*Nokomis* (YT-142)	*Sicard* (DM-21)
Chew (DD-106)	*Oglala* (CM-4)	*Solace* (AH-5)
Cinchona (YN-7)	*Oklahoma* (BB-37)	*Sotoyomo* (YT-9)
Cockatoo (AMc-8)	*Ontario* (AT-13)	*Sumner* (AG-32)
Cockenoe (YN-47)	*Osceola* (YT-129)	*Sunnadin* (AT-28)
Condor (AMc-14)	*Patterson* (DD-392)	*Swan* (AVP-7)
Conyngham (DD-371)	*Pelias* (AS-14)	*Taney* (PG-37) (USCG)†
Crossbill (AMc-9)	*Pennsylvania* (BB-38)	*Tangier* (AV-8)
Cummings (DD-365)	*Perry* (DMS-17)	*Tautog* (SS-199)
Curtiss (AV-4)	*Phelps* (DD-360)	*Tennessee* (BB-43)
Dale (DD-353)	*Phoenix* (CL-46)*	*Tern* (AM-31)
Detroit (CL-8)	*Preble* (DM-20)	*Thornton* (AVD-11)
Dewey (DD-349)	*Pruitt* (DM-22)	*Tiger* (PC-152) (USCG)
Dobbin (AD-3)	PT-20	*Tracy* (DM-19)
Dolphin (SS-169)	PT-21	*Trever* (DMS-16)
Downes (DD-375)	PT-22	*Tucker* (DD-374)
Farragut (DD-348)	PT-23	*Turkey* (AM-13)
Gamble (DM-15)	PT-24	*Utah* (AG-16)
Grebe (AM-43)	PT-25	*Vega* (AK-17)
Helena (CL-50)	PT-26	*Vestal* (AR-4)
Helm (DD-388)	PT-27	*Vireo* (AM-52)
Henley (DD-391)	PT-28	*Wapello* (YN-56)
Hoga (YT-146)	PT-29	*Ward* (DD-139)
Honolulu (CL-48)	PT-30	*Wasmuth* (DMS-15)

West Virginia (BB-48)	YNg-17	YT-152
Whitney (AD-4)	YO-21	YT-153
Widgeon (ASR-1)	YO-43	YW-16
Worden (DD-352)	YP-108	*Zane* (DMS-14)
YG-15	YP-109	YO-30
YG-17	YTT-3	YO-44
YG-21	YT-119	
YMT-5	YT-130	

*The *Phoenix* (CL-46) was sold to Argentina in 1951 and renamed *General Belgrano*. On May 2, 1982, the cruiser was sunk off the Falkland Islands by a British submarine during the hostilities between the two countries over sovereignty of the Falklands. It was the first sinking of a ship by a submarine since the end of World War II.

†The *Taney*, a 327-foot-long endurance cutter, remained in U.S. service longer than any of the above-mentioned vessels. Still on active service on December 7, 1981, forty years after the attack, the *Taney* participated in memorial services at Pearl Harbor.

Whatever Happened to the *Enola Gay?*

Donated to the Smithsonian Institution by the Department of Defense, the B-29 that dropped the first atom bomb on a Japanese city was, in 1981, lying in parts in a hangar in Silver Spring, Maryland.

"I'd like to see it donated to New Jersey and have it displayed at Teterboro Airport. It was my plane and I lived in that state all my life," noted Captain Robert Lewis, the ship's commander. Lewis was obliged to take part in the Hiroshima mission as co-pilot in his own plane when the 509th Composite Group's commander Colonel Paul Tibbets elected to participate in the flight.

When asked about the naming of the plane, Lewis replied, "The naming of the plane was reserved for the ship's commanding officer, and that was me. I would have named it *Pearl Harbor* or *Indianapolis* after the U.S. Navy cruiser that delivered the uranium to Tinian Island and was then sunk by a Japanese sub. That was the greatest single naval loss we ever suffered at sea." Tibbets named the plane after his mother.

"That B-29, my B-29, came off the assembly line in Omaha, Nebraska, on June 16, 1945, and was christened by a young lady named Dorothy Norgood," Lewis added. He said this last bit of information is not common knowledge. "I'm sure Tibbets doesn't even know that!" (from a personal conversation with the author on December 12, 1981.)

The 22 Largest Battleships in World War II

Until the Japanese attack on Pearl Harbor the navies of the world considered battleships the ultimate sea weapon; and the larger and heavier they were was supposed to indicate something about a country's sea power. Ironically, the Japanese launched the two largest battleships ever built. But her aircraft carriers were the weapon she depended on for the initiation of hostilities with the U.S., and it was U.S. aircraft carriers that turned the tide of war in the Pacific. It is interesting to note that while Japan's *Yamato*-class battleships were by far the heaviest, the United States' *Iowa*-class dreadnoughts were the longest.

Ship/Country	Tons	Length
Yamato, Japan	72,809	862
Musashi, Japan	72,809	862
Iowa, United States	55,710	887
New Jersey, United States	55,710	887
Missouri, United States	55,710	887
Wisconsin, United States	55,710	887
Bismarck, Germany	50,153	823
Tirpitz, Germany	50,153	823
Richelieu, France	47,500	812
Jean Bart, France	47,500	812
Hood, Great Britain	46,200	860
North Carolina, United States	44,800	729
Washington, United States	44,800	729
King George V, Great Britain	44,780	754
Prince of Wales, Great Britain	44,780	754
Duke of York, Great Britain	44,780	754
Anson, Great Britain	44,780	754
Howe, Great Britain	44,780	754
Nagato, Japan	42,785	725
Mutsu, Japan	42,785	725
Tennessee, United States	40,500	624
California, United States	40,500	624

The U.S.S. *Arizona*

Compared to these 40,000-plus giants, the most famous U.S. battleship was small. The third American ship to carry the name *Arizona* was placed in commission in 1916 and had a normal displacement of 31,400 tons and was 608 feet long. Of the approximately 1,550 Navy and Marine Corps personnel aboard her on December 7, 1941, only 289 survived. A campaign to raise $500,000 for a memorial was begun in 1957 and included a benefit performance by entertainer Elvis Presley as well as support from the popular television show *This Is Your Life* and from newspapers across the country. The memorial, dedicated on Memorial Day 1962, spans the *Arizona*, which was never raised from its watery grave.

U.S. Army Photo

Did Eva Braun and Hitler's Daughter Escape?

The November 1981 issue of the British Medical Association's *News Review* published the findings of a ten-year study on the World War II records of Adolf Hitler and his mistress Eva Braun, including dental evidence by a California research team that cast doubt on her death. According to the report, Hitler's dental records matched those of one of the thirteen bodies found near the bunker in Berlin on twenty-six points, including a unique window crown. The report said the odontological data for the female body presumed to be Eva Braun's did not agree with her personal records. The report stated further that if Eva Braun died in the bunker she may be buried elsewhere. It also pointed to the possibility that she may have escaped. A German U-boat, U-977, was the last German ship to surrender on August 17, 1945—more than three months after the war had ended. It surrendered in Argentina. It immediately became suspect of having transported Hitler or other ranking Nazis out of Germany. The controversy as to why this U-boat remained at large for so long after the end of hostilities has never been settled, according to doubters and those who believe it carried Eva Braun and others to freedom. In the accompanying photo, Hitler and Eva are shown with a child, Uschi, who was thought to have been Hitler's daughter.

The 20 Leading U-Boat Commanders of the German Kriegsmarine*

As with fighter pilots, the U-boat commanders dominated their area of warfare. It is interesting to note that the United States' top submarine commander, Richard O'Kane, would place seventh in the German top twenty U-boat commanders based on the number of ships sunk.

Commander/U-Boat	Ships Sunk	Number of Patrols
Otto Kretschmer, U-23 and U-99	45	16
Wolfgang Luth, U-9, U-138, U-43, U-181	44	14
Joachim Schepko, U-3, U-19, U-100	39	14
Erich Topp, U-57, U-552	35	13
Victor Schutze, U-25, U-103	34	7
Heinrich Liebe, U-38	30	9
Karl F. Merten, U-68	29	5
Guenther Prien, U-47	29	10
Joh. Mohr, U-124	29	6
Georg Lassen, U-160	28	4
Carl Emmermann, U-172	27	5
Herbert Schultze, U-48	26	8
Werner Henke, U-515	26	6
Heinrich Bleichrodt, U-48, U-109	25	8
Robert Gysae, U-98, U-177	25	8
Klaus Scholtz, U-108	24	8
Reinhard Hardegen, U-147, U-123	23	1
H. Lehmann-Willenbroch, U-5, U-96, U-256	22	10
Engelbert Endrass, U-46, U-567	22	9
Ernst Kals, U-130	19	5

*Based on number of ships sunk. Gross tons considered only for ranking when number of ships is equal. Other commanders who sank nineteen ships are not included if total tonnage was below 138,500.

FACT   Several towns in Florida refused to respond to blackout precautions in early 1942 when German U-boats were enjoying what they called the American Hunting Season and the Happy Time. During this period U-boats were sinking ships silhouetted against the U.S. coast. In one two-week period U-boats sank twenty-five ships. Towns were reluctant to turn off their lights, as it would have an adverse effect on the tourist trade.

Q. How many Japanese submarines were in the Advance Expeditionary Force that attacked Pearl Harbor?

A. Twenty-seven, five of which carried midget two-man submarines. This one is shown on display at Bellows Field, Oahu, Hawaii. The midgets made long voyages "piggy-back" on larger subs and were set loose as they neared their target.

The 20 Leading Submarine Commanders of the United States Navy*

Commander/Submarine	Ships Sunk	Number of Patrols
Richard H. O'Kane, *Tang*	31	5
Eugéne B. Fluckey, *Barb*	25	5
Slade D. Cutter, *Seahorse*	21	4
Samuel D. Dealey, *Harder*	20½	6
William S. Post, Jr., *Gudgeon* and *Spot*	19	7
Reuben T. Whitaker, S-44 and *Flasher*	18½	5
Walter T. Griffith, *Bowfin* and *Bullhead*	17	5
Dudley W. Morton, R-5 and *Wahoo*	17	6
John E. Lee, S-12, *Grayling* and *Croaker*	16	10
William B. Sieglaff, *Tautog* and *Tench*	15	7
Edward E. Shelby, *Sunfish*	14	5
Norvell G. Ward, *Guardfish*	14	5
Gordon W. Underwood, *Spadefish*	14	3
John S. Coye, Jr., *Silversides*	14	6
Glynn R. Donaho, *Flying Fish* and *Picuda*	14	7
George E. Porter, Jr., *Bluefish* and *Sennet*	14	6
Henry G. Munson, S-38, *Crevalle* and *Rasher*	13	9
Robert E. Dornin, *Trigger*	13	3
Charles O. Triebel, S-15 and *Snook*	13	8
Royce L. Gross, *Seawolf* and *Boarfish*	13½	7

*Based on number of ships sunk. Gross tons sunk considered only for ranking when number of ships is equal. Other commanders who sank thirteen ships are not included if total tonnage was below 80,000.

The Leading Fighter Pilots, All Nations

To earn the distinction of being an ace a pilot had to score a minimum of five "kills," or victories. As difficult as that was, the list of all the aces would fill several pages (there were 330 in the U.S. Navy alone). Those listed here are aces who earned the title *five times over or more,* meaning a minimum of twenty-five "kills." In addition, thirty-eight German fighter Aces *scored over 100 "kills,"* making them the unchallenged super aces of the war. In the interest of brevity, only German super aces with more than 250 kills each have been listed.

Fighter Ace/Nationality	*Number of Kills*
Erich Hartmann, Germany	352
Gerhard Barkhorn, Germany	301
Gunther Rall, Germany	275
Otto Kittel, Germany	267
Walther Nowotny, Germany	255
Hiroyishi Nishizawa, Japan	87*
Shoichi Sugita, Japan	80*
Hans H. Wind, Finland	75
Saburo Sakai, Japan	64†
Ivan Kozhedub, Russia	62
Aleksandr Pokryshkin, Russia	59
Grigorii Rechkalov, Russia	58
Hiromichi Shinohara, Japan	58
Nikolai Gulaev, Russia	57
Waturo Nakamichi, Japan	55
Takeo Okumura, Japan	54
Naoshi Kanno, Japan	52
Kirill Yevstigneev, Russia	52
Satoshi Anabuki, Japan	51
Yasuhiko Kuroe, Japan	51
Dimitrii Glinka, Russia	50
Aleksandr Klubov, Russia	50
Ivan Pilipenko, Russia	48
Arsenii Vorozheikin, Russia	46
Vasilii Kubarev, Russia	46
Nikolai Skomorokhov, Russia	46
J. Pattle, South Africa	41
Richard I. Bong, U.S.A.	40
Thomas B. McGuire, U.S.A.	38
J. E. Johnson, Great Britain	38
A. G. Malan, South Africa	35
David McCampbell, U.S.A.	34
P. H. Closterman, France	33
B. Finucane, Ireland	32

*Some works credit Shoichi Sugita with 120 kills and Nishizawa with 103.

†Saburo Sakai has been credited with 80 kills in another work. (Though this author is satisfied that the figures given here are correct, the discrepancies have been pointed out because they do exist.)

Fighter Ace/Nationality	Number of Kills
G. F. Beurling, Canada	31⅓
Frances S. Gabreski, U.S.A.	31
J. R. D. Graham, Great Britain	29
R. R. S. Tuck, Great Britain	29
C. R. Caldwell, Australia	28½
Gregory Boyington, U.S.A.	28
J. Frantisek, Czechoslovakia	28
Robert S. Johnson, U.S.A.	28
J. H. Lacey, Great Britain	28
C. F. Gray, New Zealand	27½
Charles H. MacDonald, U.S.A.	27
George E. Preddy, U.S.A.	26
E. S. Lock, Great Britain	26
Joseph J. Foss, U.S.A.	26
Robert M. Hanson, U.S.A.	25

Musée de la Guerre Photo

Q. Identify the only two Luftwaffe pilots to attack Allied troops during the initial Normandy landings.

A. Colonel Josef "Pips" Priller and Sergeant Heinz Wodarczyk. All other German aircraft had been moved back from the French coast to avoid destruction from regular Allied bombing. The unit this lone Luftwaffe pair belonged to was the 26th Fighter Wing. Here Priller tells another Luftwaffe officer about the daring flight.

Bibliography

Ambrose, Stephen E. *The Supreme Commander: The War Years of General Dwight D. Eisenhower.* New York: Doubleday, 1970.

Angelucci, Enzo. *Airplanes from the Dawn of Flight to the Present Day.* New York: McGraw-Hill, 1973.

Aron, Robert. *De Gaulle Before Paris: The Liberation of France, June–August 1944.* New York: Putnam, 1962.

Aster, Sidney. *1939: The Making of the Second World War.* New York: Simon and Schuster, 1974.

Bazna, Elyesa. *I Was Cicero.* New York: Harper & Row, 1962.

Bekker, Cajus. *The Luftwaffe War Diaries.* New York: Doubleday, 1968.

————. *Hitler's Naval War.* New York: Doubleday, 1974.

Blair, Clay, Jr. *Silent Victory.* New York: Lippincott, 1975.

Boyington, Gregory. *Baa Baa Black Sheep.* New York: Putnam, 1958.

Bradley, Omar N. *A Soldier's Story.* New York: Henry Holt, 1951.

Brown, Anthony Cave. *Bodyguard of Lies.* New York: Harper & Row, 1975.

Buchanan, A. Russell. *The United States and World War II.* New York: Harper & Row, 1964.

Bullock, Alan. *Hitler—A Study in Tyranny.* New York: Harper & Row, 1963.

Butcher, Harry. *My Three Years with Eisenhower.* New York: Simon and Schuster, 1946.

Calvocoressi, Peter, and Wint, Guy. *Total War.* New York: Pantheon, 1972.

Catton, Bruce. *The War Lords of Washington.* New York: Harcourt Brace, 1948.

Churchill, Winston S. *The Second World War.* Boston: Houghton Mifflin, 1948–53.

Clark, Alan. *Barbarossa: The Russian-German Conflict, 1941–1945.* New York: Morrow, 1965.

Collier, Basil, *Japan at War.* London: Sidgwick and Jackson, 1975.

Collins, Larry, and Lapierre, Dominique. *Is Paris Burning?* New York: Simon and Schuster, 1965.

Daley, Robert. *An American Saga: Juan Trippe and His Pan American Empire.* New York: Random House, 1980.

Dean, John R. *The Strange Alliance: The Story of Our Efforts at Wartime Cooperation with Russia.* New York: Viking, 1947.

De Gaulle, Charles. *War Memoirs*. New York: Simon and Schuster, 1964.

Deighton, Len. *Blitzkrieg*. New York: Knopf, 1980.

Delmer, Sefton. *The Counterfeit Spy*. New York: Harper & Row, 1971.

Dissette, Edward, and Adamson, Hans Christian. *Guerrilla Submarines*. New York: Bantam Books, 1980.

Dulles, Allen W. *The Craft of Intelligence*. New York: Harper & Row, 1963.

————. *The Secret Surrender*. New York: Harper & Row, 1966.

Eisenhower, Dwight D. *Crusade in Europe*. New York: Avon, 1968.

Elson, Robert. *Prelude to War*. New York: Time/Life, 1976.

Epstein, Helen. *Children of the Holocaust*. New York: Putnam, 1979.

Essame, Hubert, and Belfield, E. M. G. *Normandy Bridgehead*. New York: Ballantine, 1970.

Farago, Ladislas. *The Broken Seal*. New York: Random House, 1967.

————. *The Game of the Foxes*. New York: McKay, 1971.

Fleming, Peter. *Operation Sea Lion*. New York: Simon and Schuster, 1957.

Ford, Corey. *Donovan of OSS*. Boston: Little, Brown, 1970.

Fuller, J. F. C. *The Second World War, 1939–1945*. New York: Duell, Sloan & Pearce, 1949.

Gavin, James M. *On to Berlin*. New York: Viking, 1978.

Goebbels, Joseph. *Diaries of Joseph Goebbels, 1942–1943*. New York: Doubleday, 1948.

Goralski, Robert. *World War II Almanac, 1939–1945*. New York: Putnam, 1981.

Hughes, Terry, and Costello, John. *The Battle of the Atlantic*. New York: Dial, 1977.

Innis, W. Joe, with Bunton, Bill. *In Pursuit of the Awa Maru*. New York: Bantam Books, 1981.

Irving, David. *The German Atomic Bomb*. New York: Simon and Schuster, 1968.

Jackson, Stanley. *The Savoy: The Romance of a Great Hotel*. London: Frederick Muller, 1964.

Jackson, W. G. F. *The Battle for Italy*. London: Batsford, 1967.

Kahn, David, *The Codebreakers*. New York: Macmillan, 1967.

Kaufman, Louis; Fitzgerald, Barbara; and Sewell, Tom. *Mo Berg: Athlete, Scholar, Spy*. Boston: Little, Brown, 1974.

Keil, Sally Van Wagenen. *Those Wonderful Women in Their Flying Machines*. New York: Rawson, Wade, 1979.

Kimmel, Husband E. *Admiral Kimmel's Story*. Chicago: Henry Regnery, 1955.

King, Ernest J., and Whitehill, W. M. *Fleet Admiral King*. New York: Norton, 1952.

Kitchen, Ruben P., Jr. *Pacific Carrier*. New York: Zebra Books, 1980.

Kowalski, Isaac. *A Secret Press in Nazi Europe*. New York: Shengold, 1978.

Kramarz, Joachim. *Stauffenberg: The Life and Death of an Officer*. London: Deutsch, 1967.

Lawson, Ted W. *Thirty Seconds over Tokyo*. New York: Random House, 1943.

Leahy, W. *I Was There*. New York: Whittlesey, 1950.

Le Vien, Jack, and Lord, John. *Winston Churchill: The Valiant Years*. New York: Bernard Geis, 1962.

Longmate, Norman. *If Britain Had Failed*. New York: Stein & Day, 1974.

Lord, Walter. *Day of Infamy.* New York: Henry Holt, 1957.

McKee, Alexander. *Last Round Against Rommel.* New York: New American Library, 1964.

Manchester, William. *American Caesar: Douglas MacArthur, 1880–1964.* Boston: Little, Brown, 1978.

Manvell, Roger, and Fraenkel, Heinrich. *The Canaris Conspiracy.* New York: McKay, 1969.

Marshall, Samuel. *Night Drop.* Boston: Little, Brown, 1962.

Mason, David. *Who's Who in World War II.* Boston: Little, Brown, 1978.

————. *U-Boat: The Secret Menace.* New York: Ballantine, 1968.

Michel, Henri. *The Shadow War.* New York: Harper & Row, 1973.

Michel, Jean. *Dora: The Nazi Concentration Camp Where Modern Space Technology Was Born and 30,000 Prisoners Died.* New York: Holt, Rinehart and Winston, 1980.

Mikesh, Robert C. *Japan's World War II Balloon Bomb Attacks on North America.* Washington: Smithsonian Institution Press, 1973.

Mollo, Andrew. *A Pictorial History of the SS.* New York: Bonanza, 1979.

Montagu, Ewen. *The Man Who Never Was.* Philadelphia: Lippincott, 1954.

Morella, Joe; Epstein, Edward Z.; and Griggs, John. *The Films of World War II.* New York: Citadel/Lyle Stuart, 1975.

Morison, Samuel E. *The History of United States Naval Operations in World War II.* 14 vols. Boston: Little, Brown, 1947–62.

Page, Geoffrey. *Tale of a Guinea Pig.* New York: Bantam, 1981.

Patton, George S., Jr. *War As I Knew It.* Boston: Houghton Mifflin, 1947.

Payne, Robert. *The Life and Death of Adolf Hitler.* New York: Praeger, 1973.

Pearcy, Arthur. *DC-3.* New York: Ballantine, 1975.

Peniakoff, Vladimir. *Popski's Private Army.* New York: Bantam, 1980.

Popov, Dusko. *Spy-Counterspy.* New York: Grosset & Dunlap, 1974.

Ryan, Cornelius. *The Longest Day.* New York: Simon and Schuster, 1959.

————. *A Bridge Too Far.* New York: Simon and Schuster, 1974.

————. *The Last Battle.* New York: Simon and Schuster, 1966.

Schaeffer, Heinz. *U-Boat 977.* New York: Norton, 1953.

Sherrod, Robert. *Tarawa.* New York: Duell, Sloan & Pearce, 1944.

Shirer, William L. *The Rise and Fall of the Third Reich.* New York: Simon and Schuster, 1960.

Simms, Edward H. *American Aces.* New York: Harper Brothers, 1958.

Smith, Liz. *The Mother Book.* New York: Doubleday, 1978.

Speer, Albert. *Inside the Third Reich.* New York: Avon, 1970.

Stagg, J. M. *Forecast for Overload.* New York: Norton, 1972.

Strong, Sir Kenneth. *Intelligence at the Top.* New York: Doubleday, 1969.

Sulzberger, C. L. *The American Heritage Picture History of World War II.* New York: American Heritage, 1966.

Sunderman, James F. *World War II in the Air.* New York: Franklin Watts, 1962.

Sutton, Horace. *Travelers.* New York: Morrow, 1980.

TerHorst, Jerald F., and Albertazzie, Ralph. *The Flying White House.* New York: Coward, McCann & Geoghegan, 1979.

Thomson, David. *Europe Since Napoleon.* New York: Knopf, 1960.

Toland, John. *The Last 100 Days*. New York: Random House, 1965.

Tregaskis, Richard. *Guadalcanal Diary*. New York: Random House, 1943.

Truman, Harry S. *Memoirs*. New York: Doubleday, 1958.

Wallechinsky, David; Wallace, Amy; and Wallace, Irving. *The People's Almanac Presents the Book of Predictions*. New York: Morrow, 1981.

Whiting, Charles. *Hitler's Werewolves*. New York: Bantam, 1973.

————. *The Hunt for Martin Bormann*. New York: Ballantine, 1973.

————. *Patton*. New York: Ballantine, 1971.

Wiener, Jan G. *The Assassination of Heydrich*. New York: Pyramid, 1969.

Williams, Eric. *The Wooden Horse*. New York: Bantam, 1980.

Winterbotham, Frederick W. *The Ultra Secret*. New York: Harper & Row, 1974.

Young, Desmond. *Rommel, the Desert Fox*. New York: Harper Brothers, 1950.

THE
ULTIMATE
WWII
QUIZ BOOK
VOLUME TWO

For Marilyn, again

Contents

Introduction

As I noted in what has now become Volume 1 of *The World War II Quiz & Fact Book,* there was never a problem of what to include. I also noted that space simply did not permit the use of all the information. The problem was, and still is, what *not* to put in.

The war years, and in some cases events that followed but are directly related, remain full of historic treasures, bits of information, nostalgia, anecdotes, vignettes, all scattered throughout the millions of printed pages of war books. But the wealth of information does not end there.

Since publication of the first volume in December 1982, I have had the privilege of meeting and communicating with literally hundreds of veterans who have offered nuggets of their own. Most were Americans, but there have been many Canadians and Britons and a few French, Japanese and Germans also.

There was tremendous interest in the Naval section and the attack on Pearl Harbor. Code names and nicknames were equally popular, while most people were not too keen on bothering to remember specific dates. Consequently I have organized the material in this volume to reflect those preferences.

The Air and Land sections in this volume are as strong as in the first. Messages and Quotations, on the other hand, is smaller only because by now I may have exhausted the majority of truly memorable utterances.

For the reader seeing this work without having previously read the original volume, I hasten to note that each volume can be enjoyed without the other. There is no continuity lost, as the material skips over the period without regard to chronology.

However, occasionally I have supplied parenthetical references to specific pages in Volume 1. Their only purpose is to call attention to additional information about a particular person or event in case the reader cares to know more.

In the first volume I depended heavily upon photographs from official sources. I am delighted to note that this volume also has a generous selection of photographs taken by individuals who were kind enough to permit me to reproduce them. For the most part these were snapshots privately taken by service personnel. Three of the photo contributors, however, were wartime photographers in the Signal Corps. Appropriate credit lines are included for all photos, official and private.

Every effort has been made to publish only information that I was able to confirm from at least two other printed sources. The bibliography for this work, as with the last, is in excess of one hundred books. But if the reader discovers an error, it must be mine alone.

TIMOTHY B. BENFORD

Mountainside, New Jersey
August 1983

Posterity!! You will never know how much it cost the present generation to preserve your freedom. I hope you will make good use of it.

—U.S. President John Adams
1797

Q. What was the name of General Douglas MacArthur's private B-17?

A. *Bataan*. In the top photo, MacArthur and Admiral Thomas Kinkaid discuss the war as the general's plane wings toward New Guinea on February 27, 1944. In the bottom photo Lieutenant General Robert L. Eichelberger, commanding general of the U.S. Eighth Army, sits near the waist gun in his B-17, *Miss Em*, during a flight from Leyte to Mindoro, Philippines, on March 17, 1945.

U.S. Army Photos

Code Names

Q. What was the German code name for the plan to assassinate President Franklin D. Roosevelt?
A. Operation Long Pounce, which was said to be scheduled for execution during the Teheran Conference.

Q. What was the name Adolf Hitler used to avoid being recognized before his face was so widely known?
A. Herr Wolf.

Q. What was the Allied code name for Guadalcanal?
A. Cactus. (Volume 1, page 40)

Q. What was the name Nazi Rudolf Hess gave to authorities after his dramatic flight to and capture in Scotland on May 10, 1941?
A. Alfred Horn. Hess, who was at the time the third-highest-ranking Nazi behind Hitler and Goering, was still a prisoner in Spandau Prison, Germany, as 1983 ended.

Q. General James M. Gavin was known as
      a. Bad Jim
      b. Big Jim
      c. Slim Jim
      d) Jumpin' Jim
A. He was more commonly known as Slim Jim, but Jumpin' Jim was also a name he earned. (Volume 1, page 121)

Q. Who were the Devil's Brigade?

A. U.S. and Canadian troops under the command of U.S. General Robert T. Frederick that used unconventional tactics against the Axis forces in Italy. They were officially known as the First Special Service Force.

Q. Who were the Hell's Angels?

A. It was the name of a squadron of Flying Tigers that included the youngest and first member of the Flying Tigers killed in action, twenty-one-year-old Henry Gilbert. He was shot down over Rangoon in December 1941.

Q. What was Hell's Highway?

A. The road captured by the U.S. 82nd and 101st Airborne Divisions in Holland during Operation Market Garden. More than 20,000 Allied troops participated in the drops intended to outflank the Siegfried Line and push into the Ruhr basin.

Q. What did U.S. bomber pilots call the Happy Valley?

A. The Ruhr Valley in Germany earned the name because of the heavy anti-aircraft guns there.

Q. What did Allied pilots nickname the flight path between airfields in the Marianas Islands and Tokyo, Japan?

A. Hirohito Highway.

Q. Identify the air route nicknamed the Aluminum Trail.

A. The aircraft run over the Himalayas to China. The dubious distinction was a testimony to the several planes that never completed the flight.

Q. What was the name given to the Allied supply route from Antwerp, Belgium, to the northern battlefronts in Europe?

A. The ABC Express, not to be confused with the Red Ball Express, which was the route for supplies from the Normandy beaches inland.

Q. Which unit was known as the Black Bulls?

A. The British 79th Armoured Division.

Q. Identify the spy Ian Fleming is said to have used as a model for James Bond, the character in the novel and film series.

A. Fleming, who was a British intelligence agent himself, is said to have based his fictional agent on the life of a key double agent under his charge, Dusko Popov. Popov, who died at age seventy in France in 1981, published his memoirs, *Spy-Counterspy*, in 1974.

Q. What was British Prime Minister Winston Churchill's code name for telephone calls to U.S. President Franklin D. Roosevelt?
> a. Colonel Warden
> b. Former Naval Person
> c. John Martin

A. He was John Martin on the phone, Former Naval Person in written communication with FDR and Colonel Warden in British military and diplomatic codes. (Volume 1, pages 34 and 45)

Q. What was the special attachment U.S. and RAF crews had for the Gibson Girl?

A. It was a vital part of their survival equipment. A radio transmitter that broadcast SOS messages, it saved the lives of numerous aircrews shot down over water.

Q. Who was Josip Broz?

A. Better known as Tito, he was head of the resistance forces (communist) in Yugoslavia.

Q. Which U.S. general had a Piper Cub named the *Missouri Mule*?
> a. Dwight D. Eisenhower
> b. Douglas MacArthur
> c. Omar Bradley
> d. George C. Marshall

A. General Omar Bradley.

FACT Ian Fleming, author of the James Bond series, named his estate on the Caribbean island of Jamaica Golden Eye after the war. He took the name from British Prime Minister Winston Churchill's plan to secure Gibraltar if the Spanish had joined the Axis in the war. Fleming, as a member of the British intelligence system, was involved in the plan. (Volume 1, page 162)

Q. Who was Max Heilinger?

A. It was the fictitious name the SS used to establish a bank account in which they deposited money, gold and jewels taken from European Jews.

Q. What was Klim?

A. Milk, backwards. It was the powdered milk U.S. troops learned to live with.

Q. What was Meyer's Hunting Horn?

A. The name Berliners gave to air-raid sirens. Hermann Goering, who was among other things Chief Huntsman and Game Warden of the Reich, had once said that if Allied bombs fell on Germany people could call him Meyer.

Q. What did Hitler intend to rename Berlin after its planned modernization by architect Albert Speer?
>   a. Teutonia
>   b. Germania
>   c. Europa

A. Germania.

Q. What were the Japanese "windship weapons"?

A. The paper balloons and rubberized-silk balloons that Japan launched against the northwestern U.S. The first of more than 9,000 balloons carrying incendiary and anti-personnel bombs was launched on November 3, 1944. Six Americans were killed, and the balloons reached as far east as Michigan. The Smithsonian Institution has one of the paper versions on display. It was recovered at Echo, Oregon, on March 13, 1945.

Q. What was the most powerful artillery gun created by any nation and used in the war?

A. A monstrous gun developed by the Germans that could project a 2½-ton shell over three miles. The shells, twenty-four inches wide, were capable of going through eight to nine feet of concrete. Nicknamed Karl after its designer, General Karl Becker, the gun was used against the Russians.

USIS Photo

Q. What was the name of Edward R. Murrow's radio program from London?
A. *London After Dark.* (Volume 1, page 130)

Q. Who were the BAMs?
A. The U.S. Marine Corps simply called females in its ranks Women Marines. However, not wanting to be outdone by WACs, WAVES, WAFs and WASPs, some enterprising leathernecks coined the term BAMs — which stood for Broad-Assed Marines. The women, however, called the men HAMs, or Hairy-Assed Marines.

Q. What was the name of Bill Mauldin's jeep, which he converted into a mobile art studio?
A. Mauldin, the creator of "Willie and Joe," dubbed the jeep *Jeanie.*

Q. What did U.S. Admiral Chester Nimitz name his jeep?
A. USS *Hush Hush.* In Navy tradition it was painted battleship gray.

Q. Name the popular U.S. general who used a C-47 plane named *Mary Q.*
A. Omar Bradley.

Q. President Franklin D. Roosevelt's private plane, a C-87, was named:
       a. France
       b. Commando
       c. Sacred Cow
       d. Jingle Jangle
A. FDR's plane was the *Sacred Cow.* French General Charles de Gaulle's C-56 was *France* and British Prime Minister Winston Churchill's LB-30 was *Commando.* Elliott Roosevelt, the President's son, piloted a B-17 named *Jingle Jangle.*

FACT Nazi propagandists took full advantage of the name a U.S. B-17 bomber crew had given their plane and had painted on their jackets. When they were forced to bail out over Germany and were captured, the Nazis released stories that the U.S. Army Air Force was employing Chicago gangsters to bomb German cities. The name of the plane, and on the flight jackets, was *Murder Inc.*

Q. The German code name for the plan to infiltrate Allied lines in U.S. uniforms during the Battle of the Bulge was the same as the code name Erwin Rommel gave to his command car in North Africa. What was it?

      a. Grief

      b. Chaos

      c. Surprise

A. Operation Grief, which initially disrupted U.S. forces but did not accomplish the amount of harm the Germans expected.

Q. What was the name of Benito Mussolini's horse?

A. The Duce's white stallion was named Atlantico.

Q. What was the name of U.S. General Jonathan Wainwright's horse?

A. Joseph Conrad. When food supplies had been exhausted on Bataan in 1942, U.S. troops ate the horse.

Q. Match these leaders with the names of their private trains:

a) General Alfred Jodl	*Bayonet*
b) Adolf Hitler	*Steiermark*
c) Hermann Goering	*Asia*
d) General Dwight D. Eisenhower	*Atlas*
e) Heinrich Himmler	*Amerika*

A. Jodl had *Atlas*; Hitler rode in *Amerika*; Goering preferred *Asia*; Ike picked *Bayonet*; and Himmler's was *Steiermark*.

Q. What was the name of Adolf Hitler's yacht?

A. *Grille*.

Q. Who was known as the Rommel of the jungle?

A. Japanese General Tomoyuki Yamashita, because of his dynamic and resourceful leadership. Unlike Rommel, however, he managed also to gain a reputation for cruelty.

FACT At the outbreak of war the U.S. was the only major power that did not have an organized intelligence operation.

Q. What was the name of the brothel the SS ran for foreign diplomats and other VIP's in Berlin?

A. The Kitty Salon.

Q. What were Liberty Steaks?

A. The popular hamburger, which was renamed as a home-front propaganda move in the U.S. to avoid having to call them what sounded distinctly German.

Q. Identify the U.S. Army Air Force unit that was nicknamed the Forgotten Air Force.

A. Because they felt the U.S. Eighth Army Air Force received all the glory and publicity, the troops in the Fifteenth Army Air Force gave themselves the nickname.

Q. Identify the two code names used for the British operation to employ a look-alike for Field Marshal Bernard Law Montgomery.

A. Operation Hambone and Operation Copperhead. The individual selected was an actor, E. Clifton-James, who later wrote a book about his role and portrayed himself in the movie *I Was Monty's Double*. Fellow actor Colonel David Niven solicited Clifton-James for the job. The ruse was terminated when the actor had a difficult time giving up tobacco and alcohol. Monty didn't smoke or drink.

Q. What popular song had the Germans rewritten the words for and played over the air for Allied troops to hear less than forty-eight hours before the Normandy landings?

A. "I Double Dare You." The new lyrics read, in part: "I double dare you to venture too near...I double dare you to try and invade."

Q. The trio of Sherman tanks, under the command of Captain Raymond Dronne, that were the first Allied tanks to enter Paris in 1944 were named after Napoleon's battles. Name them.

A. The tanks, which clanked along the same route that Bonaparte had taken in his return from Elba, were *Montmirail*, *Romilly* and *Champaubert*. Their arrival within the city limits of Paris was on August 24, 1944. In photo at left, the first tank passes through the Porte d'Italie (the Italian Door) entrance to the city.

Metro Photo

Q. Identify the U.S. song whose music was pirated by the Nazis for their "Sieg Heil" march.

A. The Harvard "Fight" song.

Q. Name the popular song written on December 7, 1941, by Charles Tobias and Clifford Friend.

A. "We Did It Before (and We Can Do It Again)."

Q. Identify the Swedish female singer who was known as the voice of Lili Marlene to both the Allied and Axis troops.

A. Lala Andersen, who sang in Berlin cabarets during the war years. (Volume 1, page 87)

Q. Name the female singer known to British troops as the Forces' Sweetheart.

A. Vera Lynn. Her theme song was "We'll Meet Again."

Q. Identify the U.S. entertainer nicknamed the Allied V-2.

A. Dinah Shore. The name stuck after a reporter called her a bombshell.

Q. Who was known as Miss Spark Plug?

A. U.S. Army Colonel Oveta Culp Hobby, commander of the WACs.

Q. Name the woman who was known as the Mother of the WAVES.

A. Senator Margaret Chase Smith, who was one of the prime supporters of a more active role for women in the U.S. Navy.

Q. What was the name of the children's section of the Communist movement in Italy?

A. Koba, which was Joseph Stalin's childhood nickname.

FACT In May 1982, ABC News broadcast evidence that a Soviet code book found on a Finnish battlefield after World War II permitted the U.S. to break the Soviet spy codes. It was information gained from this effort that led the FBI to put Ethel and Julius Rosenberg under surveillance, but this fact was not revealed, since the U.S. didn't want the Soviets to know it had broken the codes. The Rosenbergs were convicted and executed in 1951 for espionage.

Q. Identify the Allied campaign that German propaganda radio broadcaster Axis Sally derided by calling it "the largest self-supporting
prisoner-of-war camp in the world."
A. Mildred E. Gillars, known as Axis Sally, used the expression to
underscore the inability of the Allies to break out from the beaches
of Anzio, Italy, for a considerable time after the initial invasion.
(Volume 1, pages 35 and 129)

Q. Besides Axis Sally, another female propaganda broadcaster for the
Nazis was:
  a. Stuttgart Steffie
  b. Nuremberg Nancy
  c. Berlin Betty
  d. Luftwaffe Lucy
A. Berlin Betty, whose voice became well known to Allied troops in
North Africa.

Q. Who was the Nazi propaganda broadcaster known as Mr. O.K.?
A. Max O. Koischwitz, a naturalized U.S. citizen who returned to Ger-
many in 1939 but never quite gained the notoriety of William Joyce,
Lord Haw Haw.

Q. Who was known as the Humbug of Hamburg?
  a. Joseph Goebbels
  b. Hermann Goering
  c. William Joyce (Lord Haw Haw)
A. The name belonged to William Joyce, an American-born British subject who broadcast propaganda for Germany. (Volume 1, page 35)

Q. Who was Lady Haw Haw?
A. German propaganda broadcaster Jane Anderson. Born in America,
she was active in both the Spanish Civil War and the first 2½ years
of World War II.

Q. Who was known as the Most Feared Man in Europe?
A. German super commando Otto Skorzeny. (Volume 1, page 80)

FACT The Wehrmacht used a delousing powder that was named Russia.

Q. Who was known as the Bitch of Buchenwald?
A. Ilse Koch, wife of Karl Koch, commandant of the Büchenwald concentration camp from 1937 to 1942. She was convicted of crimes against humanity for her part in several tortures and murders. She committed suicide while in a German prison during the mid-1960s while serving a life sentence for war crimes.

Q. Who was the Beast of Belsen?
A. Josef Kramer, commander of the concentration camp, who was executed for crimes against humanity.

Q. Who was known as the Angel of Death of Auschwitz?
A. Dr. Josef Mengele, who performed a variety of experiments on human beings with little regard for their pain or suffering. His present whereabouts, like that of Martin Bormann, remains a mystery.

Q. Identify the European Resistance movement leader known as the King of Shadows.
A. Frenchman Jean Moulin, because of his ability to appear and vanish in the dark of night. (Volume 1, page 81)

Q. Who was nicknamed the Fuehrer's Fireman?
A. Field Marshal Walther Model. He earned the name as a result of Hitler repeatedly giving him charge of difficult situations.

Q. Identify the high-ranking Nazi nicknamed the Flying Tailor by other Nazis.
A. Because of his large wardrobe of uniforms, Reichsmarschall Hermann Goering earned the name.

Q. Name the Luftwaffe fighter ace known as the Star of Africa.
A. Jans J. Marseille, who is credited with scoring seventeen enemy "kills" in a single day. His total was 158.

FACT Actor John Banner, who is best known for his portrayal of Sergeant Schultz in the television series *Hogan's Heroes*, was a Jew who left Austria after the Nazis took over the country in 1938. During the war he posed for U.S. recruiting posters.

Q. Identify the German fighter ace known as the Blond Knight.

A. The ace of aces, of all nations, Erich Hartmann, with 352 "kills." (Volume 1, page 214)

Q. Who was known as the Iron Man of Malta?

A. Canadian fighter ace George F. Beurling, who scored thirty-one "kills." Twenty-nine of them were earned when Malta was cited as the "most bombed spot on earth."

Q. Identify the U.S. Army Air Force unit known as the Flying Buccaneers.

A. Established on February 5, 1942, under the command of Lieutenant General George C. Kenney, the Fifth Army Air Force was the Flying Buccaneers.

Q. Who were the Flying Knights?

A. The squadron of P-38s under the command of Major Richard I. Bong in the Fifth Army Air Force. Bong was the top U.S. ace of the war with forty "kills."

Q. Who were the Lone Eagles?

A. The members of the all-black 99th Pursuit Fighter Squadron.

Q. Identify the homosexual member of Adolf Hitler's inner circle who was called "Fraulein Anna" by others in the group.

A. Deputy Fuehrer Rudolf Hess, who was also known as the Brown Mouse. (Volume 1, pages 106, 144 and 195)

Q. Who were known as Iron Ass and Stone Ass?

A. General Curtis LeMay was the former while V. M. Molotov was the latter.

FACT On June 24, 1947, a Boise, Idaho, businessman named Kenneth Arnold sighted what he described as unidentified flying objects that looked like "pie plates skipping over the water" near Mount Rainier, Washington. Newspaper reporters coined the term "flying saucers." However, Allied pilots reported similar sightings during the war, and these UFO's were known as foo-fighters. Pilots reporting them were often removed from flight duty.

Q. Identify the U.S. ship known as the Ship That Wouldn't Die.

A. The aircraft carrier USS *Franklin* (CV-13) earned the name as a result of surviving the third-greatest U.S. naval disaster ever, yet managing to travel some 12,000 miles from the coast of Japan to Brooklyn Navy Yard for repairs. More than 830 crewmen died as a result of the March 19, 1945, battle off Japan. The greatest single loss of U.S. Navy personnel (1,177) at one time was aboard the USS *Arizona* (BB-39) at Pearl Harbor. The greatest single loss of U.S. Navy personnel at sea was the sinking of the USS *Indianapolis* (nearly 900 lives), on July 30, 1945. (Volume 1, page 114)

Q. Which U.S. aircraft carrier was known as the Blue Ghost?

A. The USS *Lexington* (CV-16), which was launched five weeks after her namesake (CV-2) was sunk. The nickname came about from the fact that she was not painted in a camouflage pattern.

Q. Name the ship known as the Galloping Ghost of the Java Coast.

A. The heavy cruiser USS *Houston*, which was reported sunk twice by the Japanese, including once in the Battle of the Java Sea. She was finally sunk on March 1, 1942, along with the Australian cruiser HMAS *Perth*, in Sunda Strait.

Q. Identify the U.S. ship nicknamed the Galloping Ghost of the Oahu Coast.

A. Also known as the Old Lady and the Big E, the aircraft carrier USS *Enterprise* (CV-6) enjoyed the nickname. After the war the *Enterprise* remained in the mothball fleet stationed at Bayonne, New Jersey. She made her last sea voyage from the Brooklyn Navy Yard to the former Federal Shipyard in Kearny, New Jersey, on August 22, 1958, where she was cut up for scrap after having been sold for $561,333. Efforts to convert the ship into a memorial, under the direction of Admiral William F. Halsey, were unsuccessful.

Q. What was Operation Magic Carpet?

A. The name given to the U.S. operation to return overseas personnel to the United States at the end of the war. The ships involved were called the Magic Carpet Fleet. Scenes such as the one at left were eagerly awaited in all theaters of the war.

Exclusive Photo by Joseph De Caro

Q. Which U.S. unit was nicknamed the Ghost Corps?
A. The U.S. XX Corps, Third Army.

Q. Which ship was known as the First Lady of the Third Fleet?
A. The 52,000-ton battleship USS *Iowa* (BB-61).

Q. Identify the U.S. Navy officer nicknamed the Oil King of the Pacific for his ability to supply ships.
A. Commodore Augustine H. Gray.

Q. Identify the ship known as the Fightingest Ship in the Royal Canadian Navy.
A. Commissioned in August 1943, the Canadian destroyer HMCS *Haida* saw action in the English Channel and the Bay of Biscay. She is credited with destroying fourteen enemy ships. She is now a memorial open to the public at Ontario, Canada.

Q. Identify the naval engagement that is called the Japanese Pearl Harbor.
A. The U.S. attack against the Japanese at Truk on February 16–17, 1944. American planes, based on aircraft carriers, inflicted serious damage on the Japanese. However, the heaviest Japanese ships lost in the strike were light cruisers (*Naga* and *Agano*) and a training cruiser (*Katori*). The *Agano* was actually sunk by a U.S. submarine.

Q. What was known as the Concrete Battleship?
A. U.S. Fort Drum in Manila Bay, the Philippines. It was located approximately five miles from Corregidor.

Q. What four detachments were identified by the code names Concrete, Granite, Iron and Steel during one of history's most daring assaults in May 1940?
A. The four detachments that assaulted the Belgian Fort Eben Emael. (Volume 1, page 125)

FACT William Hitler, a nephew of Adolf Hitler, was in the U.S. Navy during the war. He changed his name upon returning to the U.S. after the war.

Q. Identify the U.S. Navy ship nicknamed the Pirate of the Pacific.
A. The USS *Kidd* (DD-661), which was commissioned in April 1943.
   After reaching the eastern Pacific, she participated in every major
   naval campaign until the end of the war, and is now on public view
   as a memorial in Baton Rouge, Louisiana.

Q. Name "the ship that was always there."
A. The slogan, and reputation, belonged to the battleship USS
   Washington (BB-56), which won thirteen battle stars in the war.

Q. Identify the ship known as Battleship X until information about
   her joining the fleet had been declassified.
A. The USS *South Dakota* (BB-57).

Q. Identify the U.S. aircraft carrier known as the Old Covered Wagon.
A. The USS *Langley* (CV-1), which was converted into a seaplane
   tender.

Q. What was the nickname of the aircraft carrier USS *Lexington*
   (CV-2)?
A. Lady Lex. She was the first U.S. aircraft carrier lost in the war,
   sunk by friendly fire after being badly damaged in the Battle of
   the Coral Sea in May 1942.

Q. What was the French luxury liner *Normandie* renamed after it was
   seized by the U.S.?
A. The S.S. *Lafayette*. However, it burned at dockside in New York
   in February 1942 and had to be scrapped.

Q. Which U.S. ship was known as the Sweet Pea?
A. The USS *Portland* (CA-33), a veteran of twenty-four major actions
   against Japan. She was also the first ship in the U.S. Navy to carry
   that city's name.

FACT In a classic case of mistaken identity, shipments of wartime
     materiel destined for Milne Bay, New Guinea, wound up being
     sent to Fall River, Massachusetts, where they remained unac-
     counted for for a considerable time. The code name for Milne Bay
     was Fall River.

Q. Which U.S. Navy vessel was nicknamed the One-Ship Fleet?
A. The cruiser USS *Salt Lake City*, because of her many single engagements of the enemy in the Pacific.

Q. Identify the U.S. Navy vessels known as mosquito boats.
A. The name applied to PT boats. The Japanese referred to them as Green Dragons.

Q. Which two Japanese ships were the Green Dragon and the Flying Dragon?
A. Two of the six aircraft carriers that took part in the attack on Pearl Harbor, *Soryu* and *Hiryu*, respectively.

Q. What was the nickname of the U.S. submarine USS *Jack*?
A. Jack the Tanker Killer, because she sank four enemy tankers in a single day.

Q. General Pershing was nicknamed Black Jack in World War I. Name the U.S. admiral given the same nickname in World War II.
A. Admiral Frank (Black Jack) Fletcher.

Q. During the German occupation what were the cut-in-half taxis drawn by humans or horses in Paris called?
A. Velo-Taxis. Usually the driver pulled the vehicle by using a bike.

Q. Identify the plane known by Luftwaffe and RAF pilots alike as Goering's Folly.
A. The Messerschmitt BF-110, a twin-engine fighter that was too slow to compete with British fighters.

FACT During the Battle of the Bulge, U.S. General Omar Bradley was challenged by American troops on the lookout for Germans dressed in U.S. uniforms. He was asked to name the capital of Illinois, and correctly responded "Springfield"; the scrimmage position of a guard in football, to which he replied, "Between the center and tackle." However, on three separate challenges he failed to identify the husband of pinup girl and movie star Betty Grable. Despite not knowing that it was bandleader Harry James, Bradley was given passage.

Q. What was the name of the secret road constructed to transport tanks and armor to the hills above Cassino, Italy?
A. Cavendish Road.

Q. What were the GI Joe Diners?
A. Food and rest stops along U.S. supply routes in Europe where canned rations could be exchanged for hot meals.

Q. What was the name of the powder explosive developed by the Allies that could actually be mixed with water, baked and eaten?
A. Because of its strong resemblance to flour and its ability to be digested, in necessity, it was known as Aunt Jemima, with a bow to the famous pancake mix.

Q. What was the code name for the U.S. invasion of Okinawa on April 1, 1945?
A. Operation Iceberg. (Volume 1, pages 132, 134, 157, 179, 186 and 205)

Q. What was the U.S. code name for the invasion of Iwo Jima in 1945?
A. Operation Detachment. (Volume 1, pages x, 3, 27, 60, 85, 125 and 135)

Q. What was the code name for the U.S. Second Marine Division assault on Tarawa in November 1943?
    a. Operation Long Bow
    b. Operation Long Arm
    c. Operation Long Legs
    d. Operation Longsuit
A. Operation Longsuit. (Volume 1, pages 45, 69, 83 and 118)

Q. Who was the individual credited with the actual breakthrough that resulted in the U.S. reading of the Japanese Purple Code?
A. While Colonel William F. Friedman is generally regarded as the individual most responsible for breaking the Purple Code (after nearly twenty months of work), it was the genius of a civilian cryptanalyst, Harry Larry Clark, who triggered the actual breakthrough.

FACT Mikado, Michigan, changed its name to MacArthur, Michigan, after the Japanese attack on Pearl Harbor.

Q. Who advised the Japanese that the U.S. was reading their code messages?

A. Nazi Heinrich Stahmer, the individual who had been entrusted by Hitler to negotiate the Tripartite Pact in Tokyo. Stahmer passed this information on to the Japanese Foreign Ministry in May 1941, but Japan could not believe it possible and, therefore, did not change the codes.

Q. What was the Mechelen Incident?

A. It relates to partially burned documents that outlined German intentions against Belgium. A German plane lost its way on January 10, 1940, and crashed in Belgium. The information salvaged confirmed the thrust intended against the British and French expeditionary forces. Had the Allies fully believed the documents, Germany's advances could have been stopped cold.

Q. What was the name of the German plan to seize the Suez Canal?

A. Part of the overall German objective to take Egypt, the plan was Operation Aida.

Q. What was the Knutsford Affair?

A. The name given to the incident in which U.S. General George S. Patton referred to the U.S. and British destinies to "rule the world" and thereby offended our French and Russian allies.

Q. Who were the Jedburghs?

A. The special teams of one American, a Briton and a Frenchman who worked with the French Maquis.

Q. What was Sho-Go, the Japanese plan for Operation Victory?

A. The plan for crushing any Allied attempt to retake the Philippines.

Q. What was the code name for British General Bernard Montgomery's Lightfoot operations in North Africa during 1942?
    a. Old Bailey
    b. Bertram
    c. Big Ben

A. It was Operation Bertram, the El Alamein offensive. Here a German tank crew surrenders as infantry rush their tank during the campaign.

Imperial War Museum Photo

Q. Name the plane commanded by USAAF Captain Ted Lawson in Doolittle's raid.

A. The *Ruptured Duck*. Lawson wrote the best-selling book *Thirty Seconds over Tokyo*.

Q. Which Allied invasion beaches were code-named Cent, Dime and Joss?
  a. Guadalcanal
  b. Okinawa
  c. Sicily

A. Sicily. Okinawa beaches were Blue and Purple, and Red was the code name for Guadalcanal. Other invasions that had Red beaches include Attu, Dieppe, Saipan, Salerno and Tarawa, either as single objectives or part of a multibeach invasion. (Volume 1, pages 45 and 76)

Q. What was Operation Red?

A. The second and final phase of the German Battle for France. It began as the Dunkirk evacuation ended.

Q. Name the German plan to kidnap Marshal Tito in 1944.

A. Operation Knight's Move, which employed commandos in gliders who swept in but failed to get him.

Q. What was the code name for the U.S. plan to reach Hechingen, Germany, and capture as many German atomic scientists as possible before any of the other Allies?

A. Operation Humbug.

Q. What was the name of the German scheme to counterfeit British currency and bank notes?

A. Operation Bernhard. It was the brainchild of Alfred Naujocks, the SS officer who was in command of the fabricated incident at Gleiwitz, Poland, which the Nazis used as a reason for invading Poland. (Volume 1, page 79)

FACT The French forces under De Gaulle, which had been known as the Free French, were renamed the Fighting French in mid-July 1942.

Q. What was the Italian three-ton light tank (L-3-33/5) irreverently called? (Note: this is the tank that Franco's troops used in the Spanish Civil War and the Italians used unsuccessfully in Libya.)

A. Sardine Can. It was no match for the most modest anti-tank weapons.

Q. What were *grilles de Cointets*?

A. Mobile metal tank traps, named after their inventor, which were designed to assist the Allies during the campaign in Europe prior to Dunkirk.

Q. What term did British Prime Minister Neville Chamberlain use to describe the lull between the declarations of war in September 1939 and open hostilities in the spring of 1940?

A. To Chamberlain it was the Twilight War, while in Germany it was known as the Sitting War (Sitzkrieg).

Q. Who is credited with coining the phrase Phony War?
> a. Winston S. Churchill
> b. William Borah
> c. George S. Patton
> d. Joseph Goebbels

A. U.S. Senator William Borah used the term to describe the period after the European Allies declared war on Germany in September 1939 and the lull that followed until hostilities broke out on a large scale in the spring of 1940.

Q. What was the German code name for the plan to annex the unoccupied area of France after the armistice?

A. Attila.

Q. What was Operation Titanic?

A. The code name for the Allied airborne deception tactics during the D-Day invasion.

FACT Germany benefited greatly from the Phony War inasmuch as by May 10, 1940, when open hostilities broke out, it had mustered 157 divisions. This was forty-nine more than it had on September 1, 1939, when it invaded Poland.

Q. Identify the participants involved in a May 1940 conversation between France and London which was conducted in Hindustani to prevent the Germans from monitoring it.

A. Prime Minister Winston Churchill ordered General Ismay to telephone London and request the Cabinet meet at once to consider a telegram he was sending dealing with continued aid to the French. Ismay arranged for an Indian Army officer to deliver the unusual message. Churchill and Ismay were among a British group in France conducting strategy meetings.

Q. What was known as the German Pak?

A. The term is an abbreviation of *Panzerabwehrkanon*, or anti-tank gun. Anti-tank crews were referred to as Panzerjaeger (tank hunters), which gave an offensive psychological name to a defensive force.

Q. What was the German nickname for the dive-bombing aircraft known as *Sturzkampfflugzeug*?

A. The Junkers Ju-87 was known by both the Allies and the Axis as the Stuka, which is an abbreviation of the German word for dive bomber.

Q. Who was General John C. H. "Courthouse" Lee?

A. Deputy commander under General Dwight D. Eisenhower for European Theater of Operations (ETOUSA).

Q. What was Operation Aphrodite?

A. The secret mission in which Lieutenant Joseph P. Kennedy, Jr. was killed. The objective was to destroy German submarine pens at St. Nazaire and Lorient on the French coast. (Volume 1, page 89)

FACT Elizabeth Windsor, an eighteen-year-old member of the British Auxiliary Territorial Service in 1944, was an automobile mechanic who had a trick played on her by His Majesty King George VI. The King had removed the distributor from a car that the young woman was attempting to get started as part of her final test in a heavy mechanics course. He finally told her the reason she had been unsuccessful and she easily passed the test. Second Subaltern Elizabeth Alexandra Mary Windsor is better known to the world today as Queen Elizabeth II.

Q. Identify the U.S. official who was code-named Mary by the Germans.
    a. William Donovan
    b. Harry Hopkins
    c. Charles A. Lindbergh
A. Wild Bill Donovan, head of the OSS.

Q. What other code name, besides Valkyrie, was the plan to kill Adolf Hitler known by?
A. The July 20, 1944, plot was also called Malaparte. (Volume 1, pages 53 and 85)

Q. What was the German code name for the attack against the Soviets at the Kursk salient in July 1943?
A. Operation Citadel, which resulted in the largest tank and armored battle in history. More than 3,600 tanks and armored vehicles were involved.

Q. What was the name of the British-inspired plan to deceive the Germans as to where the Allies would land during Operation Overlord?
A. Operation Bodyguard, which was intended to convince the Germans that the invasion would be at Calais rather than Normandy.

Q. What was the objective of Operation Dracula?
A. The Allied capture of Rangoon in May 1945.

Q. What was Operation Strangle?
A. The air support that the Allies employed prior to Operation Diadem in an effort to sever German supply routes around Rome. (Volume 1, page 53)

Q. What was the code name for the German effort to land spies in New York and other areas of the U.S. in 1942?
A. Operation Pegasus.

FACT To confuse Japanese who were listening to U.S. Marine Corps radio transmissions in the Pacific during the war, the Corps employed more than 300 Navajo-speaking American Indians as radio code talkers.

Q. What was the German code name for the plan that led to the creation of the Afrika Korps?
A. Operation Sunflower (Sunnenblume). It was intended to use a German force to defend Tripoli.

Q. What was Operation Shoestring?
A. The unofficial name U.S. Marines gave to the Guadalcanal campaign because of the severe shortages of supplies, particularly as they were required by Marine Corps Aviation.

Q. Identify the code name for the British plan to keep the 7th Australian Division in the Nile delta for a possible attack on Rhodes and Leros, Greece.
A. Operation Mandible.

Q. What was the Allied code name for transporting Canadian troops from the Mediterranean theater to Great Britain in advance of the Normandy invasion in 1944?
      a. Operation Gold Coast
      b. Operation Goldfake
      c. Operation Golden Nugget
A. Operation Goldfake.

Q. What was the German code name for plans to invade Norway?
A. Weseruebung (Exercise Weser). The plan for the attack was Case N (for north).

Q. What was the code name for the Allied air raid on Hamburg that produced the infamous fire storms?
A. Operation Gomorrah. (Volume 1, pages 12, 147)

Q. What was the name of the British attack on the French naval fleet at Oran in July 1940?
A. Operation Catapult.

Q. What was Operation Violet?
A. The action by the French Resistance in cutting German communication lines in concert with the Normandy invasion.

Q. What was the name of the Norwegian resistance organization that opposed the Nazis?

A. Milorg. For the most part, Norwegians who were anti-Hitler were known as Jossingers while the pro-Hitler Norwegians were called Quislings. Vidkun Quisling was a Norwegian Nazi who is considered the country's greatest traitor. The use of his name in reference to a group, an individual or an act is understood to indicate treason.

Q. Who described the combination of land, air and sea forces working together in war as "triphibian" strategy?

A. British Prime Minister Winston S. Churchill.

Q. What was the task of the commando team known by the code name Anthropoid?

A. The two-man team of Josef Gabcik and Jan Kubis was sent into Czechoslovakia in 1941 to assassinate SS General Reinhard Heydrich. The mission succeeded. (Volume 1, page 85)

Q. Who was nicknamed Cottonhead?
      a. General Matthew B. Ridgway
      b. Prime Minister Neville Chamberlain
      c. Admiral Chester Nimitz
      d. General Theodore Roosevelt, Jr.

A. Admiral Chester Nimitz.

Q. When the Japanese captured Wake Island they rechristened it Otori Shima. What is the English translation?

A. Bird Island.

Q. What was calvados?

A. The apple brandy from Normandy that was the unofficial drink for victory toasts throughout France on June 6, 1944.

FACT The year 1941 was the Year of the Snake in the Buddhist fortune calendar cycle of twelve years. Though any connection with the evil disposition of the reptile and the ambitions of Japan was not made in the empire, the connection was quickly seized upon by Allied propagandists after December 7, 1941.

Q. What was the German code name for the effort to land spies in the U.S. via submarines?
A. Operation Pastorius.

Q. What was the code name for the U.S. attack on the Japanese Navy at Truk in February 1944?
       a. Operation Pearl
       b. Operation Revenge
       c. Operation Hailstone
       d. Operation Glad
A. Operation Hailstone.

Q. What was Operation Flintlock?
A. The U.S. attack on Kwajalein, the largest atoll in the world (18 miles wide by 78 miles long) in January 1943. (Volume 1, page 79)

Q. Identify the European country where an intelligence operation known as the Alliance of Animals worked against the Germans.
A. France. The individuals in the group used animal code names.

Q. What was the code name of Britain's King George VI?
A. General Lyon.

Q. What did Batter Up and Play Ball mean with regard to Operation Torch in 1942?
A. The former indicated that Allied troops were meeting resistance from the French in North Africa, while the latter ordered the Allies to attack.

Q. What was the German code name for the conquest of Gibraltar?
A. Operation Felix.

Q. What were the troops under General Bernard Law Montgomery in the Africa campaign known as?
A. The Desert Rats, a name they earned before Montgomery took command. In this North African photo, Montgomery, left, and an aide are seen talking to General Ritter von Thoma, commander of the Afrika Korps, shortly after his capture.

U.S. Army Photo

Q. What was the name of the proposed pontoon airfield the British seriously considered building off the coast of France to support the Normandy landings?

A. Lily, which never went beyond the development stage.

Q. Who is known as the man who cut a hole in the Atlantic Wall?

A. British General and tank strategist Sir Percy Hobart. His armor designs, such as the flail tank, were instrumental in establishing Allied beachheads in Normandy in 1944.

Q. In Japanese telephone conversations between Tokyo and Washington in 1941, what were the code words used for President Franklin D. Roosevelt and Secretary of State Cordell Hull?

A. FDR was referred to as Miss Kimiko, while Hull was Miss Fumeko. By introducing these and other code names into a seemingly innocuous telephone call, the Japanese Foreign Ministry was able to get an instant reading from its ambassadors in Washington as to the progress of the peace talks. The United States was Minami in the code, and the Army was Tokugawa.

Q. Who were known as the Plus Four?

A. The term was coined by the wife of Secretary of War Henry L. Stimson and meant to indicate her husband, Secretary of State Cordell Hull, Secretary of the Navy Frank Knox, and Secretary of the Treasury Henry Morgenthau, Jr. The implication was that President Roosevelt and his adviser Harry Hopkins frequently met with these men at the same time. Hence a meeting would involve FDR, Hopkins, Plus Four.

Q. What was the British code name for the torpedo-bombing attack on Italian ships at Taranto?

A. Operation Judgement.

FACT U.S. troops enjoyed free outgoing mail service although all enlisted personnel mail was subject to censorship. Officers, on the other hand, were relied on to observe security restrictions and only spot checks of their mail took place. The quickest way to send or receive a letter was by V-mail, a special form which was microfilmed and reconstituted at the receiving end.

Q. To the Germans it was called *Rudeltaktik*, to the British it was...?
A. *Rudeltaktik*, or "pack tactics," was known to the British as the U-boat wolf packs.

Q. What was the name of the Allied army that was almost totally fabricated to deceive the Germans into thinking the invasion of Europe would come at the Pas de Calais rather than Normandy in 1944?
A. FUSAG — First United States Army Group.

Q. What was STAVKA?
A. The Russian Army High Command.

Q. What was the code word the British used in 1939 to advise intelligence agents that war with Germany was unavoidable?
A. Halberd, which was sent in August 1939.

Q. What was the Gun Club in the U.S. Navy?
A. The unofficial name that proponents of aircraft carriers gave to the proponents of battleships as the primary naval weapon.

Q. Who were the Hiwis?
A. Soviet troops who fought with the Nazis against Stalin's Red Army.

Q. What did the U.S. Marines nickname Mount Suribachi on Iwo Jima?
A. Hotrocks. (Volume 1, pages 3, 27, 60, 85, 125 and 135)

Q. What were known as Hun Sleds by the Dutch?
A. The radio detection vehicles used by the Germans to locate Resistance transmitters.

Q. What did the Allies call the underground radio operation in Luxembourg that furnished misinformation to the Nazis?
A. Operation Annie, which broadcast legitimate German news and information as a means of deceiving German troops when it broadcast misinformation.

Q. What did the term Seabees stand for?
A. Construction battalions, also called CB's. (Volume 1, page 105)

Q. Name the U.S. general that the Japanese called the Beast.

A. Army Air Force General George C. Kenney, the officer who commanded air personnel in the southwest Pacific and creator of the parachute fragmentation bomb.

Q. Who was nicknamed the Major of St.-Lô, France?

A. U.S. Army Major Thomas D. Howie, who was killed in combat there and became a symbol for all other U.S. casualties. (Volume 1, pages 34 and 179)

Q. Who was Swift Heinz?

A. German General Heinz Guderian. The nickname was first applied by his own troops during the German thrust toward the English Channel in 1940.

Q. What was Audie Murphy's nickname?

A. The most decorated U.S. soldier ever by the time he was twenty years old, Audie Murphy was called Baby. (Volume 1, page 105)

Q. Identify the two Allied intelligence personnel known as Big Bill and Little Bill.

A. William Stephenson, who was also known as Intrepid, was the head of British intelligence in New York and was Little Bill. William Donovan, the chief of the American OSS and the first recipient of the four highest U.S. decorations, was known as both Big Bill and Wild Bill. The decorations: Congressional Medal of Honor, Distinguished Service Cross, Distinguished Service Medal and the National Security Medal.

Q. Identify the naval battle that British military theorist Basil Liddell Hart called Strategic Overstretch and became known in postwar Japan as Victory Disease.

A. The Battle of the Coral Sea, because of its boldness and slight chance of success for Japan. (Volume 1, pages 31, 171 and 173)

FACT Much is made of the harsh winter the Germans faced in their Russian campaign in 1941. "General Winter" was considered the Soviet reserve secret weapon. It was the coldest winter in 140 years.

Q. Name the German aircraft nicknamed Iron Annie.
A. The Ju-52 transport.

Q. What did the Morse code message KDHP mean when sent by the U.S. Merchant Marine?
A. It was similar to an SOS in that it indicated the sending ship had been hit by torpedoes.

Q. Identify the U.S. general who used the code name Howe during the North Africa invasion:
    a. George S. Patton
    b. Dwight D. Eisenhower
    c. James M. Gavin
A. General Eisenhower, whose more frequently used code name was Duckpin. (Volume 1, page 13)

Q. What was the GAPSALS?
A. The Give a Pint, Save a Life Society formed by radio personality Arthur Godfrey.

Q. What was the code name of the planned, but not executed, Allied attack on Hitler's headquarters at Berchtesgaden in support of the Allied invasion of Normandy?
A. Operation Hellbound, which was to be carried out by the U.S. Fifteenth Army Air Force based in Italy. It was feared that the Germans would conclude from the attack that the Allies had broken German codes.

Q. What was FIDO?
A. The name for the Allied system of eliminating fog at airstrips in England: Fog Investigation and Dispersal Operation. By using pipes to pump gas that was then ignited and burned off the heavy fog, the Allies managed to keep the airstrips open.

FACT The term Nasos, not Nazis, was the original abbreviation for the National Socialist German Workers' Party. However, German writer Konrad Heiden, who had little use for them, bastardized Nasos into Nazi as a means of poking fun at them. Nazi is derived from a Bavarian word that means "simple-minded."

Q. What was the nickname the leathernecks on Guadalcanal gave to Henderson Field?

A. Bull's Eye, because it was so frequently hit by the Japanese.

Q. What did the word asdic stand for? (Asdic was the British equivalent of sonar.)

A. At the end of World War I, the Royal Navy was assisted in its efforts to combat German U-boats by Allied scientists who were part of the Anti-Submarine Detection Investigation Committee, hence the name asdic.

Q. What was a *Pillenwerfer*?

A. A device created to thwart sonar from Allied anti-submarine vessels. It ejected small gas bubbles that returned an echo similar to a submarine's.

Q. What was Operation Bronx Shipments?

A. The code name for the transfer of material needed for the atomic bomb from the U.S. to Tinian Island in July 1945 aboard the cruiser *Indianapolis*.

Q. What was Huff Duff?

A. The High-Frequency Direction-Finding equipment which the Allies developed to locate German U-boats.

Q. What were Hedgehogs?

A. Anti-submarine cluster weapons consisting of two dozen individual bombs attached to a single projectile. They opened into a spread pattern, thereby increasing greatly the chances of striking a target. The concept was first developed by the Royal Navy at the suggestion of U.S. Navy Captain Paul Hammond.

Q. Identify the two Allied commanders nicknamed Bomber and Tooey.

A. Sir Arthur Harris of the RAF was Bomber and General Carl Spaatz was Tooey. Spaatz (right) joins British Air Chief Marshal Sir Arthur Tedder (left) and Soviet Deputy Commander in Chief Georgi K. Zhukov in a toast at Russian headquarters in Berlin on May 7, 1945, to celebrate the German surrender.

U.S. Army Photo

Q. What was an Anderson Shelter?

A. A simple, cheap and quickly erected structure of concrete and corrugated iron widely used in private gardens throughout Britain to protect civilians during air raids. It was credited with saving thousands of lives and was designed by Scottish engineer Sir William Paterson and inspired by Sir John Anderson.

Q. What was the code name for U.S. troops stationed in Ireland:
  - a. Force Green
  - b. Shamrock
  - c. Magnet

A. Magnet

Q. What was Mackerel the German code name for?

A. Ireland.

Q. What was the Allied code name for Ho Chi Minh, a U.S. ally during the war and adversary in the 1960s?
  - a. Lucifer
  - b. Lucius
  - c. Lulu

A. Ho Chi Minh of Vietnam was known as Lucius.

Q. Who or what were the Maquis?

A. The name identified the French Resistance fighters.

Q. Name the U.S. fighter ace whose plane was named *Marge*.
  - a. Pappy Boyington
  - b. Richard Bong
  - c. Thomas B. McGuire
  - d. David McCampbell

A. Richard Bong's P-38 was *Marge*. (Volume 1, page 214)

Q. What nickname did U.S. Marines give to leatherneck fliers?

A. Airedales. The term was popular with the ground support crews.

Q. What was the code name for the U.S. offensive in Burma that had as its objective securing the Burma Road?

A. Operation Galahad.

Q. What were Kriegies?

A. Allied prisoners of war. The term is a short version of the German word for war captive.

Q. What was the Kreisau Circle?

A. The anti-Hitler movement that wanted to get rid of him by non-violent means. The majority of its members were rounded up and executed after the July 20, 1944, plot to kill Hitler failed.

Q. What was the code name for the British airborne invasion of Sicily?
  a. Ladybird
  b. Ladbroke
  c. Ladbrine

A. Ladbroke.

Q. Which Pacific amphibious invasion was nicknamed Love Day by the U.S. Marines?

A. The April 1, 1945, invasion of Okinawa (Operation Iceberg), because of the moderate to light resistance at first.

Q. What did the British come to call the destruction of secret papers in Cairo on the day it appeared that Rommel would soon overrun the Egyptian capital?

A. Ash Wednesday, because they burned everything and anything they could, rather than chance it falling into German hands.

Q. What was the code name of the RAF plan to raid the prison in Amiens, France, in 1944 in the hope the disruption would result in Allied escapes?

A. Operation Jericho, which succeeded in permitting more than 245 persons to escape. Many of them were facing death sentences from the Gestapo.

Q. What was the Allied code name for the Philippine Islands?
  a. Excalibur
  b. Excelsior
  c. Expedient

A. Excelsior.

The War on Land

Q. Identify the most decorated unit ever in U.S. history.

A. The 442nd Regimental Combat Team, whose motto was "Go for Broke," consisted of Japanese-American volunteers, won 4,667 major medals, awards and citations, including 560 Silver Stars — 28 of which had oak-leaf clusters — 4,000 Bronze Stars, 52 Distinguished Service Crosses and one Medal of Honor, plus 54 other decorations. It also held the distinction of never having a case of desertion. The majority of soldiers in this unit served while their relatives in the U.S. were being held in the infamous detention centers and camps created by the panic after Pearl Harbor.

Q. Name the only two professional sports that were prohibited during the war.

A. Automobile racing, because of its consumption of fuel, and horse racing, which was ruled as nonessential to the war effort.

Q. Who was Winston Churchill's double?

A. Alfred Chenfalls, who was killed in the same plane crash that took the life of actor Leslie Howard. (Volume 1, page 76)

FACT The American flag first flown over Berlin in July 1945 had also flown over the U.S. Capitol in Washington the day the U.S. declared war on Japan, December 8, 1941. (Volume 1, page 2)

Q. Identify the two German divisions that made up the Afrika Korps.
A. The 5th Light (which became the 21st Panzer) and the 15th Panzer. Erwin Rommel was named commander on February 6, 1941, of only these two divisions. Later his command included, in addition to the Afrika Korps, the 90th Light and six Italian divisions. He arrived in Tripoli on February 12, 1941.

Q. Who was Adolf Hitler's favorite actress?
    a. Shirley Temple
    b. Marlene Dietrich
    c. Greta Garbo
    d. Gloria Swanson
A. Der Fuehrer liked Greta Garbo.

Q. Identify the major U.S. city mayor who made propaganda broadcasts to the Italians urging them to dispose of Mussolini and join the Allied cause?
A. Fiorello LaGuardia of New York City, an American veteran of the First World War.

Q. Name the legendary U.S. industrialist whose framed photograph was frequently seen on Adolf Hitler's desk.
A. Automotive pioneer Henry Ford, who also kept a framed photo of the Nazi leader on his desk in Dearborn, Michigan. In *Mein Kampf* Hitler included some anti-Semitic views attributed to Ford.

Q. Name the only major league baseball player who served in both world wars.
A. Hank Gowdy, who was a member of the New York Giants and Boston Braves between 1910 and 1930.

Q. Who designed the camouflage print for U.S. service uniforms?
A. Norvell Gillespie, the garden editor of *Better Homes and Gardens* magazine. (Volume 1, page 83)

FACT German rocket expert Wernher von Braun failed mathematics and physics while attending school at the French Gymnasium. However, he subsequently mastered both subjects in later years.

Q. Who preceded General Hideki Tojo as prime minister of Japan?

A. Prince Konoye, who resigned in October 1941 after President Franklin D. Roosevelt rejected his plea for a summit meeting. Both the prince and Emperor Hirohito were anxious to avert war, while Tojo and the Supreme War Council thought war was the only solution to Japan's problems. In photo above, Tojo is seen in captivity awaiting the Tokyo War Crimes trials.

Exclusive Photo by George Schroth

FACT The Allies tried 199 persons during the International War Crimes trials at Nuremberg. Of these thirty-six received death sentences, five took their own lives while the trials were in progress, twenty-two were sentenced to life in prison, 103 got lesser terms and thirty-eight were acquitted. Crimes against humanity performed in occupied countries accounted for other trials in the specific countries involved for other defendants.

Q. Who wrote the script for the recruitment film *Women in Defense* that was intended to encourage female enlistments?

A. Mrs. Franklin D. Roosevelt. Katharine Hepburn did the narration.

Q. Identify the first member of the U.S. Senate to enlist and face combat in the war.

A. Senator Henry Cabot Lodge II of Massachusetts, who served in North Africa. Representative Lyndon B. Johnson of Texas was the first congressman to enlist. (Volume 1, page 93)

Q. Identify the wartime leader who rejected a German offer of a prisoner exchange that included the return of his own son.

A. Joseph Stalin. His son Jacob eventually died in a German prison camp.

Q. Who produced the Voice of America radio show?
>   a. Arthur Godfrey
>   b. John Houseman
>   c. Edward R. Murrow

A. John Houseman, best known now for his investment commercials on TV and as the star of the TV series *Paper Chase*.

Q. Identify the Republican member of President Franklin D. Roosevelt's Cabinet during the war who had been the GOP vice presidential candidate in 1936 against the Roosevelt ticket.

A. A World War I Army veteran who attained the rank of major (but was constantly called Colonel afterwards for some unknown reason), Secretary of the Navy Frank Knox was one of two prominent Republicans in Democrat Roosevelt's Cabinet. The other was Secretary of War Henry L. Stimson, a former Rough Rider with Teddy Roosevelt.

Q. Identify the avenue in Paris where the Germans marched 250 troops behind a band almost every day during the occupation.

A. The Champs-Elysées, playing military music. The tune most frequently heard was Prussia's Glory. In photo above, U.S. troops follow the same route of march immediately following the City of Light's liberation.

U.S. Army Photo

Q. Name the high-ranking military and political figure that Heinrich Himmler discredited by presenting evidence showing his wife to be a former prostitute.

A. Field Marshal and Reich War Minister Werner von Blomberg. Hitler had been a witness at his wedding only weeks earlier. The scandal forced Blomberg's resignation.

Q. How did Himmler manage to eliminate German Army Chief of Staff General Werner von Fritsch?

A. With fabricated evidence "proving" he was a homosexual.

Q. Name the Nazi whose wife cited thirty women as mistresses when she tried unsuccessfully to divorce him in 1938.

A. Joseph Goebbels. Hitler forbade the divorce.

Q. Identify the wartime boat designer/manufacturer who earned a reputation for building boats for rum runners and bootleggers prior to the war.

A. A. J. Higgins, Jr., whose most touted effort was the Higgins Boat landing craft.

Q. Identify the U.S. Marine Corps Japanese language interpreter who is credited with capturing over half of the prisoners on Saipan in June and July 1944.

A. Guy Gabaldan, whose military exploits were depicted in the movie *Hell to Eternity*. Gabaldan was with the 2nd Marine Division. (Volume 1, pages 105 and 199)

Q. What was the highest German decoration in the war?
A. The Knight's Cross.

FACT Adolf Hitler married his mistress Eva Braun shortly before they allegedly took their own lives. However, no less than five other top-ranking Nazis had mistresses but failed to follow suit. The men, and their women, were:

      Heinrich Himmler and Hedwig Potthast
      Joseph Goebbels and Lida Baarova
      Martin Bormann and Manja Behrens
      Josef Mengele and Irma Griese
      Adolf Eichmann and Maria Masenbucher

FACT The cavalry remained a functioning part of U.S. armed forces throughout the war with the continued operation of cavalry school at Fort Riley, Kansas. However, what is believed to be the last mounted action involved the 26th Cavalry Regiment against the Japanese in January 1942 in the Philippines as U.S. forces retreated to Bataan. During the siege of the fortress cavalry horses were slaughtered for food.

Q. Name the dog who was a USMC mascot and made the amphibious landings on Iwo Jima with the 4th and 5th Marine divisions.

A. George, who was apparently one of several hundred canine mascots U.S. troops took into combat with them. In photo above, two U.S. Army servicemen rest somewhere in the Pacific with a four-legged friend.

Exclusive Photo Courtesy of Mrs. Frank F. Wall

Q. Who was Fritz Kuhn?
A. Chief of the German American Bund.

Q. Name the first Hollywood actor drafted in the war.
    a. Ronald Reagan
    b. Jimmy Stewart
    c. Clark Gable
    d. Sterling Holloway
A. Sterling Holloway.

Q. Identify the eight British air and naval bases transferred to the U.S. by agreement on March 27, 1941.
A. The eight were Antigua, Bahamas, Bermuda, British Guiana, Jamaica, St. Lucia, Newfoundland and Trinidad.

Q. Identify the two French units that fought so bravely that the German victors gave them an honor guard after the battle for Lille, Loos and Haubourdin.
A. The French IV and V Corps. German General Waeger was so impressed that he permitted French General Molinier to retain his staff car. The incident took place after the successful German campaign against Cassel and Monts des Flandres in May 1940.

Q. Identify the only U.S. army that had written orders mentioning Berlin as an objective.
A. The Ninth Army in a document entitled "Letter of Instructions, #20." Commanding Lieutenant General William Simpson was aware that other armies in the Twelfth Army Group (First and Third) had received instructions that did not include the phrase "advance on Berlin." He believed his army had been selected to beat the Russians, and everybody else, there.

Q. Identify the first German army to surrender to U.S. troops.
A. On May 9, 1945, the Fifth Panzer Army under the command of General Gustav von Vaerst surrendered to General Omar Bradley, one day after Germany officially surrendered in the war. (The first German army to surrender in the war was the Sixth Army under Field Marshal von Paulus, which surrendered to the Russians at Stalingrad.)

Q. Why were so many senior German officers absent from their units when the Normandy invasion began?

A. They had been summoned to Rennes in Brittany for war games, which were to include a paratroop assault and sea landings at Normandy. The date of the games was June 6.

> **FACT** The first GI barber shop on the Normandy beaches was operated by Victor Lombardo approximately 1,000 feet from the shoreline on Utah Beach. In photo above, Lombardo, who was with the Quartermaster Corps, tends to the needs of dental technician Sam Kravetz of the 1st Engineer Special Brigade.
>
> *Exclusive Photo Courtesy of Murray D. Lombardo*

FACT Of the nearly 3 million Allied troops massed in England for the Normandy invasion, 176,475 personnel actually took part in the initial assaults. They brought support equipment including 20,111 vehicles.

Q. Who made the greatest advances on D-Day, the British or Americans?
A. The British. However, they were unable to capture their principal objective, Caen, for more than six weeks.

Q. What was German Army strength in the Cherbourg area of Normandy on D-Day?
A. Approximately 40,000 men.

Q. What were Allied casualties during the twenty-four hours of D-Day?
A. Between 10,000 and 12,000, of which 6,603 were U.S.; 946 Canadians; and the rest British, French and other Allies. The British have never released official figures.

Q. What were German Army Group B casualties in the first month after the Normandy invasion?
A. According to its commander, Rommel, "28 generals, 354 commanders and approximately 250,000 men."

Q. What was the purpose of the 2nd and 5th Rangers' assignment to scale the nearly vertical 100-foot cliffs on Normandy at Pointe du Hoc?
A. Their objective was to knock out six long-range guns capable of hitting either Omaha or Utah Beach. Of the 225 Rangers who participated, 135 were casualties. Ironically the guns had not yet been installed and were still en route.

Q. Which sector of "Bloody Omaha" Beach had the fiercest fighting?
A. Dog Green. Casualties, such as those of Company C of the 2nd Ranger Battalion, which lost fifty-eight of its seventy men, were widespread.

FACT The Allies used a plastic explosive that resembled cow manure in appearance as a road vehicle land mine.

Q. Identify the first U.S. military forces to set foot inside Tokyo.
A. Admiral Lewis Smith Parks, commander of Submarine Squadron
Twenty, arrived at Tokyo to participate in the surrender ceremonies
and made a secret visit to the Emperor's Palace before General
Douglas MacArthur. In photo above, tank 30 of A Company is seen
at Sasebo Naval Base. It was the first tank ashore in the amphibious
landing of the U.S. 5th Marine Division at Kyushu. Hitching a ride
on the tank are members of the infantry of the 26th Regiment, 5th
Division.

U.S. Marine Corps Photo

Q. What is the name of the French hamlet in Normandy behind the sand dunes and the beach the Allies code-named Utah?
A. La Madeleine.

Q. Who appeared on Sword Beach on D-Day to welcome the invading British troops?
A. The mayor of Colleville-sur-Orne, replete with a bright brass helmet and proper formal clothes. His village was about one mile inland.

Q. Name the ten U.S. Japanese Relocation Center camps where U.S. citizens were sent following the panic of Pearl Harbor and held throughout the war.
A. The ten camps were Gila River and Poston in Arizona; Manzanar and Tule Lake in California; Granada, Colorado; Topaz, Utah; Heart Mountain, Wyoming; Minidoka, Idaho; and Rohwer and Jerome in Arkansas. (Volume 1, page 73)

Q. Which member of Hitler's inner circle was born in Cairo, Egypt?
A. Rudolf Hess.

Q. Identify the first person executed by the British for treason during the war.
A. George T. Armstrong, a sailor in the Royal Navy who passed on information to the Germans via their consul in New York. Captured by the FBI he was turned over to the British and was hanged on July 9, 1941.

Q. Name the first member of Parliament killed in the war.
A. Ronald Cartland, who died in 1940. He was the brother of romance novelist Barbara Cartland. She, in turn, is related by marriage to Princess Diana, wife of British Crown Prince Charles.

FACT John Amery, son of British Parliament member Leopold Amery, was executed in 1945 for treason after trying to recruit British internees in Germany to fight against the Soviet Union. It was his father's stinging denunciation of Prime Minister Neville Chamberlain that ushered in the collapse of that government. (Volume 1, page 62)

FACT A handful of British advocates of tank and armored warfare prior to war were not taken as seriously as it was later proved they should have been. Captain B. H. Liddell Hart, Colonel J. F. C. Fuller, General Sir Frederick (Tim) Pile and General Sir Percy Hobart were among them. The outspoken Hobart managed to offend his superiors to such a degree that he was actually forced to serve as a corporal in his local Home Guard during a period when his theories were considered unfounded. He is credited with developing flame-throwing tanks, ditch-crossing tanks, pillbox-smashing tanks and others, which his detractors called "funnies." The Germans, however, appreciated and copied many of his ideas.

Q. Where and when was the greatest tank battle in history?

A. At the Kursk salient in the Soviet Union between the Germans and Russians from July 4 to 22, 1943. More than 3,600 tanks were involved.

FACT The cost of an American M-3 tank in 1941 was under $34,000, just about the U.S. price of a Mercedes in 1981. However, by 1981 the price tag on an XMI tank was over $2 million.

U.S. Army Photo

> **FACT** Nazi Germany built two giant tanks called Mammoths that they
> tested in June 1944. These vehicles were thirty feet long, weighed
> 185 tons and had steel plating 9½ inches thick. Unfortunately
> they ruined any roads they were driven on, crushing cobblestone
> into powder. When they traveled on dirt roads they sank deep
> into the earth. Designed by automaker Dr. Ferdinand Porsche,
> they were destroyed by the Germans at Kummersdorf in late 1944
> so they would not fall into the hands of the advancing Allies.

Q. Name the U.S. Army chaplain that General George S. Patton
ordered to write a prayer for good weather.

A. While Patton was preparing to move units of the Third Army toward
Bastogne to relieve the 101st Airborne during the Battle of the
Bulge in 1944, he ordered Chaplain James H. O'Neill to write a
prayer so the weather would improve and he could make rapid progress. The prayer was written, Patton read it, the weather improved
and the chaplain was given a Bronze Star by the general.

Q. Identify the only two types of tanks that had six-man crews.

A. The U.S. M3 Lee/Grant 31-ton, 18′6″ long tanks (4,924 made) and
the German 74.8-ton, 22′3″ long Elephant (90 made). The Elephant
had the lowest production of any tank in the war.

Q. What was the strength of a German Leichte Divisionen (light division) as compared to a panzer division?

A. A light division had two motorized rifle regiments and a single tank
battalion for a total of 80 tanks. A panzer division had 324 tanks.
Figures given are tactical strengths in 1940 and may have
changed as the war progressed.

> **FACT** The German panzer divisions' swift victories over the French in
> 1940 were partially due to the tactical planning and refueling
> techniques they employed. French tanks were slowly refueled by
> tankers while the Germans accomplished the same results using
> handier "jerricans." During the battle for the Meuse, for instance,
> the French 1st Armored Division (156 tanks) was virtually wiped
> out as it refueled. It was surprised and attacked by the XV Panzer
> Corps.

FACT The Soviets had more than four times the number of tanks than the Germans. In all, Russia used more than 21,000 tanks in the war.

Q. What distinction does Nazi Rudolf Hess hold with regard to the Tower of London.

A. He is the last person to have been incarcerated there. (Volume 1, pages 106, 144 and 195)

Q. Identify the first British officer to win a Victoria Cross in the war.

A. Army Captain Harold Ervine-Andrews of the Lancashire Regiment at Dunkirk in 1940.

Q. In which area of combat readiness did France and Germany have the greatest contrast at the outbreak of war in 1939?

A. The French had seven motorized divisions, while the German Army had only four. A fifth, however, was made up of the Waffen (military) SS. In addition, Germany had six panzer (armored) divisions for which the French had nothing comparable. In photo above, a tank that did not survive the liberation of Paris in August 1944 rests on the fringe of the Place de la Concorde.

Author's Collection

FACT General Hideki Tojo resigned as Japanese Premier on July 20, 1944, the same day that the German generals' plot to kill Hitler failed. (Volume 1, pages 55 and 85)

Q. Where were the few remaining survivors who were arrested for the plot to kill Hitler kept?

A. Lehrterstrasse Prison, in Berlin. Approximately 7,000 persons were initially arrested. Just over 5,000 were quickly executed.

Q. After war began in Europe, when was the first attempt made on Hitler's life?

A. Slightly over two months later, November 8, 1939, when a bomb exploded in a Munich beer hall, killing nine people. Hitler had left the area less than a half hour earlier.

Q. Who was the last person to see Adolf Hitler alive?

A. His valet, Heinz Linge.

Q. Identify the two cities selected to be host to the Olympics in 1940 and 1944.

A. After Berlin in 1936, Tokyo was to host the 1940 games while London had been selected for the event in 1944. Neither was held.

Q. Name the two Jews on the German Olympic Team of 1936.

A. Rudi Ball on the soccer squad and Helene Mayer in fencing.

Q. Identify the first U.S. outpost to fall to enemy hands in the war.

A. Guam, where 153 U.S. Marines armed with nothing larger than .30-caliber machine guns tried to hold back a Japanese invasion force of 6,000 troops in early December 1941. It was not recaptured until August 1944.

Q. Who was Hitler's personal secretary?

A. Gertrude Junge.

FACT A plan to assassinate Adolf Hitler by using a telescopic rifle was termed "unsportsmanlike" by the British in 1940. The idea was proffered by Lieutenant General Sir Frank Mason-MacFarlane, who had been a military attaché in Berlin prior to hostilities.

Q. Who was the first U.S. Army paratrooper killed in combat?
A. Private John T. MacKall, who was killed by aerial gunfire while still in the aircraft taking him to the North Africa Theater of Operations. The plane that attacked was French.

Q. Name the first U.S. airborne officer killed in combat.
A. Lieutenant Walter W. Kiser, USMC, on Gavutu Island in August 1942 when the 1st Parachute Battalion landed on the northeast coast. However, the 1st Parachute Battalion invaded via the sea rather than from aircraft, since the island was too far for a controlled air drop.

FACT Mohammed Riza Pahlevi became the Shah of Iran upon the abdication of his father on September 16, 1941. He remained in power until January 16, 1979, when he was asked to leave the country by a newly formed government under Shahpur Bakhtiar. During World War II, Iran proved to be a desired R and R stop for Allied troops. Here a U.S. MP makes the rounds of a brothel in Arak in October 1944.

U.S. Army Photo

FACT The American armed forces were the highest paid in the war. A U.S. Army staff sergeant earned as much as a British Army captain. A U.S. private serving overseas earned sixty dollars per month, roughly three times as much as his British counterpart. (Volume 1, page 60)

Q. Identify the first airborne attack using sappers.
A. The German assault on Fort Eben Emael, Belgium, led by Captain Walter Koch. His engineer troops captured nine installations during the first ten minutes in what was considered the strongest fort in the world. Koch and the 424 men of his unit used 42 gliders to execute the stunning assault in May 1940.

Q. Name the Polish division that fought on the side of the Soviets.
A. The Kosciusko Division.

Q. Name the German divisions made up of pro-Nazi Dutch and Norwegian volunteers.
A. Nederland and Nordland.

Q. Name the Nazi concentration camp commander who was tried and found guilty by the SS of stealing from the state and then executed.
A. Karl Koch, commander of Buchenwald. He was charged and convicted of diverting personal property of inmates for his own use.

Q. Identify the last U.S. Marine to leave Wake Island in 1941 (he was also the first to return when it was surrendered).
A. Colonel Walter Bayler, who left aboard a U.S. Navy PBY on December 21, 1941, and returned in September 1945.

Q. Who was Hitler's interpreter?
A. Dr. Paul Schmidt, who assisted during Hitler's meetings with Chamberlain, Mussolini, Franco and Japanese Foreign Minister Yosuke Matsuoka.

Q. Which U.S. unit holds the distinction of being the first ground troops to see combat in Asia?
A. The 5307th Composite Group, known as Merrill's Marauders.

Q. How many Japanese troops were evacuated from Guadalcanal in February 1942?

A. Approximately 12,000 troops were rescued by destroyers from Cape Esperance at the northwestern end of the island. Efforts to use transport ships proved unsuccessful. Above, the wrecked *Kyusyu Maru* is beached, while at bottom, trio of GI's pause for a photo session near another Japanese transport.

Exclusive Photos by Ben Lebowitz

Q. Identify the German unit that wore enemy uniforms in order to capture objectives at Gennep, Nijmegen and Roermond, in Holland, in 1940.

A. The Brandenburg Detachment, which was specially trained in such tactics. They succeeded in capturing the bridge at Gennep but failed in the other two attempts. As the war progressed, such tactics became much more regular by both the Allies and Axis powers.

Q. Name the only two Latin American nations that had combat troops in action during the war.

A. Brazil and Mexico.

Q. Name the Philippine President who had been his country's most decorated soldier in the war.

A. Ferdinand E. Marcos.

Q. Who headed the Philippine puppet government established by the Japanese in October 1943?

A. Jose Laurel, a wealthy nationalist known for his anti-American sentiments.

Q. Who was the ranking Canadian overseas commander in the war?

A. General Andrew G. McNaughton.

Q. Name the only U.S. corps commander in the war who was a National Guard officer.

A. Major General Raymond S. McLain, who commanded the XIX Corps.

Q. Which country holds the distinction of capturing the greatest number of enemy troops in one place at one time?

A. Germany. It captured more than 500,000 Russian troops at Kiev on September 16, 1941. (Soviet figures claim 527,000 captured while German files indicate over 660,000.

FACT The U.S. Marine Corps strength when the country entered the war in December 1941 was 65,000 officers and enlisted men. It hit its peak strength in August 1945, when the total had risen to 485,113. At full strength the Corps had six divisions and five aircraft wings. In addition, 23,000 women served in the Corps.

Q. Identify the Marine Corps unit that was assigned the task of capturing Mount Suribachi, Iwo Jima, in February 1945.

A. Colonel Harry B. Liversedge's 28th Marines. It was personnel from this unit that raised the American flag, a scene captured so dramatically by Associated Press photographer Joe Rosenthal. The photo won the Pulitzer Prize in journalism for Rosenthal and inspired the U.S. Marine Corps War Memorial by sculptor Felix de Weldon.

Q. Who was General Eisenhower able to reach on his red, green and black telephones from his bedroom in England?

A. The red phone scrambled calls with Washington. On the green phone he reached Winston Churchill. His chief of staff was the voice on the black phone.

Q. Who was the Soviet Union's top propagandist?

A. Ilya Ehrenburg, who is credited with writing the infamous "Kill! Kill!" anti-German copy that was printed and broadcast to Soviet troops. Sign above reflects a similar sentiment by U.S. troops against the Japanese. Scene was on Guadalcanal.

Exclusive Photo by Ben Lebowitz

Q. Where and when was the first stand-up land fight between the U.S. and the Japanese?

A. At Tenaru River on Guadalcanal. It revealed that the Marines were more than able to fight the Japanese on their chosen terrain and beat them.

Q. Identify the Hollywood director who won two Academy Awards for documentaries he made during the war.

A. John Ford, who won Oscars for *December Seventh* and *The Battle of Midway*. (Ford filmed Doolittle's planes as they left the USS *Hornet* for the raid on Tokyo.)

Q. Identify the first U.S. correspondent to land on the Normandy beaches on D-Day, June 6, 1944.

A. Warren H. Kennet, a military writer with the now defunct *Newark News* (New Jersey), had the honor. A 44-year newspaper veteran, Kennet died in March 1982. He also had been the only newsman present when the German 19th and 24th armies surrendered to New Jersey's 44th Infantry during the war.

Q. Identify the U.S. newsman credited with creating the nickname Merrill's Marauders as it applied to the 5307th Composite Group.
- a. Ernie Pyle
- b. Bill Mauldin
- c. Jim Shepley
- d. Edward R. Murrow

A. Jim Shepley of Time-Life, Inc.

Q. How did the premature message of the liberation of Paris come to be broadcast?

A. CBS newsman Charles Collingwood had tape-recorded the story in advance and forwarded it to London for use at the appropriate time. However a mixup resulted in its being broadcast on August 23, 1944, two full days before the actual liberation. It was carried throughout the world.

FACT All eleven starting members of Montana State University's 1940–41 football team were killed in the war.

FACT Iva Ikuko Toguri d'Aquino was an American citizen who was visiting a sick relative in Japan when war broke out. A graduate of UCLA with a degree in zoology, she chose to work in the Japanese Broadcasting Company rather than be assigned to work in a factory. Although she insists she was not Tokyo Rose, she received a ten-year prison term for treason after the war plus a $10,000 fine. President Gerald Ford pardoned her in January 1977. The value of the sultry messages broadcast to U.S. troops in the Pacific by Tokyo Rose has always been questioned, since many servicemen enjoyed the music she played and found her remarks laughable. Iva d'Aquino is seen here in custody, shortly after the war ended, tending to a garden in the prison compound.

Exclusive Photo by George Schroth

Q. Name the *Stars and Stripes* staffer who along with another GI entered Berlin in April 1945, before Germany surrendered.

A. Ernie Leiser, who was accompanied by an Army soldier identified as Mack Morris.

Q. Who was Colonel Blimp?

A. The British cartoon character often used to satirize life in the Empire. He was the product of David Low and appeared in the *Evening Standard*.

Q. Identify the British cartoon character used in World War I that was also employed in World War II.

A. Created by cartoonist Bruce Bairnsfather, "Old Bill" brought the same kind of morale and visual points to British military and civilian personnel as Bill Mauldin's "Willie and Joe" did to U.S. troops.

Q. Who created the cartoon character Sad Sack?

A. George Baker, while on the staff of *Yank* magazine. He had worked for Walt Disney prior to being drafted. His better-known Disney animated films include *Bambi*, *Dumbo* and *Pinocchio*. (Vol I, page 127)

Q. Identify the German newspaper reporter who spied on the Japanese for the Russians, was captured in 1941 and hanged in 1944.

A. Richard Sorge, considered by many to have been the most productive spy up till that time.

Q. Identify the American author who managed to get on a Nazi death list because of his treatment of Adolf Hitler's sex life in the book *Inside Europe*.

A. John Gunther, who outlived Hitler and the Nazis.

Q. What was the name of the 32-page booklet all U.S. servicemen received prior to arriving in Britain?

A. *A Short Guide to Great Britain*, which warned of such social blunders as stealing a British soldier's girl and spending money too freely. It also noted: "The British don't know how to make a good cup of coffee. You don't know how to make a good cup of tea. It is an even swap."

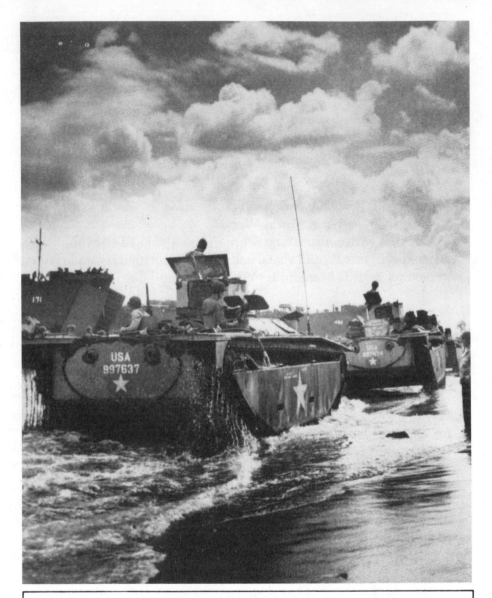

FACT More than 56,000 Japanese died during the 1944 campaign to liberate the Philippines by the Allies. Allied losses were slightly under 3,000. Only 389 Japanese were taken prisoner. In photo above, two huge U.S. Army Alligators move forward toward Japanese positions on Leyte Island. The U.S. Navy LSTs in the picture were manned by Coast Guard personnel.

U.S. Coast Guard Photo

> **FACT** Adolf Hitler became a millionaire as a result of the royalties he earned from his book *Mein Kampf*. The first part of the book was written while he was in Landsberg Prison in 1925, but he added considerably more afterward. Once he came to power, Hitler arranged for copies to be given to newlyweds in the Reich, and it was this widespread distribution that increased his wealth.

Q. Identify the Swedish businessman who spied on the Nazis for the U.S. and was the subject of the book and movie titled *The Counterfeit Traitor*.

A. Eric Erickson, who died in January 1983 at the age of ninety-two. He was so convincing in his role as a pro-Nazi that he lost most of his friends. He was instrumental in passing German synthetic oil secrets on to the Allies. After the war he was honored for his work and invited to meet President Harry S. Truman.

Q. In what city did Anne Frank live when she was caught?

A. Amsterdam, Holland.

Q. Name the city Hitler intended to designate as the new German capital when the war ended.

A. Linz, Austria, his boyhood city.

Q. What was the distance the Afrika Korps was forced to cover in its retreat from El Alamein?

A. Approximately 1,750 miles. It was one of the longest retreats in history.

Q. Where were the majority of German torpedoes manufactured?

A. In the Paris suburb of Saint-Cloud in an underground factory code-named Pilz (mushroom). Though Germany required fewer torpedoes after 1943, Pilz production did not drop off. By the time Paris was liberated, Pilz contained an enormous stockpile of these never-to-be-used weapons.

Q. Who is credited with being the leader of the first organized resistance movement in occupied Europe?

A. General Draza Mihajlovic of Yugoslavia. He not only fought the Nazis, but at times also fought against Tito's partisans.

FACT Martin Bormann, who was sentenced to death in absentia by the
Nuremberg War Crimes trials and whose whereabouts are still
undetermined, began a program of transporting gold, jewels and
art treasures to South America toward the end of 1943. The boo-
ty was transported in U-boats, and much of it is thought to have
gotten to Argentina, where it was used to finance the later ar-
rivals and provide sanctuary for numerous Nazis who are believed
to still be there.

Q. Where did the French officially surrender to the Germans on June
21, 1940?

A. At Compiègne and, by Hitler's request, in the same train car in which
the French had accepted Germany's surrender on "the eleventh hour
of the eleventh day of the eleventh month" in 1918. In this photo
Hitler and other ranking Nazis are seen leaving the train car.

Ullstein Photo

> **FACT** Over 100 Soviet combat photographers lost their lives filming the war. One effort, the total filming of twenty-four hours of the war on June 13, 1943, involved nearly 250 cameramen who recorded the conflict from 140 vantage points and produced an eight-reel film that packed movie houses in the U.S. and Britain as well as Russia. The title: *Day of War*.

Q. Besides Lidice, name the other Czech town that the Nazis destroyed in revenge for the assassination of SS General Reinhard Heydrich.

A. Levzacky. (Volume 1, page 85)

Q. Where were General Eisenhower's headquarters during the preparation of the North Africa invasion?

A. Eisenhower set up headquarters on Gibraltar on November 5, 1942.

Q. What was located in the Collège Moderne et Technique in Reims, France?

A. Supreme Headquarters of the Allied Expeditionary Forces (SHAEF), Eisenhower's actual office.

Q. Name the U.S. general who was headquartered in the Ivory Tower.

A. General Douglas MacArthur, in Port Moresby, Papua.

Q. What building, described as a miniature Versailles, once stood at 73 Wilhelmstrasse in Berlin?

A. The palace that had served as the official residence of German presidents prior to the Third Reich. Hitler's Chancellery was at 77 Wilhelmstrasse.

Q. Which branch of the German military had its headquarters at Shell House in Berlin?

A. The Oberkommando der Kriegsmarine (Navy High Command).

Q. Where was the first Jewish ghetto established in Poland in World War II?

A. In Lodz. Totally enclosed and kept secure by the Nazi SS, it came into being in April 1940.

> **FACT** The largest Japanese spy ring was not in the U.S. but in Mexico, where it kept tabs on the U.S. Atlantic Fleet.

FACT The hands on the clock tower at Hiroshima, Japan, stopped at
8:15 A.M. on August 1, 1945. Coincidentally, five days later at the
same time, the first atom bomb ever released over a populated
area struck the city. The photo above is one of the earliest taken
after U.S. troops entered the city and shows the ruins of the
domed Agricultural Exhibition Hall in a rare angle from behind.
It remains today as a memorial for the first victims of an atomic
attack.

Exclusive Photo by George Schroth

FACT Japan tried to build an atomic bomb during the war and the Nazis agreed to help them. However, the Allied navies were able to prevent shipments of uranium from reaching Japan. Prime Minister Hideki Tojo reportedly ordered Toranosuke Kawashina, a former army colonel, to launch an atom bomb project in January 1943, because Tojo felt the war might be decided by atomic bombs. Germany actually sent two tons of uranium to Japan via U-boat but it was sunk before arriving. The top nuclear physicist on the Japanese project was Hideki Yukawa, who won the Nobel Prize in 1949 for his discoveries about the atom. His nuclear energy research had begun in 1941.

Q. Identify the town in Germany where the Nazis conducted efforts to produce an atomic chain reaction.

A. Haigerloch.

Q. Identify the city in the southern United States that employed illiterates as sanitation men as part of national security during the war.

A. Oak Ridge, Tennessee, where the government conducted atomic research projects. It was believed that if classified information that might escape shredding found its way into the garbage collection, illiterate sanitation employees would be unable to compromise security.

Q. Where was the first German killed in Paris by the underground? When?

A. In the Barbes metro station in 1942. He was shot by a Frenchman, Pierre Fabien.

FACT The same day the French government of Paul Reynaud fell in Paris (June 16, 1940) Frédéric Joliot-Curie, the son-in-law of Madame Curie, watched the British ship *Broompark* sail from France with 410 pounds of heavy water that he had removed from Norway. Joliot-Curie had done experiments in producing an explosion from atomic fission, which required heavy water. During the insurrection in Paris in August 1944, Joliot-Curie contributed sulfuric acid and potassium chlorate for Molotov Cocktails he and others would use against the Germans. His efforts and earlier experiments with atomic fission were considered a vital link in the eventual production of an atomic bomb.

FACT On August 7, 1945, the day after the U.S. dropped the first atom
bomb, Stalin summoned five top Soviet physicists and ordered
them to catch up with the U.S. in atomic research and development. On July 10 1949, the U.S.S.R. detonated its first atom
bomb.

Q. Who was the first non-Chinese general ever to be in command of
Chinese troops?
A. General Joseph W. (Vinegar Joe) Stilwell, of the United States. He
commanded the Chinese Fifth and Sixth armies in Burma in 1942.
Waiting to board an aircraft that will take them to Chungking, China,
in this September 1944 photo are Stilwell, Major General Patrick J.
Hurley and Major General Daniel I. Sultan.

U.S. Army Photo

> **FACT** General von Senger und Etterlin, the German commander responsible for defending Monte Cassino, was a lay member of the Benedictines. The monastery was also Benedictine, and the only area to survive without damage was the crypt where St. Benedict is buried.

Q. Who had been selected to head the German government by the plotters in the July 20, 1944, failed attempt to kill Adolf Hitler?
    a. Field Marshal Erwin Rommel
    b. Admiral Karl Doenitz
    c. Prince Louis Ferdinand
    d. Admiral Wilhelm Canaris
A. Prince Ferdinand, a co-conspirator in the plot and a high-ranking employee of Lufthansa, who was the grandson of Kaiser Wilhelm II. (Volume 1, page 85)

Q. Who was the German general also considered as Hitler's replacement if the July 20, 1944, plot had been successful.
A. General Ludwig Beck, who had served as chief of staff in 1938 and was openly anti-Nazi.

Q. Name the Israeli general who holds the distinction of being buried at the U.S. Military Academy at West Point.
A. David (Mickey) Marcus, who was a U.S. Army colonel in World War II and afterwards became Israel's first general since biblical times. He was shot by an Israeli soldier in 1948, when he failed to properly identify himself in a restricted area. His life was the subject of the book and movie *Cast a Giant Shadow*.

Q. Identify the church in Prague where the assassins of SS General Reinhard Heydrich hid.
A. Karl Borromaeus Church. (Volume 1, page 85)

Q. Identify the first German general to become a casualty after the Allied invasion of Normandy.
A. Wilhelm Falley, commander of the 91st Infantry Division at Normandy on D-Day, June 6, 1944, was fatally wounded by members of the 508th Parachute Infantry Regiment.

Q. Identify the U.S. Army lieutenant general who was the first choice to be commander of American forces in Europe. (Note: Eisenhower was second choice and got the job when this officer was killed in a plane crash.)

A. Lieutenant General Frank M. Andrews, who was killed in Iceland in 1943.

Q. Identify the first U.S. army activated overseas during the war.

A. The Fifth Army under General Mark Clark.

> **FACT** Bernard Law Montgomery was not Britain's first choice to command the Eighth Army in North Africa. Lieutenant General W. H. E. Gott, who was scheduled to assume command, was killed on August 8, 1942, and Lieutenant General Montgomery was picked as a replacement. By the time Montgomery and U.S. General William K. Harrison, Jr., exchanged pleasantries in England in April 1944, Montgomery had become a British living legend.
>
> *U.S. Army Photo*

> **FACT** General Dwight D. Eisenhower's first choice to command the 21st
> Army Group for Operation Overlord, the Normandy invasion,
> was British General Sir Harold Alexander. However, Prime
> Minister Winston S. Churchill had other plans for the able general
> and overruled Ike. Churchill hoped that Alexander, as commander
> of the 15th Army Group in Italy, could take Rome and eventual-
> ly open the way to the Balkans. As a result the 21st Army Group
> command was given to Bernard Law Montgomery.

Q. Identify the general who was relieved of command of U.S. Army
II Corps after the German victory at Kasserine Pass, North Africa.
A. Major General Lloyd R. Fredenhall.

Q. Identify the U.S. Army general who was removed from command
and reappointed to it the same day during the Battle of the Bulge.
A. General Robert Hasbrouck, 7th Armored Division.

Q. Identify the high-ranking Nazi who became an SS general after being dishonorably discharged from the German Navy.
A. Reinhard Heydrich.

Q. Identify the first U.S. Marine Corps officer to attain four-star rank.
A. General Thomas Holcomb, who commanded the Corps from 1936
to 1944.

Q. Identify the only U.S. Marine Corps officer to ever command a field
army.
A. Major General Roy S. Geiger, a naval aviator, who was second in
command to U.S. Army General Simon B. Buckner, Jr., when
Buckner was killed during the battle for Okinawa. Geiger immediately assumed command of the Tenth Army.

Q. When General Mark Clark's Fifth Army captured Rome from the
south it was only the third time the Eternal City had been successfully assaulted from that direction. *Bonus Question:* Name the other
two conquerors and when they did it.
A. In A.D. 536 General Belisarius of the Eastern Empire became the
first, and the feat was not duplicated until 1849, when Giuseppe
Garibaldi took Rome from the south and ended papal rule.

FACT Kaiser Wilhelm II, who led Germany in World War I, despised
Hitler. However, one of his sons, a devout Nazi, became an SS
general. The Kaiser did, nonetheless, send Hitler a congratulatory
wire after the fall of France. He took particular delight in the
reuse of the old train car as the site of the capitulation. Above,
the Kaiser's statue in Koblenz hangs upside down from its
pedestal. The monument was destroyed during the U.S. Third
Army's battle for the city in 1945.

U.S. Army Photo

Q. Why did Hitler replace General Heinz Guderian as Chief of the General Staff in 1945 as the Allies closed in on Berlin?

A. Because of a confrontation between them on March 27, 1945, in which Guderian told Hitler the frank truth about the strength of the German armies expected to defend Berlin. It has been described as a loud, rough exchange that made others present fear Guderian would be arrested for insubordination.

Q. Identify the three British generals who were captured by Rommel's Afrika Korps when their driver got lost in the desert and drove up to an enemy patrol.

A. Generals Richard N. O'Connor, Philip Neame and Carton de Wiart, on April 6, 1941. O'Connor escaped from an Italian POW camp later in the war and commanded the VIII Corps during the Normandy invasion in June 1944.

Q. What distinction do U.S. Army privates C. H. Kuhl and P. G. Bennett hold?

A. They share the dubious honor of having been slapped by General George S. Patton in 1943. Kuhl was slapped on August 3 and Bennett on August 10.

Q. How many hours after General Douglas MacArthur had been notified of the Pearl Harbor raid was Manila attacked?

A. Between eight and nine hours. Yet, as at air bases in Pearl Harbor, his planes remained on the ground and were easy targets.

Q. Identify the Italian and Greek army commanders who faced each other when Italy invaded Greece on October 28, 1940.

A. General Sebastiano Visconti-Prasca, in command of the Ninth and Eleventh Italian armies and General Alexander Papagos who led the Greek forces. The Italians put nearly 88,000 troops against the Greek forces reported to be 150,000 strong.

FACT U.S. General Douglas MacArthur's mother apparently had a difficult time accepting that her child was a boy. Until he was eight years old she kept him dressed in skirts and wearing his hair in long curls.

FACT Of the 4,800 German troops in Colonel Dietrich von Choltitz's command during the battle of Sebastopol, only 347 survived. As a general, von Choltitz was the commander of Greater Paris, which turned out to be his last command. (Volume 1, pages 18, 48 and 126)

Q. Identify the first German officer to land in Holland and the Low Countries when the invasion started on May 10, 1940.

A. Lieutenant Colonel (later general) Dietrich von Choltitz, hero of Sebastopol and the man who disobeyed Hitler's order to destroy Paris. In this August 26, 1944, photo, von Choltitz is being interrogated by U.S. Army Major Sterling H. Abernathy after Paris was liberated.

U.S. Army Photo

Q. Whom did General von Choltitz relieve as commander of Paris?
A. General Hans von Boinseburg-Lengsfeld.

Q. Identify the German military intelligence officer whom the Russians offered a $250,000 reward for.
A. General Reinhard Gehlen, known as the Spy of the Century, who was an expert on the East. When he lost favor with Hitler he escaped to the West and turned over all his files on the Red Army to the U.S. (Volume 1, page 36)

Q. Name the U.S. general most responsible for creating the hysteria and panic that led to the confinement of Japanese-Americans in relocation centers.
A. Lieutenant General John L. DeWitt who told the Secretary of War that the Japanese in the U.S. were preparing sabotage: "The very fact that no sabotage has taken place to date is a disturbing and confirming indication that such action will be taken...the Japanese race is an enemy race...racial strains are undiluted." The subsequent relocation is one of the darkest moments in the history of the democracy.

Q. Who did the initial planning for the Normandy invasion?
A. Lieutenant General Sir Frederick Morgan, Eisenhower's assistant chief of staff.

Q. Who was the British commander on Crete when the Germans invaded in 1941?
A. General Bernard Freyberg, who controlled a garrison of 42,000 British and Greek troops. He was forced to evacuate within two weeks after the German assaults. About 18,000 troops managed to get off the island.

FACT Polish General Maczek's 10th Armored Brigade, which escaped from Poland after the Nazi victory, managed to escape from France after that country began negotiations with the Germans for an armistice. Maczek marched his troops across France and embarked for England. They returned to France with the Allied invasion of Normandy in 1944. In all 24,300 Poles, 5,000 Czechs and 163 Belgian troops made it to England before the armistice.

Q. Identify the French town where General Charles de Gaulle made his first speech after the Normandy invasion.

A. De Gaulle addressed a gathering at Bayeux, France, on June 14, 1944.

Q. Identify the twenty-nine-year-old Free French general in Paris whom de Gaulle charged with gaining control of the Resistance to avoid an unauthorized insurrection?

A. Jacques Chaban-Delmas.

Q. Who was the commander of the Free French Forces of the Interior (FFI) before the liberation of Paris?

A. General Pierre Koenig.

FACT In an effort to repair relations with French General Charles de Gaulle, Supreme Allied Commander Dwight D. Eisenhower designated the 2nd French Armored Division to head the advance toward the liberation of Paris. It was the only French division in Europe. In this photo Major Jacques Massu and chauffeur prepare to enter the outskirts of the city.

Archives Laffont Photo

Q. Name the first SS general to be given command of an army.
A. General Paul Hausser, who had been a lieutenant general in the regular army before joining the SS. He commanded the 7th Army during the Normandy invasion.

Q. Identify the relatively obscure German general whom Hitler put in command of the invasion of Norway.
A. General Nikolaus von Falkenhorst, who, being told his assignment, studied a travel guidebook before presenting a plan of action to Hitler.

Q. Identify the two U.S. generals who actually directed traffic as the troops from Utah Beach began moving inland.
A. Major General Raymond Barton and Brigadier General Theodore Roosevelt, both of the 4th Division.

Q. What became of the American general who at a cocktail party in London in April 1944 carelessly told other officers that the invasion of Europe would take place before June 15?
A. A classmate of Dwight Eisenhower's, he was demoted to colonel, removed from command and sent back to the U.S. He retired.

Q. What was the fate of the British colonel who in April 1944 hinted to civilian friends that the D-Day landings would take place at Normandy.
A. As with the American general who had also been indiscreet, he was demoted and removed from his command. However, he became a member of Parliament after the war.

Q. Name the German general who was considered the third best panzer commander after Guderian and Rommel.
A. General Hasso von Manteuffel.

FACT Contrary to popular belief, James M. Gavin of the 82nd Airborne Division was not the youngest serviceman to become a general in the U.S. Army during the war. Thirty-four-year-old Gerald J. Higgins became a brigadier general in the 101st Airborne. (Volume 1, page 121)

Q. Identify the de Gaulle who arrived in a liberated Paris before the famous general.

A. His son, Philippe, a lieutenant with the 2nd French Armored.

Q. What was Montgomery's objective in the Sicily campaign?
   a. Palermo
   b. Messina
   c. Agrigento

A. Messina, which was taken by Patton, who also took Palermo, Agrigento and, for that matter, most of Sicily.

Q. Who commanded the First French Army, formed after liberation?

A. General Jean de Lattre de Tassigny. One hundred thousand strong, it was part of General Jacob Devers' Sixth Army Group and marched into Germany over some of the most difficult European countryside including the Black Forest and the Vosges. In this picture, some First Army troops in the Mulhouse area of France in November 1944 decorated a jeep with a captured picture of Hitler to which they added their own sentiments.

U.S. Army Photo

FACT U.S. General Omar Bradley, who graduated from West Point in 1915, did not receive his first field command until after the U.S. entered the war in 1941.

Q. Identify the U.S. general who literally lost his pants while being chased by Vichy French police.
   a. George S. Patton
   b. Maxwell B. Taylor
   c. Mark Clark
A. While running from the police after having made a secret visit to North Africa, and removing his pants prior to jumping into a rowboat which was to take him to a waiting submarine, General Mark Clark lost his trousers.

Q. Who replaced the Tojo government in Japan when it fell after the loss of Saipan?
A. General Kuniaki Koiso headed a cabinet that took over the reins of government.

Q. Where did the unauthorized embroidered insignia patches worn by bazooka paratroopers of the 82nd Airborne come from?
A. They were made by nuns in Trapani, Sicily, after the value of bazooka fire gained new respect. James Gavin, commander of the 505th Regimental Combat Team, ordered them.

Q. Identify the only American to hold the rank of field marshal.
A. General of the Army Douglas MacArthur had the rank bestowed upon him by the Philippine, not U.S., government. However, the five-star rank of U.S. services is equal to that of field marshal. (See table of comparative ranks in Appendix.)

Q. Name the German general from whom Hitler took over as Commander-in-Chief of the German army in December 1941.
A. General Walther von Brauchitsch, who had been CIC since 1938. His popularity with Hitler was at its zenith in the early stages of the war with victories in Poland, France and the Low Countries. Once the difficulties of war against Russia became obvious he fell out of favor. However, his early successes earned him a cover on *Time* magazine in 1939.

Q. Who was the one-armed German general that Hitler pulled out of the Stalingrad campaign?
A. General Hans Hube of the Sixth Army.

Q. Identify the location of the first Japanese beachhead in the Philippines campaign in 1941.
A. At Aparri, in the north of Luzon.

Q. Identify the commander of the U.S. Sixth Army for the invasion of Lingayen Gulf, Luzon Island, the Philippines, in 1945.
A. Lieutenant General Walter Krueger, left, shown prior to the invasion with Vice Admiral Thomas Kinkaid, 7th Fleet commander, aboard one of the ships that would carry U.S. troops against the 250,000-man force of Japanese General Yamashita.

U.S. Army Photo

Q. Who was the Japanese defender of the Philippine archipelago?
A. Field Marshal Hisaichi Terauchi.

Q. Who succeeded Marshal Pietro Badoglio as Italian Army Chief of Staff?
A. Ugo Cavallero. Badoglio resigned as a result of the military failures the Italians suffered in Greece. Cavallero replaced him on December 6, 1940.

Q. What was the highest military award in the Soviet Union?
A. Hero of the Soviet Union.

Q. What rank did gold epaulettes with a one-inch-across star indicate on Russian Army uniforms?
A. Field marshal.

Q. Name the three German field marshals who commanded the trio of army groups that invaded Russia on June 22, 1941.
A. Wilhelm von Leeb, Army Group North; Fedor von Bock, Army Group Center; Gerd von Rundstedt, Army Group South.

Q. Identify the first and last men to be named field marshals by Hitler.
A. Werner von Blomberg was the first in 1936, and Ritter von Greim was the last in 1945. In all, Hitler promoted twenty-five generals to field marshal.

Q. Who was the youngest field marshal in German military history?
A. Erwin Rommel, age 50. Hitler elevated him to the position after his stunning successes in North Africa against the British.

Q. Identify the soldier to whom Hitler gave a three-pound gold baton eighteen inches long.
A. Rommel in 1942. However the field marshal never was seen publicly with it after that.

FACT Axis prisoners of war were, for the most part, treated in accordance with the provisions of the Geneva Convention in British and U.S. prison camps. However, prisoners of war in Russian camps experienced an 85 percent mortality rate.

Q. Name the SS general in Rome whom Adolf Hitler ordered to kidnap Pope Pius XII.

A. General Karl Wolff, the playboy SS chief in Italy. Hitler summoned Wolff to Rastenburg on September 12, 1944, two days after the German occupation of Rome, and told him to "...occupy Vatican City...and take the Pope and the Curia to the North. I do not want him to fall into the hands of the Allies."

FACT After the war, German courts found twenty-five SS and Army generals guilty of war crimes and executed them. The Allied powers sentenced another fifty-seven to death. An astonishing total of 101 committed suicide during the war. As a result of combat deaths, accidents, natural causes and the above-mentioned war-crimes convictions and suicides, Germany lost 901 men who had been general officers during the war years. Above, a Nazi Volkssturm (People's Army) general lies on the floor of the Leipzig City Hall after taking his own life rather than surrendering to the U.S. First Army on April 19, 1945. The scene is eighty miles southwest of Berlin.

Ullstein Photo

Q. How many generals did the U.S. have compared to the Germans?
A. Germany had a total of 3,363 generals during the war while the U.S. had just over 1,500.

Q. Identify the Hungarian dictator whose son was kidnapped by Otto Skorzeny to guarantee Hungary's support of Nazi goals.
A. Admiral Miklos Horthy. (Volume 1, page 80)

Q. Name the two European leaders Hitler earmarked for kidnapping after the successful commando raid in Italy that resulted in the rescue of Mussolini.
A. Pétain of France and Tito of Yugoslavia.

Q. Identify the geographic area that was scheduled along with the Marshall Islands to be the target of the first U.S. offensive against Japan in February 1942.
A. Wake Island. However, lacking aircraft carrier support from the USS *Lexington* (CV-2) because of a refueling problem, the attack was only carried out on the Marshalls.

Q. Who was the Gestapo chief in France in August 1944?
A. Karl Oberg.

Q. Identify the first U.S. serviceman to land from a troopship in Great Britain after the U.S. entered the war.
A. Private First Class Melburn Hencke, on January 26, 1942.

Q. Identify the first U.S. soldier to set foot on French soil once the U.S. got into the war.
A. U.S. Army Corporal Frank M. Koons, who was an American Ranger in the Dieppe, France, raid. The first U.S. soldier to land in France during the Normandy invasion, June 6, 1944, was a member of the 101st Airborne Division Pathfinders, Frank L. Lillyman.

FACT Technical Sergeant Milton Shenton of the U.S. Army's 4th Division had the distinction of being point man for the division when it broke across Utah Beach on D-Day and again when they were part of the forces that liberated Paris.

Q. Identify the American singer voted the most popular by troops during the war.

     a. Bing Crosby

     b. Frank Sinatra (shown above)

     c. Kate Smith

     d. Roy Acuff

A. Country-Western singer Roy Acuff.

Exclusive Photo by Joseph De Caro

FACT The United States is the greatest haven for Nazi war criminals, according to estimates of various organizations that continue to hunt such people. In the first thirty-six years following the end of World War II, the U.S. managed to deport only one accused Nazi while it is estimated that upwards of 3,000 others are still living in the country.

Q. Identify the wartime European monarch who fled the Nazis, joined the RAF, eventually worked in public relations in New York, and is the only European monarch buried in the U.S.

A. King Peter II of Yugoslavia who fled ten days after being crowned king in 1941, when the Nazis invaded his country. The British backed Tito as the leader of postwar Yugoslavia, and Peter thus became a king without a country. He died in Denver, Colorado, on November 4, 1970, and is buried in Libertyville, Illinois.

Q. When was Ethiopian Emperor Haile Selassie returned to his country's throne?

A. On May 5, 1941, exactly five years after the Italians had conquered Addis Ababa, the capital.

Q. Where did the Italian royal family re-establish itself after it fled from Rome in September of 1943?

A. Brindisi, far south of Rome. They feared capture by the Germans whom they had just deserted as allies.

Q. Name the song the U.S. 28th Infantry Division marched to on the Champs-Elysées in Paris when they were requested to march in a liberation parade before resuming their advance.

A. "Khaki Bill."

FACT Less than 10 percent of the people considered war criminals for their part in the Nazi extermination camps have ever been brought to justice. According to the West German government, it took approximately 25,000 people to operate the camps. A small portion of them reached freedom through ODESSA, the secret escape organization for former SS members. However, the vast majority of war criminals passed themselves off as refugees at displaced persons camps when the war ended, thereby gaining freedom.

Q. Identify the first U.S. soldier to cross the Ludendorff Bridge at Remagen and set foot on German soil.

A. Sergeant Alexander A. Drabik, a butcher from Holland, Ohio, led a platoon through a barrage of artillery fire at 4 P.M. on March 7, 1945. He was a member of the 9th Armored Division, First Army. In photo above, Private Leroy Johnson of Lakewood, New York, operates a traffic control telephone to direct traffic across the treadway pontoon bridge from Remagen to Erpel, Germany, on March 17, the same day the Ludendorff bridge crumbled. (Volume 1, page 77)

U.S. Army Photo

> **FACT** In an extraordinary move, unequaled in world history, Britain suggested a union with France that would create a new country out of what had been two. The blueprint for the merger was outlined in the Declaration of Franco-British Union, which General Charles de Gaulle read over a phone from London to French Premier Paul Reynaud. De Gaulle and other Frenchmen worked it out with British leaders in the hope that such a union would bolster the morale of the French and make it impossible for France to negotiate a separate armistice or peace with Germany as long as the British Isles remained free. It never came to pass.

Q. Identify the British diplomat, and future prime minister, who was heavily involved in the Allied plan to capture Rome by using airborne troops.

A. Harold Macmillan. Eisenhower had also given approval for Macmillan to be involved in the actual operation, but it never came to pass.

Q. Who was Lieutenant Colonel Hellmuth Meyer?

A. The senior officer in charge of Germany's counterintelligence staff on the European invasion front prior to and during D-Day. The staff was able to intercept calls by military police jeeps over one hundred miles away in England.

Q. Who was the first public official named by de Gaulle in Paris, even before liberation?

A. Charles Luizet, appointed to replace Prefect of Police Amédée Bussière. Luizet had parachuted into France on August 12. He assumed his job on August 19.

> **FACT** When U.S. troops occupied Sicily they learned that there was a serious interest among some Sicilians in having the island become the forty-ninth state in the U.S. By 1947 the effort had come to the point that a Sicilian bandit named Salvatore Giuliano wrote to President Harry S. Truman and asked for help in liberating Sicily. The movement attracted many nationalists who resented Rome's treatment and also sought protection from what they considered a communist takeover of Italy. The separatist cause became a thing of the past by the 1950s as various leaders were unable to unify and settle differences among themselves.

Q. What location became known as the Argonne of World War II?

A. The Hurtgen Forest near Aachen, Germany, because of the heavy casualties sustained during the campaign. Aachen was the first German city captured by American troops. In the photo above, soldiers of the 2nd Battalion, 26th Infantry, are seen involved in street-by-street fighting in Aachen.

U.S. Army Photo

FACT During the invasion of the Low Countries (May 10, 1940) the German commander of the 22nd Infantry Division, General Graf von Sponeck, was so convinced that he would receive a request for an audience from Dutch Queen Wilhelmina that he set out on the campaign in full-dress uniform. His objective was The Hague and also the submission and cooperation of the Dutch Crown. Sponeck did not get his meeting with the queen but instead was wounded in the fierce battle.

Q. Who followed French Premier Daladier as leader of France when he resigned?

A. Paul Reynaud, who proved to be no better than Daladier in coping with the German war machine. (Reynaud was replaced by Henri Pétain, Marshal of France, hero of Verdun in the First World War, on May 17, 1940.)

Q. Who was Germany's ambassador to France at the time of the liberation of Paris?

A. Otto Abetz.

Q. From where did Vichy French Prime Minister Pierre Laval depart from Paris? How? When?

A. From the Hôtel de Matignon, residence of the country's prime ministers on August 17, 1944. The Germans provided an SS-chauffeured car (a Hotchkiss) to take him to Germany.

Q. Identify the first member of the Vichy French government to be tried and found guilty of collaboration.

A. Former Minister of the Interior Pierre Pucheau, who was tried by a military court in Algiers in 1944 and sentenced to death.

Q. Where was Leon Trotsky killed and how?

A. The Russian revolutionary, who, along with Lenin and Stalin, was an architect of communism in 1917, was killed by a Spanish communist in Mexico City on August 21, 1940.

FACT Neville Chamberlain, whose handling of the early war effort and prewar negotiations led to his resignation, died on November 10, 1940, exactly six months after he was succeeded by Winston Churchill as Prime Minister. (Volume 1, pages 62, 66 and 196)

FACT Gasoline, which played such an important role in halting the German advance during the Battle of the Bulge and was at times considered as precious as water to the Allied and Axis tanks in North Africa, was needed in tremendous quantities. An armored division needed more than eight times as much gasoline as it did food and even an infantry division needed six times more gasoline than food. Convoy above is somewhere in France after D-Day.

U.S. Signal Corps Photo

FACT What is regarded as the highest bounty ever put on a human being, the sum of $1 million, was offered for the capture of Adolf Hitler by U.S. industrialist Samuel H. Church in 1940. The conditions were that Hitler be alive and unharmed and that he be tried by an international court set up by the League of Nations.

Q. When did Italy sign the armistice with the Allies?
A. September 8, 1943.

Q. How many of Berlin's 248 bridges did the Germans destroy to slow down the Russian advance on the city in April 1945?
A. Approximately 120 were destroyed.

Q. Which of the Resistance groups in France had the most military and political power?
A. The FTP (Francs-Tireurs et Partisans), which was communist.

Q. Identify the three Frenchmen executed for sabotage at the Farman aircraft works at Boulogne-Billancourt in 1940.
A. Roger and Marcel Rambaud and Maurice Lebeau, all suspected communists. They were charged with weakening locking nuts on fuel nozzles, which caused aircraft to explode in flight.

Q. Identify the European leader who was put on trial for his negligence in not preparing his country for war.
A. French Prime Minister Edouard Daladier, who at the time of his arrest had just resigned as War Minister. He had been Prime Minister when war was declared.

Q. Why were no bronze cents issued by the U.S. government in 1943?
A. The copper was needed for the war effort. Zinc-coated steel cents were issued in that year. However, a few bronze planchets were struck by error and are very rare. Likewise zinc-steel planchets that were struck in 1944 are also rare.

FACT Adolf Hitler received his Iron Cross in the First World War from a Jew, Lieutenant Hugo Gutman.

Q. What was Dwight D. Eisenhower's rank when he arrived in England
in 1942?
A. He was a lieutenant general, relatively unknown, who had been put
in charge of the invasion of North Africa, Operation Torch, by U.S.
Army Chief of Staff General George C. Marshall, In this June 14,
1944, photo at Normandy, France, Supreme Allied Commander
Eisenhower and Marshall leave an amphibious vehicle while the Air
Force's Commanding General, Henry H. (Hap) Arnold, steps down.

U.S. Army Photo

FACT The United States Marine Corps is almost always thought of with
regard to the campaigns in the Pacific. However, Marines were
also involved in the war in Europe with individuals assigned to
special missions with underground units and Resistance fighters.
On August 29, 1944, Marines from two U.S. cruisers landed on
a trio of islands near Marseilles, France, and captured German
installations. Marines also served on U.S. Navy staffs and as seagoing troops on ships during the landings in North Africa, Italy, Southern France and Normandy.

Q. Identify the two German coins that were virtually melted out of
existence because of a need for bronze and copper in airplane engine
production.

A. One- and two-pfennig copper coins, which were almost totally nonex-
istent by March 1942. At that time Germany began calling in church
bells to satisfy the production need.

Q. How much silver is in U.S. five-cent pieces minted between 1942
and 1945 and why?

A. Nickel, a critical war material, had been used in U.S. five-cent pieces
since 1866. To indicate a change of alloy in 1942–45, a large "P"
was placed above the dome of Monticello on the reverse of the coin.
Its composition is 35 percent silver, 56 percent copper and 9 percent manganese. In 1946 the old alloy of nickel and copper was again
used.

Q. Identify the only East European leader of a government in exile
whom the Soviets permitted to return home after the war.

A. Eduard Benes of Czechoslovakia.

FACT The famous U.S. Marine Corps raid on Makin Island by Carlson's
Raiders in 1942 actually worked against U.S. efforts in the Pacific
despite its much-publicized success. The leathernecks were
credited with destroying a Japanese base and killing approximately 350 enemy troops while sustaining less than forty fatalities.
However, this bold move by the U.S. prompted the Japanese to
strengthen other islands that had previously been lightly fortified.
The result was a higher cost in American lives in campaigns that
followed.

Q. What did the Germans tell the Sicilians and the Italian Army about U.S. paratroopers that made those U.S. troops so feared prior to the invasion?

A. That their units were hardened American murderers and convicts who were pardoned in exchange for fighting. The widespread practice of paratroopers shaving their heads did much to substantiate the fears when Sicilians encountered them. In wartime photo above, note that rank insignia of first paratrooper has been retouched out.

Imperial War Museum Photo

FACT Before Nazi Germany decided upon its final solution to rid itself of Jews, it had considered sending them to the island of Madagascar, where they would serve as hostages in the event the U.S. threatened to enter the war. However, transportation and logistic considerations were used as an excuse not to carry out the deportation.

Q. What use did the U.S. government find for cartridge cases between 1944 and 1946?

A. They were recycled as pennies. The color of pennies minted was slightly different on new, uncirculated coins but otherwise they were the same. The U.S. resumed using the original alloy of 1864–1942 in 1947.

Q. How many people did the Nazis transport from Paris to Germany on the last train from the French capital to the concentration camps at Ravensbruck and Buchenwald?

A. Approximately 2,450 on August 18, 1944, less than seven days before the first Allied troops entered Paris. Less than 300 of those moved survived the war.

Q. When did Hitler arrive at his bunker under the Reich Chancellery in Berlin for the last time?

A. On January 16, 1945, Hitler came to the Chancellery and remained there throughout the rest of his life.

Q. Who was Alain Perpezat?

A. The young Frenchman who had the unhappy task of delivering the message to the Resistance advising them that the Allies did not intend to liberate Paris but instead would bypass it and continue advancing on retreating German forces. Perpezat did not know the contents of the coded message, which was later reversed.

FACT Major Cyril Barclay of the British Expeditionary Forces purchased several Michelin road maps in France to assist moving his troops to Dunkirk for the evacuation. He had been unsuccessful in obtaining regulation maps from the Army. However, he was refused compensation for the expenditure inasmuch as the Army had no provisions for the retail purchase of maps.

Q. Identify the objective in North Africa that marked the first British offensive there.

A. Sidi Barrani, where General Sir Richard O'Connor's 31,000-man Western Desert Force routed the 80,000-man Italian Army by a surprise rear attack. Over 2,000 Italians were captured in the early hours of the campaign. This photo shows Australian troops in Bren carriers moving across the North African desert.

Imperial War Museum Photo

> **FACT** The Red Cross once owned and operated a company that manufac-
> tured arms. During World War II the firm of Oy Sako Ab made
> over 270 million cartridges for Finland's armed forces. When
> Soviet troops moved to take over all munitions plants in ter-
> ritories it occupied, the Finns gave the firm to the Red Cross.
> It remained under their control and manufactured arms, until
> 1962, when it changed hands again.

Q. Name the site of Rommel's first offensive against the British in
North Africa.

A. The March 24, 1941, attack by the 5th Light Division against El
Agheila in Libya.

Q. When did the British and Germans first meet in combat in North
Africa?

A. February 27, 1941.

Q. Identify the Polish Brigade that along with British troops relieved
the Australians at Tobruk in October 1941.

A. The Polish Carpathian Brigade.

Q. Name the three countries that were represented by troops in every
theater of the war.

A. All were Allies: The United States, Great Britain and New Zealand.

Q. Identify the first Canadian woman at sea during the war.

A. Fern Blodgett, who earned the distinction in June 1941, when she
became a radio operator on the Norwegian cargo ship *Mosdale*.

Q. When did the U.S. announce its neutrality in the European war?

A. September 5, 1939.

> **FACT** Canada did not send draftees overseas until January 1945. There
> was strong objection to the draft in Canada, and as a result more
> than 10 percent of the 60,000 draftees were AWOL when the ships
> departed from Halifax. However, 13,000 Canadian draftees served
> in the European theater. Prior to their country's entry into the
> war, Canadian volunteers served with distinction in the RAF and
> Royal Navy.

FACT The first entire division to receive a Presidential Unit Citation was the 101st Airborne. The photo above was taken during the official presentation and review on March 15, 1945, in France. In the rear of the jeep are General Dwight D. Eisenhower, Supreme Allied Commander, and General Maxwell D. Taylor, commanding general. Deputy Division Commander Brigadier General G. J. Higgins is in front. Driver is unidentified. (Author's note: Photo negative was "flopped" during official processing. As a result steering wheel is on wrong side and jeep ident numbers are backwards!)

U.S. Army Photo

> **FACT** During the British drive to Benghazi they captured over 130,000
> Italian troops in North Africa.

Q. How did Austrian-born Adolf Hitler become a German citizen?

A. Wilhelm Frick, while Premier of Thuringia, did the honors by making Hitler a German citizen. Frick went on to become the Nazi Minister of the Interior, Protector of Bohemia and Moravia.

Q. Name the future Pope who passed on intelligence to the American OSS while he was a monsignor in the Vatican.

A. Pope Paul VI, Monsignor Giovanni Montini.

Q. Name the French priest who headed up a Resistance group that manufactured passports, identity cards and other documents in his Marseilles monastery.

A. Father Benoit-Marie de Bourg d'Ire of the Capuchin order. The false documents were used to help Jews, both French and foreign, escape capture by the Nazis and Vichy government. When Italy defected to the Allies and the Germans swept into the Italian-occupied zone of France, Father Benoit moved his operation to Rome.

Q. Who was Monsignor Hugh O'Flaherty?

A. The Vatican cleric who organized an underground network of safe houses and escape routes for Allied prisoners of war who had escaped from the Germans.

Q. Who was Winston Churchill's doctor?

A. Charles Moran.

Q. Who was Adolf Hitler's doctor?

A. Theodor Morell.

Q. Identify the site of the first Allied land victory in the war.

A. Narvik, Norway, on May 28, 1940, when the French Foreign Legion captured the port from the Germans.

> **FACT** New Zealand provided a higher proportion of its population (under
> 3 million) for war service than any other dominion.

Q. Identify the city that received the greatest number of German V-1
and V-2 bombings.
  a. Coventry
  b. London
  c. Antwerp
  d. Southampton
A. Antwerp, Belgium, which was hit over 3,700 times. London was hit
a total of 2,936 times. (Volume 1, pages 27, 151, 153 and 160)

Exclusive Photo by Joseph Niechwiadowicz

The Air War

Q. Identify the 1636 Olympic Gold Medal winner who participated in the Battle of Britain as a wing commander.

A. Major Gotthardt Handrick, who was a wing commander in the Luft-waffe, not the RAF. He won top Olympic honors in the Pentathlon.

Q. Identify the first U.S. pilot to become an ace in two wars.

A. Although some historians consider the Spanish Civil War as a part of or related to World War II, it was in fact a totally separate conflict. A. J. Baumler, an American veteran of the Spanish war, scored eight kills during action in the CBI Theater.

Q. Identify the first U.S. pilot to equal Captain Eddie Rickenbacker's World War I mark by scoring twenty-six "kills."

A. USMC fighter ace Joe Foss, who also won the Medal of Honor for action over Guadalcanal.

Q. Identify the U.S. Army Air Force general who began his service career as an enlisted man and is credited with shooting down Hermann Goering in World War I.

A. General George C. Kenney.

Q. What was the Japanese Army version of kamikaze called?

A. Tokko tai. Kamikaze indicated Japanese Navy suicide planes only.

Q. .When was Buckingham Palace bombed?
A. On September 13, 1940. The plane that did it was subsequently shot down by RAF Sergeant-Pilot Ginger Lacey of the 501st Squadron. Commissioned later in the war, Lacey became an ace more than five times over, with twenty-eight "kills."

Q. What was the original name for the U.S. P-51 Mustang fighter?
   a. Colt
   b. Apache
   c. Thunderbird
   d. War Horse
A. It was Apache.

Q. Identify the U.S. pilot credited with shooting down Japanese Admiral Isoroku Yamamoto.
A. Captain Thomas G. Lanphier.

Q. Identify the Japanese air ace credited with shooting down Captain Colin P. Kelly, Jr., America's first publicized hero.
A. Saburo Sakai, who is credited with a total of sixty-four "kills" and ranks as Japan's third-highest-scoring ace. (Volume 1, page 214)

Q. Who was the most successful jet pilot ace of the war?
A. Lieutenant Colonel Heinz Bar. Ranked ninth overall among Germany's air aces, Bar scored sixteen "kills" flying the Me-262. His combined total was 220 "kills." Remarkably, he survived being shot down himself eighteen times.

Q. Identify the pilot who flew more than 2,530 sorties and is credited with destroying over 500 enemy tanks.
A. Luftwaffe fighter ace Hans Ulrich Rudel. His total of sorties is the record in the war.

Q. What was the nickname of the U.S.-built Grumman F6F aircraft?
A. The Hellcat, which only saw service in the Pacific Theater. Closeup photo at left is of a Hellcat from the aircraft carrier USS *Saratoga* (CV-3).

Exclusive Photo by Tom Christie

Q. In service slang what did SNAFU stand for?

A. Situation Normal, All Fouled Up. Military personnel were known, however, to substitute a different term for the next to last word. Photo above shows the fuselage of a USAAF bomber at Fenton Field, Australia, with appropriate artwork and the name *SNAFU II*. Kindred slang included: FUBAR (Fouled Up Beyond All Recognition), FUMTU (Fouled Up More Than Usual) and JANFU (Joint Army-Navy Foul Up).

Exclusive Photo by Harold D. Zahler

Q. Identify the high-scoring U.S. air ace who was shot down by Japan's second-highest-scoring ace in action over Los Negros in the Philippines in January 1945.

A. Thomas B. McGuire, Jr., whose score of thirty-eight "kills" was surpassed only by Richard Bong (forty). McGuire was shot down and killed by Shoichi Sugita, Japan's second-ranked ace with eighty "kills." (See footnote on controversial scores for Sugita and Hiroyishi Nishizawa, Volume 1, page 214.)

Q. Identify the Japanese pilot credited with shooting down "Pappy" Boyington.

A. Gregory Boyington, the colorful USMC pilot who was the fifth-ranked U.S. ace in the war (twenty-eight "kills"), was shot down by Masajiro Kawato on January 3, 1944. (Volume 1, page 215)

Q. Name the U.S. serviceman who became the first member of the Army Air Force to bomb Berlin, Rome and Tokyo.

A. Sergeant Kurt Hermann who served with both the Twelfth and Eighth Air forces in Europe. In the Pacific he was assigned to B-29s that bombed Tokyo. He flew more than 105 missions before being reported missing in action in the Pacific.

Q. Identify the future U.S. Vice President who was shot down as a U.S. Navy pilot over Iwo Jima and rescued by submarine.

A. George Bush. The sub that saved him was the USS *Finback*.

FACT The Luftwaffe organized and operated what is considered one of the most successful Trojan Horse operations in the history of warfare with the formation of Kampfgeschwader 200 (KG-200). This extremely secret group penetrated Allied air space by using captured U.S., British and Russian aircraft, complete with flight crews that spoke the appropriate language, dressed in enemy uniforms and passed as Allied fliers. They were used for depositing spies on foreign soil, photo recon and for attacking Allied units that they attached themselves to, usually on return legs from bombing missions over Europe. There were no less than forty-eight KG-200 bases operating out of eleven countries and flying almost everything in the Allied arsenal including B-17s, B-24s, P-51s, Spitfires and Mosquitoes.

Q. What was the Allied code name for Guadalcanal?
A. Cactus, and the pilots who used Henderson Field were called the Cactus Air Force. In this photo, a Japanese Betty bomber rests amid the skeletons of palm trees after it crash-landed. (Volume 1, page 40)

Exclusive Photo by Ben Lebowitz

Q. Identify the Japanese fighter that was modified and produced as a kamikaze toward the end of the war.
A. The Mitsubishi Zero-Sen, known to the Allies as the Zeke. Only 465 Zekes out of nearly 10,450 produced ever became kamikazes. The one in photo above is seen in the water off Guadalcanal.

Exclusive Photo by Ben Lebowitz

Q. Identify the first U.S. armed forces airman to shoot down a German plane.
A. Lieutenant Samuel F. Junkin, USAAF, during the raid on Dieppe, France, August 19, 1942.

Q. Identify the pilot of the first B-17 lost in combat.
A. U.S. Army Air Force Captain Colin P. Kelly, Jr., on December 10, 1941.

Q. Identify the first U.S. pilot to make use of the airfield on Iwo Jima in 1945.
A. Captain Raymond Malo, on March 4, 1945, in a B-29 named *Dinah Might*, was the first of approximately 2,400 emergency landings by U.S. aircrews on Iwo Jima. (Volume 1, pages 3, 27, 60, 85, 125 and 135)

Q. Identify the only member of the RAF to be awarded a Victoria Cross in 1940 for air battle over Britain.
A. Fighter pilot Lieutenant James B. Nicholson. He received it posthumously for attacking a German squadron while his own plane was on fire.

Q. Who was the first fighter pilot to score over 100 "kills"?
A. Lieutenant Colonel Werner Molders of the Luftwaffe. He was also the first pilot to be decorated with the Knight's Cross with oak leaves, swords, and diamonds — Germany's highest award. He was killed in a crash while a passenger in a plane in November 1941, en route to funeral services for General Ernst Udet. By the end of the war thirty-eight German fighter aces scored 100 or more "kills," something no other country in the war was able to do.

Q. What was unusual about the U.S. 99th Fighter Squadron?
A. It was the first Army Air Force unit made up totally of blacks.

FACT The dreaded German fighter Me-109 (Messerschmitt) used American-made propellers and British-made wing slats early in the war.

FACT The largest planned crash landing by the USAAF during the war took place on July 15, 1942, when two B-17s and six P-38Fs were forced down on Greenland because of fake German weather reports which caused them to run low on fuel. The planes had been on their way to Great Britain from Maine, but the crews spent the next ten days on the ice cap before being rescued just forty-five miles from the Arctic Circle. Still there, and believed to be under thirty-five to forty feet of snow, the six P-38Fs are the goal of an extraordinary recovery expedition sponsored by the R. J. Reynolds Tobacco Company. No effort will be made to recover the B-17s. If successful, the team will have more than doubled the number of P-38s left in the world. Of the 9,600 made, only five survived. In photo above, Lieutenant Robert H. Wilson relaxes on his P-38F Lightning. One landed with gear down and promptly flipped. The other five skidded down with gear up, preventing eventual takeoffs. The photo was taken by J. Brad McManus, the first to land.

Photo by J. Brad McManus

Q. Identify the U.S. pilot who shot down four Japanese planes on December 7, 1941.

A. George Welch, who was the first member of the U.S. armed forces to score four "kills" in a single day.

Q. Name the only person to ever become a triple ace in one day by scoring fifteen "kills."

A. Major Wilhelm Batz of the Luftwaffe against the Russians in 1942. He was ranked sixth overall among German aces with 237 "kills."

Q. What was the greatest number of enemy planes ever shot down in a single day by a U.S. pilot and name him?

A. Nine Japanese planes were shot down on October 24, 1944, by U.S. Navy pilot David McCampbell.

Q. Name the first American pilot to become an ace by scoring five "kills" in one day.

A. On December 25, 1941, Robert Hedman, a volunteer pilot with the Flying Tigers, accomplished the feat. However, the first U.S. armed forces pilot to score five "kills" in one day was Lieutenant Edward (Butch) O'Hare on February 20, 1942. Chicago's O'Hare International Airport was named in his honor. (Volume 1, page 138)

Q. Identify the only American killed in the war who is buried in St. Paul's Cathedral in London.

A. William M. Fiske III, who was the first American to join the Royal Air Force, was killed on August 16, 1940.

Q. Identify the British general who was killed in a plane crash and is buried in Arlington National Cemetery in the U.S.

A. Major General Orde Wingate, who along with several Americans died on March 24, 1944, in Burma. Because identification was impossible, all of the victims were buried in a common grave at Arlington.

FACT U.S. General Henry H. Arnold learned how to fly from the Wright brothers. He was the first five-star general in the Army Air Force and among the first five fliers in the Army Air Corps.

Q. Identify the Luftwaffe ace who had a likeness of Mickey Mouse painted on his fighter.

A. Adolf Galland. He was one of thirty-eight German aces to score more than 100 "kills." His personal score was 103. The practice of naming aircraft and illustrating the names with art was common to both Allied and Axis air forces. The two U.S. bombers in photos above were at Fenton Field, Australia. Harold D. Zahler, who took the previous photo of *SNAFU II* and the one of *Satan's Secretary*, managed to have himself snapped next to *Puss & Boots*.

Exclusive Photos by Harold D. Zahler

Q. Identify the most decorated bomber pilot in the Luftwaffe.
    a. Gerhard Barkhorn
    b. Werner Baumbach
    c. Heinz Wodarczyk

A. Oberleutnant Werner Baumbach, who at one time was the commander of the dreaded Kampfgeschwader 200 (KG 200), the Luftwaffe organization that flew captured U.S. and British aircraft. Barkhorn was Germany's second-leading fighter ace (with 301 kills), while Wodarczyk was one of two Luftwaffe pilots who managed to attack Allied troops during D-Day. The other was "Pips" Priller. (Volume 1, page 215)

Q. Name the three Japanese cities that were targets of the final air raid of the war.

A. The three cities bombed by U.S. B-29s were Kumagaya, Isesaki and Akita. The raid took place on August 14, 1945, the same day Japan agreed to surrender unconditionally.

Q. Identify the first British aircraft type to be shot down in the war.

A. A Wellington bomber on September 7, 1639, while it was preparing to bomb the German battle cruiser *Gneisenau*.

Q. Identify the Polish fighter plane that was never used by the Polish but was purchased by the air forces of Greece, Bulgaria, Turkey and Rumania.

A. The P.Z.L. P-24f, first produced in 1634.

Q. Where was the first major training ground of U.S. airborne pathfinder units?

A. At Biscari Airfield in Sicily.

FACT U.S. Army Air Force personnel assigned as heavy bomber crews fought odds of nine to one that they would become casualties in the European Theater of Operations. Casualty rates for heavy bomber crews were almost three times as great as for medium bomber crews and just under twice the rate of casualties sustained by fighter pilots.

FACT German fighter planes shot down or damaged 145 out of 178 Allied planes that attacked the oil refineries in German-occupied Rumania on August 1, 1943. Of the 1,733 U.S. personnel flying the B-24s, 446 were killed. Only thirty-three of the planes ever saw combat again.

Q. Name the American B-24 Liberator that was found in a state of near perfect preservation in the Libyan desert in May 1959.

A. The *Lady Be Good*, which was reported missing on April 4, 1943. It was first sighted on November 9, 1958, from the air by geologists Ronald McLean and S. V. Sykes. After apparently overshooting their base, the crew was forced to land in the desert when their fuel expired. They perished as they were making their way across the desert on foot. Remarkable photo above captures the instant of a flak burst as seen from the top turret of a B-24 Liberator en route to raid the Ploesti oil fields in Rumania. Plane in photo is from Group 456, Squad 746, Fifteenth Air Force.

Exclusive Photo from Mrs. Kenneth L. Boughner

Q. Identify the last U.S. aircraft type involved in action in the war.

A. Although the war with Japan ended August 15, 1945 (but September 2 is celebrated as VJ-Day since that is when the surrender was signed), a B-32 aircraft on a photo reconnaissance mission over Japan on August 18 was engaged by Japanese fighters. One U.S. airman was killed and two others were wounded. The B-32 involved was named *Hobo Queen II*. (Volume 1, page 140)

Q. When did U.S. Marine Corps pilots shoot down their first and last enemy planes in the war?

A. Japanese planes at Wake Island were the first, and Japanese planes at Okinawa were the last. Between those battles, USMC pilots scored 2,355 "kills," which resulted in 121 aces, including five who scored twenty or more "kills."

Q. Besides the December 7, 1941, attack on Pearl Harbor, when else did Japanese aircraft bomb the Hawaiian Islands during the war?

A. On March 5, 1942, three Kawanishi H8K2 flying boats, unable to locate Pearl Harbor, dropped their bombs elsewhere on Oahu. Visibility was bad.

Q. What was the reconnaissance version of the B-29 known as?

A. Produced in limited quantity toward the end of the war, it was identified as the F-13.

Q. Identify the first U.S. aviation unit to operate on Japanese soil.

A. The war with Japan ended on August 15, 1945, and the surrender was signed aboard the battleship USS *Missouri* (BB-63) in Tokyo Bay on September 2. Five days later, U.S. Marine Corps aircraft began using the airfield at Yokosuka. The particular group gaining the distinction was Marine Aircraft Group 31. No U.S. aircraft operated from Japanese homeland bases during the hostilities.

FACT Allied bomber raids against Germany suffered heavy losses between August 1942 and December 1943 for lack of adequate long-range fighter escorts. During one week in October 1943, the Allies lost 153 planes to the Germans.

Q. Identify the future U.S senator and presidential candidate who piloted
a B-24 named *Dakota Queen* in the Fifteenth Air Force.
A. George McGovern of the 455th Bomber Group. In photo above, a
"box" of B-24s wing toward the oil fields in Ploesti, Rumania.

Exclusive Photo from Mrs. Kenneth L. Boughner

Q. What was the name of the B-25 that Congressman/Lieutenant Commander Lyndon B. Johnson was aboard when it was reportedly attacked by Japanese aircraft over New Guinea?
A. *Heckling Hare.* The future President was the only person aboard
the aircraft to be awarded the Silver Star for the action. (Volume
1, page 63)

Q. Who succeeded General Hans Jeschonnek as Luftwaffe chief of staff
in 1943?
A. General Gunther Korten. (Volume 1, page 12)

Q. Who was "Sailor" Malan?
A. The South African pilot who became the third-highest ace in the
RAF with thirty-five "kills." He was the first pilot to receive both
the Distinguished Flying Cross (with bars) and the Distinguished
Service Order. His full name was Adolph G. Malan. (Volume 1, page
214)

Q. Identify the type of aircraft that Bruno Mussolini, the Italian dictator's son, was killed testing in 1639.

A. The Piaggio P-108B, a four-engine heavy bomber which was often compared to the U.S. B-17. It was Italy's only four-engine heavy bomber of the war but produced in such low quantity (fifty-five) that it had little impact.

Q. Where did the U.S. Navy planes that arrived at Pearl Harbor during the December 7, 1941, attack come from?

A. The aircraft carrier USS *Enterprise* (CV-6), which was returning from a trip to Wake Island. There were eighteen planes.

Q. Who flew the first Bloch 174 light bomber–reconnaissance aircraft into action for France against Germany?

A. French civil aviation pioneer and noted writer Antoine de Saint-Exupéry on March 29, 1940.

Q. What did Mikhail Gurevich and Artem Mikoyan contribute to the war effort?

A. They were the designers of the MiG fighter plane, which made its debut in 1940.

Q. Identify the Allied power that had the only jet fighter plane to see combat against the Luftwaffe during the war.

A. Great Britain, with its Meteor. It is reported to have entered combat nearly a month before the Messerschmitt-262 jet.

Q. Name the first five U.S. Army Air Force sergeants ever to fly in combat as pilots.

A. Despite regulations that only commissioned officers could act as pilots the following five men did fly against the Luftwaffe in 1944: John Ferguson of Bayside, New York; Dennis L. A. Johns, of Jackson, Michigan; Daniel L. Richards, of Long Beach, California; Donald E. Dempsey, of Elyria, Ohio; and William C. Arney, of Buffalo, New York.

FACT The German Messerchmitt-262 jet had a top speed of 540 miles per hour.

FACT When Japanese fighters shot off most of the right wing of this Chinese National Aviation Corporation DC-3, the company used the wing of a DC-2 to replace it and flew the plane to safety. It was promptly nicknamed the DC-2½.

McDonnell-Douglas Photo

FACT In one of the most unusual cases of revenge recorded by either side in the war, U.S. Army Air Force Lieutenant Harold Fisher plotted to locate and shoot down the Italian pilot who had shot him down in 1943 using a decoy American P-38 fighter. The U.S. plane was being used by the Italians in very much the same way the German KG-200 units used captured Allied aircraft to infiltrate Allied formations and then shoot down as many as possible. The incident so infuriated Fisher he managed to equip a B-17 with additional armament and use himself as bait for the decoy P-38. Fisher learned the name of his nemesis, Guido Rossi, and the fact that Rossi's wife was now behind Allied lines. He had her name and likeness painted on the plane's nose. A short time after Fisher began trying to bait Rossi he was successful. When Rossi began an air-to-air radio exchange with Fisher, the U.S. pilot told the Italian pilot that he named his plane after a woman he had been living with — then identified her. As Fisher expected, Rossi put his previous tactics aside and came at the B-17 directly. Fisher shot him down and Rossi was picked up and became a prisoner of war. The bizarre episode won Fisher the Distinguished Flying Cross.

Q. Identify the U.S. serviceman listed as the first American to be killed in action in the Pacific.

A. U.S. Navy Ensign Manuel Gonzalez, a pilot from the aircraft carrier USS *Enterprise* (CV-6), on December 7, 1941.

Q. What was necessary to become a member of the Goldfish Club?

A. An Allied airman who was picked out of the sea after being shot down qualified.

Q. Identify the first type of German aircraft shot down in the war.

A. A Junkers-87 Stuka during the invasion of Poland. Polish Air Force fighter pilot Wladyslaw Gnys is credited with doing it. He became a member of the RAF after fleeing from Poland.

Q. What was the name of the airstrip on Betio Island, Tarawa?

      a. Haskins Field

      b. Hasset Field

      c. Hawkins Field

A. Named after USMC Medal of Honor winner Lieutenant William Hawkins, who died on Tarawa, the airstrip was Hawkins Field. (Volume 1, page 137)

Q. Who was General Dwight D. Eisenhower's pilot?

A. Captain Larry Hansen.

Q. Name the first ace in the Flying Tigers?

      a. Claire Chennault

      b. Richard Bong

      c. Duke Hedman

A. Duke Hedman, who scored his five "kills" on December 25, 1941.

FACT The world-famous Baedeker travel guide books were used by the Luftwaffe to select important targets for bombing in Britain. They publicly announced that buildings that Baedeker had given three stars to would be primary targets. German troops also used Baedeker guides during land campaigns in Europe in areas where their military maps were incomplete. (Volume 1, page 164)

Q. Name the U.S. Army Air Force officer who defected to Germany in order to fight the Soviets.

A. Lieutenant Martin J. Monti, who crossed sides in October 1944 by flying his fighter to Vienna. The Nazis accepted him but rather than letting him join the Luftwaffe they gave him command of an SS unit made up largely of Americans. After the war Monti was tried for treason and given a twenty-five-year prison term.

Q. What was the Allied code name for the air raids on the Benedictine Abbey at Cassino in March 1944?
  a. Operation Hemingway
  b. Operation Deighton
  c. Operation Ludlum
  d. Operation Uris

A. Operation Ludlum, which was named after the USAAF officer who signaled the attack after several postponements due to bad weather.

Q. Who was the commander of Luftflotte 3 on the Western Front in 1944?

A. General Field Marshal Hugo Sperrle.

Q. How many tons of bombs did Britain drop on Germany?

A. Just over 645,920 tons.

Q. How many air raids did Berlin sustain during the war?

A. The British and American air forces conducted 363 raids over a period of three years and eight months.

FACT If it became necessary to drop a third atom bomb on Japan, the city that would have been the target was Tokyo. On August 10, 1945, the day after the bomb was dropped on Nagasaki, U.S. planes dropped counterfeit Japanese yen warning that a third bomb would be dropped unless Japan surrendered. The obverse of the money was authentic-looking while the reverse side carried the third-bomb message. Tokyo was not mentioned as the intended target. This view of Tokyo is from the top of the Finance Building looking toward the Imperial Palace (extreme left) and the Daitchi Building (center).

Exclusive Photo by George Schroth

Q. What was the nickname of the C-47?

A. The Gooney Bird. The C-47 and the other derivative of the DC-3, the R4D, were the mainstay of the U.S. Carrier Command and served as troop and cargo transports, hospital ships and also as bombers and gliders.

McDonnell-Douglas Photo

FACT The C-47 military version of the DC-3 was produced at a rate of 1.8 aircraft per hour at the peak of mass production. In total, Douglas Aircraft (now McDonnell-Douglas) produced 10,196 C-47s at plants in California and Oklahoma. In photo above the seventy-one female assemblers who worked on the 2,000th plane in Long Beach took time to sign it and get their picture taken.

McDonnell-Douglas Photo

Q. Identify the Japanese aircraft that was almost an exact duplicate of the U.S. DC-3.

A. The L2D.

Q. Who was the highest-scoring ace in the Flying Tigers?
  a. Richard Bong
  ·b. Pappy Boyington
  c. Bob Neale
  d. Claire Chennault

A. Neale, who scored sixteen "kills" while a member of the Flying Tigers.

Q. Identify the mountain in Oregon that was hit by bombs dropped by a Japanese plane.

A. Mount Emily, on September 9, 1942, by Lieutenant Nobuo Fujita. He was launched by catapult from the submarine I-25. He is the only military member of a foreign power to have done this during the war. (Volume 1, page 160)

Q. Name the Japanese prisoner of war camp where VIP prisoners, including Pappy Boyington, were held.

A. Ofuna.

Q. Who was the commander in chief of the Soviet Air Force?

A. Marshal Alexander A. Novikov.

Q. What was deflection shooting?

A. The art of squirting gunfire ahead of an enemy aircraft. Its success depended on hair-trigger judgment of the angles, speeds and distances that separated two planes traveling in different directions at more than six miles per minute.

Q. Who was France's top air ace of the war?

A. Marcel Albert, with twenty-three "kills."

FACT U.S. Navy fighter ace Lieutenant Edward (Butch) O'Hare was killed in action by friendly fire. He was mistaken by the rear gunner of a TBF for Japanese during a night mission and was shot down. (Volume 1, page 138)

Q. Identify the first German city to be hit by 4,000-pound bombs.
A. Emden, on March 31, 1941.

Q. Besides the Ju-87 Stukas, identify the other two German aircraft that dominated the skies over Poland in 1639.
A. Two medium bombers, the Dornier Do-17 and the Heinkel He-111.

Q. What were British and German air losses during the evacuation of Dunkirk?
A. The RAF lost 106 planes vs. 156 for Germany.

Q. Where and when was the first RAF 1,000-plane raid on a German city?
A. May 1942, when 1,130 planes hit Cologne.

Q. Where did Britain suffer its first civilian casualties as a result of a German air raid?
A. In the Orkney Islands on March 16, 1940, when the Luftwaffe bombed the location.

Q. When did the Allied "fire raid" on Hamburg take place?
A. July 1943.

Q. Who was the top Soviet air ace in the war?
A. Major Ivan N. Khozedub with sixty-two "kills."

Q. Who was Norway's top ace of the war?
A. Svein Heglund, with fifteen "kills" while a member of the RAF.

Q. Who was the top Yugoslavian air ace of the war?
A. Critan Galic, with thirty-six "kills." (Author's note: he was inadvertently omitted from list of the top aces that appears in Volume 1, page 214.)

Q. What was the nickname of the version of the C-47 (DC-3) that had 41-foot-long pontoons?
A. The Duck. The tremendous pontoons on the amphibious transport were the longest ever made.

McDonnell-Douglas Photo

Q. Where did the Japanese surrender delegation first come in physical contact with American forces?

A. On Ie Shima in August 1945 when several members of the advance delegation landed there to make preparations for the actual surrender. In top photo the delegation is met by unidentified American military personnel. In bottom photo flight crews from Japanese Betty bombers pose with an American interpreter (front row, second from left).

Photos by George M. Barclay

Naval Operations and Sea Battles

Q. Who was Isoroku Takano?

A. Born on April 4, 1884, Isoroku Takano was thirty-two years old when he was adopted into another Japanese family (as was the custom in order to prevent a family name from dying if there were no male heirs). His name, Isoroku, is spelled with the ideographs of the numbers 56, which was the age of his natural father when Isoroku was born, and they indicated the pride the older man had in fathering a son at that age. With his adoption, Isoroku took the name of his new family and, in so doing, guaranteed it a place in Japanese world history. As Isoroku Yamamoto he will be remembered as one of Japan's greatest admirals.

Q. Identify the only U.S. Navy officer ever to be court-martialed for losing a ship in war.

A. Captain Charles McVay, commanding officer of the cruiser USS *Indianapolis*, which was sunk on July 30, 1945, by Japanese submarine I-58. It was the greatest loss of life (883) on the high seas ever sustained by the U.S. Navy.

Q. Identify the famous naval battle incorrectly named for a location other than where it was actually fought.

    a. Leyte Gulf

    b. Coral Sea

    c. Philippine Sea

A. The Battle of the Coral Sea was not fought there but rather in the Solomon Sea, on May 7 and 8, 1942. It was Japan's first defeat of the war. (Volume 1, pages 31, 171 and 173)

Q. Identify the German U-boat captain who attempted to sink the luxury liner *Queen Elizabeth*.

A. Horst Kessler of U-704. (Volume 1, page 57)

Q. Identify the four chaplains who gave up their life preservers to troops on the SS *Dorchester* as she sank in 1942.

A. George L. Fox, Clark V. Poling, John P. Washington and Alexander D. Goode.

Q. Name the twelve-year-old boy who managed to enlist in the U.S. Navy and served on the battleship USS *South Dakota* (BB-57).

A. Calvin Graham, who won a Bronze Star and a Purple Heart before the Navy found out how old he was, served aboard the battleship nicknamed Old Nameless.

Q. Name the only Japanese battleship to survive the war.

A. The 42,785-ton *Nagato*. The 725-foot-long warship was the nineteenth largest battleship in the war. (Volume 1, page 210).

Q. Name the only German aircraft carrier in the war years.

A. The *Graf Zeppelin*. Its keel was laid in 1938, but the ship was not finished before the end of the war and it did not see action.

Q. Identify the only British aircraft carrier to make it through the war.

A. HMS *Furious*, which was originally a cruiser and then converted to a carrier.

Q. Identify the ships' bands who were finalists Saturday night, December 6, 1941, in "The Battle of Music" at Pearl Harbor.

A. The bands from the following ships: USS *Pennsylvania*, USS *Tennessee*, USS *Argonne* and USS *Detroit*. The *Arizona*'s band had been eliminated.

Q. Where were Japan's midget submarines designed and made?

A. They were designed in Germany but built in Japan. In photo, a midget sub captured at Pearl Harbor is seen on display in New York City's Times Square during the war.

Exclusive Photo by George Schroth

Q. Who said, "There will always be an *England* in the U.S. Navy"?

A. U.S. Admiral Ernest King, with reference to the destroyer escort USS *England* that sank six Japanese submarines in twelve days and was seriously damaged by kamikazes off Okinawa in 1945. In photo above, Admiral King is seen at the Red Arrow in London on June 15, 1944.

U.S. Army Photo

> **FACT** The first ship sunk in the war, the Cunard Line's *Athenia*, was featured in the movie *Arise My Love*.

Q. Identify the U.S. ship that sank five enemy submarines in eight days.
A. The destroyer escort USS *England*, under the command of Lieutenant Commander W. B. Pendleton in May 1944 in the Pacific. Actually Pendleton's ship totaled six subs during the last twelve days of the month.

Q. When was the first U.S. submarine sunk in the Atlantic?
A. On January 24, 1942, the S-26 was rammed and sunk off Panama.

Q. Although the "social consumption of alcoholic beverages" was strictly prohibited aboard all U.S. Navy ships, it was a regulation that was often and easily circumvented. What did the submariners call their supply of spirits (allegedly intended for medicinal use)?
A. Depth-charge whiskey. Most veterans of the Silent Service remember their boats having a good supply on hand.

Q. Name the U-boat commander who sank the British passenger liner *Athenia* in September 1939:
    a. Otto Kretschmer
    b. Fritz Lemp
    c. Erich Topp
    d. Gunther Prien
A. Lieutenant Fritz Lemp. The others are the first-, fourth-, and eighth-highest-scoring U-boat commanders, respectively. (Volume 1, page 212)

> **FACT** The magnitude of Hitler's crimes against humanity are historically documented. However, one incident for which he was blamed by Allied propagandists is in fact false. The sinking of the British liner *Athenia* on the first day of war (September 1, 1939) was an act contrary to his orders not to attack passenger liners. The embarrassing mistake by U-30 resulted in German propagandists turning the tables and blaming the sinking on the British themselves.

FACT According to JANAC (Joint Army-Navy Assessment Committee), the official investigating team that tallied losses at the end of the war, U.S. forces sank approximately 10 million tons of Japanese shipping, including 8 million tons of merchant ships. U.S. submarines sank more than half of the combined tonnage, precisely 54.6 percent, for 5.3 million tons (1,314 ships). Land-based and carrier aircraft were credited with a third of the total (929 ships for 3 million tons), while the remaining 1.4 million tons were sunk by surface craft, mines and miscellaneous causes.

FACT The last ship present at Pearl Harbor on December 7, 1941, to be sunk in hostile action was the former USS *Phoenix* (CL-46), which the U.S. sold to Argentina in 1951. Renamed the *General Belgrano*, she was sunk by a British submarine on May 2, 1982, off the Falkland Islands during the conflict between those two nations. In this February 28, 1944, photo, Vice Admiral Thomas C. Kinkaid and General Douglas MacArthur are seen on the flag bridge of the *Phoenix* during the bombardment of Los Negros Island. Colonel Lloyd Lehrbas, an aide to MacArthur, is at extreme right. Photo was taken by Pfc. Gae Falilace.

U.S. Army Photo

Q. Name two submarines that sank Soviet ships by mistake during the war.

A. In February 1943 the USS *Sawfish* sank the *Kola* and the *Ilmen*, while in May of that year the USS *Sundlance* sank the *Bella Russa*. In all three sinkings, the Soviet ships were mistaken for Japanese.

Q. Name the U.S. submarine that incorrectly identified the Navy salvage ship USS *Extractor* and sank her on January 23, 1945.

A. The USS *Guardfish*.

Q. Who was the only U.S. submarine skipper relieved of command of a *Japanese* submarine for cause?

A. Hiram Cassedy, who had been assigned to accept the surrender at sea of one of three I-class subs designed and built to torpedo the Panama Canal. He violated strict orders not to take souvenirs by passing out Japanese swords. Admiral William Halsey removed him from command.

Q. What distinction does British Royal Navy Captain Donald Macintyre hold?

A. A prominent U-boat hunter, Captain Macintyre captured Germany's most successful U-boat commander ever, Otto Kretschmer, in March 1941. As commander of U-23 and U-99, Kretschmer sank forty-five ships during sixteen patrols. (Volume 1, page 212)

Q. How was the USS *Juneau* sunk?

A. By torpedoes from Japanese submarine I-26. The *Juneau* was the ship on which the five Sullivan brothers perished. (Volume 1, page 177)

FACT For every U.S. surface-ship sailor lost in the war, six U.S. submariners lost their lives. Although the 1,700 U.S. submarine war patrols were responsible for more than half of Japan's sea losses (nearly one half million Japanese), the cost in U.S. lives was the heaviest ratio of any branch of the U.S. armed forces, including the Marines. One out of every seven U.S. submariners died — 3,505 officers and enlisted men and one out of every five submarines was lost. In the Pacific forty-nine were sunk and in the Atlantic three. (Volume 1, pages 174-175)

FACT The first U.S. Navy PT boat, #9, arrived in New York from Great Britain two days after World War II had begun in September 1939. It had been purchased there by Henry R. Sutphen, executive vice president of the Electric Boat Company, which had its Elco Naval Division in Bayonne, New Jersey. The Navy took delivery of its first boat (PT #9) in June 1940 from Elco. By the time Pearl Harbor was attacked, several manufacturers were offering designs in what were called the Plywood Derbys of 1941. Sutphen used his British-purchased boat as a model for the hundreds of others made at the Elco facility.

Author's Collection

Q. Identify the U.S. submarine that has the distinction of sinking three enemy submarines in as many days.
    a. USS *Tang*
    b. USS *Batfish*
    c. USS *Ling*

A. In February 1945, on her sixth war patrol, the USS *Batfish* encountered three of the four known Japanese submarines around the Philippines and sank them in three days. No other submarine of any navy had done that before, or since. *Batfish* is now a memorial exhibit in Muskogee, Oklahoma, while USS *Ling* is on exhibit in Hackensack, New Jersey. (See Appendix.)

Q. Name the only U.S. submarine credited with sinking a battleship in the war and name the battleship.
A. The USS *Sealion II* sank the Japanese battleship *Kongo* off Foochow, China, on November 21, 1944. The American submarine was under the command of Commander G. T. Reich.

Q. Identify the U.S. submarine credited with sinking the first Japanese destroyer in the war.
A. The SS-44, which sank the *Kako* on August 10, 1942.

Q. Identify the first submarine sunk by aircraft fire during the war.
A. The Italian submarine *Argonauta*, on June 28, 1940, by a British Sunderland.

Q. Name the first Japanese submarine sunk by aircraft fire in the war.
A. The I-70 on December 10, 1941, by planes from the USS *Enterprise* (CV-6).

FACT German naval hero and U-boat captain Gunther Prien sank a 15,500-ton British passenger ship, the *Arandora Star*, in July 1940, some nine months after his daring penetration of Scapa Flow and subsequent sinking of the battleship HMS *Royal Oak*. While his action against the British at Scapa Flow did much to raise German morale, his sinking of the *Arandora Star* had a reverse effect. The British ship was transporting some 1,500 German and Italian prisoners to Canada. (Volume 1, page 164)

Q. Of the ten armed merchantmen that Germany used on the high seas during the war, which was the last one to survive?

A. The *Michel*, which was sunk by the submarine USS *Tarpon* off Japan in October 1943. Merchantmen raiders accounted for 133 Allied ship sinkings, totaling 830,000 tons. Only one of the ten was charged with actions not permitted by international law or the rules of war, and its captain was tried as a war criminal.

Q. Identify the first member of the U.S. Submarine Service to win the Medal of Honor.

A. Commander Howard Gilmore, CO of the USS *Growler* was posthumously given the award in 1943. Gilmore ordered his officers to clear the bridge of the submarine while he remained on deck to maneuver the *Growler* to safety after it had rammed a Japanese gunboat. Injured in the exchange of gunfire that followed, Gilmore gave his last order to the officer of the deck: "Take her down." The *Growler* dived, seriously damaged, and escaped to safety. Commander Gilmore remained topside.

Q. Name the first Japanese submarine to be sunk as a result of Hedgehog, or cluster bomb, fire.

A. The I-175 on February 5, 1944. Hedgehogs, and a smaller version called Mousetraps, were adopted by the U.S. Navy in 1942. They consisted of clusters of bombs that broke into a pattern after being fired from a surface ship.

Q. Name the Japanese submarine that sank off Truk as a result of a sailor failing to secure one of its torpedo doors.

A. The I-169 which was forced to perform an emergency dive from attacking U.S. planes. The sub crew perished after several unsuccessful efforts to refloat her.

FACT Germany's second-highest-scoring U-boat captain, Wolfgang Luth, was accidentally shot and killed by a sentry for failing to properly identify himself near the headquarters of Admiral Karl Doenitz. Luth commanded four different U-boats in the war, made fourteen patrols and sank forty-four enemy ships, just one short of tying Otto Kretschmer's record.

> **FACT** Twenty percent of the German U-boat fleet was lost as a result of British air and naval fire in March 1941. The German casualties included several veteran U-boat commanders.

Q. Identify the first U.S. ship sunk on the high seas by a Japanese submarine.

A. The SS *Cynthia Olson*, approximately 750 miles from the West Coast on December 7, 1941, by submarine I-26.

Q. Identify the German U-boat credited with sinking the first Allied warship, HMS *Courageous*, in the war.

A. U-29, under the command of Otto Schuhart, sank the aircraft carrier on September 17, 1939. Royal Navy records note that 519 members of the 22,500-ton ship's crew perished.

Q. Identify the only U.S. submarine sunk by a Japanese submarine in the war.

A. The USS *Corvina* on November 16, 1943, off Truk by the I-176.

Q. Identify the first U.S. submarine to sink a Japanese submarine in the war.

A. The USS *Gudgeon*, under the command of Lieutenant Commander Joseph Grenfell, sank the I-173 on January 27, 1942. Another skipper of this boat, William S. Post, Jr., recorded the fifth-highest number of enemy ships sunk (nineteen) between his service on the *Gudgeon* and the USS *Spot*. (Volume 1, page 213)

Q. Name the U.S. submarine credited with sinking the last Japanese submarine in the war.

A. The USS *Spikefish*, which sank the I-373 on August 13, 1945, two days before the war ended. Japan lost over 130 submarines as opposed to 52 lost by the U.S. in the war. (Volume 1, pages 174,175)

Q. Name the U.S. submarine that fired the last torpedo and is credited with sinking the last Japanese combatant ship in the war, on August 14, 1945.

A. The USS *Torsk* (AG SS-423), which was commissioned in December 1944. In 1972, she became a submarine memorial and is open to the public at Baltimore, Maryland.

> **FACT** Japanese kamikaze and Tokko Tai suicide planes sank thirty-four
> U.S. ships at a cost of 1,228 pilots for Japan.

Q. Identify the two submarines involved in the only U.S. underwater
collision of the war.

A. The USS *Hoe* and USS *Flounder* apparently needed more room to
navigate than they had off Indochina and managed to make contact on February 23, 1945. Neither sub sank.

Q. Identify the Japanese ship credited with sinking the aircraft carrier USS *Wasp* (CV-7).

A. Submarine I-19 hit the *Wasp* with torpedoes near Espiritu Santo
on September 15, 1942, and the carrier had to be finished off by
friendly fire from U.S. destroyers. Commander of the I-19 was
Takaichi Kinashi, Japan's leading submarine commander. (Volume
1, page 179)

Q. Identify the first U.S. ship to be sunk in U.S. coastal waters in the war.

A. The USS *Jacob Jones*, a destroyer, off New Jersey on February 28,
1942. It was torpedoed by U-578.

Q. Identify the only U.S. ship sunk by the Japanese Kaitens (human
suicide torpedoes).

A. The SS *Mississinewa* in October 1944.

Q. Identify the future U.S. President who was director of physical educa-
tion aboard the aircraft carrier USS *Monterey*:

    a. John F. Kennedy

    b. Lyndon B. Johnson

    c. Richard M. Nixon

    d. Gerald R. Ford

    e. Jimmy Carter

A. It was Gerald R. Ford. He was also the carrier's assistant navigation
officer. All five of the above choices were Navy men and served as
President *consecutively* after Dwight D. Eisenhower, an Army man.

Q. Which country lost the greatest number of hospital ships during the war?
A. Italy, which lost eight.

Q. Name the first U.S. Navy ship designated as an escort aircraft carrier, or baby flattop.
A. The converted cargo ship SS *Mormacmail* became the USS *Long Island*.

Q. Identify the U.S. Navy admiral who holds the unfortunate distinction of having two aircraft carriers lost while he was aboard them.
A. Admiral Frank J. Fletcher, winner of the Medal of Honor in 1914 for the Vera Cruz campaign, lost the USS *Yorktown* (CV-5) and USS *Lexington* (CV-2).

Q. Identify the last Japanese admiral to command a major force against the U.S. Navy in the war.
A. Admiral Seiichi Ito, who led a ten-ship action against the U.S. during the Okinawa campaign in April 1945. He was killed aboard his flagship the 72,809-ton battleship *Yamato*. (Volume 1, page 210)

Q. Identify the two U.S. admirals with the same last name who participated in the war in the Pacific.
A. Admirals Clifton Sprague and Thomas Sprague.

Q. Identify the ship that holds the record for wartime crossings of the Atlantic.
A. The Norwegian flag cargo ship *Mosdale*. It made the dangerous crossing ninety-eight times.

FACT Japan lost a total of twelve aircraft carriers in four naval battles: Coral Sea, May 7–8, 1942; Midway, June 3–6, 1942; Marianas, June 18–20, 1944; and Leyte, October 23–26, 1944. These losses are considered critical in the reversal of Japan's supremacy of the skies in the Pacific. At the outbreak of war, December 7, 1941, Japan had over 3,500 aircraft vs. fewer than 1,300 Allied aircraft in the war area. The U.S. lost three aircraft carriers in the same four battles.

> **FACT** During her forty months of combat in the war the USS *North Carolina* (BB-55) was reported sunk six times by Japanese propagandists, the USS *South Dakota* (BB-57) five times.

Q. Identify the first U.S. battleship to launch an aircraft from her decks. (Note: This took place *pre*-World War II).

A. The USS *Texas* (BB-35), which is a veteran of both world wars. Commissioned in 1914, she became a state shrine in 1948, the first battleship so designated by a state, and is open to the public at San Jacinto State Park, Texas.

Q. Identify the only U.S. battleship to sink a Japanese battleship in the war.

A. The USS *Washington* (BB-56), which sank the *Kirishima* on November 15, 1944, off Savo Island in the Solomons.

Q. Identify the two Japanese battleships that participated with the fleet that attacked Pearl Harbor.

A. *Hiei* and *Kirishima*. In all there were thirty-one ships in the attack fleet.

Q. Identify the U.S. Navy ship that President Franklin Roosevelt traveled on for the Middle East conferences in Cairo and Teheran.
  a. *Augusta*
  b. *Iowa*
  c. *Missouri*

A. The battleship USS *Iowa* (BB-61).

Q. Identify the only state in the U.S. that has never had a battleship named after it.

A. Montana. Work was started on a battleship to be named USS *Montana* for World War I, and in World War II a *Montana*-class was also begun, but in both cases the wars ended before the ships were built and christened.

Q. Identify the only U.S. warship that was present both at Pearl Harbor on December 7, 1941, and at Normandy on D-Day, June 6, 1944.
A. The battleship USS *Nevada* (BB-36). In photo at left, she is settling and burning at Pearl Harbor. Note fireboat alongside.

U.S. Navy Photo

FACT A mission from the Japanese Naval Air Force visited Taranto in May 1941 and was given a detailed account of how aircraft from British carriers had attacked the Italian ships there. It is highly likely that what they learned was used in Pearl Harbor.

Q. Identify the U.S. warship nicknamed the *Mighty Moo*.
A. The aircraft carrier USS *Cowpens* (CVL-25). The *Mighty Mo* was the battleship USS *Missouri* (BB-63).

Q. Who was the commander of the battleship USS *Missouri* (BB-63) during the Japanese surrender ceremonies in Tokyo Bay?
A. Captain Murry S. Stuart.

Q. Identify the U.S. warship that transported the Japanese surrender delegation from Tokyo to the USS *Missouri* (BB-63).
A. The destroyer USS *Lansdowne*.

Q. Identify the first battleship to be sunk by an attack from dive-bombing planes.
      a. HMS *Ark Royal*
      b. USS *Arizona*
      c. *Marat* (USSR)
A. The Soviet battleship *Marat* was sunk by German dive-bombers while in the port of Kronstadt in September 1941.

Q. Name the U.S. ship credited with firing the first and last American 16-inch shells in the war.
A. The USS *Massachusetts* (BB-59). The first was fired in November 1942 during Operation Torch and the last in 1945 at Honshu, Japan. She is now part of the warships exhibit open to the public at Battleship Cove, Fall River, Massachusetts.

Q. Who was the commanding officer of the German battleship *Bismarck*?
      a. Hans Langsdorff
      b. Ernest Lindemann
      c. Hans Ulrich Rudel
A. Lindemann. Langsdorff was captain of the *Graf Spee*, and Rudel was a Luftwaffe air ace. (Volume 1, pages 139 and 169)

Q. Name the two most memorable actions undertaken by Force F of the British Royal Navy.

A. The sinking of the *Bismarck* and the sinking of the French fleet at Oran.

Q. What were Japanese losses as a result of sinking the British dreadnoughts *Prince of Wales* and *Repulse*?

A. It cost the Japanese three aircraft to eliminate the 35,000-ton *Prince of Wales* and the 32,000-ton *Repulse* in the Gulf of Siam.

Q. Which country launched the first successful attack on enemy ships by aircraft-carrier planes?

A. The British, with planes from the carrier *Illustrious* against the Italians at Taranto. The battleships *Conte de Cavour*, *Littorio* and *Duilio* were so badly damaged they were unable to return to action until the war was nearly over. They represented almost half of the Italian battleship fleet.

Q. Who was the last commander-in-chief of the German Navy in the war?
   a. Admiral Hans Georg von Friedeberg
   b. Admiral Karl Doenitz
   c. Admiral Erich Raeder

A. Von Friedeberg, who killed himself after signing the surrender papers.

Q. Name the Italian admiral who became chief of the Navy upon the resignation of Admiral Domenico Cavagnari.

A. Admiral Arturo Riccardi, on December 8, 1940.

Q. Who was commander-in-chief of the Soviet Navy?

A. Admiral Nikolai G. Kuznetsov.

FACT Royal Navy Captain J. C. Leach of HMS *Prince of Wales* was one of two survivors out of eleven men on her bridge when a shell from the *Bismarck* hit her on May 24, 1941. Captain Leach was less fortunate on December 10 and lost his life when the Japanese sank the *Prince of Wales* and HMS *Repulse*.

Q. Identify the U.S. destroyer that fired the coup de grace to the disabled aircraft carrier USS *Lexington* (CV-2) on May 8, 1942.
A. The USS *Phelps*.

Q. Identify the two Royal Navy personnel who are credited with defusing the first German magnetic mine discovered in the Thames estuary on November 23, 1939.
A. Lieutenant Commander J. G. D. Ouvry and Chief Petty Officer Baldwin. Between November and December 1939, fifty-nine Allied and neutral ships (203,513 tons) were sunk by the magnetic mines.

Q. Did the Allies or the Germans have superiority on the seas at the outbreak of war in 1939?
A. The Allies were by far the stronger sea force. There were 676 ships built or launched for the Allies as opposed to 130 ships for Germany.

Q. What distinction does the Liberty Ship SS *Benjamin Warner* hold?
A. She was the last Liberty Ship built. Some 2,740 others preceded her, starting with the first, SS *Patrick Henry*, in September 1941.

Q. Identify the only remaining U.S. Liberty Ship.
A. The SS *Jeremiah O'Brian*, built in May 1943. It is now a memorial in San Francisco.

Q. Name the first Liberty Ship to be launched ten days after the keel was laid.
A. SS *Joseph N. Teal*, in October 1942.

Q. Name the first black to be named captain of a U.S. Liberty Ship.
A. Captain Hugh Mulzac, who commanded the SS *Booker T. Washington*.

Q. What were the names of the Greek battleships *Kilkis* and *Lemnos* when they were in commission as part of the U.S. Navy?
A. The *Kilkis* had been the USS *Mississippi* and the *Lemnos* was the old USS *Idaho*, whose newer namesake (BB-42) is seen here on April 1, 1945, off Okinawa.

U.S. Marine Corps Photo

> **FACT** Out of the crew of 1,421 aboard HMS *Hood*, only three survived the fatal engagement with the German battleship *Bismarck*.

Q. What distinction does the Japanese heavy cruiser *Mikuma* hold?

A. It is credited with sinking the greatest number of sister Japanese ships in the war. On February 27–28, 1942, the *Mikuma* sank four Japanese transports while trying to hit the USS *Houston*.

Q. Name the first Japanese surface ship sunk in the war.

A. The destroyer *Kisaragi* at Wake Island on December 11, 1941.

Q. Name the first Japanese ship to be scuttled in the war.

A. The 36,500-ton aircraft carrier *Akagi*, which was sunk by friendly fire after receiving serious damage in the Battle of Midway. It had been the flagship during the Japanese attack on Pearl Harbor. (Volume 1, pages 161 and 183)

Q. Name the two Japanese cruisers that took part in the attack on Pearl Harbor.

A. The *Chikuma* and the *Tone*. The first was sunk off Samar, the Philippines, by ship and aircraft fire on October 25, 1944, and the second off Kure, Japan, by aircraft on July 28, 1945.

Q. Name the Australian heavy cruiser that was hit by five Japanese kamikaze planes during the Okinawa campaign yet remained in action.

A. HMAS *Australia*.

Q. Who was the first American casualty, other than Air Force, in the war in Europe?

A. Lieutenant Colonel Loren B. Hillsinger during the raid on Dieppe in 1942. He was aboard the destroyer *Berkley* and lost a leg when the ship was bombed by the Luftwaffe.

Q. Name the U.S. admiral in command of the Saipan invasion.

A. Admiral Raymond Spruance, whose 535-ship armada brought 127,000 Marine and Army troops there on June 15, 1944. Here Spruance, left, and Admirals King and Nimitz inspect the island on July 17, 1944.

U.S. Marine Corps Photo

Q. Identify the most decorated ship in U.S. Navy history.

A. The 27,000-ton aircraft carrier USS *Franklin* (CV-13), which spent several years after the war in the mothball fleet stationed at Bayonne, New Jersey, until she was decommissioned and sold for scrap in 1947. Her navigation bridge is on exhibit as a permanent memorial in Norfolk, Virginia.

Q. Identify the first U.S. Navy captain to rise through the ranks to command an aircraft carrier.

A. Captain Leslie E. Gehres, who received the Navy Cross for saving the USS *Franklin* (CV-13) after it was seriously damaged and was considered lost.

Q. Who was the captain of the USS *Hornet* (CV-8) when Colonel (later General) Jimmy Doolittle launched his famous raid on Tokyo?

A. Captain (later Admiral) Marc Mitscher. (Volume 1, page 176)

Q. Identify the other U.S. aircraft carrier that escorted the USS *Hornet* (CV-8) during the Doolittle raid.

A. The USS *Enterprise* (CV-6).

Q. Which side was able to claim victory in the Battle of the Coral Sea?

A. As far as the naval battle is concerned, the U.S. and Japan fought to a tie, each lost a carrier — the USS *Lexington* (CV-2) and the *Shoho*. However, Japan's invasion of Australia was thwarted.

Q. Name the first two U.S. aircraft carriers to be converted from battle cruiser hulls.

A. The USS *Lexington* (CV-2) and USS *Saratoga* (CV-3), as a result of language in the Washington Naval Disarmament Treaty after World War I. The U.S. was permitted to convert two existing hulls into aircraft carriers of 33,000 tons each. In reality both topped out at just over 36,000 tons when "legal" modifications were added. In photo at left, the *Sara* is seen off Iwo Jima on February 21, 1945, after being seriously damaged by seven direct bomb hits. The damage shown was caused by two kamikaze planes.

Exclusive Photo by Tom Christie

Q. What were the ships that participated in the evacuation at Dunkirk called?

A. The Mosquito Armada.

Q. Who is credited with the success of the Dunkirk evacuation in May 1940?

A. Vice Admiral Sir Bertram Ramsay. Four years later Ramsay used his talents for mobilizing ships in the execution of the Normandy invasion.

Q. How long did it take to remove Allied troops from Dunkirk?

A. The rescue fleet continually crossed the English Channel for nine days.

Q. What is considered Britain's first naval victory in the war?

A. The hunt and offensive actions against the pocket battleship *Graf Spee*.

Q. Who was the oldest officer on active duty with the Japanese Navy when hostilities began in December 1941?

A. Admiral Osami Nagano, chief of the naval general staff. He had studied at Harvard, served as an attaché in Washington and considered New York City his second home. He was sixty-two years old.

Q. U.S. Admiral William F. Halsey signed the papers awarding the Navy and Marine Corps Medal to which future President of the United States?

A. John F. Kennedy, for his heroic actions after the sinking of the PT-109. (Volume 1, pages 175, 177)

FACT During the war, U.S. Admiral William F. Halsey made a remark about riding in Tokyo on the Emperor's horse, and several western U.S. cities presented him with saddles. In photo at left, Halsey presents a saddle to the U.S. Naval Academy Museum on November 27, 1945. Happy officer in center is museum director Captain Harry A. Baldridge, and on the right is the Superintendent of the Academy, Vice Admiral Aubrey Fitch. The saddle was made by Fred Lohlein of Bools and Butler Saddlery and presented by the Chamber of Commerce of Reno, Nevada.

U.S. Naval Academy Museum Photo

Q. What ship led the first convoy to approach the Normandy beaches for the D-Day invasion?

A. The USS *Corry*, a destroyer under the command of Lieutenant Commander George D. Hoffman.

Q. Under what conditions did the German Navy lose the destroyers *Leberecht Maass* and *Max Schultz* in the North Sea on February 22, 1940?

A. Because Germany, like Italy, did not have coordinated air and sea support but instead had an "autonomous air arm," communications often did not exist. Luftwaffe Stukas bombed and sank the *Leberecht Maass* and caused the *Max Schultz* to try to escape by sailing into a minefield, which proved fatal.

Q. How many ships did Germany lose during the battle for Norway?

A. Twenty-one ships were actually sunk, including eight submarines, three cruisers and ten destroyers. Several other ships were damaged badly.

Q. Name the British destroyer that rammed the German cruiser *Hipper* off Trondheim on April 9, 1940.
　　a. HMS *Glowworm*
　　b. HMS *Glower*
　　c. HMS *Glassfish*

A. The HMS *Glowworm*, after being fatally hit by fire from the *Hipper*, managed to ram her attacker and signal a warning that the German fleet was at sea. *Glowworm* survivors were rescued by the *Hipper*.

Q. Who commanded Halsey's Task Force 16 at Midway?

A. Rear Admiral Raymond A. Spruance, because Halsey had developed a rash and was in the hospital.

FACT According to U.S. Navy historian Admiral Samuel Eliot Morison, the nickname Bull was attached to Admiral William F. Halsey by a newsman. However, nobody who knew Halsey personally ever called him that, even though the corruption of the name Bill was not intended to be derogatory.

FACT Italian Navy Lieutenant Luigi Durand de la Penne was captured by the British after the two-man torpedo he had directed at the battleship HMS *Valiant* damaged but did not sink the warship. In 1945, with the Italians now on the side of the Allies, de la Penne was among several naval officers awarded medals for bravery. He received a medal for his action against the HMS *Valiant* in 1941. The medal was presented by Royal Navy Captain Charles Morgan, the man who had been in command of the *Valiant* at the time of de la Penne's attack.

Q. Which of the British armed services, the RAF or the Royal Navy, suffered the greater number of fatalities?

A. The Royal Navy lost 50,758 personnel, while the RAF counted 69,606 killed. The Army, however, had 144,079 killed or missing.

Q. Name the British-built destroyer that saw action as part of the German Navy.

A. *Hermes*, which the British had given to the Greeks, only to have it captured by the Germans. (Not to be confused with HMS *Hermes*, the British aircraft carrier that was the last British warship sunk in the war.)

Q. Identify the three Italian cruisers sunk by British planes during the Battle of Cape Matapan off southern Greece.

A. The *Fiume*, *Pola* and *Zara*. The Italians also lost two destroyers. Over 2,400 Italian sailors died, while the British lost one Swordfish torpedo bomber.

Q. Identify the British and German commanders who were both killed during the sea battle for Narvik, Norway, on April 10, 1940.

A. Captain B. A. W. Warburton-Lee, commander of the British 2nd Destroyer Flotilla, and Commander Paul Bonte of the German destroyer force. Both sides lost two destroyers.

Q. Identify the two old coastal defense ships of Norway that defied a German surrender demand on April 8, 1940, and were promptly blown out of the water.

A. The *Eidsvold* and the *Norge* challenged the German invasion force heading for the port of Narvik.

Q. Identify the U.S. aircraft carrier that former major-league baseball star pitcher George Earnshaw served aboard as a gunnery officer.

A. Lieutenant Commander George Earnshaw, ace right-hander for Connie Mack's Philadelphia Athletics during the late 1920s and early 1930s, served aboard the USS *Yorktown* (CV-10).

Q. Identify the only surviving U.S. destroyer of the USS *Allen M. Sumner* class.

A. The USS *Laffey* (DD-724), which is part of the famous ship display at Patriots Point Naval and Maritime Museum in Charleston, South Carolina. (See listing of WWII ship memorials in appendix.)

Q. Name the ship that carried U.S. General Douglas MacArthur back to the Philippine Islands so he could keep his promise to return.

A. The cruiser USS *Nashville*, on October 20, 1944.

Q. Pound for pound, which type of craft was the most heavily armed in the U.S. Navy fleet?

A. The swift, deadly and highly maneuverable PT boats.

Q. Identify the U.S. ship that survived the heaviest air attack of the Pacific war against a single vessel.

A. The USS *Laffey* (DD-724) which battled twenty-two attacking Japanese planes for seventy-nine minutes off Okinawa on April 16, 1945. Five kamikazes scored direct hits, as did three bombs. The *Laffey* shot down eleven of the attacking planes and suffered over 30 percent casualties.

Q. What was the purpose of Foxer devices used by merchant marine ships?

A. They caused sufficient noise to confuse German torpedoes. Towed behind ships, they made more noise than ship propellers and made acoustic torpedoes run amok.

FACT Ernie Pyle, the distinguished news correspondent who was killed on Ie Shima and buried there, now rests in the Punchbowl, Oahu, Hawaii, between two unknowns. He merited interment there not as a war correspondent but as a U.S. Navy veteran of World War I.

> **FACT** The USS *Arizona* (BB-39), considered America's most famous battleship and now a permanent memorial to the U.S. personnel who died during the December 7, 1941, attack on Pearl Harbor, was seen in a 1934 Hollywood movie, *Here Comes The Navy*, starring Jimmy Cagney and Pat O'Brien. (Volume 1, pages 164, 182, 190, 198 and 210).

Q. How many of the fifty U.S. destroyers that President Roosevelt sent to the British actually saw service in the Royal Navy?

A. Seven of them went to the Canadian Navy, two others were manned by Norwegian crews, leaving forty-one that the Royal Navy crewed with British sailors.

Q. Who was the Royal Navy commander for the raid on Dieppe, France, in August 1942?

A. Admiral John Hughes-Hallett.

Q. Identify the U.S. Navy ensign who is credited with being the first person to sight the Japanese at Pearl Harbor.

A. Ensign R. C. McCloy, who was aboard the minesweeper USS *Condor* (AMc-14) and reported seeing the conning tower of a submarine. It turned out to be one of the midget subs and was subsequently sunk by the destroyer USS *Ward* (DD-139). (Volume 1, pages 181 and 183)

> **FACT** Three U.S. Navy men whose names would later be linked forever with World War II were involved in the first successful crossing of the Atlantic using flying boats in 1919. Marc Mitscher, Patrick Bellinger and John C. Towers were members of the crews of three NC-4 aircraft that departed Rockaway Beach, New York, on May 18. Only one of the 68-foot-long planes completed the trip, and it was commanded by Lieutenant Commander Albert C. Reed. Nicknamed Nancys, the plywood and fabric craft had a wingspan of 128 feet, making them the largest aircraft in the world at the time. Years later Bellinger would tell the world America was at war with his famous "Air Raid Pearl Harbor, this is no drill." Mitscher would achieve fame as a carrier task force commander, and Towers would become one of the most vocal members of Congress to fight for a U.S. Navy Air Force.

———— FACT ————

Many of the key Japanese officers involved in the planning and execution of the Pearl Harbor attack on December 7 lost their lives during the war. With the exception of Minoru Genda, who was the tactical planner, and Flight Leader Mitsuo Fuchida, whose "Tora! Tora! Tora!" initiated hostilities, here is the fate of some of the others:

• *Admiral Isoroku Yamamoto*, the man who insisted that any war with the U.S. begin with the destruction of the U.S. fleet at Pearl Harbor, was aboard a plane shot down by U.S. airmen over Bougainville, April 18, 1943.

• *Vice Admiral Chuichi Nagumo*, commander-in-chief, 1st Air Fleet (the senior officer present in the attack fleet), was killed in action at Saipan.

• *Rear Admiral Tamon Yamaguchi*, commander-in-chief, 2nd Carrier Division, died aboard his aircraft carrier during the Battle of Midway.

• *Rear Admiral Matome Ugaki*, chief of staff to Yamamoto and the man who wrote the historic "Climb Mount Niitaka" message signaling the irrevocable order to attack Pearl Harbor, died piloting a kamikaze plane on the last day of the war.

• *Lieutenant Commander Kakuiche Takahashi*, leader of the dive-bombers in the first wave, was killed on May 2, 1942, in the Battle of the Coral Sea.

• *Lieutenant Commander Shigemaru Murata*, leader of the torpedo bombers in the first wave, was killed in battle at Santa Cruz, October 26-27, 1942.

• *Lieutenant Commander Takashige Egusa*, leader of the dive-bombers in the second wave, was killed over Saipan.

• *Lieutenant Commander Shigeru Itaya*, leader of the first wave of fighter planes, was shot down by mistake by Japanese Army planes over the Kuriles.

• *Lieutenant Commander Shigekazu Shimazaki*, commander of the second-wave attack force, was killed on January 9, 1945, off the Philippines.

Of the two major participants who survived, Genda went on to become a lieutenant general and later serve as a member in the upper house of the Diet (the Japanese equivalent of the U.S. Senate). Fuchida, as noted elsewhere in this volume, converted to Christianity and toured overseas extensively as a nondenominational evangelist.

Special Pearl Harbor Quiz

After the publication of the original volume of this book, we quickly discovered that the single event in the war that generated the most interest and that people seemed to be most fascinated about is the December 7, 1941, attack on Pearl Harbor. This section contains contributions from veterans, students of history and military buffs from across the U.S. who took the time to send along their particular favorites. Nearly half of the material that follows came from those sources. Additional Pearl Harbor related material is in Volume 1, pages 30, 33, 54, 59, 60, 107, 135, 139, 144, 146, 163, 164, 165, 166, 167, 168, 181, 183, 184, 185, 187, 193 and 213. In addition, the complete listing of all 145 U.S. Navy and U.S. Coast Guard ships involved appears in that volume on pages 208–209.

> Personnel of your Naval Intelligence Service should be advised that because of the fact that from past experience shows [sic] the Axis Powers often begin activities in a particular field on Saturdays and Sundays or on national holidays of the country concerned they should take steps on such days to see that proper watches and precautions are in effect.
> —An April 1, 1941 alert from U.S. Naval Intelligence, Washington.

Q. Identify the first U.S. ship in Pearl Harbor to be hit by a Japanese torpedo.
A. The USS *Oklahoma* (BB-37). The torpedo was fired by torpedo-plane pilot Inichi Goto.

Q. What was the U.S. code name for Japan prior to hostilities?
A. Orange. The term was used in practically all communications, codes and tactical planning.

FACT Commander Mitsuo Fuchida, the leader of the air attack on Pearl Harbor with the utterance of "Tora! Tora! Tora!" was en route to Hiroshima by plane on August 6, 1945, and saw the mushroom cloud rise above his homeland when the U.S. dropped the atom bomb. Fuchida was also aboard the battleship USS *Missouri* (BB-63) to witness the surrender ceremonies the following September. He is believed to be the only person present at *all three* historic events. After the war he became a convert to Christianity and frequently visited the United States. This photo was taken the day before the surrender.

Author's Collection

> **FACT** Two leading air officers in the Japanese attack on Pearl Harbor
> wore red underwear and red shirts in order to conceal any injuries
> they might sustain during the raid. Flight Leader Mitsuo
> Fuchida, the overall attack commander, and Lieutenant Com-
> mander Shigemaru Murata, leader of the torpedo bombers in the
> first wave, reasoned that if they became wounded their blood
> would not show up against the red. Their intention was to pre-
> vent demoralizing other flying officers.

Q. Identify the Japanese officer involved in the Pearl Harbor attack
who admired Adolf Hitler so much that he grew a toothbrush
mustache.

A. The man whose "Tora! Tora! Tora!" signaled the start of the attack, Commander Mitsuo Fuchida.

Q. Identify the last U.S. ship to sortie in Pearl Harbor on December
7, 1941.

A. The cruiser USS *St. Louis* (CL-49), which ran at twenty-two knots
in an eight-knot zone in order to clear the channel at 10:04 A.M. She
immediately had to take evasive action to avoid two torpedoes fired
from a Japanese midget submarine. The fish struck the coral reef
near the channel entrance, and *St. Louis* returned fire at the sub,
believing they hit the conning tower.

Q. Identify the bandleader aboard the USS *Nevada* (BB-36) who conducted his musicians through the final notes of "The Star Spangled
Banner" while under attack in Pearl Harbor.

A. Oden McMillan, who reportedly picked up the tempo somewhat as
enemy fire hit the ship.

Q. What was the Japanese name for its formidable Pearl Harbor strike
force?

A. Kido Butai.

Q. Who was the second-highest-ranking U.S. Navy officer stationed
at Pearl Harbor on December 7?

A. Vice Admiral William Satterlee Pye, outranked only by Admiral
Husband E. Kimmel. While in the War Plans Division in
Washington, Pye drafted the U.S. Navy's war plan for the Pacific.

Q. Identify the American who captured the first prisoner of war after the attack on Pearl Harbor, and name the prisoner.

A. U.S. Army Sergeant David M. Akui captured the commander of a midget submarine that had difficulties and drifted near the Kaneohe-Bellows Field area of Oahu, Hawaii, on December 7, 1941. Unsuccessful in an effort to scuttle the boat, and weakened from exhaustion, Ensign Kazuo Sakamaki passed out in the water and awoke on a beach with Sergeant Akui standing over him. The incident took place late in the evening of the attack, making Sakamaki prisoner of war #1.

Q. Identify the Japanese admiral who was nicknamed King Kong by his own sailors.

A. Rear Admiral Chuichi Hara, commander of the Fifth Carrier Division, which included the aircraft carriers *Shokaku* and *Zuikaku*. He was one of three carrier division commanders who participated in the attack on Pearl Harbor.

Q. After the deaths of Admiral Kidd and Captain Van Valkenburgh aboard the USS *Arizona* (BB-39), who issued the order to abandon ship?

A. Lieutenant Commander Samuel G. Fuqua.

FACT The Imperial Japanese Navy General Staff, under Admiral Osami Nagano, opposed Admiral Yamamoto's plan to attack Pearl Harbor as being too risky and continued to question Yamamoto up to the very last minute as to whether he could be sure the U.S. fleet would be there. It was the powerful and confident personage of Yamamoto himself that conquered any fears and managed to get the IJN General Staff to permit executing the attack. However, this was all predicated upon the fact that Japan continued to get assurances from its consulate in Oahu that the fleet remained stationed there. When the U.S. government ordered all twenty-four German consulates in the U.S. closed, plus all Italian consulates, during June 1941, Japan feared that as a member of the Tripartite Pact it would also face similar closures. It is believed that under such conditions (the lack of espionage revealing the presence of the U.S. fleet) the IJN General Staff may well have canceled Yamamoto's plan to attack Pearl Harbor. However, for several political reasons, the U.S. government did not close the Japanese consulates.

> **FACT** Joseph C. Grew was the U.S. Ambassador to Japan for nearly a decade and was the ranking member of the diplomatic corps when Pearl Harbor was attacked. Partially deaf, he never managed to master Japanese. However, his wife, Alice, spoke it fluently. She was the granddaughter of Commodore Perry.

Q. Identify the U.S. Navy ship that happened to be in the berth at Battleship Row that was usually occupied by the battleship USS *Pennsylvania* (BB-38).

A. The minelayer USS *Oglala* (CM-4) was at Dock 1010 instead of the *Pennsylvania*, which was in dry dock across the harbor. *Oglala* was outboard the cruiser USS *Helena* (CL-50). *Oglala* was the flagship of Rear Admiral William Rhea Furlong, commander of Battle Forces Pacific (service vessels), and it was Furlong who gave the order to the fleet, "All ships in harbor sortie," as the Japanese attack began.

Q. What did the following mean: *Higashi no kazeame*?

A. It is the original Japanese quote of the famous "East wind, rain" message. It was sent to Japanese Ambassador Nomura on November 29, 1941, by the Foreign Office in Tokyo. "East wind rain" meant Japanese-U.S. relations were in danger.

Q. Identify the radio station in Hawaii that, because it was broadcasting all night to guide in U.S. B-17s from the mainland, was used by the Japanese task force as a guide to Pearl Harbor, Oahu, on December 6–7, 1941.

A. Radio station KGMB, which normally did not broadcast all night.

Q. What was the name of the radar station on Oahu that sighted the Japanese planes heading for the attack on the morning of December 7?

A. Opana Mobile Radar Station. It was staffed on that day by U.S. Army privates Joseph L. Lockard and George E. Elliott. They were due to go off duty at 7 A.M. but remained later to watch an unusual blip that had just appeared. The sighting was reported to the Army's Information Center. However, Lieutenant Kermit Tyler, the pursuit officer who had the authority to "intercept enemy planes," was convinced that the blip was the flight of U.S. B-17s expected from the mainland.

Q. Who was Tadao Fuchikami?

A. The RCA motorcycle messenger in Honolulu who delivered the Western Union telegram from Washington advising General Short and Admiral Kimmel that the Japanese were issuing an ultimatum at "1 P.M. Eastern Standard Time today..." (7:30 A.M. in Honolulu). It had been received by Honolulu RCA twenty-two minutes before the attack but not delivered until four hours later. It took another three hours to decode.

Q. Besides the eight battleships in Pearl Harbor on December 7, identify the other two that Admiral Kimmel had requested be sent there earlier in the year.

A. During a meeting in The White House with President Roosevelt on June 9, 1941, Kimmel asked his Commander-in-Chief for the USS *North Carolina* (BB-55) and USS *Washington* (BB-56) since Japan at the time had more battleships in the Pacific than the U.S. did. Fortunately, FDR did not comply.

Q. Besides the attacking Japanese planes, what else hindered the efforts of the Ford Island Fire Brigade to contain or control the numerous fires?

A. When the USS *Arizona* (BB-39) sank, she settled on the island's main water lines, resulting in a complete loss of pressure.

FACT On May 12, 1941, some seven months before the Japanese attack on Pearl Harbor, the U.S. Army and Navy held what were described as "the greatest war drills ever staged" in the Hawaiian Islands. Army bombers "attacked" enemy aircraft carriers several hundred miles at sea just as one carrier was preparing to launch planes against the islands. In an ironic note a formation of twenty-one B-17s landed on Oahu from the mainland while the "attack" was under way. The war games contained many phases and options and continued for two weeks, with the U.S. forces gaining the upper hand. The Navy had held similar games involving a Pearl Harbor attack by enemy aircraft carriers in 1933 and in 1939. In the 1939 exercise, aircraft from the carrier USS *Saratoga* (CV-3) succeeded in a surprise attack on a Sunday morning. The attacking aircraft "sank" several ships at anchor in Pearl Harbor and attacked Hickam, Wheeler and Ford Island airfields before returning safely to their carrier.

> **FACT** A Gallup Poll taken in September 1941 reflected that 70 percent of the American population was willing to risk war with Japan. A poll taken in July had shown that 51 percent held that attitude.

Q. Who was the commander of the aircraft carrier USS *Enterprise* (CV-6) when it missed being in Pearl Harbor during the December 7 attack?

    a. William F. Halsey
    b. Raymond Spruance
    c. Kelly Turner
    d. George Murray

A. Captain George Murray was the commander. Admiral Halsey was also aboard.

Q. Other than the submarine contact made on the morning of December 7, what was the earliest contact U.S. forces had indicating possible hostile submarines in Hawaiian waters?

A. On December 5, the destroyers USS *Selfridge* (DD-357) and *Ralph Talbot* (DD-390) made underwater contact with what the *Talbot* commander reported as a submarine about five miles off Pearl Harbor. He requested but was denied permission to depth-charge with the explanation that it was not a sub but a blackfish. "If this is a blackfish, it has a motorboat up its stern!" he reportedly responded. That same night Admiral William F. Halsey's task force was advised that a submarine had been reported on December 4 just south of Hawaii.

Q. What distinction does U.S. Army nurse Ann Fox hold with regard to the December 7 attack on Pearl Harbor?

A. She received the first Purple Heart presented to a woman in the war as a result of injuries she received at Hickam Field.

Q. On February 11, 1941, Admiral Husband E. Kimmel, commander-in-chief of the U.S. Fleet in Hawaii, issued a letter to his command that said, in part, "a declaration of war might be preceded by — "

    a. a surprise attack on ships in Pearl Harbor
    b. a surprise submarine attack on ships in operating area
    c. a combination of these two

A. *All three* caveats were included in his letter.

> **FACT** Lieutenant Colonel Kendall (Wooch) Fielder became intelligence
> officer (G-2) on the staff of General Walter C. Short in July 1941,
> a scant five months before the Pearl Harbor attack. He had no
> prior intelligence duty and had not previously served under Short.

Q. What was the name of the annual charity dinner-dance held on Oahu
on December 6, and attended by General Short and several other
U.S. Army staff personnel?

A. Ann Etzler's Cabaret. It was staged at the Schofield Barracks Officers' Club.

Q. Identify the Roosevelt Administration Cabinet member who flew
to Pearl Harbor on December 9, 1941.

A. Secretary of the Navy Frank Knox arrived at Kaneohe Bay on
December 11. Upon returning to Washington, Knox gave FDR a
complete report of his meetings with Admiral Kimmel, General
Short and other key military personnel, plus an evaluation of the
damage.

Q. What were Japan's estimates of its own losses with regard to the
attack on Pearl Harbor?
    a. It expected less than 10 percent losses
    b. One-third of their task force
    c. Approximately 50 percent of ships and planes

A. It was estimated that one-third of the task force would be lost, but
that such a cost was necessary. In actuality not a single surface
ship was lost, but the submarine fleet did sustain losses.

Q. Who called Pearl Harbor a "God-damn mousetrap"?

A. Admiral Kimmel's predecessor, Admiral James O. Richardson,
because of its long, narrow channel entrance that required capital
ships to enter it one at a time.

> **Q.** Who said, "What a target that would make!" upon seeing the U.S.
> fleet all lit up at Pearl Harbor on the night of December 6, 1941?
> **A.** Lieutenant General Walter C. Short, the U.S. Army commander on
> Oahu, while returning home with his wife and his intelligence officer
> (G-2), Lieutenant Colonel Kendall J. Fielder, after attending a party.
>
> *U.S. Army Photo*

Q. Identify the U.S. commander who on September 20, 1941, submitted a plan calling for joint Army-Navy exercise drills to train against a potential Japanese carrier-based air attack.

A. Major General Frederick L. Martin, commander of the Hawaiian Air Force. He suggested the "games" take place November 17–22. At the time he made the request, the Japanese were themselves considering either November 16 or 23 as the date for the attack. Martin's request was not acted upon favorably.

Q. Identify the two U.S. officers who in March 1941 were charged with the task of creating a joint Army-Navy plan in the event of an attack on Oahu or U.S. fleet ships in Hawaiian waters.

A. Rear Admiral Patrick N. L. Bellinger and Major General Frederick Martin, who authored the famous Martin-Bellinger Report. Both were based in Hawaii. Among highlights of the report are observations such as

- A successful, sudden raid against our ships and naval installations on Oahu might prevent effective offensive action by our forces in the Western Pacific for a long period.
- It appears possible that Orange [the U.S. code for Japan] submarines and/or an Orange fast raiding force might arrive in Hawaiian waters with no prior warning from our intelligence service.
- Orange might send into this area one or more submarines and/or one or more fast raiding forces composed of carriers supported by fast cruisers.
- A declaration of war might be preceded by: A surprise submarine attack on ships in the operating area. A surprise attack on Oahu, including ships and installations in Pearl Harbor.
- It appears that the most likely and dangerous form of attack on Oahu would be an air attack...such an attack would most likely be launched from one or more carriers which would probably approach inside of three hundred miles.
- Any single submarine attack might indicate the presence of a considerable undiscovered surface force...
- In a dawn air attack there is a high probability that it could be delivered as a complete surprise...

> **FACT** In the 1925 novel *The Great Pacific War*, author Hector C. Bywater detailed a fictitious account of a Japanese surprise attack against the U.S. fleet at Pearl Harbor. The novel was reportedly used in the Japanese Navy War College.

Q. Where did Japanese Consul General Kiichi Gunji, based in Hawaii, get his information on the size, numbers and movements of the U.S. fleet?

A. The information he was requested to get by Tokyo regularly appeared in the news pages of Honolulu newspapers, which included the names and exact arrival and departure times of fleet ships. This data, public information in Hawaii, became classified the moment it arrived in Japan. In addition, the Japanese consulate's treasurer, Kohichi Seki, used a copy of *Jane's Fighting Ships* to scout and identify vessels of the fleet.

Q. Though much is made of the fact that the U.S. was reading Japanese codes prior to Pearl Harbor, how many Purple decoding machines did the U.S. actually have?

A. In 1941 the U.S. had only eight such machines. Four were in Washington (two each for the Army and Navy), one went to the Philippines and two were sent to London (in exchange for Ultra intelligence we were receiving from the British). That left one machine, and it was slated for Hawaii. However, Washington wanted it, and it was known that London was also interested in a third machine. At the expense of Hawaii, and as a compromise with Washington, the machine was sent to the British.

Q. What were the Japanese J codes?

A. These were what the U.S. considered lower-grade codes between the Foreign Ministry and several of its consulates, including Honolulu. The U.S. had broken and was reading them from the summer of 1940. The J codes are not to be confused with the so-called Purple Code. The significance of the J codes, particularly one known as J-19, is that the U.S. was fully aware of Tokyo's interest in the position and/or movement of the U.S. fleet based in Hawaii. In early December 1941, the Japanese consulate in Hawaii changed from the J code to the PA-K2 code.

Q. What was the "bomb plot" message?

A. A request from Tokyo to its agents on Oahu to divide the area of Pearl Harbor into a grid when referring to locations in further communication. It was intercepted by U.S. intelligence on September 24 but not translated until October 9. At the time it was considered by most U.S. military personnel involved as an example of the extreme detail the Japanese were famous for and not as a grid pattern for an attack.

Q. To whom or what did Japan credit the sinking of the battleship USS *Arizona* (BB-39)?

A. Contrary to facts, Japan first reported — and continued to report through the spring of 1942 — that the *Arizona* was sunk by one of its midget submarines. However, Japanese Petty Officer Noboru Kanai, considered the top horizontal bombardier in the Imperial Navy, is believed to have dropped the bomb that sank the USS *Arizona* (BB-39) at Pearl Harbor. Experts, however, disagree as to whether the bomb actually went down the smokestack or struck the ship in a vulnerable position. Kanai lost his life during the battle for Wake Island.

Q. How did the medical staffs at Pearl Harbor indicate which injured personnel had already been given morphine so that double injections were not given?

A. Those already injected got Mercurochrome marks on their foreheads. More than 300 casualties arrived at the medical facilities of Patrol Wing Two within the first half hour of the attack.

Q. Identify the only U.S. Navy submariner wounded in the attack on Pearl Harbor.

A. Seaman Second Class G. A. Myers, who was hit by Japanese aircraft fire while aboard the USS *Cachalot* (SS-170).

Q. How much damage did the city of Honolulu sustain in the attack on Pearl Harbor on December 7, 1941?

A. Approximately $500,000 worth of damage, which was the result of U.S. anti-aircraft fire, not Japanese bombs. Upwards of forty explosions rocked the city.

U.S. Army Photo

Q. Identify the U.S. battleship at Pearl Harbor on December 7 that had several of her manholes open (either removed or loosened) in preparation for inspection the following day.

A. The USS *California* (BB-44), flagship of Vice Admiral William S. Pye. As a result of the open manholes the *California* nearly capsized after being hit by two torpedoes. Water poured into the fuel system and cut off light and power. However, Ensign Edgar M. Fain immediately directed counterflooding measures, which are considered to have saved the ship.

Q. Why did Kichisaburo Nomura, the Japanese Ambassador to the U.S., request on August 4, 1941, that Japan send veteran diplomat Saburo Kurusu to Washington as a special envoy to assist with efforts to secure a "final attempt at peace"?

A. Kurusu, who as Japanese Ambassador to Germany signed the Tripartite Pact, was thought of with great respect and confidence in Japanese government circles. In addition, he was married to an American woman and spoke idiomatic English, affording him the guarantee that he could not be misunderstood nor misinterpret anything said to him by the Americans.

Q. Identify the communications problem the Japanese had to overcome in preparation for the attack on Pearl Harbor.

A. Prior to 1941, Japan had never had a Navy fighter plane involved in action more than 100 miles from its home base or aircraft carrier because their radiotelephone communications system was unable to function beyond that distance. Throughout the summer of 1941, Japanese Navy pilots and communications personnel had to become proficient in Morse code in order to sustain communications during the planned Pearl Harbor attack.

Q. What distinction does U.S. Navy Lieutenant William W. Outerbridge hold?

A. He was the first American to sink a Japanese warship in 1941. As commander of the destroyer USS *Ward* (DD-139), he sighted and depth-charged a Japanese midget submarine near Pearl Harbor on the morning of December 7, nearly an hour before the enemy air attack.

FACT The American opinion of the Japanese prior to, and even after, Pearl Harbor, saw them as a backward, ignorant race. However, it was not commonly known that several leading Japanese officers had attended some of the finest universities and colleges in the U.S. Some Ivy League participants in the Pearl Harbor attack included Yamamoto and Nagano (Harvard); Yamaguchi (Princeton); and Arima (Yale). Likewise, in Europe, a number of German generals had studied at Oxford and other English schools.

Q. After the attack on Pearl Harbor, to what port did the Japanese fleet return?
A. Hiroshima, on December 23, 1941.

Q. When did Japan formally declare that a state of war existed with the U.S.?
A. At 1600 EST on December 7, 1941, Japan announced that it was at war with the U.S. and the British Empire. This was some three hours after the attack on Pearl Harbor.

Q. Who did Japanese Commander Minoru Genda consider the "torpedo ace of the Japanese Navy"?
A. The man he selected to be leader of the torpedo bombers in the first wave against Pearl Harbor, Lieutenant Commander Shigemaru Murata.

Q. Who was Lieutenant Commander Takeshige Egusa?
A. He was the leader of the dive bombers in the second wave of the attack on Pearl Harbor and, according to tactical planner Commander Minoru Genda, "the number-one dive-bombing pilot in all Japan."

Q. Name the Japanese admiral who commanded the Sixth Fleet (submarines) in the Pearl Harbor attack.
A. Vice Admiral Mitsumi Shimizu.

Q. Identify the U.S. armed forces commander who pleaded with the U.S. War Department for bombproof aircraft repair facilities on September 10, 1941, which he called "vital to the continued functioning of the Hawaiian Air Force during an attack on Oahu."
A. Lieutenant General Walter C. Short.

Q. Identify the U.S. naval officer who wrote a memorandum entitled "Steps to be Taken in Case of American-Japanese War Within the Next Twenty-Four Hours."

A. Admiral Husband E. Kimmel, CINCUS. In a meeting with aides on December 6, Kimmel updated the prophetic memo.

Q. Who sent the first message out reporting the attack on Pearl Harbor, Bellinger or Ramsey?

A. As noted in Volume 1, page 59, Rear Admiral Patrick Bellinger has been credited with the historic message: "Air raid, Pearl Harbor — This is no drill," at 7:58 A.M. Bellinger is named as the officer in Samuel Eliot Morison's *The Two-Ocean War* and Walter Lord's *Day of Infamy*. A third source that credits Admiral Bellinger is Lieutenant Colonel Eddy Bauer in the 24-volume *Illustrated World War II Encyclopedia*. However, in *At Dawn We Slept*, author Gordon Prange claims Lieutenant Commander Logan C. Ramsey sent the message out, also at 7:58, but in this message "no" is replaced by "not." It is interesting to note that Ramsey was with a Lieutenant Richard Ballinger near the radio room of the Ford Island command center at this point in the attack and reportedly ran into the room to order radiomen on duty to send out the message. There were at least two other messages, similar in content, sent over the air in the immediate minutes reported here.

Q. Who said, "The Japs wouldn't dare attack Hawaii."?

A. U.S. Army Chief of Staff General George C. Marshall, to Secretary of War Henry L. Stimson on April 23, 1941.

Q. Who was the commander of the Southeast Asia Theater?

A. Lord Louis Mountbatten, first row center, cousin of the British King. In this photo with four American officers whose names would forever be linked to December 7, 1941, Mountbatten is shown visiting the Hawaiian Islands when he was commander of the British aircraft carrier *Illustrious*. The others: General Walter C. Short, U.S. Army commander; Admiral Husband E. Kimmel, U.S. Navy commander; General Frederick L. Martin, commander of the Hawaiian Air Force; and Admiral Patrick N. L. Bellinger, whose message "Air raid Pearl Harbor. This is no drill" would be the first news of the attack to reach Washington.

U.S. Army Photo

Q. Identify the island that served as the training center for the attack on Pearl Harbor.

A. Kyushu, the southernmost of the four main Japanese islands. Ariake Bay, frequently the home of the fleet, had a resemblance to Pearl Harbor.

Q. Prior to its extensive training, why were Japan's horizontal bombers considered a poor risk, or a minimally effective force, with regard to the attack on Pearl Harbor?

A. The Japanese used a modified version of the German Boyco bombsight, critically inferior to the Norden bombsight used by the U.S. The accuracy of the Japanese Boyco depended almost totally upon the expertise of the bombardier and pilot working together as a team.

Q. Who correctly guessed that the unusual wording of the fourteen-part Japanese message breaking diplomatic relations at 1 P.M. Washington time on December 7 indicated that hostilities against Pearl Harbor were nearly certain?

A. Commander Arthur H. McCollum, Lieutenant Commander A. D. Kramer, both of Naval Intelligence, and Colonel Rufus S. Bratton of Army Intelligence. The time in Pearl Harbor would be 7:30 A.M.

Q. When did U.S. forces in the Pacific receive the "war warning" from Washington that said in part, "An aggressive move by Japan is expected within the next few days"?

A. On November 27, 1941.

Q. Who said, "If war eventuates with Japan, it is believed easily possible that hostilities would be initiated by a surprise attack upon the fleet or the naval base at Pearl Harbor"?

A. Secretary of the Navy Frank Knox in a letter to Secretary of War Henry L. Stimson on January 24, 1941, some eleven months before the attack. The letter, which was actually written by Rear Admiral Richmond Kelly Turner and approved by Admiral Stark (before being given to Knox to sign), continued: "In my opinion the inherent possibilities of a major disaster to the fleet or naval base warrant taking every step, as rapidly as can be done, that will increase the joint readiness of the Army and Navy to withstand a raid of the character mentioned above."

> **FACT** On December 2, 1941, Lieutenant Ellsworth A. Hosner and another staff member of the 12th Naval District Intelligence (San Francisco) Office detected radio signals in the Pacific they thought could be from the Japanese fleet, which had been missing since late November. Their commander, Captain Richard T. McCollough, a friend of President Roosevelt, was advised. They continued to track the signals and on December 6 established that the position was about 400 miles north of Oahu.

Q. Who said, "Hawaii would be a fine place from which to watch a Japanese-American war"?

A. Takeo Yoshikawa, a trained Japanese intelligence agent who functioned at the consulate in Hawaii under the name of Tadashi Morimura. When he made the statement to Kohichi Seki, the Japanese consulate's treasurer and the man who had reported the movements of the U.S. fleet prior to Yoshikawa's arrival there, neither man knew anything about the planned attack on Pearl Harbor.

Q. Who said, "The only real answer was for the fleet not to be in Pearl Harbor when the attack came"?

A. Admiral Husband E. Kimmel, CINCUS, to Admiral Harold R. Stark, CNO, in a meeting in Washington on June 13, 1941, attended also by Secretary of the Navy Frank Knox. Kimmel said the congestion of ships, fuel oil storage and repair facilities in Pearl Harbor invited an "attack, particularly from the air." With the fleet in port, Kimmel said, it would take at least three hours to sortie. "The only real answer was for the fleet not to be in Pearl Harbor when the attack came," he added.

Q. Who said the following about the defense of Pearl Harbor: "It must be remembered too that a single submarine attack may indicate the presence of a considerable surface force...accompanied by a carrier"?

A. Admiral Husband E. Kimmel to Rear Admiral Claude C. Bloch, the man he named as naval base defense commander for Pearl Harbor in February 1941. At 6:45 A.M on December 7, the destroyer USS *Ward* (DD-139) depth-charged and sank a Japanese submarine more than an hour before the attack. A second sub was sunk at 0700 by a Catalina flying boat.

> **FACT** The Navy and Army commanders at Pearl Harbor, Admiral Husband E. Kimmel and General Walter C. Short, assumed their commands within days of each other in February 1941. Kimmel's tour began on February 1, while Short took over on February 7.

Q. Who said, "In view of the Japanese situation, the Navy is concerned with the security of the fleet in Hawaii...They are in the situation where they must guard against a surprise or trick attack"?

A. General George C. Marshall, U.S. Army Chief of Staff to high-ranking U.S. Army staff personnel on February 25, 1941. He continued: "We also have information regarding the possible use of torpedo planes. There is the possible introduction of Japanese carrier-based planes." Eight days later Marshall urged General Walter C. Short to send him a review of the Hawaii defenses against possible air attack, calling it "a matter of first priority."

Q. Who said, "The Japanese will not go to war with the United States. We are too big, too powerful and too strong"? When?

A. Vice Admiral William Satterlee Pye, on Oahu, Hawaii, December 6, 1941. Pye was the second-highest-ranking U.S. Navy officer at Pearl Harbor.

Q. Who said, "They [Japan] will attack right here" during a conversation about Japanese intentions on December 6, 1941, in Pearl Harbor?

A. Ensign Fred Hall, the assistant communications officer aboard the USS *Vestal* (AR-4). His prophetic statement was interjected into a conversation among other officers in the wardroom. However, nobody bothered to ask him when or why the attack would take place. The following morning Hall was the officer of the deck and pulled the general quarters signal at 7:55 A.M. as the Japanese attack began.

> **Q.** What were Japanese losses in the Pearl Harbor attack?
> **A.** In terms of human life, fifty-five fliers and nine midget submariners, plus an unknown number aboard an I-class submarine. Of the 432 planes that participated in the raid, twenty-nine were downed. In this photo, Lieutenant Fusata Iida, who crashed at Kaneohe Bay, is buried with honor by U.S. military personnel on Hawaii.
>
> *U.S. Navy Photo*

> **FACT** Admiral Husband E. Kimmel came from a Kentucky family with a West Point military tradition. Upon failing to gain admittance to the Point, he tried and succeeded in being admitted to the Naval Academy, where he graduated thirteenth in a class of sixty-two. His wife was the daughter of an admiral who was the brother of Admiral Thomas C. Kinkaid. Kimmel served as an aide to the then Secretary of the Navy, Franklin D. Roosevelt, for a brief time.

Q. Who said "This means war"?

A. President Franklin D. Roosevelt, on December 6, 1941, after reading the thirteen-part message Tokyo had sent to its ambassadors in Washington. (The copy FDR read was not the official communication which would not be delivered until the following day, but the result of U.S. code-breaking activity.) The fourteenth part had not been seen by the President at this time.

Q. Who said, "To make victory certain, we would have to march into Washington and dictate the terms of peace in the White House"?

A. Taken out of context, the above statement was made by Admiral Isoroku Yamamoto in a letter to Japanese ultranationalist Ryoichi Sasakawa prior to the Pearl Harbor attack. The excerpt was later used by U.S. nationalists to foster the belief that Yamamoto intended to invade the U.S. and capture Washington, D.C. In its entirety, the paragraph was actually a sarcastic cut at Japan's extreme right. Yamamoto was telling them the U.S. was not a hollow giant. It continued: "I wonder if our politicians, among whom armchair arguments about war are being glibly bandied about in the name of state politics, have confidence as to the final outcome and are prepared to make the necessary sacrifices."

Q. Who said, "If we are going into a war, why don't we have machine guns"?

A. Major Truman H. Landon to Major General Henry H. (Hap) Arnold when he and other members of the crews of the 38th and 88th Reconnaissance squadrons were about to fly to Clark Field, the Philippines, to deliver B-17s. Arnold had said, "War is imminent. You may run into a war during your flight." The planes, which were stripped to conserve fuel, had a scheduled stop at Hickam Field, Oahu, Hawaii, on December 7, 1941.

Q. Who said, "Our most likely enemy, Orange [Japan], can probably employ a maximum of six carriers against Oahu"?

A. Colonel William E. Farthing, commander of the Fifth Bombardment Group, Hickam Field, Hawaii, in what is known as the Farthing Report. Farthing completed the report on July 10, 1941. Its intent was to analyze the use of bombardment aviation as a defense for Hawaii. It also noted that "the early morning attack is, therefore, the best plan of action to the enemy."

Q. Who said, "I feel that a surprise attack [submarine, air or combined] on Pearl Harbor is a possibility"?

A. Admiral Husband E. Kimmel, Cincus, on February 18, 1941, in a letter to Admiral Harold R. Stark, CNO.

Q. Who said, "My Peruvian colleague told a member of my staff that he heard...that Japanese military forces planned...to attempt a surprise attack on Pearl Harbor"?

A. Considered one of the most remarkable dispatches ever sent by a U.S. diplomat, U.S. Ambassador to Japan Joseph C. Grew sent the above to the State Department within *a month after Admiral Yamamoto first disclosed to anyone* his bold plan for attacking Pearl Harbor in January 1941. However, it received only token interest in official circles, since Japanese fiction writers had used the theme of attacking Pearl Harbor for several years and the report was considered just an unfounded rumor based on such tales. Nonetheless, on February 1, 1941, the Office of Naval Intelligence paraphrased the ambassador's dispatch and forwarded it to Admiral Husband E. Kimmel in Hawaii.

FACT General Hein Ter Poorten, commander of the Netherlands East Indies Army, advised the U.S. military observer in Java, Brigadier General Elliott Thorpe, in early December 1941, that his intelligence staff had intercepted a Japanese code which stated that Japan would attack Hawaii, the Philippines, Malaya and Thailand shortly. He further noted that the signal for hostilities against the U.S. would be the message "East wind, rain." General Thorpe sent this information to Washington along with three others on the same subject, but Washington's reply requested he send no further information on the subject.

FACT Captain Johan Ranneft, the Dutch naval attaché in Washington, was told on December 6, 1941, that two Japanese aircraft carriers were proceeding east between Japan and Hawaii. While at the Office of U.S. Naval Intelligence, he asked where the carriers were. An officer placed a finger on a wall chart and indicated a position between 300 and 400 miles northwest of Honolulu.

Q. Who said, "Do you mean to say that they [the Japanese fleet] could be rounding Diamond Head this minute and you wouldn't know?"

A. Admiral Husband E. Kimmel to his intelligence officer on Oahu on December 2, 1941, five days before the infamous attack, when the officer informed Kimmel that the Japanese carrier force that left its home waters in late November was still "missing" to U.S. plotters.

Q. Who said, "My impression of the Hawaiian [Pearl Harbor] problem has been that if no serious harm is done us during the *first six hours* of known hostilities, thereafter the existing defenses would discourage an enemy against the hazard of an attack"?

A. U.S. Army Chief of Staff George C. Marshall, who never considered that Japan could inflict the kind of harm he feared in the *first six minutes* (author's italics).

Q. Who said, "No, thanks, Betty, I feel I can get it through quickly enough," to whom concerning the final warning message to Pearl Harbor the morning of December 7?

A. General George Marshall in a telephone call to Admiral Harold R. (Betty) Stark. Marshall marked the message "First Priority — Secret," and it was sent by Western Union rather than through the U.S. Navy's rapid transmission system that Stark had offered. The message was "The Japanese are presenting at 1 P.M. Eastern Standard Time today what amounts to an ultimatum. Also they are under orders to destroy their code machine immediately. Just what significance the hour set may have we do not know, but be on the alert accordingly." It arrived on Oahu at the Western Union office and was delivered some time after the attack began. It was not completely decoded until seven hours after the attack had begun, and only then did General Short and Admiral Kimmel receive copies of it.

Q. Who said, "An attack upon these [Hawaiian] islands is not impossible and in certain situations it might not be improbable"?

A. Lieutenant General Walter C. Short, the U.S. Army commander in Hawaii, in an address at the University of Hawaii on August 12, 1941.

Q. Who said, "If I were in charge in Washington I would relieve Kimmel at once. It doesn't make any difference why a man fails in the Navy, he has failed"?

A. Admiral Husband E. Kimmel, speaking about himself and his expected fate, to two staff members after the Pearl Harbor attack.

Q. To whom was the following said in Moscow by a Japanese newsman on December 7: "So sorry, we sank your fleet this morning. Supposing we are at war"?

A. To American newsman C. L. Sulzberger at the Grand Hotel in Moscow.

Q. Who said: "Today all of us are in the same boat with you and the people of the Empire and it is a ship which will not and cannot be sunk"?

A. President Franklin D. Roosevelt to Prime Minister Winston S. Churchill on December 8, 1941, shortly after Congress declared war on Japan.

Q. Who asked FDR, "How did they catch us with our pants down, Mr. President?" upon hearing details of the Pearl Harbor attack on December 7?

A. Senator Thomas Connally (Democrat of Texas) on the evening of the attack when Cabinet and congressional leaders met with FDR.

FACT After Pearl Harbor, critics repeatedly asked why the U.S. fleet was in port rather than out at sea. The simple answer was a critical fuel shortage. Admiral Kimmel wanted to keep two task forces at sea at all times while only one remained in port at a time. However, all fuel for the fleet had to be brought to Hawaii from the U.S. mainland, and only four of the Pacific fleet's tankers were capable of fueling ships at sea. As an example of fuel consumption, it is noted that a single destroyer at sea was capable of consuming its entire fuel supply in thirty hours.

Messages and Quotations

Q. "A lot of Moxey" (earlier spelled "Moxie" when it was attributed to a soft drink), referred to whom or what?

A. RAF Squadron Leader E. L. Moxey, the designer of a disarming device for bombs, was regarded as an exceptionally courageous individual for his dangerous work.

Q. "Dear Kitty:" Who began each writing with that salutation?

A. Anne Frank, who began entries in her diary that way. The house she and her family hid in for two years is in Amsterdam, Holland. Open to the public, it remains exactly as it was on the day they were arrested in 1944.

Q. Who said, "Before we're through with 'em, the Japanese language will be spoken only in hell"?

A. U.S. Rear Admiral William F. Halsey, from the bridge of the aircraft carrier USS *Enterprise* (CV-6) as he returned to Pearl Harbor and saw the destruction of the U.S. fleet.

Q. Who said, "This is not the end. It is not even the beginning of the end. But it is, perhaps, the end of the beginning"?

A. British Prime Minister Winston S. Churchill as he referred to the British victory over Rommel at El Alamein during a November 10, 1942, speech.

Q. Who is credited with coining the phrase the "United Nations"?

A. President Franklin D. Roosevelt.

Q. Who said; "I have…a reactionary Army and a Christian Navy"?
A. Adolf Hitler, whose description of the three branches of the Wehrmacht began, "I have a National Socialist Air Force, a reactionary…"

Q. Who said, "Guts, as well as guns, win battles"?
A. U.S. Admiral Harold R. Stark.

Q. Who said, "The highest obligation and privilege of citizenship is that of bearing arms for one's country"?
A. U.S. General George S. Patton.

Q. Who said, "Send us more Japs"?
A. While Wake Island was under a fierce attack by the Japanese in December 1941, the U.S. Navy began assembling a relief expedition from Pearl Harbor, but the plan was soon abandoned because of the admitted weakened condition of U.S. forces at Pearl. As a result, Pearl Harbor sent a radio message to the U.S. Marines on Wake. "Is there anything we can provide?" it asked. The leathernecks' reply was "Send us more Japs."

Q. Who said, "No one doubts that the British and American naval forces now in the Far East could easily destroy the Japanese Navy"?
A. The *Atlanta Constitution*, on September 20, 1941. It was typical of optimistic remarks that appeared in many newspapers across the country, which did not consider Japan a strong potential enemy.

Q. Who said, "If there were ever men and a fleet ready for any emergency it's Uncle Sam's fighting ships"?
A. The *Honolulu Advertiser*, on February 1, 1941, less than a month after Japanese Admiral Yamamoto first discussed the idea of attacking the U.S. fleet at Pearl Harbor.

FACT U.S. General Douglas MacArthur took maximum advantage of his famous "I shall return" utterance upon leaving the Philippines. He had cigarettes and candy bars imprinted with the initials I.S.R. (I Shall Return) and sent to the islands by submarines during the Japanese occupation.

Q. What was the historic battle cry in the streets of Paris that signified
the insurrection against German occupation in August 1944?

A. *Aux barricades!* Here a French woman, wearing a German helmet on
her head and the Croix de Lorraine armband, prepares for the battle
near the Prefecture of Police.

Roughol Photo

Q. Who said, "It now turns out that Japan was one of our customers who wasn't right"?

A. In a play on words (the customer is *always* right) the *Arkansas Gazette* made the comment after the Japanese attack on Pearl Harbor.

Q. Who said, "He's a hero! Already he has massacred seven microphones, and he's still going..." about General Charles de Gaulle and his radio broadcasts urging Frenchmen to join the Free French?

A. The Roman daily newspaper *Il Travaso*.

Q. Who said, "You can get a man down quicker by hitting on the same tooth than by hitting him all over"?

A. U.S. Admiral Forest Sherman.

Q. Who said, "All the Axis is hearing the tolling of the bells, and we are doing the rope pulling"?

      a. Admiral William F. Halsey, Jr.
      b. Prime Minister Winston S. Churchill
      c. President Franklin D. Roosevelt

A. Admiral Halsey.

Q. Who said, "Don't tell me it can't be done...go out there and do it"?

A. U.S. General Lucian K. Truscott.

Q. Who said, "To defeat the enemy, come to grips with him and fight him"?

      a. Field Marshal Erwin Rommel
      b. General George S. Patton
      c. Admiral Chester Nimitz
      d. General Omar N. Bradley

A. Admiral Chester Nimitz.

Q. Who said, "The chief impression you get from watching the German Army at work...is a gigantic, impersonal war machine, run as coolly and efficiently as our automobile industry in Detroit"?

A. American journalist William L. Shirer, who covered the early stages of the war from Germany. After the war, Shirer wrote *The Rise and Fall of The Third Reich*.

Q. About whom did U.S. General Mark Clark say, "A more gallant fighting organization never existed"?

a. British commandos

b. American airborne troops

c. French Expeditionary Corps

d. Italian marines

A. The Expeditionary Corps, made up of Moroccans, Algerians and French Nationals, formed by French General Alphonse Juin in North Africa.

U.S. Army Photo

Q. Who said, "There is no one more frustrated than a newspaperman with a story he can't get out"?

A. General Mark Clark, commander of the U.S. Fifth Army at the final briefing before the invasion of Italy. He expected that facilities would be arranged for the press shortly after the "quick victory."

Q. Who said, "Stand fast! We're staying here. Marines don't retreat"?

A. Lieutenant Robert Glenn, USMC, on Iwo Jima.

Q. Who said, "Aim not only to hit first, but to keep hitting, and oftener than the other fellow"?

A. U.S. Admiral Ernest J. King

Q. Who said, "I shall send in my resignation as an Italian if anyone objects to our fighting the Greeks"?

A. Benito Mussolini to Count Ciano when questioned whether the Duce had discussed the attack on Greece with Marshal Badoglio.

Q. Who said, "It is criminal to take part in a war which, disguised as a war for the preservation of democracy, is nothing but a war for the destruction of National Socialism"?
        a. U.S. pacifist Father Conlon
        b. Soviet diplomat V. I. Molotov
        c. Deputy Fuehrer Rudolf Hess

A. Molotov, underscoring the "joint fight of Germany and the Soviet Union against the capitalist powers of the West," on October 31, 1939.

Q. Who said, "We will win only by fighting"?
        a. Dwight D. Eisenhower
        b. Chester Nimitz
        c. Winston Churchill

A. U.S. Admiral Chester Nimitz.

Q. Who said "I'm an officer of the Fifth Army Headquarters. I guess I can play, can't I?" to a group of officers and enlisted man having a game of softball in Morocco?

A. General Mark Clark, who landed his Piper Cub on a field where the game was in progress. He managed to play at first base.

FACT Swiss-German actor Emil Jannings, who won the first-ever
Academy Award for Best Actor (1927–28) for his work in *The
Last Command* and *The Way of All Flesh*, made propaganda films
for Germany during the war.

Q. Who said, "I shall do as Bertoldo did. He accepted the death sentence
on the condition that he could choose the tree on which he was to
be hanged. Needless to say, he never found that tree"?
A. Italian dictator Benito Mussolini to Count Galeazzo Ciano in ex-
plaining how he would agree to enter the war but reserve for himself
the choice of the moment. The conversation took place on April 2,
1940.

Q. Who said, "Cease firing, but if any enemy planes appear, shoot 'em
down in a friendly fashion"?
A. U.S. Admiral William F. Halsey, Jr., in August 1945, after Japan announced it had accepted the Allied terms for surrender.

Q. Who said, "[It was] a submarine without a periscope" in describing
the headquarters of French General Gamelin in 1940?
A. French General Charles de Gaulle. The remark referred to Gamelin's
failure to have adequate radio contact with his army in the field.

Q. Who said, "We shall never forget that it was our submarines that
held the lines against the enemy while our fleets replaced losses and
repaired wounds"?
A. U.S. Admiral Chester W. Nimitz.

Q. Who said, "A serious day, rich in crises. It seems that we are in
trouble"?
A. German Field Marshal Fedor von Bock, in his diary on June 6, 1940,
commenting on the unexpected resistance his troops were receiving from the French. The quote could also have been used four years
to the day later as the Allies stormed the beaches at Normandy.

Q. What did the message "Execute Pontiam" signify to the troops on
Corregidor in 1942?
A. Sent by General Jonathan Wainwright to all commands, it notified
them of the surrender to the Japanese on May 6.

Q. Who said, "Three demoralizing factors, inactivity, propaganda and drink," were responsible for the rapid German victory over the French in 1940?

A. Colonel A. Goutard, in his book *The War of Lost Opportunities*, to describe the general state of mind of the twenty divisions France fielded in 1940.

Q. Who said, "Even if he is 4F he can feel like a hero," and about what?

A. New York department store Lord & Taylor, as part of its campaign to sell "Ike Jackets" to civilians. The jacket was a copy of the one first worn by General Dwight D. Eisenhower and created especially for him.

Q. Name the Rumanian dictator who said, "You can't even shoot straight!" as a firing squad's efforts to execute him failed on the first attempt?

A. Ion Antonescu. He had aligned himself with the Axis out of a violent hate of the Soviets. Not only did the first attempt to execute him fail, but a second one did as well. The commanding officer of the Soviet firing squad was required to give him the coup de grace.

Q. Who wrote the following to one of Britain's leading advocates of tank warfare: "To Captain B. H. Liddell Hart from one of his disciples in tank affairs"?

A. Germany's foremost tank warfare strategist General Heinz Guderian. The inscription appears on a photograph Guderian gave Hart prior to the outbreak of war. Hart also received a similar tribute from German General Hasso von Manteuffel.

FACT The 1942 movie *Mrs. Miniver* had a tremendous effect on American public opinion and is considered to have been of great value in increasing the empathy of Americans for the British. It portrayed the quiet heroism of entire families, housewives, the middle class and the wealthy. It included scenes of the evacuation of Dunkirk and generally depicted the British in the stereotypes many Americans held. President Franklin D. Roosevelt was so touched by the closing monologue that he had it printed on leaflets and dropped over occupied Europe. The film premiered on June 4, 1942, two years to the day that Winston Churchill had made his Fight on the Beaches speech.

Q. Who said, "Three demoralizing factors, inactivity, propaganda and drink," were responsible for the rapid German victory over the French in 1940?

A. Colonel A. Goutard, in his book *The War of Lost Opportunities*, to describe the general state of mind of the twenty divisions France fielded in 1940.

Q. Who said, "Even if he is 4F he can feel like a hero," and about what?

A. New York department store Lord & Taylor, as part of its campaign to sell "Ike Jackets" to civilians. The jacket was a copy of the one first worn by General Dwight D. Eisenhower and created especially for him.

Q. Name the Rumanian dictator who said, "You can't even shoot straight!" as a firing squad's efforts to execute him failed on the first attempt?

A. Ion Antonescu. He had aligned himself with the Axis out of a violent hate of the Soviets. Not only did the first attempt to execute him fail, but a second one did as well. The commanding officer of the Soviet firing squad was required to give him the coup de grace.

Q. Who wrote the following to one of Britain's leading advocates of tank warfare: "To Captain B. H. Liddell Hart from one of his disciples in tank affairs"?

A. Germany's foremost tank warfare strategist General Heinz Guderian. The inscription appears on a photograph Guderian gave Hart prior to the outbreak of war. Hart also received a similar tribute from German General Hasso von Manteuffel.

FACT The 1942 movie *Mrs. Miniver* had a tremendous effect on American public opinion and is considered to have been of great value in increasing the empathy of Americans for the British. It portrayed the quiet heroism of entire families, housewives, the middle class and the wealthy. It included scenes of the evacuation of Dunkirk and generally depicted the British in the stereotypes many Americans held. President Franklin D. Roosevelt was so touched by the closing monologue that he had it printed on leaflets and dropped over occupied Europe. The film premiered on June 4, 1942, two years to the day that Winston Churchill had made his Fight on the Beaches speech.

Q. Who said, "Hit 'em where they ain't"?

A. Though it is doubtful that the very proper General Douglas MacArthur would have phrased it that way, the remark sums up his tactics of assaulting Japanese islands.

Q. Who said, "There is nothing so unpleasant as partisan warfare. It is perhaps very important not to make reprisals on hostages at the first outbreak of partisan warfare"?

A. German Field Marshal Erwin Rommel. The quote appears as an entry in his diary of September 2, 1942. In 1944, Rommel protested to Hitler about the massacre of French civilians at Oradour-sur-Glane by the SS Das Reich Panzer Division and demanded exemplary punishment for those responsible. Hitler's response was a violent rebuff.

Q. Who said, "I have no intention of carrying out that order," referring to any possible order that would require France to turn her fleet over to Germany after the armistice.

A. French Admiral Jean François Darlan, in a letter to Vice Admiral Le Luc on May 28, 1940. If the order ever came, he said, he wanted all able ships to put to sea and make for the nearest British port.

Q. Who said, "Everything that flies is my concern"?

A. The commander of the Luftwaffe, Hermann Goering.

Q. Who said, "He who tortures animals wounds the feelings of the German people"?

A. The author may have been Reichsmarschall Hermann Goering, in whose office the legend hung.

FACT The 12,000-acre Bialowieza National Park in Poland is the result of conservation efforts undertaken by German Reichsmarschall Hermann Goering. As Master of the German Forests (one of many titles), he took steps to ensure that the devastation the area received at the hands of German troops was reversed. Goering had the forest restocked with animals and put a strict limit on hunting. The park is considered the largest remaining area of the primeval forest that once covered much of Europe.

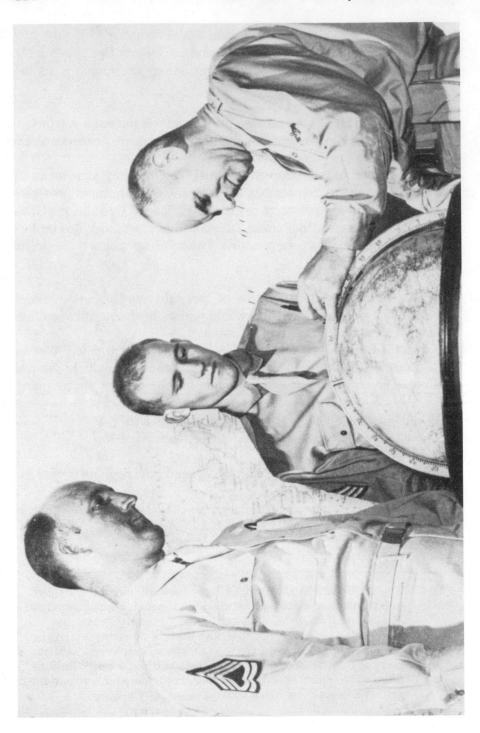

FACT By August 1940, Britain's Home Guard contained one million volunteers. However, it was nearly impossible to arm them. Guns, swords and ammunition were taken from military museums and war memorials, and unlikely sources such as the Drury Lane Theatre contributed a dozen old, rusty rifles. The task of arming the Home Guard was so difficult for a time that cutlasses from the days of Admiral Nelson were actually given out.

Q. Who said, "I don't think much of the name 'Local Defense Volunteers,' I think 'Home Guard' would be better"?

A. Prime Minister Winston S. Churchill, who continued: "Don't hesitate to change on account of having already made armlets, etc., if it is thought the title of Home Guard would be more compulsive."

Q. Who said, "Appallingly shameful; appallingly stupid" in reference to the British attack on the French fleet in Mers el-Kebir?

A. British Admiral of the Fleet Sir John H. D. Cunningham, in 1962. In 1940, Admiral Cunningham was faced with a similar prospect when he received orders to eliminate the French ships (Force X) in the eastern Mediterranean. Instead he worked out a demobilizing program with French Admiral Godfroy that removed the ships as a possible threat without the loss of lives.

Q. Who called the years between the two world wars "that period of exhaustion which has been described as peace"?

A. British Prime Minister Winston S. Churchill.

Q. Who said, "Fighter planes win battles, but photo reconnaissance wins wars"?

A. U.S. General Hap Arnold.

Q. Who said, "They flew from Shangri-La," when asked where the planes that participated in the Doolittle raid came from?

A. President Franklin D. Roosevelt, in an effort to protect the identity and position of the aircraft carrier USS *Hornet* (CV-8). By the time Jimmy Doolittle and two of the men who participated in the raid, Sergeant Eldred V. Scott (left) and Sergeant David J. Thatcher, got together for this 1942 photo, the Army Air Force flying legend was Brigadier General James H. Doolittle.

U.S. Army Photo

Q. Who said, "Anything new, Georges"?

A. Amédée Bussière, prefect of the Paris Police Department, to his valet on the morning of August 19, 1944, upon awakening. The reply was "Yes...they have come back." The "they" was the police force, which had been on strike. That morning they gathered to capture the Prefecture of Police building, the central point in the insurrection to liberate Paris. In photo above, a policeman and other members of the Free French Forces of the Interior, attempting to get to the Prefecture later in the day, meet German opposition at Pont Neuf, one of the bridges that cross the Seine.

U.S. Army Photo

> **FACT** Dusko Popov, a German spy whom the British compromised and turned into a double agent, was chased out of the U.S. by J. Edgar Hoover, who said, "I can catch spies without you or anybody else's help." The Germans had sent Popov to the U.S. in August 1941 to get information about Pearl Harbor for the Japanese. Popov told the British, who in turn told the U.S., but Hoover was not interested and sent the double agent packing.

Q. Who said, "It appears the peacock will be on time"?
A. U.S. Admiral William F. Halsey, Jr., authorizing U.S. P-38 aircraft to intercept and shoot down the aircraft carrying Japanese Admiral Isoroku Yamamoto in April 1943. The last part read, "Fan his tail."

Q. Who said, "The issue is in doubt"?
A. USMC Major James Devereaux. It was the last message sent from Wake Island before it was overrun by the Japanese.

Q. Who said, "The second best air force was no more use than the second best hand at poker"?
A. U.S. General Henry Harley Arnold.

Q. Who said, "Sighted sub, sank same"?
      a. Lieutenant Commander Robert Dixon
      b. Captain Fred M. Smith
      c. Lieutenant Donald F. Mason
A. Dixon reported sinking the Japanese aircraft carrier *Shoho* with "Scratch one flattop." Smith, flying a P-38, radioed "Saw steamer, strafed same, sank same, some sight, signed Smith." Mason, in a Lockheed Hudson in March 1942, reported "Sighted sub, sank same."

Q. Who said, "Just sight, track, shoot and sink"?
A. Commander Dudley W. Morton of the submarine USS *Wahoo* (SS-238).

Q. Who said, "Expended four torpedoes and one Jap destroyer"?
A. U.S. Navy Commander Sam Dealy, upon reporting the sinking of the *Ikazuki* by the submarine USS *Harder*.

Appendix

Ships have always held a fascination for sailors and non-sailors alike. Enshrined warships from past conflicts going as far back as the American Revolution have, over the decades, remained to fascinate anew each generation that views them. It is therefore not surprising that fighting ships from World War II that have been maintained as memorials draw increasing numbers of visitors each year.

Battlefield memorials mark the very earth where this nation first won its independence and then more than four score years later preserved it. Bunker Hill, Yorktown, Saratoga, Lexington, Bull Run and Gettysburg are but a representative few. Yet it is impossible to mark locations on the high seas where our nation's fate so often hung in the balance.

So we've done the next best thing. We've preserved the ships. Not all of them, to be sure, and probably far too few. As you move through the pages of this section it is worth reflecting for a moment that these World War II warships have been saved from being recycled as scrap in almost all cases by what began as the dedicated and determined efforts of small groups of people.

We've culled the records of memorials, commissions and commemorative displays and hope we have compiled as complete a list of U.S. World War II ships as exists anywhere.

But as we did this we couldn't help thinking about those great ships that were not so fortunate. The USS *Enterprise* (CV-6) and USS *Nevada* (BB-36) immediately come to mind. The former was sold for scrap and the latter ended up as a target ship for atomic bomb testing off Bikini atoll.

What follows is a listing of ships that are open to public view. The first thirteen are fairly complete and include photos. Beyond that we've condensed the information either in the interest of brevity or because of incomplete or insufficient information.

USS *Alabama* (BB-60) and USS *Drum* (SS-228)

Located at Battleship Alabama Memorial Park, Battleship Parkway, Mobile, Alabama. Open to visitors 8 A.M. until sunset every day of the year except Christmas. Parking is one dollar and admission for persons twelve years or older is $3.50; under twelve years, $1.50; under six years old there is no charge. Group rates available for ten or more. Armed forces personnel admitted free. Tours are not conducted. Visitors receive printed numbered tour guides which correspond to numbered arrows on the two ships. The site also includes a P-51 Mustang, a gull-winged Corsair and other aircraft and historic ships. Approximately 300,000 people visit the memorial annually. The single admission covers all memorial attractions and there is a gift shop on the premises.

The 35,000-ton USS *Alabama* is a sister ship to the USS *Massachusetts*, USS *Indiana* and USS *South Dakota*. She was launched at the Norfolk Naval Shipyard, Portsmouth, Virginia, on February 16, 1942, while General Douglas MacArthur's troops were fighting on Bataan. She eventually won nine battle stars in World War II for action in the Gilberts, Marshalls, Pacific raids, Hollandia, Marianas, Western Carolines, Leyte, Okinawa and Japan.

The submarine USS *Drum* was launched on May 12, 1941, and earned twelve battle stars on thirteen war patrols and is credited with sinking fifteen enemy ships for a total of 80,580 tons of shipping. She sank the Japanese seaplane tender *Mizuho* and three cargo ships on her first patrol between April 14 and June 12, 1942.

USS *Arizona* (BB-39)

Located exactly where it was on December 7, 1941, Battleship Row, Ford Island, Pearl Harbor, Oahu, Hawaii. The USS *Arizona* Memorial spans the sunken hull of the battleship which is resting in thirty-eight feet of water. The U.S. Navy conducts daily free tours on a first-come, first-served basis, which also include a documentary film about the Japanese attack. At present there are also four civilian tour boats making daily tours for a nominal fee, but they do not debark passengers at the memorial itself, something the Navy tour does. Navy tour passengers can visit the three sections of the memorial: the museum room, which houses mementos of the ship; the assembly area, capable of accommodating 200 persons for ceremonies; and the shrine room, where names of the 1,177 U.S. personnel killed on the ship are engraved on a marble wall. The civilian boats tour the harbor and play tapes that explain the action on the morning of the attack and pause alongside the memorial for a moment of silence. Well over one million people visit the USS *Arizona* Memorial annually. It is the most popular tourist attraction in Hawaii.

The USS *Arizona* was launched at the New York Navy Yard on June 19, 1915, and commissioned on October 17, 1916. She was a member of the honor escort that brought President Woodrow Wilson to France for the 1918 Paris Peace Conference. Throughout the 1920s she was the mightiest ship of the U.S. fleet and was modernized between the wars. On April 2, 1940, she was assigned to duty at Pearl Harbor. She left the U.S. west coast for the last time in 1941, reaching Pearl Harbor on July 8, 1941.

The ship is no longer in commission, but in memory of the men who lost their lives on the "Day that will live in infamy" the Navy has granted special permission for the American flag to fly over the USS *Arizona*.

USS *Becuna* (SS-319) and USS *Olympia*

Located at Penn's Landing, Delaware Avenue and Spruce Street, Philadelphia, Pennsylvania. Open to visitors from 10 A.M. to 4:30 P.M. seven
days a week except Christmas and New Year's Day. Summer hours are
extended until 6 P.M. Admission is $2.50 for adults and $1.25 for
children under twelve years of age. Information on group rates available.
Purchases made in the ship's store help to preserve these two historic
ships. One particularly interesting item is souvenir coins made from
the *Olympia*'s propellers, priced at $7.50 each.

Though the senior attraction here is the USS *Olympia* we begin this
listing with the World War II submarine USS *Becuna*, a guppy-class
boat that was commissioned on May 27, 1944. She served as the submarine flagship of the Southwest Pacific Fleet under General Douglas
MacArthur. The *Becuna* earned four battle stars in five war patrols
and also received a Presidential Unit Citation. After a postwar refit,
she continued to see active duty in the Atlantic and Mediterranean
during the Korean and Vietnam wars. She was decommissioned on October 1, 1969. The *Becuna* is the last of her type open for public exhibit.

Naval buffs and military historians need little introduction to the
USS *Olympia*. Launched on November 5, 1892, and retired on
September 1, 1922, she played a part in all the major American actions
that marked this country as a world power.

Commodore Dewey stood on her bridge on May 1, 1898, found himself
eyeball-to-eyeball with the Spanish fleet off the Philippine Islands and
uttered the historic "You may fire when you are ready, Gridley," thus
exploding the Battle of Manila Bay into history. Her log includes delivering the peace-keeping force to Murmansk, Russia, in 1918, service as
flagship for U.S. Navy ships in the eastern Mediterranean, flagship for
the North Atlantic Squadron and service as a training ship for An-
napolis midshipmen.

USS *Bowfin* (SS-287)

Located at 11 Arizona Memorial Drive, Honolulu, Hawaii. Open to visitors every day 9:30 A.M. to 4:30 P.M. Adult admission is three dollars and children between six and twelve years can board the boat for a dollar. Children under six years of age are not permitted aboard the *Bowfin*. No federal or state funds are used for the maintenance. The exhibit is operated by the Pacific Fleet Submarine Memorial Association as a memorial to the fifty-two U.S. submarines and 3,505 submariners of World War II who are considered "still on patrol." Visitors are provided with lightweight radio wands which receive transcribed narratives at stations throughout the submarine. Additionally, tour guides are in the boat to answer questions. The gift shop offers fairly priced items and the volunteer staff is pleasant.

The USS *Bowfin* was launched at Portsmouth, New Hampshire, on December 7, 1942, the first anniversary of the Pearl Harbor attack. She was commissioned on May 1, 1943. During her nine war patrols between August 1943 and August 1945, the USS *Bowfin* sank 179,946 tons of enemy shipping (forty-four ships), and one of her commanders, Walter T. Griffith, ranks as the seventh-highest-scoring American submarine commander in the war (he is credited with seventeen ships while serving on the *Bowfin* and USS *Bullhead*). The USS *Bowfin* earned eight battle stars and both the Presidential Unit Citation and the Navy Unit Commendation.

The USS *Bowfin* saw a variety of assignments after World War II and was finally decommissioned in December 1971. Rather than see this fierce fighting boat sold for scrap and possibly end up being recycled into razor blades, a small group in Hawaii formed the association that persuaded the U.S. Navy to give them the boat, and the result is this exhibit.

USS *Croaker* (SS-246)

Located at the Fort Griswold Moorings, 359 Thames Street, Groton, Connecticut. Open to visitors from April 15 to October 15 from 9 A.M. to 5 P.M. with the last tour starting at 4:30 P.M. From October 16 to April 14, it is open from 9 A.M. but closes at 3 P.M. That is also the hour of the last tour. Adults pay three dollars admission; children from five to eleven pay $1.50; children under five may board free with an adult. Military personnel in uniform are admitted free. There are group rates for ten or more, pre-scheduled, arriving together. The guided tour takes approximately one half hour. The exhibit has a snack bar–restaurant and gift shop.

The USS *Croaker* was commissioned at the U.S. Naval Submarine Base, Groton, Connecticut, on April 21, 1944. She participated in six war patrols in the Pacific and is credited with sinking a Japanese cruiser, four tankers, two freighters, two escort craft, a minesweeper and an ammunition ship.

After World War II the *Croaker* returned to Connecticut and participated as an active member of the fleet until she was stricken from the record in 1971. She is maintained by the Submarine Memorial Association, Incorporated, which is also involved in obtaining the world's first nuclear-powered submarine, the USS *Nautilus*, as a permanent national monument exhibit near the USS *Croaker*. Information about this effort is available from the association. (The *Nautilus* was built at the nearby Electric Boat Division of General Dynamics.)

USS *Intrepid* (CV-11)

Located at Pier 86 on West 46th Street in New York City. The Intrepid Sea-Air-Space Museum offers considerably more than an exciting visit to one of the only two U.S. World War II aircraft carriers open to visitors, since it combines exhibits that feature other areas of interest noted in its name. From June 1 to September 30, it is open from 10 A.M. until 8 P.M. and between October 1 and May 31, it closes one hour earlier. However, the ticket office closes at 6 P.M. and 5 P.M., respectively. Adult admission is five dollars, children $2.50, senior citizens four dollars and groups of ten or more are four dollars for adults, and two dollars for those eighteen and younger.

Built in 1943 in Newport News, Virginia, at a cost of $44 million, the *Intrepid* carried 360 officers and 3,008 enlisted men during wartime service. She was nicknamed the Fighting I but because she was the most frequently hit U.S. ship in the war she became known as the Evil I. Her combat record would easily fill several pages. Planes from her decks sank the two largest battleships (72,809 tons) ever built, the *Yamato* and *Musashi*. In the 1960s she was the prime recovery ship during two Mercury and Gemini space missions.

The museum section of the exhibit (on the hangar deck) features four theme halls: the United States Navy Hall uses special effects to recreate the excitement of carrier aviation and puts an emphasis on the modern peacekeeping Navy; Intrepid Hall takes visitors back to the action of World War II; Pioneer Hall details man's early probes into the sky with flight; Technologies Hall covers the great advances in sea, air and space that have had a profound influence on the twentieth century. The Flight Deck includes many historic aircraft. The Intrepid Sea-Air-Space Museum opened to the public in the summer of 1982, and new exhibits are being added regularly.

USS *Kidd* (DD-661)

Located in Baton Rouge, Louisiana. Opened daily to the public for the first time in June 1983. Admission for adults is three dollars for touring the *Kidd*, but there will be no charge for admission to a proposed $2.5 million museum facility being built near the ship. The museum currently has an exhibit on display at the Louisiana Arts and Sciences Center, also at this location. The Louisiana Naval War Memorial Commission expects that a good number of the 200,000 annual visitors to the Arts and Sciences Center will also visit the USS *Kidd* and the museum. A gift shop and snack bar are planned for the complex.

Commissioned in April 1943, the *Kidd* saw heavy action in World War II. She was involved in every major naval campaign in the Pacific and earned four battle stars. Engagements she was involved in included Okinawa, Leyte, the Gilberts, Marshalls and the Philippines. Her nickname is the Pirate of the Pacific. She earned four more battle stars for her service during the Korean War.

The USS *Kidd* was decommissioned in 1964 and became part of the Atlantic Reserve Fleet until 1982, when ownership was transferred to the Louisiana Naval War Memorial Commission. Accompanying photo was taken during her days of active service.

USS *Ling* (SS-297)

Located in Borg Park on the Hackensack River at the intersection of Court and River Streets, Hackensack, New Jersey. Admission for adults is two dollars, for children twelve and under it is one dollar. A discount of 25 percent is offered to groups of fifteen and up. Tours are conducted seven days a week from June to September from 10:15 A.M. on, with the last tour starting at 5 P.M. Between October and May the last tour goes off at 4 P.M. There is a gift shop and exhibit of nautical items of interest. Money raised through the boat tours and the gift shop is used by the non-profit Submarine Memorial Association to maintain the exhibits, which, besides the USS *Ling*, include several missiles, torpedoes, mines and anchors. The boat is heated for winter touring.

The USS *Ling* was commissioned on June 8, 1945, and managed to get in one Atlantic war patrol before the war ended. She is the last of the fleet-type submarines that patrolled American shores in the war years and was built by the Cramp Shipbuilding Company and outfitted at the Boston Navy Yard. She was decommissioned on October 26, 1946, and became part of the New London Group, Atlantic Reserve Fleet, until she was reactivated as a Submarine Naval Reserve training vessel in 1960.

In December 1962, the *Ling* was converted from an SS to an AGSS submarine and served as one of the most elaborate and authentic training aids in the world. She was decommissioned for a second, and final, time in December 1971. She arrived in Hackensack at her present berth on January 13, 1973.

While on active service, she carried a complement of ninety-five officers and men and an armament capacity of twenty-four torpedoes.

USS *Massachusetts* (BB-59)

Located at Battleship Cove, Fall River, Massachusetts, at Exit 5, I-95. The battleship is the main attraction of an exhibit that includes five other ships and a marine museum. All six attractions are open throughout the year except Thanksgiving and Christmas, from 9 A.M. to 5 P.M. and until 8 P.M. between June 30 and Labor Day. Admission is $4.50 for adults, $2.50 for children six to thirteen, and tots two to five get in for seventy-five cents. Group rates are available upon request.

The museum contains 131 beautifully executed ship models ranging in size from a half inch to twelve feet long. At several locations visitors can press a button and hear background information about the particular exhibit being viewed.

The other ships at Battleship Cove include the destroyer USS *Joseph P. Kennedy* (DD-850); the submarine USS *Lionfish* (SS-298); a PT boat; the gunboat *Asheville*; and the bow of the cruiser USS *Fall River* (CA-131).

The USS *Massachusetts* holds the distinction of being the first battleship to fire 16-inch guns at the enemy in World War II, in the Atlantic, and the last to fire them, this time in the Pacific. From that first volley until the last, she traveled over 225,000 miles and participated in thirty-five battles. Her nickname is Big Mamie.

The USS *Massachusetts* is the official state memorial to those who gave their lives in all branches of the service during World War II. The memorial area contains the names of the more than 13,000 Bay State residents who died in the war. The destroyer USS *Joseph P. Kennedy* is the official state memorial to the more than 4,500 who died in the Korean and Vietnam conflicts.

USS *Missouri* (BB-63)

Located at the Puget Sound Naval Shipyard, Bremerton, Washington. Of all the ships in this section the battleship USS *Missouri* is the only one that is still the property of the U.S. Navy. She is preserved as part of the mothball fleet. There is no charge to board and visit her, and normal visiting hours from Memorial Day to Labor Day are 10 A.M. to 8 P.M. At other times hours are noon to 4 P.M. There is a refreshment stand at the site, and souvenirs are available.

We should note that if Congress approves funding for reactivation of this mighty battleship during 1983 it will join the USS *New Jersey* as part of the active fleet.

The USS *Missouri* was built at the New York Naval Shipyard and was launched on January 29, 1944. She was commissioned on June 11 of that year and remained in service until being decommissioned on February 26, 1955. She transited the Panama Canal and entered the western Pacific in January 1945.

The *Missouri* participated in operations against Okinawa, Iwo Jima and the Japanese mainland. It was on her decks, while in Tokyo Bay on September 2, 1945, that the instrument of surrender was signed by the representatives of the Japanese government, thus ending World War II.

Between 225,000 and 250,000 people visit the USS *Missouri* annually.

USS *North Carolina* (BB-55)

Located in Wilmington, North Carolina. The *North Carolina* is open every day of the year from 8 A.M. to 8 P.M. in the summer and closes at sunset during other times. Admission for those twelve and over is $2.50; children six to eleven, one dollar; and those five and under are free. A discount for groups of twenty or more is available when all tickets are purchased at once. A sound-and-light spectacular titled "The Immortal Showboat" (from her nickname) is presented nightly at 9 P.M. in the summer. It depicts her World War II record, replete with the majestic roar of the 16-inch guns. Admission for the show is $1.50 for adults; seventy-five cents for children six to eleven; and free for those five or under. Group discounts are available.

The USS *North Carolina* was the third U.S. Navy ship to bear that name. Her keel was laid at the Brooklyn Navy Yard on Navy Day, October 27, 1937, and she was launched on June 13, 1940. On April 9, 1941, she was commissioned. During her forty months in combat zones in World War II, the Showboat was reported sunk six times by Tokyo Rose.

She participated in the following Asiatic-Pacific campaigns: Guadalcanal and Tulagi; eastern Solomons; Gilbert Islands; Tarawa; Makin; Marshalls; Kwajalein; Roi; Namur; Guam; Saipan; Palau; Yap; Ulithi; Woleai; Satawan; Ponape; New Guinea; Aitape; Tanahmerah Bay; Humboldt Bay; Marianas; Tinian; Philippines; Iwo Jima; Honshu; Nansei; Shoto; Okinawa; Kerama-retto; Kyushu and the Inland Sea, among others.

The USS *North Carolina* Battleship Memorial is dedicated to the 10,000 state residents who died in World War II.

USS *Texas* (BB-35)

Located at Battleground Road, San Jacinto State Park, La Porte, Texas. Open to visitors from 10 A.M. to 5 P.M. every day of the year. Admission charges are three dollars for adults; two dollars for senior citizens; one dollar for those between six and eighteen. A gift shop is located aboard ship, and a snack bar is nearby as are several restaurants. Approximately 240,000 people visit the Grand Old Lady annually.

Commissioned in 1914 at Norfolk, Virginia, as a Dreadnought-class battleship, she saw action in both world wars. In World War II she made her combat debut in Operation Torch, the North African invasion, and participated in Operation Overlord, the D-Day invasion of Normandy. In the Pacific she made her presence felt at Iwo Jima and Okinawa. She is the third U.S. Navy ship named for the state of Texas. After the Japanese surrender, the USS *Texas* was one of the ships in the Magic Carpet Fleet that returned U.S. servicemen to the States.

Also enshrined at San Jacinto State Park along with the USS *Texas* is the USS *Cabrilla* (SS-288), a World War II submarine that sank 38,767 tons of enemy shipping during six of her eight war patrols.

Fleet Admiral Chester W. Nimitz was present at the dedication ceremonies when the USS *Texas* went on public display in 1948. The effort to preserve the *Texas* was the first such undertaking to create a ship-and-shore memorial to a state's naval namesake and encouraged other groups to create similar exhibits.

The San Jacinto State Park is a short drive by freeway from downtown Houston.

USS *Yorktown* (CV-10)

Located at Patriots Point, Charleston Harbor, South Carolina. the Fighting Lady is the main attraction at this exhibit that includes three other ships and several aircraft. Open daily to visitors from 9 A.M. to 6 P.M. (daylight saving time) and 9 A.M. to 5 P.M. (standard time). Admission is five dollars for adults; three dollars for children six to eleven; $4.50 for senior citizens and military personnel in uniform. Group rates are also available.

The ship's theater regularly shows the movie *The Fighting Lady*. There is a gift shop and restaurant.

The aircraft carrier USS *Yorktown* received the traditional champagne christening on April 15, 1943, at Newport News, Virginia. Mrs. Eleanor Roosevelt did the honors. Some ten months later the *Yorktown* celebrated the 7,000th landing on her decks. Her total landings in World War II alone were 31,170. The Fighting Lady earned fifteen battle stars during which time she was clearly the carrier to beat in the rivalries that always exist in any navy. She set records for the fastest launches and recoveries of aircraft and the heaviest flying schedules. She also set a record in shooting down 14½ enemy aircraft, while her planes accounted for 458 enemy planes in the air and 695 on the ground. She earned a presidential unit citation and several other awards. Truk, the Marianas, the Philippines, Iwo Jima, Okinawa, et al. — she was there.

Besides this great carrier, visitors can also see the destroyer USS *Laffey* (DD-724), hit by more Japanese kamikaze planes than any other ship in one battle; the World War II submarine USS *Clamagore* (SS-343); the world's first nuclear-powered merchant ship, the *Savannah*; plus aircraft, including a B-25 and eight others.

USS *Hazard* (AM-240)

Located at the Greater Omaha Marina, 2000 North 25th Street, East Omaha, Nebraska. Admission for adults is one dollar and children seventy-five-cents. Information on hours visitors may board is available by calling (402) 341-0550. In addition to the minesweeper USS *Hazard*, the Greater Omaha Marina also exhibits the post–World War II submarine USS *Marlin* (SST-2) and a McDonnell Douglas A-4 Skyhawk. There is a restaurant and lounge, golf-driving range, trailer campgrounds, three boat-launch ramps. The *Hazard* is the largest ship that has traveled this far inland, making the trek from Orange, Texas, to Omaha — a distance of 2,000 miles — in twenty-nine days. She now rests at the marina on the Missouri River.

The USS *Hazard* was launched on May 21, 1944, at Winslow, Washington, and commissioned on October 31, 1944. She screened convoys and swept mines at Eniwetok, the Philippines, Okinawa, Kerama-retto, the East China Sea, the Yellow Sea and Jinsen, Korea.

USS *Pampanito* (AG SS-383)

Located at Fisherman's Wharf in San Francisco, California. Admission is three dollars for adults; two dollars for juniors (twelve to eighteen) and seniors (over sixty-five); one dollar for children. She is open daily from 10 A.M. to 10 P.M.

The *Pampanito* was built at Portsmouth Naval Shipyard, New Hampshire, and was commissioned on November 6, 1943. She sank five enemy ships totaling 27,288 tons during her six war patrols. She rescued seventy-three Australian and British POW's after she and the USS *Sealion* sank two Japanese ships that were transporting them to labor camps.

FACT The American Battle Monuments Commission in Washington, D.C., administers U.S. Military cemeteries overseas. There are fourteen cemeteries on foreign soil where U.S. armed forces personnel killed in World War II are buried. The largest is near Manila, the Philippines, which has 17,208 graves and commemorates an additional 36,279 persons missing in action. The smallest is at Rhone, France, which has 861 graves and commemorates 293 missing personnel. A fifteenth cemetery, originally dedicated to personnel killed in the First World War at Suresnes, France, also has the graves of twenty-four unknown American dead from World War II.

Other Ships Open to Visitors

USS *Batfish* (AG SS-310), Muskogee, Oklahoma
USS *Cavalla* (AG SS-244), Galveston, Texas
USS *Cobia* (AG SS-245), Manitowoc, Wisconsin
USS *Codd* (SS-224), Cleveland, Ohio
USS *Inaugural* (AM-242), St. Louis, Missouri
PT 619, Memphis, Tennessee
USS *Little Rock* (CLG-4), Buffalo, New York
USS *Requin* (AG SS-481), Tampa, Florida
USS *Silversides* (SS-236), Chicago, Illinois
USS *Stewart* (DE-238), Galveston, Texas
USS *The Sullivans* (DDG-537), Buffalo, New York
USS *Torsk* (AS SS-423), Baltimore, Maryland
USS *Utah* (BB-31), Pearl Harbor, Oahu, Hawaii
U-505 (captured German submarine), Chicago, Illinois

Comparative German and American Officer Ranks

U.S. Army	*Wehrmacht*	*SS (Schutz Staffeln)*
General of the Army	Generalfeldmarschall	SS Reichsfuehrer
General	Generaloberst	Oberstgruppenfuehrer
Lieutenant General	General	Obergruppenfuehrer
Major General	Generalleutnant	Gruppenfuehrer
Brigadier General	Generalmajor	Brigadefuehrer
———	———	Oberfuehrer
Colonel	Oberst	Standartenfuehrer
Lieutenant Colonel	Oberstleutnant	Obersturmbannfuehrer
Major	Major	Sturmbannfuehrer
Captain	Hauptmann	Hauptsturmfuehrer
First Lieutenant	Oberleutnant	Obersturmfuehrer
Second Lieutenant	Leutnant	Untersturmfuehrer
Warrant Officer	Unteroffizer	Hauptscharfuehrer

————————————————The McAuliffe Christmas Card————————————————

"Merry Christmas" from General Anthony C. McAuliffe

The 101st Airborne Division was totally surrounded by German units on Christmas Eve 1944 in Bastogne. McAuliffe's famous reply to the German surrender ultimatum ranks among the great quotes of that or any other war for its stunning simplicity. However, McAuliffe was not quite so abrupt with his own men when he circulated a mimeographed "greeting card" that December 24. Included in the text was the surrender ultimatum which the Germans typed on a captured American typewriter. Reprinted below, sans official letterhead, is General McAuliffe's Christmas message:

HEADQUARTERS 101ST AIRBORNE DIVISION
Office of the Division Commander

24 December 1944

What's Merry about all this, you ask? We're fighting — it's cold, we aren't home. All true but what has the proud Eagle Division accomplished with its worthy comrades of the 10th Armored Division, the 705th Tank Destroyer Battalion and all the rest? Just this: We have stopped cold everything that has been thrown at us from the North, East, South and West. We have identifications from four German Panzer Divisions, two German Infantry Divisions and one German Parachute Division. These units, spearheading the last desperate German lunge, were headed straight west for key points when the Eagle Division was hurriedly ordered to stem the advance. How effectively this was done will be written in history; not alone in our Division's glorious history but in World history. The Germans actually did surround us, their radios blared our doom. Their Commander demanded our surrender in the following impudent arrogance.

FACT The U.S. sustained a greater number of casualties during the Battle of the Bulge than U.S. forces under General MacArthur sustained throughout the entire war.

December 22nd 1944

"To the U.S.A. Commander of the encircled town of Bastogne.

"The fortune of war is changing. This time the U.S.A. forces in and near Bastogne have been encircled by strong German armored units. More German armored units have crossed the river Ourthe near Ortheuville, have taken Marche and reached St. Hubert by passing through Hombres-Sibret-Tillet. Libramont is in German hands.

"There is only one possibility to save the encircled U.S.A. Troop from total annihilation: that is the honorable surrender of the encircled town. In order to think it over, a term of two hours will be granted beginning with the presentation of this note.

"If this proposal should be rejected one German Artillery Corps and six heavy A. A. Battalions are ready to annihilate the U.S.A. Troops in and near Bastogne. The order for firing will be given immediately after this two hour's term.

"All the serious civilian losses caused by this Artillery fire would not correspond with the well known American humanity.

The German Commander"

The German Commander received the following reply:

22 December 1944

"To the German Commander: N U T S !

The American Commander"

Allied Troops are counterattacking in force. We continue to hold Bastogne. By holding Bastogne we assure the success of the Allied Armies. We know that our Division Commander, General Taylor, will say: "Well Done!"

We are giving our country and our loved ones at home a worthy Christmas present and being privileged to take part in this gallant feat of arms are truly making ourselves a Merry Christmas.

(signed)
McAULIFFE,
Commanding.

——————————— Instrument of German Surrender ———————————

World War II began in the early morning hours of September 1, 1939, and for Germany, who started it, it ended in the early morning hours of May 7, 1945. At 0241 hours that day in Rheims, France, the unconditional surrender of "all forces on land, sea, and air" under German authority was signed. The text of that document is reprinted below minus the signatures.

Only this text in English is authoritative

ACT OF MILITARY SURRENDER

1. We the undersigned, acting by authority of the German High Command, hereby surrender unconditionally to the Supreme Commander, Allied Expeditionary Force and simultaneously to the Soviet High Command all forces on land, sea, and in the air who are at this date under German control.

2. The German High Command will at once issue orders to all German military, naval and air authorities and to all forces under German control to cease active operations at 2301 hours Central European time on 8 May and to remain in the positions occupied at that time. No ship, vessel, or aircraft is to be scuttled, or any damage done to their hull, machinery or equipment.

3. The German High Command will at once issue to the appropriate commanders, and ensure the carrying out of any further orders issued by the Supreme Commander, Allied Expeditionary Force and by the Soviet High Command.

4. This act of military surrender is without prejudice to, and will be superseded by any general instrument of surrender imposed by, or on behalf of the United Nations and applicable to GERMANY and the German armed forces as a whole.

5. In the event of the German High Command or any of the forces under their control failing to act in accordance with this Act of Surrender, the Supreme Commander, Allied Expeditionary Force and the Soviet High Command will take such punitive or other action as they deem appropriate.

Signed at Rheims, France, at 0241 hours on the 7th day of May, 1945.

──────Medal of Honor Recipients in World War II──────

The Medal of Honor is the highest award the United States government can give for military valor. Because it is conferred by the President in the name of the Congress, it is commonly called the Congressional Medal of Honor (CMH).

It is bestowed on an individual who distinguishes himself "conspicuously by gallantry and intrepidity at the risk of his life above and beyond the call of duty."

The award was conceived in the 1860s and first presented in 1863.

In their provisions for judging whether an individual is entitled to the Medal of Honor, each of the armed services has set up regulations that permit no margin of doubt or error. The deed of the person must be proven by the incontestable evidence of at least two eyewitnesses; it must be so outstanding that it clearly distinguishes his gallantry beyond the call of duty from lesser forms of bravery; it must involve the risk of life; and it must be the type of deed which, if it had not been done, would not subject the individual to any justified criticism.

A history of the Medal of Honor with a list of all recipients from 1863 to 1978 is available from the Superintendent of Documents, U.S. Government Printing Office, Washington, D.C. 20402, for a fee. The list that follows includes all World War II recipients up through October 1983.

Name, Rank, Organization	For Action In or At	Date of Action
Adams, Lucian, Army, Staff Sgt.	St. Die, France	28 Oct. 1944
*Agerholm, Harold C., U.S.M.C., Pfc.	Saipan, Marianas	7 July 1944
Anderson, Beaufort T., Army, Tech. Sgt.	Okinawa	13 Apr. 1945
*Anderson, Richard B., U.S.M.C., Pfc.	Marshall Islands	1 Feb. 1944
*Antolak, Sylvester, Army, Sgt.	Italy	24 May 1944
Antrim, Richard N., Navy, Cmdr.	East Indies	Apr. 1942
Atkins, Thomas E., Army, Pfc.	Philippines	10 Mar. 1945
*Bailey, Kenneth D., U.S.M.C., Maj.	Guadalcanal	12 Sept. 1942
*Baker, Addison E., Army, Lt. Col.	Rumania	1 Aug. 1943

*An asterisk indicates posthumous award.

Name, Rank, Organization	For Action In or At	Date of Action
*Baker, Thomas A., Army, Sgt.	Saipan, Marianas	19 June–7 July 1944
Barfoot, Van T., Army, 2nd Lt.	Carano, Italy	23 May 1944
Barrett, Carlton W., Army, Pvt.	France	6 June 1944
Basilone, John, U.S.M.C., Sgt.	Guadalcanal	24–25 Oct. 1942
*Bauer, Harold W., U.S.M.C., Lt. Col.	South Pacific	10 May–14 Nov. 1942
*Bausell, Lewis K., U.S.M.C., Cpl.	Peleliu Island	15 Sept. 1944
*Beaudoin, Raymond O., Army, 1st Lt.	Germany	6 Apr. 1945
Bell, Bernard P., Army, Tech. Sgt.	France	18 Dec. 1944
Bender, Stanley, Army, Staff Sgt.	France	17 Aug. 1944
*Benjamin, George, Jr., Army, Pfc.	Philippines	21 Dec. 1944
Bennett, Edward A., Army, Cpl.	Germany	1 Feb. 1945
*Bennion, Mervyn S., Navy, Capt.	Pearl Harbor	7 Dec. 1941
*Berry, Charles J., U.S.M.C., Cpl.	Iwo Jima	3 Mar. 1945
Bertoldo, Vito R., Army, Mstr. Sgt.	France	9–10 Jan. 1945
Beyer, Arthur O., Army, Cpl.	Belgium	15 Jan. 1945
*Bianchi, Willibald C., Army, 1st Lt.	Philippines	3 Feb. 1942
Biddle, Melvin E., Army, Pfc.	Belgium	23–24 Dec. 1944
*Bigelow, Elmer C., Navy, Seaman 1/C	Philippines	14 Feb. 1945
Bjorklund, Arnold L., Army, 1st Lt.	Italy	13 Sept. 1943
Bloch, Orville E., Army, 1st Lt.	Italy	22 Sept. 1944
Bolden, Paul L., Army, Staff Sgt.	Belgium	23 Dec. 1944
Bolton, Cecil H., Army, 1st Lt.	Holland	2 Nov. 1944
Bong, Richard I., Army Air Corps, Maj.	Borneo/Leyte	10 Oct.–15 Nov. 1944
*Bonnyman, Alexander, Jr., U.S.M.C., 1st Lt.	Gilbert Islands	20–22 Nov. 1943
*Booker, Robert D., Army, Pvt.	Tunisia	9 Apr. 1943
*Bordelon, William J., U.S.M.C., Sgt.	Gilbert Islands	20 Nov. 1943
*Boyce, George W. G., Jr., Army, 2nd Lt.	New Guinea	23 July 1944
Boyington, Gregory, U.S.M.C., Maj.	Solomon Islands	12 Sept.–3 Jan. 1944
Briles, Herschel F., Army, Staff Sgt.	Germany	20 Nov. 1944
Britt, Maurice L., Army, Capt.	Italy	10 Nov. 1943
*Brostrom, Leonard C., Army, Pfc.	Philippines	28 Oct. 1944
Brown, Bobbie E., Army, Capt.	Germany	8 Oct. 1944
Bulkeley, John D., Navy, Lt. Cmdr.	Philippines	7 Dec./10 Apr. 1942
Burke, Frank, Army, 1st Lt.	Germany	17 Apr. 1945

Q. Who was the first *enlisted* man in the U.S. armed forces to win the Medal of Honor?

A. USMC Sergeant John Basilone for action on Guadalcanal in 1942. He was killed in 1945 on Iwo Jima.

Q. Name the only father and son to both win the Medal of Honor.
A. General Douglas MacArthur in World War II and his father in the War Between the States.

Name, Rank, Organization	For Action In or At	Date of Action
*Burr, Elmer J., Army, 1st Sgt.	New Guinea	24 Dec. 1942
Burr, Herbert H., Army, Staff Sgt.	Germany	19 Mar. 1945
Burt, James M., Army, Capt.	Germany	13 Oct. 1944
Bush, Richard E., U.S.M.C., Cpl.	Okinawa	16 Apr. 1945
Bush, Robert E., Navy, Med. Corpsman	Okinawa	2 May 1945
*Butts, John E., Army, 2nd Lt.	France	14, 16, 23 June 1944
*Caddy, William R., U.S.M.C., Pfc.	Iwo Jima	3 Mar. 1945
*Callaghan, Daniel J., Navy, Rear Adm.	Savo Island	12–13 Nov. 1942
Calugas, Jose, Army, Sgt.	Philippines	16 Jan. 1942
*Cannon, George H., U.S.M.C., 1st Lt.	Midway	7 Dec. 1941
*Carey, Alvin P., Army, Staff Sgt.	France	23 Aug. 1944
*Carey, Charles F., Jr., Army, Tech. Sgt.	France	8–9 Jan. 1945
Carr, Chris, Army, Sgt.	Italy	1–2 Oct. 1944

(legally changed from Christos H. Karaberis, name under which medal was awarded)

*Carswell, H. S., Jr., Army Air Corps, Maj.	S. China Sea	26 Oct. 1944
Casamento, Anthony, U.S.M.C., Cpl.	Guadalcanal	1 Nov. 1942
*Castle, Frederick W.,		
Army Air Corps., Brig. Gen./Asst. Cmdr.	Germany	24 Dec. 1944
Chambers, Justice M., U.S.M.C., Col.	Iwo Jima	19–22 Feb. 1945
*Cheli, Ralph, Army Air Corps, Maj.	New Guinea	18 Aug. 1943
Childers, Ernest, Army, 2nd Lt.	Italy	22 Sept. 1943
Choate, Clyde L., Army, Staff Sgt.	France	25 Oct. 1944
*Christensen, Dale E., Army, 2nd Lt.	New Guinea	16–19 July 1944
*Christian, Herbert F., Army, Pvt.	Italy	2–3 June 1944
*Cicchetti, Joseph J., Army, Pfc.	Philippines	9 Feb. 1945
Clark, Francis J., Army, Tech. Sgt.	Luxembourg	12 Sept. 1944
Colalillo, Mike, Army, Pfc.	Germany	7 Apr. 1945
*Cole, Darrell S., U.S.M.C., Sgt.	Iwo Jima	19 Feb. 1945
*Cole, Robert G., Army (Airborne), Lt. Col.	France	11 June 1944
Connor, James P., Army, Sgt.	France	15 Aug. 1944
Cooley, Raymond H., Army, Staff Sgt.	Philippines	24 Feb. 1945
Coolidge, Charles H., Army, Tech. Sgt.	France	24–27 Oct. 1944
*Courtney, Henry A., Jr., U.S.M.C., Maj.	Ryukyu Islands	14–15 May 1945
*Cowan, Richard E., Army, Pfc.	Belgium	17 Dec. 1944
Craft, Clarence B.. Army, Pfc.	Okinawa	31 May 1945

Name, Rank, Organization	For Action In or At	Date of Action
*Craig, Robert, Army, 2nd Lt.	Sicily	11 July 1943
*Crain, Morris E., Army, Tech. Sgt.	France	13 Mar. 1945
*Craw, Demas T., Army Air Corps, Col.	French Morocco	8 Nov. 1942
Crawford, William J., Army, Pvt.	Italy	13 Sept. 1943
Crews, John R., Army, Staff Sgt.	Germany	8 Apr. 1945
*Cromwell, John P., Navy, Capt.	Pacific	19 Nov. 1943
Currey, Francis S., Army, Sgt.	Belgium	21 Dec. 1944
Dahlgren, Edward C., Army, 2nd Lt.	France	11 Feb. 1945
Dalessondro, Peter J., Army, Tech. Sgt.	Germany	22 Dec. 1944
Daly, Michael J., Army, Capt.	Nuremberg, Germany	18 Apr. 1945
*Damato, Anthony P., U.S.M.C., Cpl.	Marshall Islands	19–20 Feb. 1944
*David, Albert L., Navy, Lt. (jg)	French West Africa	4 June 1944
Davis, Charles W., Army, Maj.	Guadalcanal	12 Jan. 1943
*Davis, George F., Navy, Cmdr.	Philippines	6 Jan. 1945
*Dealey, Samuel D., Navy, Cmdr.	Enemy waters	Various dates
DeBlanc, Jefferson J., U.S.M.C., Capt.	Solomon Islands	31 Jan. 1943
*DeFranzo, Arthur F., Army, Staff Sgt.	Vaubadon, France	10 June 1944
*DeGlopper, Charles N., Army, Pfc.	France	9 June 1944
*Deleau, Emile, Jr., Army, Sgt.	Oberhoffen, France	1–2 Feb. 1945
Dervishian, Ernest H., Army, 2nd Lt.	Cisterna, Italy	23 May 1944
*Diamond, James H., Army, Pfc.	Philippines	8–14 May 1945
*Dietz, Robert H., Army, Staff Sgt.	Kirchain, Germany	29 Mar. 1945
Doolittle, James H., Army, Brig. Gen.	Japan	9 June 1942
Doss, Desmond T., Army, Pfc.	Okinawa	29 Apr.–21 May 1945
Drowley, Jesse R., Army, Staff Sgt.	Solomon Islands	30 Jan. 1944
Dunham, Russell E., Army, Tech. Sgt.	France	8 Jan. 1945
Dunlop, Robert H., U.S.M.C., Capt.	Iwo Jima	20–21 Feb. 1945
*Dutko, John W., Army, Pfc.	Italy	23 May 1944
*Dyess, Aquilla J., U.S.M.C., Lt. Col.	Marshall Islands	1–2 Feb. 1944
Edson, Merritt A., U.S.M.C., Col.	Solomon Islands	13–14 Sept. 1942

FACT American propaganda frequently called the Japanese kamikaze, or suicide plane, pilots fanatics, while at the same time U.S. military personnel who performed similarly were regarded as heroes. Captain Richard E. Fleming, a U.S. Marine Corps pilot, posthumously received the Medal of Honor for diving his flaming bomber onto the deck of the Japanese cruiser *Mikuma* during the Battle of Midway. Some reference works report his act as the first such personal sacrifice in the Pacific war.

Q. Who was the most decorated U.S. paratrooper in the war?

A. Sergeant Leonard A. Funk, 508th Parachute Infantry Regiment, 82nd Airborne Division, who received the Medal of Honor, the Distinguished Service Cross and several other decorations. (See Volume 1, page 105).

Name, Rank, Organization	For Action In or At	Date of Action
Ehlers, Walter D., Army, Staff Sgt.	France	9–10 June 1944
*Elrod, Henry T., U.S.M.C., Capt.	Wake Island	8–23 Dec. 1941
*Endl, Gerald L., Army, Staff Sgt.	New Guinea	11 July 1944
*Epperson, Harold G., U.S.M.C., Pfc.	Saipan, Marianas	25 June 1944
Erwin, Henry E., Army Air Corps, Staff Sgt.	Koriyama, Japan	12 Apr. 1945
*Eubanks, Ray E., Army, Sgt.	Dutch New Guinea	23 July 1944
*Evans, Ernest E., Navy, Cmdr.	Samar	25 Oct. 1944
Everhart, Forrest E., Army, Tech. Sgt.	Kerling, France	12 Nov. 1944
*Fardy, John P., U.S.M.C., Cpl.	Okinawa	7 May 1945
*Femoyer, Robert E., Army Air Corps, 2nd Lt.	Merseburg, Germany	2 Nov. 1944
Fields, James H., Army, 1st Lt.	France	27 Sept. 1944
Finn, John W., Navy, Lt.	Kaneche Bay, Hawaii	7 Dec. 1941
Fisher, Almond E., Army, 2nd Lt.	France	12–13 Sept. 1944
*Flaherty, Francis C., Navy, Ens.	Pearl Harbor	7 Dec. 1941
*Fleming, Richard E., U.S.M.C., Capt.	Midway	4–5 June 1942
Fluckey, Eugene B., Navy, Cmdr.	Coast of China	19 Dec.–15 Feb. 1945
Foss, Joseph J., U.S.M.C., Capt.	Guadalcanal	9 Oct.–19 Nov. 1942 15–23 Jan. 1943
*Foster, William A., Marine Res., Pfc.	Okinawa	2 May 1945
*Fournier, William G., Army, Sgt.	Guadalcanal	10 Jan. 1943
*Fowler, Thomas W., Army, 2nd Lt.	Carano, Italy	23 May 1944
*Fryar, Elmer E., Army, Pvt.	Philippines	8 Dec. 1944
Funk, Leonard A., Jr., Army, 1st Sgt.	Belgium	29 Jan. 1945
Fuqua, Samuel G., Navy, Capt.	Pearl Harbor	7 Dec. 1941
Galer, Robert E., U.S.M.C., Maj.	Solomon Islands	Various dates
*Galt, William W., Army, Capt.	Italy	29 May 1944
*Gammon, Archer T., Army, Staff Sgt.	Belgium	11 Jan. 1945
Garcia, Marcario, Army, Staff Sgt.	Germany	27 Nov. 1944
Garman, Harold A., Army, Pvt.	France	25 Aug. 1944
Gary, Donald A., Navy, Lt. (jg)	Kobe, Japan	19 Mar. 1945
Gerstung, Robert E., Army, Tech. Sgt.	Berg, Germany	19 Dec. 1944
*Gibson, Eric G., Army, T/5	Italy	28 Jan. 1944
*Gilmore, Howard W., Navy, Cmdr.	Southwest Pacific	10 Jan.–7 Feb. 1943

> **FACT** One of the widest-held pieces of misinformation concerning the war is that Captain Colin P. Kelly, Jr., received the Medal of Honor for his actions following the sinking of the Japanese battleship *Haruna*. Kelly did not sink the battleship nor did he receive the CMH. The *Haruna* was sunk by aircraft off Kure, Japan, on July 28, 1945. Kelly was awarded a posthumous Distinguished Service Cross for remaining in his aircraft while his B-17 crew bailed out on December 10, 1942.

Name, Rank, Organization	For Action In or At	Date of Action
*Gonsalves, Harold, U.S.M.C., Pfc.	Okinawa	15 Apr. 1945
*Gonzales, David M., Army, Pfc.	Philippines	25 Apr. 1945
Gordon, Nathan G., Navy, Lt.	Bismarck Sea	15 Feb. 1944
*Gott, Donald J., Army Air Corps, 1st Lt.	Germany	9 Nov. 1944
*Grabiarz, William J., Army, Pfc.	Philippines	23 Feb. 1945
*Gray, Ross F., U.S.M.C., Sgt.	Iwo Jima	21 Feb. 1945
Gregg, Stephen R., Army, 2nd Lt.	France	27 Aug. 1944
*Gruennert, Kenneth E., Army, Sgt.	Buna, New Guinea	24 Dec. 1942
*Gurke, Henry, U.S.M.C., Pfc.	Solomon Islands	9 Nov. 1943
Hall, George J., Army, Staff Sgt.	Anzio, Italy	23 May 1944
*Hall, Lewis, Army, T/5	Guadalcanal	10 Jan. 1943
Hall, William E., Navy, Lt. (jg)	Coral Sea	7–8 May 1942
*Hallman, Sherwood H., Army, Staff Sgt.	France	13 Sept. 1944
*Halyburton, W. D., Jr., Navy, Pharm. Mate	Okinawa	10 May 1945
Hamilton, Pierpont M., Army Air Corps, Maj.	French Morocco	8 Nov. 1942
*Hammerberg, Owen, Navy, Boatswain's Mate	Pearl Harbor	17 Feb. 1945
*Hansen, Dale M., U.S.M.C., Pvt.	Okinawa	7 May 1945
*Hanson, Robert M., U.S.M.C., 1st Lt.	Bougainville	1 Nov. 1943
*Harmon, Roy W., Army, Sgt.	Casaglia	12 July 1944
*Harr, Harry R., Army, Cpl.	Philippines	5 June 1945
Harrell, William G., U.S.M.C., Sgt	Iwo Jima	3 Mar. 1945
*Harris, James L., Army, 2nd Lt.	Vagney, France	7 Oct. 1944
*Hastings, Joe R., Army, Pfc.	Germany	14 May 1945
*Hauge, Louis J., Jr., U.S.M.C., Cpl.	Ryukyus	14 May 1945
Hawk, John D., Army, Sgt.	France	20 Aug. 1944
*Hawkins, William D., U.S.M.C., 1st Lt.	Gilbert Islands	20–21 Nov. 1943
Hawks, Lloyd C., Army, Pfc.	Italy	30 Jan. 1944
*Hedrick, Clinton M., Army, Tech. Sgt.	Germany	27–28 Mar. 1945
Hendrix, James R., Army, Pvt.	Belgium	26 Dec. 1944
*Henry, Robert T., Army, Pvt.	Germany	3 Dec. 1944

Name, Rank, Organization	For Action In or At	Date of Action
Herrera, Silvestre S., Army, Pfc.	France	15 Mar. 1945
Herring, Rufus G., Navy, Lt.	Iwo Jima	17 Feb. 1945
*Hill, Edwin J., Navy, Chief Boatswain	Pearl Harbor	7 Dec. 1941
Horner, Freeman V., Army Staff Sgt.	Germany	16 Nov. 1944
Howard, James H., Army Air Corps, Lt. Col.	Germany	11 Jan. 1944
Huff, Paul B., Army, Cpl.	Italy	8 Feb. 1944
*Hughes, Lloyd H., Army Air Corps, 2nd Lt.	Rumania	1 Aug. 1943
*Hutchins, J.D., Navy, Seaman 1/C	New Guinea	4 Sept. 1943
*Jachman, Isadore S., Army, Staff Sgt.	Belgium	4 Jan. 1945
Jackson, Arthur J., U.S.M.C., Pfc.	Peleliu	18 Sept. 1944
Jacobson, Douglas T., U.S.M.C., Pfc.	Iwo Jima	26 Feb. 1945
*Jerstad, John L., Army Air Corps, Maj.	Rumania	1 Aug. 1943
*Johnson, Elden H., Army, Pvt.	Italy	3 June 1944
Johnson, Leon W., Army Air Corps, Col.	Rumania	1 Aug. 1943
*Johnson, Leroy, Army, Sgt.	Philippines	15 Dec. 1944
Johnson, Oscar G., Army, Sgt.	Italy	16–18 Sept. 1944
Johnston, William J., Army, Pfc.	Italy	17–19 Feb. 1944
*Jones, Herbert C., Navy, Ens.	Pearl Harbor	7 Dec. 1941
*Julian, Joseph R., U.S.M.C., Sgt.	Iwo Jima	9 Mar. 1945
*Kandle, Victor L., Army, 1st Lt.	France	9 Oct. 1944
Kane, John R., Army Air Corps, Col.	Rumania	1 Aug. 1943
Kearby, Neel E., Army Air Corps, Col.	New Guinea	11 Oct. 1943
*Keathley, George D., Army, Staff Sgt.	Italy	14 Sept. 1944
*Kefurt, Gus, Army, Staff Sgt.	France	23–24 Dec. 1944
*Kelley, Jonah E., Army, Staff Sgt.	Germany	30–31 Jan. 1945
*Kelley, Ova A., Army, Pvt.	Philippines	8 Dec. 1944
Kelly, Charles E., Army, Cpl.	Italy	13 Sept. 1943
*Kelly, John D., Army, Tech. Sgt.	France	25 June 1944
Kelly, Thomas J., Army, Cpl.	Germany	5 Apr. 1945
*Keppler, R.J., Navy, Boatswain's Mate	Solomon Islands	12–13 Nov. 1942
Kerstetter, Dexter J., Army, Pfc.	Philippines	13 Apr. 1945
*Kessler, Patrick L., Army, Pfc.	Italy	23 May 1944
*Kidd, Isaac C., Navy, Rear Adm.	Pearl Harbor	7 Dec. 1941
*Kimbro, Truman, Army, T/4	Belgium	19 Dec. 1944

Q. Name the only Pulitzer Prize winner who also won the Medal of Honor.

A. American aviation legend Charles A. Lindbergh. (Volume 1, pages 72 and 80)

Name, Rank, Organization	For Action In or At	Date of Action
*Kiner, Harold G., Army, Pvt.	Germany	2 Oct. 1944
*Kingsley, David R., Army Air Corps, 2nd Lt.	Rumania	23 June 1944
*Kinser, Elbert L. U.S.M.C., Sgt.	Ryukyus	4 May 1945
Kisters, Gerry H., Army, 2nd Lt.	Sicily	31 July 1943
Knappenberger, Alton W., Army, Pfc.	Italy	1 Feb. 1944
*Knight, Jack L., Army, 1st Lt.	Loi–Kang, Burma	2 Feb. 1945
*Knight, R. L., Army Air Corps, 1st Lt.	Italy	24–25 Apr. 1945
*Kraus, Richard E., U.S.M.C., Pfc.	Palau Islands	5 Oct. 1944
*Krotiak, Anthony L., Army, Pfc.	Philippines	8 May 1945
*LaBelle, James D., U.S.M.C., Pfc.	Iwo Jima	8 Mar. 1945
Lawley, W. R., Jr., Army Air Corps, 1st Lt.	Over Europe	20 Feb. 1944
Laws, Robert E., Army, Staff Sgt.	Philippines	12 Jan. 1945
Lee, Daniel W., Army, 1st Lt.	France	2 Sept. 1944
Leims, John H., U.S.M.C., 2nd Lt.	Iwo Jima	7 Mar. 1945
*Leonard, Turney W., Army, 1st Lt.	Germany	4–6 Nov. 1944
*Lester, Fred F., Navy, Hosp. 1/C	Ryukyus	8 June 1945
*Lindsey, Darrel R., Army Air Corps, Capt.	France	9 Aug. 1944
Linsey, Jake W., Army, Tech. Sgt.	Germany	16 Nov. 1944
*Lindstrom, Floyd K., Army, Pfc.	Italy	11 Nov. 1943
*Lloyd, Edgar H., Army, 1st Lt.	France	14 Sept. 1944
*Lobaugh, Donald R., Army, Pvt.	New Guinea	22 July 1944
Logan, James M., Army, Sgt.	Italy	9 Sept. 1943
Lopez, Jose M., Army, Sgt.	Belgium	17 Dec. 1944
Lucas, Jacklyn H., U.S.M.C., Pfc.	Iwo Jima	20 Feb. 1945
*Lummus, Jack, U.S.M.C., 1st Lt.	Iwo Jima	8 Mar. 1945
Mabry, George L., Jr., Army, Lt. Col.	Germany	20 Nov. 1944
MacArthur, Douglas, Army, Gen.	Philippines	
MacGillivary, Charles A., Army, Sgt.	France	1 Jan. 1945
*Magrath, John D., Army, Pfc.	Italy	14 Apr. 1945
*Mann, Joe E., Army, Pfc.	Holland	18 Sept. 1944
*Martin, Harry L., U.S.M.C., 1st Lt.	Iwo Jima	26 Mar. 1945
*Martinez, Joe P., Army, Pvt.	Aleutians	26 May 1943
*Mason, Leonard F., U.S.M.C., Pfc.	Guam	22 July 1944

Q. Identify the U.S. Marine who received the last Medal of Honor
authorized by Congress *during* the war.

A. Private First Class Robert M. McTureous, Jr., for action on
Okinawa. (Congress authorized other medals *after* the actual
fighting stopped.)

Name, Rank, Organization	For Action In or At	Date of Action
*Mathies, Archibald, Army Air Corps, Sgt.	Over Europe	20 Feb. 1944
*Mathis, Jack W., Army Air Corps, 1st Lt.	Germany	18 Mar. 1943
Maxwell, Robert D., Army, T/5	France	7 Sept. 1944
*May, Martin O., Army, Pfc.	Ryukyus	19–21 Apr. 1945
Mayfield, Melvin, Army, Cpl.	Philippines	29 July 1945
McCall, Thomas E., Army, Staff Sgt.	Italy	22 Jan. 1944
McCampbell, David, Navy, Cmdr.	Philippine Sea	19 June 1944
McCandless, Bruce, Navy, Cmdr.	Savo Island	12–13 Nov. 1942
*McCard, Robert H., U.S.M.C., Gun. Sgt.	Saipan, Marianas	16 June 1944
McCarter, Lloyd G., Army, Pvt.	Philippines	16–19 Feb. 1945
McCarthy, Joseph J., U.S.M.C., Capt.	Iwo Jima	21 Feb. 1945
McCool, Richard M., Jr., Navy, Lt.	Off Okinawa	10–11 June 1945
McGaha, Charles L., Army, Mstr. Sgt.	Philippines	7 Feb. 1945
McGarity, Vernon, Army, Tech. Sgt.	Belgium	16 Dec. 1944
*McGee, William D., Army, Pvt.	Mülheim, Germany	18 Mar. 1945
*McGill, Troy A., Army, Sgt.	Los Negros Islands	4 Mar. 1944
*McGraw, Francis X., Army, Pfc.	Germany	19 Nov. 1944
*McGuire, T. B., Jr., Army Air Corps, Maj.	Philippines	25–26 Dec. 1944
McKinney, John R., Army, Sgt.	Philippines	11 May 1945
*McTureous, Robert M., Jr., U.S.M.C., Pvt.	Okinawa	7 June 1945
*McVeigh, John J., Army, Sgt.	France	29 Aug. 1944
*McWhorter, William A., Army, Pfc.	Philippines	5 Dec. 1944
Meagher, John, Army, Tech. Sgt.	Okinawa	19 June 1945
Merli, Gino J., Army, Pfc.	Belgium	4–5 Sept. 1944
*Merrell, Joseph F., Army, Pvt.	Germany	18 Apr. 1945
*Messerschmidt, Harold O., Army, Sgt.	France	17 Sept. 1944
*Metzger, W. E., Jr., Army Air Corps, 2nd Lt.	Germany	9 Nov. 1944
Michael, Edward S., Army Air Corps, 1st Lt.	Over Germany	11 Apr. 1944
*Michael, Harry J., Army, 2nd Lt.	Germany	14 Mar. 1945
*Miller, Andrew, Army, Staff Sgt.	France/Germany	16–29 Nov. 1944
Mills, James H., Army, Pvt.	Italy	24 May 1944
*Minick, John W., Army, Staff Sgt.	Germany	21 Nov. 1944
*Minue, Nicholas, Army, Pvt.	Tunisia	28 Apr. 1943
*Monteith, Jimmie W., Jr., Army, 1st Lt.	France	6 June 1944
Montgomery, Jack C., Army, 1st Lt.	Italy	22 Feb. 1944
*Moon, Harold H., Jr., Army, Pvt.	Philippines	21 Oct. 1944
Morgan, John C., Army Air Corps, 2nd Lt.	Over Europe	28 July 1943
*Moskala, Edward J., Army, Pfc.	Okinawa	9 Apr. 1945
*Mower, Charles E., Army, Sgt.	Philippines	3 Nov. 1944

Name, Rank, Organization	For Action In or At	Date of Action
*Muller, Joseph E., Army, Sgt.	Okinawa	15–16 May 1945
*Munemori, Sadao S., Army, Pfc.	Italy	5 Apr. 1945
*Munro, D. A., Coast Guard, Signalman 1/C	Guadalcanal	27 Sept. 1942
Murphy, Audie L., Army, 2nd Lt.	France	26 Jan. 1945
*Murphy, Frederick C., Army, Pfc.	Germany	18 Mar. 1945
Murray, Charles P., Jr., Army, 1st Lt.	France	16 Dec. 1944
*Nelson, William L., Army, Sgt.	Djebel Dardys	24 Apr. 1943
Neppel, Ralph G., Army, Sgt.	Birgel, Germany	14 Dec. 1944
Nett, Robert P., Army, Capt.	Philippines	14 Dec. 1944
*New, John D., U.S.M.C., Pfc.	Peleliu	25 Sept. 1944
Newman, Beryl R., Army, 1st Lt.	Cisterna, Italy	26 May 1944
*Nininger, A. R., Jr., Army, 2nd Lt.	Philippines	12 Jan. 1942
*O'Brien, William J., Army, Lt. Col.	Marianas Islands	20 June–7 July 1944
O'Callahan, J. T., Navy, Cmdr.	Japan	19 Mar. 1945
Ogden, Carlos C., Army, 1st Lt.	France	25 June 1944
O'Hare, Edward H., Navy, Lt.	Pacific	20 Feb. 1942
O'Kane, Richard H., Navy, Cmdr.	Philippines	23–24 Oct. 1944
*Olson, Arlo L., Army, Capt.	Italy	13 Oct. 1943
*Olson, Truman O., Army, Sgt.	Italy	30–31 Jan. 1944
Oresko, Nicholas, Army Mstr. Sgt.	Germany	23 Jan. 1945
*Owens, Robert A., U.S.M.C., Sgt.	Solomon Islands	1 Nov. 1943
*Ozbourn, Joseph W., U.S.M.C., Pvt.	Marianas Islands	30 July 1944
Paige, Mitchell, U.S.M.C., Sgt.	Solomon Isls.	26 Oct. 1942
*Parle, John J., Navy, Ens.	Italy	9–10 July 1943
*Parrish, Laverne, Army, T/4	Philippines	18–24 Jan. 1945
*Pease, Harl, Jr., Army Air Corps, Capt.	New Britain	6–7 Aug. 1942
*Peden, Forrest E., Army, T/5	France	3 Feb. 1945
*Pendleton, Jack J., Army, Staff Sgt.	Germany	12 Oct. 1944
*Peregory, Frank D., Army, Tech. Sgt.	France	8 June 1944
*Perez, Manuel, Jr., Army, Pfc.	Philippines	13 Feb. 1945
*Peters, George J., Army, Pvt.	Germany	24 Mar. 1945
*Peterson, George, Army, Staff Sgt.	Germany	30 Mar. 1945
*Peterson, Oscar V., Navy, Chief Watertender	Pacific	7 May 1942

Q. Name the first U.S. serviceman to be awarded a Medal of Honor in the war.

A. Lieutenant Alexander R. Nininger, Jr., killed on Luzon in the Philippines early in the war, received the citation posthumously, for action on January 12, 1942, near Abucay, Bataan.

Q. Identify the only chaplain in the war to receive a Medal of Honor.
A. U.S. Navy Chaplain Joseph O'Callahan. He earned the distinction for heroism aboard the aircraft carrier USS *Franklin* (CV-13) when the "ship that wouldn't die" went through its ordeal in March 1945.

Name, Rank, Organization	For Action In or At	Date of Action
*Petrarca, Frank J., Army, Pfc.	Solomon Islands	27 July 1943
Pharris, Jackson C., Navy, Lt.	Pearl Harbor	7 Dec. 1941
*Phelps, Wesley, U.S.M.C., Pvt.	Peleliu	4 Oct. 1944
*Phillips, George, U.S.M.C., Pvt.	Iwo Jima	14 Mar. 1945
Pierce, F. J., Navy, Pharm. Mate 1/C	Iwo Jima	15–16 Mar. 1945
*Pinder, John J., Jr., Army T/5	France	6 June 1944
Pope, Everett P., U.S.M.C., Capt.	Peleliu	19–20 Sept. 1944
*Power, John V., U.S.M.C., 1st Lt.	Namur Island	1 Feb. 1944
*Powers, John J., Navy, Lt.	Coral Sea	4–8 May 1942
Powers, Leo J., Army, Pfc.	Italy	3 Feb. 1944
Preston, Arthur M., Navy, Lt.	Halmahera Islands	16 Sept. 1944
*Prussman, Earnest W., Army, Pfc.	France	8 Sept. 1944
*Pucket, D. D., Army Air Corps, 1st Lt.	Rumania	9 July 1944
Ramage, Lawson P., Navy, Cmdr.	Pacific	31 July 1944
*Ray, Bernard J., Army, 1st Lt.	Germany	17 Nov. 1944
*Reese, James W., Army, Pvt.	Italy	5 Aug. 1943
*Reese, John N., Jr., Army, Pfc.	Philippines	9 Feb. 1945
*Reeves, Thomas J., Navy, Radio Elect.	Pearl Harbor	7 Dec. 1941
*Ricketts, Milton E., Navy, Lt.	Coral Sea	8 May 1942
*Riordan, Paul F., Army, 2nd Lt.	Italy	3–8 Feb. 1944
*Roan, Charles H., U.S.M.C., Pfc.	Palau Islands	18 Sept. 1944
*Robinson, J. E., Jr., Army, 1st Lt.	Germany	6 Apr. 1945
Rodriguez, Cleto, Army, Tech. Sgt.	Philippines	9 Feb. 1945
*Roeder, Robert E., Army, Capt.	Italy	27–28 Sept. 1944
*Rooks, Albert H., Navy, Capt.	Pacific	4–27 Feb. 1942
*Roosevelt, Theodore, Jr., Army, Brig. Gen.	France	6 June 1944
Ross, Donald Kirby, Navy, Mach.	Pearl Harbor	7 Dec. 1941
Ross, Wilburn K., Army, Pvt.	France	30 Oct. 1944
Rouh, Carlton R., U.S.M.C., 1st Lt.	Peleliu	15 Sept. 1944
Rudolph, Donald E., Army, 2nd Lt.	Philippines	5 Feb. 1945
*Ruhl, Donald J., U.S.M.C., Pfc.	Iwo Jima	19–21 Feb. 1945
Ruiz, Alejandro R. R., Army, Pfc.	Okinawa	28 Apr. 1945
*Sadowski, Joseph J., Army, Sgt.	France	14 Sept. 1944
*Sarnoski, J. R., Army Air Corps, 2nd Lt.	Solomon Islands	16 June 1943

Name, Rank, Organization	For Action In or At	Date of Action
*Sayers, Foster J., Army, Pfc.	France	12 Nov. 1944
Schaefer, Joseph E., Army, Staff Sgt.	Germany	
Schauer, Henry, Army, Pfc.	Italy	23–24 May 1944
Schonland, Herbert E., Navy, Cmdr.	Savo Island	12–13 Nov. 1943
*Schwab, Albert E., U.S.M.C., Pfc.	Okinawa	7 May 1945
*Scott, Norman, Navy, Rear Adm.	Savo Island	11–12 Oct. & 12–13 Nov. 1942
*Scott, Robert R., Navy, Machinist's Mate	Pearl Harbor	7 Dec. 1941
Scott, Robert S., Army, Capt.	Solomon Islands	29 July 1943
Shea, Charles W., Army, 2nd Lt.	Italy	12 May 1944
*Sheridan, Carl V., Army, Pfc.	Germany	26 Nov. 1944
*Shockley, William R., Army, Pfc.	Philippines	31 Mar. 1945
Shomo, William A., Army Air Corps, Maj.	Philippines	11 Jan. 1945
*Shoup, Curtis F., Army, Staff Sgt.	Belgium	7 Jan. 1945
Shoup, David M., U.S.M.C., Col.	Gilbert Islands	20–22 Nov. 1943
Sigler, Franklin E., U.S.M.C., Pvt.	Iwo Jima	14 Mar. 1945
Silk, Edward A., Army, 1st Lt.	France	23 Nov. 1944
Sjogren, John C., Army, Staff Sgt.	Philippines	23 May 1945
Skaggs, Luther, Jr., U.S.M.C., Pfc.	Marianas Islands	21–22 July 1944
Slaton, James D., Army, Cpl.	Italy	23 Sept. 1943
*Smith, Furman L., Army, Pvt.	Italy	31 May 1944
Smith, John L., U.S.M.C., Maj.	Solomon Islands	Aug.–Sept. 1942
Smith, Maynard H., Army Air Corps, Sgt.	Over Europe	1 May 1943
Soderman, William A., Army, Pfc.	Belgium	17 Dec. 1944
Sorenson, Richard K., U.S.M.C., Pvt.	Marshall Islands	1–2 Feb. 1944
*Specker, Joe C., Army, Sgt.	Italy	7 Jan. 1944
Spurrier, Junior J., Army, Staff Sgt.	France	13 Nov. 1944
*Squires, John C., Army, Sgt.	Italy	23–24 Apr. 1944

Q. Identify the U.S. pilot who is credited with shooting down seven enemy aircraft on his first mission.

A. Captain (later major) William A. Shomo received the Medal of Honor for the feat on January 11, 1945, over Luzon in the Philippines. Shomo was lead pilot in a flight of two planes on a photographic mission when they encountered a Japanese twin-engine bomber and a twelve-fighter escort. Shomo maneuvered and attacked several times and shot down seven aircraft including the bomber. The other U.S. plane shot down three, and the remaining three enemy aircraft escaped in a cloudbank. In civilian life Shomo was a mortician.

Name, Rank, Organization	For Action In or At	Date of Action
*Stein, Tony, U.S.M.C., Cpl.	Iwo Jima	19 Feb. 1945
Street, George L. III, Navy, Cmdr.	Quelpart Island	14 Apr. 1945
*Stryker, Stuart S., Army, Pfc.	Germany	24 Mar. 1945
Swett, James E., U.S.M.C., 1st Lt.	Solomon Islands	7 Apr. 1943
*Terry, Seymour W., Army, Capt.	Okinawa	11 May 1945
*Thomas, Herbert J., U.S.M.C., Sgt.	Solomon Islands	7 Nov. 1943
*Thomas, William H., Army, Pfc.	Philippines	22 Apr. 1945
*Thomason, Clyde, U.S.M.C., Sgt.	Makin Island	17–18 Aug. 1942
Thompson, Max, Army, Sgt.	Germany	18 Oct. 1944
*Thorne, Horace M., Army, Cpl.	Belgium	21 Dec. 1944
*Thorson, John F., Army, Pfc.	Philippines	28 Oct. 1944
*Timmerman, Grant F., U.S.M.C., Sgt.	Marianas Islands	8 July 1944
*Tomich, Peter, Navy, Ch. Watertender	Pearl Harbor	7 Dec. 1941
Tominac, John J., Army, 1st Lt.	France	12 Sept. 1944
*Towle, John R., Army, Pvt.	Holland	21 Sept. 1944
Treadwell, Jack L., Army, Capt.	Germany	18 Mar. 1945
*Truemper, W. E. Army Air Corps, 2nd Lt.	Over Europe	20 Feb. 1944
*Turner, Day G., Army, Sgt.	Luxembourg	8 Jan. 1945
Turner, George B., Army, Pfc.	France	3 Jan. 1945
Urban, Matt, Army, Capt.	France	14 June–3 Sept. 1944
*Valdez, Jose F., Army, Pfc.	France	25 Jan. 1945
*Vance, L. R., Jr., Army Air Corps, Lt. Col.	France	5 June 1944
Vandergrift, Alex A., U.S.M.C., Maj. Gen.	Solomon Islands	7 Aug.–9 Dec. 1942
*Van Noy, Junior, Army, Pvt.	New Guinea	17 Oct. 1943
*Van Valkenburgh, Franklin, Navy, Capt.	Pearl Harbor	7 Dec. 1941
*Van Voorhis, Bruce A., Navy, Lt. Cmdr.	Solomon Islands	6 July 1943
*Viale, Robert M., Army, 2nd Lt.	Philippines	5 Feb. 1945
*Villegas, Ysmael R., Army, Staff Sgt.	Philippines	20 Mar. 1945
Vlug, Dirk J., Army, Pfc.	Philippines	15 Dec. 1944
Vosler, F. T., Army Air Corps, Tech. Sgt.	Germany	20 Dec. 1943
Wahlen, George E., Navy, Pharm. Mate	Iwo Jima	3 Mar. 1945
Wainwright, Jonathan M., Army, Gen.	Philippines	12 Mar.–7 May 1942
*Walker, K. N., Army Air Corps, Brig. Gen.	New Britain	5 Jan. 1943
*Wallace, Herman C., Army, Pfc.	Germany	27 Feb. 1945
Walsh, Kenneth A., U.S.M.C., 1st Lt.	Solomon Islands	15 & 30 Aug. 1943
*Walsh, William G., U.S.M.C. Res., Gun/Sgt.	Iwo Jima	27 Feb. 1945
*Ward, James R., Navy, Seaman 1/C	Pearl Harbor	7 Dec. 1941
Ware, Keith L., Army, Lt. Col.	France	26 Dec. 1944
*Warner, Henry F., Army, Cpl.	Belgium	20–21 Dec. 1944

Name, Rank, Organization	For Action In or At	Date of Action
Watson, Wilson D., U.S.M.C., Pvt.	Iwo Jima	26–27 Feb. 1945
*Waugh, Robert T., Army, 1st Lt.	Italy	11–14 May 1944
Waybur, David C., Army, 1st Lt.	Italy	17 July 1943
*Weicht, Ellis R., Army, Sgt.	France	3 Dec. 1944
*Wetzel, Walter C., Army, Pfc.	Germany	3 Apr. 1945
Whiteley, Eli, Army, 1st Lt.	France	27 Dec. 1944
Whittington, Hulon B., Army, Sgt.	France	29 July 1944
Wiedorfer, Paul J., Army, Staff Sgt.	Belgium	25 Dec. 1944
*Wigle, Thomas W., Army, 2nd Lt.	Italy	14 Sept. 1944
Wilbur, William H., Army, Col.	North Africa	8 Nov. 1942
*Wilkin, Edward G., Army, Cpl.	Germany	18 Mar. 1945
*Wilkins, Raymond H., Army Air Corps, Maj.	New Britain	2 Nov. 1943
*Will, Walter J., Army, 1st Lt.	Germany	30 Mar. 1945
Williams, Hershel W., U.S.M.C., Cpl.	Volcano Islands	23 Feb. 1945
*Williams, Jack, Navy, Pharm. Mate 3/C	Volcano Islands	3 March 1945
*Willis, J. H., Navy, Pharm. Mate 1/C	Volcano Islands	28 Feb. 1945
*Wilson, Alfred L., Army, T/5	France	8 Nov. 1944
Wilson, Louis Hugh, Jr., U.S.M.C., Capt.	Guam	25–26 July 1944
*Wilson, Robert L., U.S.M.C., Pfc.	Tinian Island	4 Aug. 1944
Wise, Homer L., Army, Staff Sgt.	Italy	14 June 1944
*Witek, Frank P., U.S.M.C., Pfc.	Marianas Islands	3 Aug. 1944
*Woodford, Howard E., Army, Staff Sgt.	Philippines	6 June 1945
Young, Cassin, Navy, Cmdr.	Pearl Harbor	7 Dec. 1941
*Young, Rodger W., Army, Pvt.	Solomon Islands	31 July 1943
Zeamer, Jay, Jr., Army Air Corps, Maj.	Solomon Islands	16 June 1943
*Zussman, Raymond, Army, 2nd Lt.	France	12 Sept. 1944

Bibliography

Aldeman, Robert H. and Walton, George. *The Devil's Brigade*. Philadelphia: Chilton, 1966.

Ambrose, Stephen E. *The Supreme Commander: The War Years of General Dwight D. Eisenhower*. New York: Doubleday, 1970.

Angelucci, Enzo. *Airplanes from the Dawn of Flight to the Present Day*. New York: McGraw-Hill, 1973.

Aron, Robert. *De Gaulle Before Paris: The Liberation of France, June–August 1944*. New York: Putnam, 1962.

Aster, Sidney. *1939: The Making of the Second World War*. New York: Simon and Schuster, 1974.

Baron, Richard; Baum, Abe; and Goldhurst, Richard. *Raid! The Untold Story of Patton's Secret Mission*. New York: Putnam, 1981.

Bauer, Eddy. *Illustrated World War II Encyclopedia* (24 vols.). Monaco: Jaspard Polus, 1966. English translation printed in the United States by H. S. Stuttman, Inc.

Bazna, Elyesa. *I Was Cicero*. New York: Harper & Row, 1962.

Bekker, Cajus. *The Luftwaffe War Diaries*. New York: Doubleday, 1968.

———. *Hitler's Naval War*. New York: Doubleday, 1974.

Belote, James H., and Belote, William M. *Corregidor: The Saga of a Fortress*. New York: Harper & Row, 1967.

Blair, Clay, Jr. *Silent Victory*. New York: Lippincott, 1975.

Boyington, Gregory. *Baa Baa Black Sheep*. New York: Putnam, 1958.

Bradley, Omar N. *A Soldier's Story*. New York: Henry Holt, 1951.

Brown, Anthony Cave. *Bodyguard of Lies*. New York: Harper & Row, 1975.

Buchanan, A. Russell. *The United States and World War II*. New York: Harper & Row, 1964.

Bullock, Alan. *Hitler — A Study in Tyranny*. New York: Harper & Row, 1963.

Butcher, Harry. *My Three Years with Eisenhower*. New York: Simon and Schuster, 1946.

Calvocoressi, Peter, and Wint, Guy. *Total War*. New York: Pantheon, 1972.

Carell, Paul. *The Foxes of the Desert*. New York: Dutton, 1961.

Catton, Bruce. *The War Lords of Washington*. New York: Harcourt Brace, 1948.

Churchill, Winston S. *The Second World War*. Boston: Houghton Mifflin, 1948–53.

Clark, Alan. *Barbarossa: The Russian-German Conflict, 1941–1945*. New York: Morrow, 1965.

Collier, Basil. *Japan at War*. London: Sidgwick and Jackson, 1975.

Collins, Larry, and Lapierre, Dominique. *Is Paris Burning?* New York: Simon and Schuster, 1965.

Cortesi, Lawrence. *Operation Bismarck Sea*. Canoga Park, California: Major Books, 1977.

Daley, Robert. *An American Saga: Juan Trippe and His Pan American Empire*. New York: Random House, 1980.

Dean, John R. *The Strange Alliance: The Story of Our Efforts at Wartime Cooperation with Russia*. New York: Viking, 1947.

De Gaulle, Charles. *War Memoirs*. New York: Simon and Schuster, 1964.

Deighton, Len. *Blitzkrieg*. New York: Knopf, 1980.

Delmer, Sefton. *The Counterfeit Spy*. New York: Harper & Row, 1971.

Dissette, Edward, and Adamson, Hans Christian. *Guerrilla Submarines.* New York: Bantam Books, 1980.

Dulles, Allen W. *The Craft of Intelligence.* New York: Harper & Row, 1963.

——. *The Secret Surrender.* New York: Harper & Row, 1966.

Eisenhower, Dwight D. *Crusade in Europe.* New York: Avon, 1968.

Elson, Robert. *Prelude to War.* New York: Time/Life, 1976.

Epstein, Helen. *Children of the Holocaust.* New York: Putnam, 1979.

Essame, Hubert, and Belfield, E. M. G. *Normandy Bridgehead.* New York: Ballantine, 1970.

Farago, Ladislas. *The Broken Seal.* New York, Random House, 1967.

——. *The Game of the Foxes.* New York: McKay, 1971.

Fleming, Peter. *Operation Sea Lion.* New York: Simon and Schuster, 1957.

Ford, Corey. *Donovan of OSS.* Boston: Little, Brown, 1970.

Friedheim, Eric and Taylor, Samuel W. *Fighters Up.* Philadelphia: Macrae-Smith, 1945.

Fuller, J. F. C. *The Second World War, 1939–1945.* New York: Duell, Sloan & Pearce, 1949.

Gavin, James M. *On to Berlin.* New York: Viking, 1978.

Goebbels, Joseph. *Diaries of Joseph Goebbels, 1942–1943.* New York: Doubleday, 1948.

Goralski, Robert. *World War II Almanac, 1939–1945.* New York: Putnam, 1981.

Hirsch, Phil. *War.* New York: Pyramid Books, 1964.

Hughes, Terry, and Costello, John. *The Battle of the Atlantic.* New York: Dial, 1977.

Innis, W. Joe, with Bunton, Bill. *In Pursuit of the Awa Maru.* New York: Bantam Books, 1981.

Irving, David. *The German Atomic Bomb.* New York: Simon and Schuster, 1968.

——. *The Trail of the Fox.* New York: Dutton, 1977.

Jackson, Stanley. *The Savoy: The Romance of a Great Hotel.* London: Frederick Muller, 1964.

Jackson, W. G. F. *The Battle for Italy.* London: Batsford, 1967.

Johnson, Frank D. *United States PT Boats of World War II.* Poole, Dorset, U.K.: Blandford Press, 1980.

Kahn, David, *The Codebreakers.* New York: Macmillan, 1967.

Kaufman, Louis; Fitzgerald, Barbara; and Sewell, Tom. *Mo Berg: Athlete, Scholar, Spy.* Boston: Little, Brown, 1974.

Keegan, John. *Who Was Who in World War II.* New York: Thomas Y. Crowell, 1978.

Keil, Sally Van Wagenen. *Those Wonderful Women in Their Flying Machines.* New York: Rawson, Wade, 1979.

Kimmel, Husband E. *Admiral Kimmel's Story.* Chicago: Henry Regnery, 1955.

King, Ernest J., and Whitehill, W. M. *Fleet Admiral King.* New York: Norton, 1952.

Kitchen, Ruben P., Jr. *Pacific Carrier.* New York: Zebra Books, 1980.

Kowalski, Isaac. *A Secret Press in Nazi Europe.* New York: Shengold, 1978.

Kramarz, Joachim. *Stauffenberg: The Life and Death of an Officer.* London: Deutsch, 1967.

Kurzman, Dan. *The Race for Rome.* New York: Doubleday, 1975.

Lawson, Ted W. *Thirty Seconds over Tokyo.* New York: Random House, 1943.

Leahy, W. *I Was There.* New York: Whittlesey, 1950.

Le Vien, Jack, and Lord, John. *Winston Churchill: The Valiant Years.* New York: Bernard Geis, 1962.

Lewin, Ronald. *The American Magic.* New York: Farrar, Straus & Giroux, 1982.

Longmate, Norman. *If Britain Had Failed.* New York: Stein & Day. 1974.

Lord, Walter. *Day of Infamy.* New York: Henry Holt, 1957.

——. *Incredible Victory.* New York: Harper & Row, 1967.

McClendon, Dennis E. *The Lady Be Good.* Fallbrook, Calif. (reprinted): Aero Publishers, Inc., 1982.

McKee, Alexander. *Last Round Against Rommel.* New York: New American Library, 1964.

Manchester, William. *American Caesar: Douglas MacArthur, 1880–1964.* Boston: Little, Brown, 1978.

Manvell, Roger, and Fraenkel, Heinrich. *The Canaris Conspiracy.* New York: McKay, 1969.

Marshall, Samuel. *Night Drop*. Boston: Little, Brown, 1962.

Mason, David. *Who's Who in World War II*. Boston: Little, Brown, 1978.

——. *U-Boat: The Secret Menace*. New York: Ballantine, 1968.

Michel, Henri. *The Shadow War*. New York: Harper & Row, 1973.

Michel, Jean. *Dora: The Nazi Concentration Camp Where Modern Space Technology Was Born and 30,000 Prisoners Died*. New York: Holt, Rinehart and Winston, 1980.

Mikesh, Robert C. *Japan's World War II Balloon Bomb Attacks on North America*. Washington: Smithsonian Institution Press, 1973.

Mollo, Andrew *A Pictorial History of the SS*. New York: Bonanza, 1979.

Montagu, Ewen. *The Man Who Never Was*. Philadelphia: Lippincott, 1954.

Morella, Joe; Epstein, Edward Z.; and Griggs, John. *The Films of World War II*. New York: Citadel/Lyle Stuart, 1975.

Morison, Samuel E. *The History of United States Naval Operations in World War II* (14 vols.). Boston: Little, Brown, 1947–62.

Murphy, Robert. *Diplomat Among Warriors*. New York: Doubleday, 1964.

Page, Geoffrey. *Tale of a Guinea Pig*. New York: Bantam, 1981.

Patton, George S., Jr. *War As I Knew It*. Boston: Houghton Mifflin, 1947.

Payne, Robert. *The Life and Death of Adolf Hitler*. New York: Praeger, 1973.

Pearcy, Arthur. *DC-3*. New York: Ballantine, 1975.

Peniakoff, Vladimir. *Popski's Private Army*. New York: Bantam, 1980.

Popov, Dusko. *Spy-Counterspy*. New York: Grosset & Dunlap, 1974.

Preston, Antony. *Aircraft Carriers*. New York: Grosset & Dunlap, 1979.

Rayner, D. C. *Escort*. London: William Kimber and Company, 1955.

Ryan, Cornelius. *The Longest Day*. New York: Simon and Schuster, 1959.

——. *A Bridge Too Far*. New York: Simon and Schuster, 1974.

——. *The Last Battle*. New York: Simon and Schuster, 1966.

Schaeffer, Heinz. *U-Boat 977*. New York: Norton, 1953.

Sherrod, Robert. *Tarawa*. New York: Duell, Sloan & Pearce. 1944.

Shirer, William L. *The Rise and Fall of the Third Reich*. New York: Simon and Schuster, 1960.

Simms, Edward H. *American Aces*. New York: Harper & Brothers, 1958.

Speer, Albert. *Inside the Third Reich*. New York: Avon, 1970.

Stagg, J. M. *Forecast for Overload*. New York: Norton, 1972.

Steichen, Edward. *U.S. Navy War Photographs*. New York: Crown Publishers, 1956–1980.

Strong, Sir Kenneth. *Intelligence at the Top*. New York: Doubleday, 1969.

Sulzberger, C. L. *The American Heritage Picture History of World War II*. New York: American Heritage, 1966.

Sunderman, James F. *World War II in the Air*. New York: Franklin Watts, 1962.

TerHorst, Jerald F., and Albertazzie, Ralph. *The Flying White House*. New York: Coward, McCann & Geoghegan, 1979.

Thomson, David. *Europe Since Napoleon*. New York: Knopf, 1960.

Toland, John. *The Last 100 Days*. New York: Random House, 1965.

——. *The Rising Sun*. New York: Simon and Schuster, 1971.

Townsend, Peter. *Duel of Eagles*. New York: Simon and Schuster, 1971.

Tregaskis, Richard. *Guadalcanal Diary*. New York: Random House, 1943.

Truman, Harry S. *Memoirs*. New York: Doubleday, 1958.

Whiting, Charles. *Hitler's Werewolves*. New York: Bantam, 1973.

——. *The Hunt for Martin Bormann*. New York: Ballantine, 1973.

——. *Patton*. New York: Ballantine, 1971.

Wiener, Jan G. *The Assassination of Heydrich*. New York: Pyramid, 1969.

Williams, Eric. *The Wooden Horse*. New York: Bantam, 1980.

Winterbotham, Frederick W. *The Ultra Secret*. New York: Harper & Row, 1974.

Young, Desmond. *Rommel, the Desert Fox*. New York: Harper & Brothers, 1950.

Index